Libraries and Society

CHANDOS
INFORMATION PROFESSIONAL SERIES

Series Editor: Ruth Rikowski
(e-mail: Rikowskigr@aol.com)

Chandos' new series of books are aimed at the busy information professional. They have been specially commissioned to provide the reader with an authoritative view of current thinking. They are designed to provide easy-to-read and (most importantly) practical coverage of topics that are of interest to librarians and other information professionals. If you would like a full listing of current and forthcoming titles, please visit our website www.chandospublishing.com or e-mail info@chandospublishing.com or telephone +44 (0) 1223 499140.

New authors: we are always pleased to receive ideas for new titles; if you would like to write a book for Chandos, please contact Dr Glyn Jones on e-mail gjones@chandospublishing.com or telephone number +44 (0) 1993 848726.

Bulk orders: some organisations buy a number of copies of our books. If you are interested in doing this, we would be pleased to discuss a discount. Please e-mail info@chandospublishing.com or telephone +44 (0) 1223 499140.

Libraries and Society

*Role, responsibility and future in
an age of change*

EDITED BY
DAVID BAKER AND WENDY EVANS

CHANDOS
PUBLISHING

Oxford   Cambridge   New Delhi

Chandos Publishing
Hexagon House
Avenue 4
Station Lane
Witney
Oxford OX28 4BN
UK
Tel: +44 (0) 1993 848726
E-mail: info@chandospublishing.com
www.chandospublishing.com

Chandos Publishing is an imprint of Woodhead Publishing Limited

Woodhead Publishing Limited
80 High Street
Sawston
Cambridge CB22 3HJ
UK
Tel: +44 (0) 1223 499140
Fax: +44 (0) 1223 832819
www.woodheadpublishing.com

First published in 2011

ISBN: 978 1 84334 131 4

© The editors and the contributors, 2011

Typeset in the UK by Concerto.
Printed in the UK and USA.

Contents

Foreword

Ellen R. Tise

In the current environment of the exponential growth of information, the library, in all its forms, is the institution that is most representative of a growing and developing society. Therefore, it must be acknowledged that libraries are indispensable, as they are, by their very nature, the conduit for the capture, preservation and delivery of 'our nation's heritage, the heritage of humanity, the records of its triumphs and failures, of mankind's intellectual, scientific, and artistic achievements', as described by Vartan Gregorian, President of the Carnegie Corporation of New York in 2007.[1] Libraries have always been – and will continue in that vein to be – that societal institution that propagates democracy and growth and development. However, the inference that the exponential growth of information would decrease the problems of the world is a red herring. There are, rather, a growing divide between rich and poor, a crumbling environment and frightening health concerns, amongst others. This book by leading experts probing the changing role of the library addresses core issues to resolve a myriad of associated problems.

There is an acceptance that the library as a concept is in need of redefinition and that in this redefined paradigm there will be interrogation of the place of the library and librarians in a virtual environment. In the virtual realm, it is imperative that there be a thorough integration of interaction with librarians and libraries. Given that libraries, in whatever format, are critical for growth and development, there has to be a close examination of the role of libraries as information navigators and innovative distributors of trusted and relevant information. This publication pays significant attention to the changing role of the socially responsible library.

This changing landscape is one in which libraries' functions are dominated by the Internet and the new kinds of provision and usage that are possible in a digital world. This book investigates key aspects of digital libraries and considers the relationship between digital libraries and knowledge creation and use in different communities. It considers the view that there is an urgent need for libraries to develop a strong online presence in addition to their physical existence in order to remain relevant in today's online world – especially because they are social institutions, rooted in social communities. In keeping with the principle of social commitment is the use of social networking tools such as wikis, blogs and podcasts to deliver an efficient and effective service to the clients of the library. Libraries, as part of their social responsibility, must use available technologies to provide innovative information services to societies that are becoming ever more culturally diverse. Libraries must interrogate future scenarios and challenges, and consider their roles in supporting and celebrating diversity in society.

Because there are major drives to develop platforms for the delivery of unhindered access to information and technologies that have the capacity to realise such a commitment, libraries must leave no stone unturned in ensuring freedom of access to information. In the current technological environment, the Internet has the capacity to provide equal and equitable access to information. Such provision must be protected and developed in support of democratic processes, freedom of speech and intellectual freedom. Libraries have always been committed to challenging oppressive processes that restrict access to information, and they must continue to uphold this as a pillar of good library practice. This book examines the upholding of these freedoms to ensure positive social change in the future.

However, while the need to uphold freedom of access to information is recognised, a significant reality is the growing divide between the 'information rich' and the 'information poor'. This divide is exacerbated in the digital era, when so much more information is available than ever before but so many are deprived of even the most basic access to simple or low-level resources. The divide is not synonymous with the divide between the developed and developing worlds – it has become so infectious that it has created communities within communities even in the developed world. There is an examination, in this book, of the concept of the information poor, of the various ways in which they can emerge and the reasons for their existence; it considers the history, current position and likely future scenarios with regard to the information divide and considers how libraries can best bridge the gap between 'haves' and 'have nots'.

In the midst of this divide between the information rich and the information poor comes the birth of a new divide, the 'generation' divide, as traditional library services grow less and less popular among younger people. This generation divide is growing as Internet usage increases. However, migration to the digital and virtual environment is not the only solution, as studies suggest that there are groups of 'new generation' users of information services who have simple needs and welcome physical as much as virtual contact. This book interrogates the current needs of younger users (and non-users) of libraries and information and looks at how these may change, develop and be best satisfied in the future. Widening participation brings with it greater diversity: how will this best be accommodated?

In this changing information services paradigm – one that is influenced by rapidly changing technology – there has to be concomitant change in the education and training of the new generation of librarians. There has to be an evaluation of the future requirements of and for library and information professionals and of how the profession – and education for librarianship – needs to change in order to accommodate the challenges ahead. Experts on the issue of education and training for the new-generation librarian consider future concepts of professionalism. Further, there is an examination of the need for a different type of information professional that has been brought about by major and possibly discontinuous changes in role as a result of changes in library and information use and delivery, and of the need for ways of teaching information literacy. The concept, principles and implementation of information literacy become ever more critical in an age of abundance of information, and especially of information that has the potential to have a negative social impact. Libraries and librarians have a significant role to play in shaping future societies by imparting critical information literacy skills, so that the future generation of information seekers can differentiate between trusted and relevant information and 'negative information', and use that trusted and relevant information for the growth and development of both the individual and society at large.

This is an excellent compilation of writings by experts and will make excellent and absorbing reading. The International Federation of Library Associations (IFLA), being the leading international body representing the interests of library and information services and their users, and as an association working towards contributing to the shaping of future societies, is proud to be associated with this publication. This book contributes significant insights on the meaning of future library and information practice for the growth and development of a changing society. The changing role of libraries, librarians and library practices makes the profession dynamic and relevant in its endeavours to contribute to the shaping of future societies. It is beyond debate that information is a critical element in a developing society. Therefore, the repackaging of information and the delivery of that repackaged information in a format that is relevant to and in keeping with the trends of the day must underpin future librarianship. IFLA seeks to provide guidance to the profession on the delivery of services that shape future societies, and applauds the contribution of this publication to shaping the library and information practice of tomorrow. This book has the hallmarks of an exciting and absorbing publication.

Note

1. http://www.laurabushfoundation.org/Gregorian.pdf.

Preface

Libraries have a long and honourable history – almost as long as that of the written word; and the library as concept, collection and service has changed and developed to meet new challenges and altered environments. Underneath all the different guises in which libraries have emerged over the centuries, there remains that key, core responsibility of the library as a force for good – educational, economic and social – within society. But the world is changing rapidly, and libraries must change with their altered and altering environment if they are to maintain and, indeed, enhance their status and position for the future. This is particularly true as we move to an ever more digital world in which the Internet is all.

This book, then, aims to explore the role, responsibilities and future of libraries. We have taken a broad, international perspective and included particular contributions from Canada, Denmark, the Netherlands and the United States of America. The various chapters encompass the past, current and likely future position of the library – public, academic and special – both in the UK and more generally. Within our overall framework, we have chosen to include chapters on the key challenges facing libraries in present-day society, and notably: equity and equality of access to information; libraries, research, education and the scholarly communications process; the library as a physical space; the library user of tomorrow; the future of librarians and of librarianship as a profession; library collaboration; and the development of libraries over the next 10, 20, 30 years and beyond.

In researching for this book, we found that, while there is a wealth of material on specific aspects of the library's future role and responsibilities, there is much less currently available on the overarching issues and possible ways forward – at least in one book. We are well aware that this present publication can be only one contribution among many to the subject, but, in this context, we hope that this collection of essays by experts in the field stimulates significant further research and discourse.

All web links were correct at the time of checking (March 2011).

David Baker and Wendy Evans
March 2011

Acknowledgements

The editors are especially grateful to all who made this book possible: to the authors of the various chapters for their contributions and their willingness to be involved in the project; to Kathryn Kendon for her initial research for the book; to Glyn Jones for his support throughout the development of the proposal and the actual production of the book; to University College Plymouth St Mark and St John for its financial support; to Emma Wainman for her work in helping us with Chapter 1; to Raymond Taylor for compiling the index; and also to Claire Stevens, research assistant for the project.

List of abbreviations

ACRL	Association of College and Research Libraries
ALA	American Library Association
BBC	British Broadcasting Corporation
BIS	Department for Business, Skills and Innovation
BLS	Bureau of Labor Statistics
BPK	Body of Professional Knowledge (from CILIP)
BSI	British Standards Institution
CIBER	Centre for Information Behaviour and the Evaluation of Research
CILIP	Chartered Institute of Library and Information Professionals
CIPFA	Chartered Institute of Public Funding and Accountancy
CLIR	Council on Library and Information Resources
COUNTER	Counting Online Usage of Networked Electronic Resources
CPD	continuing professional development
CRM	customer relationship management
D4ALLnet	Design for All Network of Excellence
DBC	Danish Bibliographic Centre
DCMS	Department for Culture, Media and Sport
DCSF	Department for Children, Schools and Families
DfES	Department for Education and Skills (UK)

DfIUS	Department for Innovation, Universities and Skills
DRC	Disability Rights Commission
EA	Enterprise Architecture
EU	European Union
FOBID	Netherlands Library Forum
FTE	full time equivalent
FY	financial year
HAERVI	Higher Education Access to E-Resources in Visited Institutions
HE	higher education
HEFCE	Higher Education Funding Council for England
HEI(s)	higher education institution(s)
HEPI	Higher Education Policy Institution
HESA	Higher Education Statistics Agency
ICT	information and communications technology
IFLA	International Federation of Library Associations
ILL	inter-library loan
IMLS	Institute for Museum and Library Services
INASP	International Network for the Availability of Scientific Publications
ISO	International Organization for Standardization
IT	information technology
JANET	Joint Academic Network
JISC	Joint Information Systems Committee
KB	Koninklijke Bibliotheek (National Library of the Netherlands)
LA	Library Association
LGA	Local Government Association
LIBER	Ligue des Bibliothèques Européennes de Recherche (Association of Research Libraries in Europe)
LIC	Library and Information Commission

LIS	library and information science
LIS	library and information services
LIS	library and information studies
LISU	Library and Information Statistics Unit
LJMU	Liverpool John Moores University
LMS	Library Management System
MBA	Master of Business Administration
MIT	Massachusetts Institute of Technology
MLA	Museums, Libraries and Archives Council
MLS	Master of Library Science
MP	Member of Parliament
MUSE	Mobile Muse Network
NCES	National Center for Education Statistics
NIACE	National Institute of Adult Continuing Education
NOUN	National Open University of Nigeria
NSS	National Student Survey
NYR	National Year of Reading
OA	Open Access
OCLC	Online Computer Library Center
OECD	Organisation for Economic Co-operation and Development
OER(s)	open educational resource(s)
PC	personal computer
PEER	Publishing and the Ecology of European Research
PFI	private finance initiative
PISA	Programme for International Student Assessment
RIN	Research Information Network
RLUK	Research Libraries UK
ROI	return on investment
RPI	Retail Price Index

RSA	Royal Society for the Encouragement of Arts, Manufactures and Commerce
SCONUL	Society of College, National and University Libraries
SLA	School Libraries Association (UK)
TESSA	Teacher Education in Sub-Saharan Africa
UBC	University of British Columbia
UCISA	Universities and Colleges Information Systems Association
UK	United Kingdom
UKOLN	United Kingdom Office for Library and Information Networking
UKOU	UK Open University
UN	United Nations
UNESCO	United Nations Educational, Scientific and Cultural Organization
UNISA	University of South Africa
VAMP	Value and Impact Programme
VRE	virtual research environment
WCAG	Web Content Accessibility Guidelines
WLHC	Worcester Library and History Centre
WRR	Wetenschappelijke Raad vor het Regeringsbeleid (Scientific Council for Government Policy)
WTYL	Welcome to Your Library

List of figures, tables and case studies

Figures

Tables

Case studies

About the authors

David Baker was born in Bradford, West Yorkshire, in 1952. His first love was the church organ, which he began playing from the age of 12. By the time that he was 16, he was an Associate of the Royal College of Organists. He gained his Fellowship the following year. In 1970 he was elected Organ Scholar of Sidney Sussex College, Cambridge, graduating with a First Class Honours degree in Music three years later. He took an MMus degree from King's College, London in 1974. He then moved into library and information services, taking a Master of Library Studies degree in 1976 and a PhD in 1988. Both of these degrees were from Loughborough University. After a number of library posts at Nottingham, Leicester and Hull Universities and a lecturing role at Loughborough, he became Chief Librarian of the University of East Anglia, Norwich, in 1985. He was promoted to Director of Information Strategy and Services in 1995, and Pro Vice Chancellor in 1997. He became Principal of University College Plymouth St Mark and St John (UCP Marjon) in July 2003 and, in addition, was appointed Professor of Strategic Information Management there in July 2006. He retired as Principal at UCP Marjon in August 2009. In October 2010 he was made an Honorary Fellow of the Chartered Institute of Library and Information Professionals for his outstanding contribution to the profession.

David Baker has published widely in the field of library and information studies, with fifteen monographs and some 100 articles to his credit. He has spoken at numerous conferences, led workshops and seminars and has undertaken consultancy work in most countries in the European Union, along with work in Bulgaria, Slovenia, Ethiopia, Kuwait, Nigeria and the Sudan. In recent years, his particular professional interest has been in the strategic management of technology. He gained an MBA degree from the Open University in this subject area in 2002. He is Deputy Chair of the Joint Information Systems

Committee, also having led a number of large technology-based projects in the library and information science sector, in relation both to digital and hybrid library development and to content creation for teaching and learning. His other key professional interest and expertise has been in the field of human resources, where he has been active in major national projects. When not working he enjoys watching cricket, walking, archaeology, history, creative writing and music – as both listener and performer. He published *Digital Library Economics: an academic perspective* with Wendy Evans in 2009, and *Eve on Top: women and the experience of success in the public sector* in 2010 (with Bernadette Casey), both with Chandos. He is also collaborating with Wendy Evans on *A Handbook of Digital Library Economics,* to be published by Chandos in 2012.

Chris Batt OBE was Chief Executive of the Museums, Libraries and Archives Council (MLA), the development agency for the sector, until September 2007. Following its creation in 2000, the MLA had a pivotal role in many aspects of cultural heritage and ICT strategy. Chris originally joined national government in 1999 to lead the implementation of the highly successful £170m People's Network project and while in the role of MLA's Chief Executive continued to ensure involvement in digital futures strategy. Since late 2007, as a director of Chris Batt Consulting Ltd, his work has ranged from projects for the Joint Information Systems Committee on topics including audience studies, community engagement and the aggregation of online guidance on all aspects of the digital life cycle; a review of information and communications technology (ICT) developments in the UK's public libraries based on six published surveys of the use of technology that Chris conducted between 1985 and 1999; lecturing and contributions to books and journals. International projects and speaking engagements have included work in Australia, New Zealand, Singapore, Canada, the USA, Iceland and a dozen countries across Europe. In 1998 Chris was awarded the OBE for work in developing public ICT services in public libraries. He is currently a Senior Research Fellow at University College London's Centre for Information Behaviour and the Evaluation of Research and studying for a PhD on the modelling of public knowledge systems in the information society.

Jenny Craven worked for over 10 years as a Research Associate at the Centre for Research in Library and Information Management at Manchester Metropolitan University (MMU). During this time she worked on a wide variety of research projects, primarily concerned with Web accessibility and usability, with a particular focus on access to information by blind or visually impaired people. She also contributed to the teaching programme at MMU Department of Information and Communications. Jenny has facilitated workshops on improving library services for people with print disabilities in Chile, Mexico, Vietnam, Brazil, Sabah and Kenya for the Force Foundation Charity, which aims to improve information access for people with print impairments in developing countries and is Information Co-ordinator on the International Federation of Library Associations Standing Committee for the Section of Libraries Serving Persons with Print Disabilities. Jenny is currently working as an Assistant Information Specialist at the National Institute for Health and Clinical Excellence.

Claire Creaser has been employed at the Library and Information Statistics Unit since 1994, and was appointed Director in 2007. Claire oversees the day-to-day management of the unit and plays a key role in ensuring the quality and reliability of methods of investigation and data gathered for the various projects undertaken. Claire's main areas of interest are in the use of statistical evidence for management, with a particular focus on benchmarking; the analysis and interpretation of survey data; and scholarly communication, with reference to researcher behaviours and open access to research outputs. Recent projects include: an investigation into the provision of services for external academic library users, for the Research Information Network; a study of the use of open access journals, for Oxford Journals; mapping health and well-being activity in public libraries, for the Museums, Libraries and Archives Council; a study on the impact of open access to research outputs, for the Research Council UK; and research into the behaviour of authors and readers with respect to self-archiving and repository use. Claire takes an active role in promoting good statistical practice via a number of external committees and working groups, including as Chair of the British Standards Institution Committee for Library and Publishing Statistics, and a member of the Royal Statistical Society Statistics User Forum.

John Dolan OBE worked in business information, and then in community librarianship in St Helens in a new leisure directorate, where he led a modernisation programme for library, archive and museum services. In Birmingham he was strategic manager for Libraries and Archives, Early Years and Family Learning, the Youth Service and Adult

Education. He led on the first concept design for the Library of Birmingham. He was project leader for the strategic development of the People's Network. At the Museums, Libraries and Archives Council he worked on policy and partnership programmes for public libraries. He has contributed to national strategies for public libraries in Bulgaria and India. Recent work includes a shared services study with a group of West Midlands library authorities, a study programme for German library directors working towards a national policy on library services for new communities and the drafting of the Chartered Institute of Library and Information Professionals' *Guidelines on public libraries*. As an Associate Director of *Eye*, he was the library specialist for a feasibility study for a joint public/academic library in Southend and the subsequent consultation on the proposals. Also with *Eye*, he has worked on three regeneration projects in Nottingham focusing on community need and consultation. John Dolan was awarded an OBE for his services to libraries and information provision. He is an Honorary Fellow at the Department of Information Studies at Aberystwyth University.

Tony Durcan has been the Head of Culture, Libraries and Lifelong Learning for Newcastle City Council since 2002. Before moving to Newcastle, Tony worked for Gateshead Library and Arts Service, as Assistant Director, then as Deputy Director and latterly as Head of Libraries, Arts and Information; before that he had a variety of roles with Derbyshire Library Service, from trainee to District Librarian. Public library priorities in Newcastle have been to work with colleagues to modernise services and to create a positive profile for the Library Service within the Council. The service is now held in high regard by both the Council and external stakeholders. One of Tony's major projects has been the development of a new city library through the private finance initiative route. The Council opened its new city library, to a very positive and sustained public response, in June 2009. Tony was President of the Society of Chief Librarians from 2007 to 2009. He currently chairs the Society's Books and Reading group. He was a member of the former Advisory Council on Libraries, and a Board member for the 2008/9 Public Libraries Modernisation Review.

Judith Elkin is Deputy Vice Chancellor Emeritus, Chair of the Endowment Committee and Professor of Children's Literature at the University of Worcester, UK. She was Deputy Vice Chancellor at the University, responsible for academic and research development, from 2003 to 2009. Prior to this, she was Dean of the Faculty of Computing,

Information and English at the University of Central England in Birmingham (now Birmingham City University). Judith worked as a children's librarian for many years before moving into academia and was Head of Library Services to Children and Young People, Birmingham Public Libraries, at a time when Birmingham was a world leader in children's library development. She has written and edited a number of books, including *A Place for Children: public libraries as a major force in children's reading* (Library Association, 1999); *Focus on the Child: libraries, literacy and learning* (Library Association, 1996); *The Puffin Book of Twentieth Century Children's Stories* (Puffin, 1999) and *Free My Mind: an anthology of Black and Asian Poetry* (Hamish Hamilton and Puffin, 1992). Children's reading and literacy and the future role of libraries for children and young people remain her passion, as does living in and researching historic Worcester, where she now lives.

Wendy Evans was born in Leamington Spa, Warwickshire in 1968. Her interest in libraries began at a very early age as both parents worked in public libraries. She graduated from the University of Central England (now Birmingham City University) with an Honours degree in Librarianship and Information Studies in 1990, having spent a 'sandwich' year working in the Library at the Royal Naval Engineering College, Plymouth. She then spent a year working in the Library at the University of Plymouth before being appointed Customer Services Manager of a commercial book supplier. Having taken a career break to raise a family and to manage a self-build project in the South Hams area of Devon she took a part-time job in the library at University College Plymouth St Mark and St John in 1998. After 18 months she was promoted to Assistant Librarian (Information Technology), where she developed a keen interest in the Internet and electronic resources and was responsible for creating the library website and setting up access to an increasing number of electronic journals and databases. During this time Wendy became a chartered member of the Chartered Institute of Library and Information Professionals and also gained associate membership of the Higher Education Academy. In 2003 she was appointed to the post of Librarian and in 2005 was appointed Head of Library. Wendy has published in the fields of electronic journal and database usage and access versus ownership of journals and has recently completed *Digital Library Economics: an academic perspective* with David Baker. She is now working (with David Baker) on *A Handbook of Digital Library Economics*, to be published by Chandos in 2012.

John Feather has been Professor of Library and Information Studies at Loughborough since 1988, having worked in publishing and librarianship before moving to Loughborough. He has served as Head of Department (1990–94, 2003–6), Dean of Education and Humanities (1994–96) and Pro Vice Chancellor for Learning and Teaching (1996–2000), and is currently Dean of the Graduate School. He has been a Visiting Professor at the University of California, Los Angeles and undertaken many other international tasks for the British Council, the EU and UNESCO, among others. He was Chair of Panel 37 in the Research Assessment Exercise 2008 and is a former Chair of the British Association for Information and Library Education and Research. He was a founding Board member of the Arts and Humanities Research Council. He has served on committees and advisory bodies of learned societies, professional bodies and government and international agencies. His many publications include *A History of British Publishing* (2nd edition, 2006), and *The Information Society: a study in continuity and change* (5th edition, 2008).

Biddy Fisher first entered libraries as an 8-year-old, sitting on a hard wooden chair reading Beatrix Potter in a small branch library in North Norfolk. Her later career choice was in no way influenced by this sedentary experience and subsequently she tried working in public, academic and nursing libraries in Norfolk, Surrey, London and Yorkshire before becoming President of the Chartered Institute of Library and Information Professionals (CILIP) in 2010. Selecting 'Professionalism' as her main theme for the year, she is well aware of issues arising from keeping CILIP relevant to members and society. Biddy has contributed to the library and information science (LIS) professional press in the area of staff development, particularly mentoring and the identification of future skills needs for roles in the LIS domain. Biddy believes that the future for the LIS profession lies in a willingness to develop partnerships with organisations that recognise the need for equality of educational opportunity in society and that work to develop access to library services for learning, reading, business, leisure and fun. Biddy is known variously for her work in the Library and Information Research Group when she championed the partnership between research and evidence-based practice, as an author, for her role as an external examiner at Leeds Metropolitan University and CILIP's Chartership Board, or as a motorcyclist with a tendency to see attending an International Federation of Library Associations and Institutions conference as a good excuse for a bike ride.

José-Marie Griffiths is Vice President for Academic Affairs and University Professor at Bryant University in Rhode Island. She has a research and leadership career that spans over 30 years. Her research spans information science, technology and leadership. She has done ground-breaking work on the value and return on investment in information systems and services; on the influences of the digital revolution on the conducting of research; and on the recruitment, education and retention of the library and information professional workforce. Her accomplishments have been recognised by several prestigious appointments and awards. She has held three presidential appointments: National Science Board (2006–12), President's Information Technology Advisory Committee (2003–5) and US National Commission on Libraries and Information Science (1996–2002). She has testified before Congress and has served on blue-ribbon panels and committees for agencies including the National Academy of Sciences, the National Aeronautics and Space Administration, US Department of Energy, US Department of Commerce, US Geological Survey and the US Navy. She was elected a Fellow of the American Association for the Advancement of Science. She received the Award of Merit from the American Society for Information Science and Technology – the Society's highest honour – and the Society's Research Award. She was also named one of the Top 25 Women on the Web in 1999. Griffiths completed her undergraduate degree in Physics with honours and a PhD in Information Science from University College London.

Jonathan Harle works on international higher education policy and research at the Association of Commonwealth Universities (ACU). Much of his work is concerned with initiatives to strengthen the research base in African universities, with a particular focus on the social sciences and on library and information issues. He runs an ACU network for higher education (HE) librarians internationally and works closely with INASP (the International Network for the Availability of Scientific Information) on initiatives to support librarians and researchers in developing countries. He has authored a number of reports on research capacity issues in Africa, including a 2-year study published as *The Nairobi Report* by the British Academy and a recent study for Arcadia exploring the use of digital resources by academics and students in East and Southern Africa, and co-edits the ACU's regular policy briefing for senior HE managers. Jonathan holds an MSc in African Politics from the School of Oriental and African Studies and is a council member of the African Studies Association of the UK.

David Harris is Professor of Leisure and Education at UCP Marjon and Director of the Centre for Educational Research there. His research and teaching interests involve applying general social theory (including Critical Theory and the work of Pierre Bourdieu) to areas including distance education and popular culture. His interest in distance education began when he worked at the UK's Open University. Publications in that area range from *Openness and Closure in Distance Education* in 1987 to an entry in the *International Handbook of Distance Education* in 2008. He has recently completed a project for the UK Higher Education Academy on the design of re-usable learning objects (RLOs) for a UK open educational resources database (JORUMOpen), and has some forthcoming publications based on that project. Further details of these activities, and some examples of electronic teaching materials including RLOs, can be found on his personal experimental website, http://www.arasite.org.

Ayub Khan is Head of Library Services (Strategy) for Warwickshire Library and Information Service. He has held a number of posts in public libraries, specialising in schools, young people's and community librarianship. Ayub's most recent role was that of Principal Project Officer (Library of Birmingham), working on plans to create a new, state-of-the-art city-centre library. He also chaired the Chartered Institute of Library and Information Professionals' (CILIP) task group to create guidelines for local authority portfolio holders on public library services. Ayub has a strong interest in international librarianship and is a member of UNESCO's Culture Committee and a former member of the British Council's Knowledge and Information Advisory Board. He chairs CILIP's Equal Opportunities and Diversity panel. He is also a past president of the Career Development Group. Ayub is Vice Chair of the Society of Chief Librarians (West Midlands) and on the advisory board of the Stratford upon Avon Poetry Festival. Ayub was awarded a Centenary Medal from the Library Association in 1998 for services to librarianship and in 2003 was highly commended in the personal achievement category of the Diversity awards by CILIP. He achieved his Fellowship of the Institute in 2004. He is also a former Trustee of CILIP.

Donald W. King is Distinguished Research Professor, Bryant University, Rhode Island. Professor King, a statistician, co-founded a statistical consulting and survey research company in 1961 (Westat, Inc.) and served as chief executive of three research companies until the mid 1990s, at which time he retired. He has continued to conduct research on a *pro bono* basis since then with Drs José-Marie Griffiths and Carol Tenopir. His 50 years in research have emphasised economic cost modelling and surveys dealing with libraries and scholarly publishing. He is widely published, with 17 books, over 150 articles, chapters in books and published presentations and over 200 other formal publications. His work has been recognised by the awards of Pioneer in Science Information, Chemical Heritage Foundation; Fellow, American Statistical Association; Research Award and Award of Merit, American Society for Information Science and Technology, among many other awards and honours.

Derek Law has worked in several British universities and published and spoken at conferences extensively. Most of his work has been to do with the development of networked resources in higher education and with the creation of national information policy. This has been combined with an active professional life in organisations related to librarianship and computing. A committed internationalist, he has been involved in projects and research in over forty countries. He was awarded the Barnard Prize for contributions to Medical Informatics in 1993, Fellowship of the Royal Society of Edinburgh in 1999, an honorary degree by the Sorbonne in 2000, the International Federation of Library Associations and Institutions medal in 2003, Honorary Fellowship of the Chartered Institute of Library and Information Professionals in 2004 and was an Online Computer Library Center Distinguished Scholar in 2006. He is currently Chair of Joint Information Systems Committee Advance and continues to teach and write, as well as being a Professor at the University of Strathclyde.

Sally Maynard is a Lecturer in the Department of Information Science at Loughborough University and holds BA, MSc and PhD degrees. Before becoming a lecturer, she worked as a Research Fellow at Library and Information Statistics Unit (at Loughborough University). As a lecturer, Sally teaches a course on the subject of children's literature and librarianship and other modules in the field of publishing. She is the Editor of the journal *The New Review of Children's Literature and Librarianship* and her research is concentrated around children's literature, children's librarianship, electronic publishing and children and the changing media environment.

Hellen Niegaard graduated from the Royal School of Library and Information Science, Denmark in 1977 and also studied Theoretical

Pedagogics at the University of Copenhagen in 1983. Since 2004, Hellen has held the post of Chief Consultant with the Danish Library Association and Editor of the periodical *Danmarks Biblioteker*. Prior to that she was Chief Consultant with the Danish Library Authority (Biblioteksstyrelsen), having also held a number of senior public library positions. Hellen has written a number of publications on library space and buildings and is also an active member of a number of international working groups and committees concerned with library buildings.

Chinwe Marie Therese Nwezeh has a certificate in Cours de Français from the Université de Sorbonne Nouvelle, Paris 111; a BA degree in Education from the University of Nigeria, Nsukka; a Postgraduate Diploma in Librarianship from the University of Ibadan, Ibadan, Nigeria; a Master's degree in Education from Obafemi Awolowo University, Ile-Ife, Nigeria; a Certificate in Computer Fundamentals at Obafemi Awolowo University, Ile-Ife; Widernet Information and Communication Technology Certificate, University of Ibadan, Nigeria; Carnegie Obafemi Awolowo University-Information and Communication Technology Certificate, Obafemi Awolowo University, Ile-Ife, Nigeria as well as the Nigerian Chartered Librarian Certificate. She started the Oyo State College of Arts and Science Library, Ile-Ife, Nigeria. She later moved over to Obafemi Awolowo University Library, known as Hezekiah Oluwasanmi Library, Obafemi Awolowo University, Ile-Ife, Nigeria. She has been the Head of the Audio-visual and Africana sections, been Chief Cataloguer, and has worked in the Documents section of the Library. Chinwe Nwezeh has also been a Special Duty Librarian in Hezekiah Oluwasanmi Library, Ile-Ife. She has written many papers published in Nigerian as well as international journals. She has also made contributions to books.

Edward Oyston is currently Director of Learning and Information Services at Sheffield Hallam University, where he has worked since 1995. He has played a leading role in the creation of the learning centre concept there and in its subsequent development. His previous experience encompasses both academic and public libraries, including the roles of Senior Assistant Director of Library Services for Birmingham City Council and Head of Library Services at Dorset Institute of Higher Education. His long-standing interests have centred around the application of information systems to library service provision, from the early days of library automation to current developments in resource discovery.

Sarah Porter is Head of Innovation at the UK Joint Information Systems Committee (JISC), a post that she has held since 2005. Prior to this, Sarah was the JISC's Director for e-Learning and held posts at the University of Oxford and for the UK's National Computers in Teaching Initiative. JISC is recognised as a world leader in providing innovative information and communications technology (ICT) solutions to the UK higher education sector and engaging with a large number of national and international partners to deliver world-class infrastructure. Sarah's current role is to develop strategic ICT programmes that help to keep the UK higher education system at the forefront of research and education and to respond to the changing pressures of the current educational environment. Sarah's background is in research and learning technologies and she has a particular interest in the strategic value of ICT's potential to transform learning opportunities for undergraduates and in ICT's use to engage the public in education and cultural heritage. Sarah has presented and written widely on how ICT can transform education and research in the UK and abroad.

Bas Savenije graduated in philosophy in 1977. Since then, he has held a range of positions at Utrecht University, including Director of Strategic Planning and Director Budgeting and Control. From 1994 until 2009 he was University Librarian of Utrecht University, managing the comprehensive university library. He has initiated a pervasive innovation programme for the library, aimed at implementing and continuously improving electronic services. One of the results is an e-press within the university library for electronic publishing and archiving services.

Since June 2009 Bas has been Director General of the KB, National Library of the Netherlands. He is a member of the Board of FOBID (Netherlands Library Forum), a member of the Board of LIBER (Association of Research Libraries in Europe) and chairman of the Board of Directors of SPARC Europe (Scholarly Publishing and Academic Resources Coalition). See also http://www.kb.nl/staff/savenije.

John Tarrant graduated from the University of Hull in 1963; he continued his studies as a post-graduate and was awarded a PhD in 1966. He then took up a 2-year appointment at University College Dublin. He joined the University of East Anglia as a founding member of staff in the School of Environmental Sciences in 1968 and went on to become Dean of the School, and first Pro and then Deputy Vice Chancellor of the University. In 1995 he was appointed Vice Chancellor of the University of Huddersfield, retiring from that position at the end of 2006. He then became Secretary General of the Association of Commonwealth Universities from 2007 to 2010. The Association, as it became known in 1963, serves the interests of universities throughout the Commonwealth. There are now over 500 members from 42 countries. John Tarrant was appointed a Deputy Lieutenant for West Yorkshire in 2007. He was Chair of the Yorkshire Museums and Libraries Council from 2006 until the regional associations were closed in 2008. Professor Tarrant's research and teaching interests have been in food and agricultural policy. He has worked in the United States at Texas A and M University, the University of Nebraska, the Food Research Institute at Stanford University and the International Food Policy Research Institute in Washington, DC. He has also worked in Australia and New Zealand, Russia, China, India, Bangladesh, Thailand and Pakistan.

Ellen Tise is currently President of the International Federation of Library Associations and Institutions (IFLA) 2009–11 and the Senior Director, Library and Information Services at Stellenbosch University, South Africa. She previously held the position of University Librarian at the University of the Western Cape, Bellville, South Africa (March 2001–December 2005). Prior to this, she was Deputy University Librarian (Client Services) at the University of the Witwatersrand, Johannesburg. She also previously held the position of Systems Librarian and other positions at the University of the Western Cape, Brakpan City Library and the University of the Free State in South Africa. She served on the Governing Board and Executive Committee of IFLA (2001–5 and 2007–9); the IFLA Free Access to Information and Freedom of Expression Advisory Board (2003–5); the IFLA Africa Section Standing Committee (2001–7); and was chairperson of the National Committee for the IFLA 73rd World Library and Information Congress, held in Durban South Africa, 19–23 August 2007. She has published various articles in professional journals and is a regular speaker at national and international conferences, seminars and symposia.

Stephen Town is Director of Information and University Librarian at the University of York, UK, including responsibility for its libraries, archives and IT services. Prior to joining York, Stephen worked at Cranfield University at the Defence Academy of the UK where he was responsible for libraries, media services and e-learning development. He began his career in the National Health Service after education at Cambridge and Loughborough universities. Stephen has also been active in research and development, and in providing consultancy and advice within the UK and internationally in the fields of performance, measurement, management, strategy, information literacy and e-learning. Stephen has taught at postgraduate level in the universities of Bristol, Sheffield and Pompeu Fabra (Barcelona). Stephen was until recently Chair of SCONUL's Working Group on Performance Improvement and has led projects on benchmarking, information literacy measures, LibQUAL+ and value and impact measurement for SCONUL (the Society of College, University and National Libraries). Stephen is a member of international conference and journal editorial boards in the library evaluation field, is a member of the LibQUAL+ Steering Committee, and has presented and written widely.

David Vogt is a scientist and entrepreneur inspired by the social and cultural potentials of emerging media technologies. Within the academic world, he is Director of Digital Learning Projects in the Faculty of Education at the University of British Columbia (UBC), where he champions original applications of learning technologies. In the innovation arena David is Executive Director of the Mobile Muse Network, which undertakes collaborative applied research into mobile-social media technologies. David is also chief executive of CrowdTrust Technologies, a semantic software company focusing on Web-presence management for professionals. Across the broader community, David serves on a number of public and private boards. In his original career, David was an astronomer and Director of Observatories at UBC, and then became a Director of Science World, a public science museum in Vancouver. In 1996 he founded and became chief executive of Brainium, a pioneer of Internet-based learning and wireless devices for K-12 classrooms. More recently, David was Chief Research Officer at the New Media Innovation Centre in Vancouver. David's family life centres on awesome wife Tracy and four amazing children. He is passionate about science, technology, learning, applied research, big ideas, building anything, music, hiking, biking and friends.

Les Watson has worked in education for over 35 years as a school teacher, lecturer, Dean and Pro Vice Chancellor. As part of his work he has managed libraries and information services in several organisations. He also has considerable experience of library developments, creating the Learning Cafe, REAL@Caledonian in 2001, the award-winning Saltire Centre in 2006 and tlc@bedford for Royal Holloway University of London in 2008. He has been a member of the Board of the Joint

Information Systems Committee (JISC) and also a consultant to the JISC on virtual and physical learning spaces. Les was the lead consultant on a project developing the web-based resource Technology Rich Spaces for Learning in 2007 and produced a report on the management of open-plan technology-rich space for the JISC in 2008. He is a Fellow of the RSA (Royal Society for the Encouragement of Arts, Manufacture and Commerce), and a registered consultant with the Higher Education Academy. He is currently a freelance educational consultant on library, learning and IT issues and is a Visiting Professor of Learning Environment Development at the University of Lincoln in the UK. Further information on Les is available at http://www.leswatson.net.

Libraries, society and social responsibility

David Baker and Wendy Evans

Introduction

This chapter introduces the key themes, concepts and ideas that are at the heart of this book. It begins by summarising the many challenges that libraries – and societies more generally – face now and for the foreseeable future. It draws attention to the importance of information and communications technology (ICT) as one of the key drivers, not only in terms of infrastructure provision but also with respect to the ways in which information and content are stored, accessed and harnessed to best effect. In this context, one of the major challenges currently faced is the digital divide. Libraries have a key role in bridging the significant gap that still exists in both developing and developed countries between the information haves and have-nots. There is just as big a challenge in terms of the provision of, and easy, seamless access to, quality information and the ability of users to evaluate and exploit it efficiently and effectively. Librarians clearly have a key role here, not simply as intermediaries between resource and user, but as facilitators and teachers, reinforcing the role of libraries as a fundamental educational and cultural resource.

There is much discussion in this book about the library as a physical space. While digital developments have already changed the way we look at the library as a building, it is clear that there will continue to be a need for places where people can go to study, research, learn, interact, socialise and carry out many more functions – some of these being traditionally associated with libraries, while others are more akin to those currently undertaken in other social and public spaces.

What is the value and impact of libraries? Without robust answers to this question, it will be difficult to justify continued investment. Yet the sections of this book which focus on evaluation demonstrate that much progress still needs to be achieved if convincing cases are to be made. And they need to be made in terms of a new kind of library service that builds on globalised access and almost infinite resources, widely distributed and available to users irrespective of provenance. The need to ensure the relevance and hence the importance of libraries and the role of the professional associations is thus a key part of this book.

Future environment

Libraries – of all types – face an uncertain future (Feather, 2004; Grant, 2010).[1] Continuing global economic difficulties, as described in Chapter 3 by John Dolan and in Chapter 6 by John Dolan and Ayub Khan, for example, and increased competition from other services, and alternative means of provision mean that libraries will have to fight for resources, including through the development of strategic approaches and partnerships (Rasmussen and Jochumsen, 2003). The worldwide recession has already had an impact on library spending in the developed world, and this situation is likely to continue for some time to come. While it is not yet clear how a major financial depression will affect the demand for library services, it is widely predicted – not least by the contributors to this book – that future needs will be served in different ways than previously. This is argued to be the almost certain conclusion when one analyses the ways in which the Internet has already significantly changed the ways in which people live their lives. Digital library developments and the globalisation and (at the same time) the personalisation of information provision have already transformed demand for, and provision and usage of, library collections and services. But technology will be only one driver, albeit a very important one. As is identified in later chapters, users are becoming more demanding, more diversified and more sophisticated in their demands and requirements, while societal and political changes will also affect the way in which libraries are viewed.

Technology push

ICT has revolutionised the way in which information is created, stored, accessed and exploited, as Derek Law and Sarah Porter, amongst other contributors to this book, describe in Chapters 23 and 24 respectively. There are now many people who have never known a world without the Internet, as Jenny Craven discusses in Chapter 7. Further major developments are forecast. The considerable potential of digitised resources is widely recognised and many major projects have already come to fruition in this area (Tanner, 2010). In consequence, libraries have been transformed through technology application. But they need to be transformed further if they are to continue to be that vital force for good that has long been at their heart. Some technologies, as for example mobile devices, and types of Internet usage (most notably perhaps, at the moment, social networking) have yet to be fully exploited in terms of information access or educational, cultural and societal support (Frakas, 2008; Ashraf, Sharma and Gulati, 2010; Lucas, 2010; Ormerod, 2010). Scholarly communication is a particular area – as identified by Claire Creaser in Chapter 4 – where technology is transforming the ways in which research is supported and findings are communicated and shared (see, for example, Research Information Network, 2009; Rowlands et al., 2009). At the present time there would seem to be a clear view that electronic-only publication is the way forward, though there is no single consensus on how that will be achieved, partly because of a lack of clarity about future economic and intellectual property models. It is evident that the current financial crisis will lead to major changes, simply because the present publication pathways can no longer be afforded (Hyams, 2010). More broadly, there remains much work to be done in terms of the relationship between digital libraries and knowledge creation and use in different communities (Bishop, Van House and Butterfield, 2003) as well as the provision of high-quality, pervasive infrastructure.

Equity and equality of access

Information has always been a basic commodity, and libraries have long been relied on to provide it. The principle of free access to the resources that libraries store is one of the main foundations of a democratic society (Usherwood and Linley, 2000; Usherwood, 2007; Morozow, 2009; Ivey,

2010). Access to information is easier than ever, but not for all.[2] The Internet, in particular, can both facilitate and inhibit equitable access to information, though inequalities existed even before the digital age came into being (Yu, 2006). This is as true in developed as in developing nations, for we now live in the time of a digital divide 'where technology and access to information can separate the haves from the have-nots' (Malnig, 2008). There is a significant inequality and inequity of library provision globally. On the one hand, as John Feather points out in Chapter 5, access to information has never been easier. On the other hand, as discussed by a number of the authors in this book, there are greater inequities and inequalities in terms of the ability to access and use the information provided than ever before. In the UK, for example, there remains (at the time of writing, at least) a well-established series of library networks – public, academic, private – that serve both the information and leisure needs of the bulk of the population mainly free at point of use, even if not everyone takes full advantage of the services offered (McNicol, 2004; Goulding, 2006), though even here a digital divide exists,[3] with many millions never having used the Internet.[4] The same is true for much of the western world (see, for example, Choudrie et al., 2010; Kinney, 2010; Min, 2010; Vicente and López, 2010), though, sadly, the picture is less positive in other parts of the globe (see, for example, King Whyte, 2010), and even in richer countries there is an unacceptable unevenness in the take-up, if not the provision of, library collections and services (see, for example, Ellcessor, 2010; Jaeger et al., 2010).

Doraiswamy (2010) stresses the need for public libraries to provide a place where people can go to socialise, view exhibitions and access information on an equal footing with the next person. She asks the question 'what would happen to the informational and recreational reading needs of the less-privileged if public libraries ceased to exist? Such an effect would affect the economic, social and political development of the entire country [USA]. The importance of public libraries in providing information to both the rich and the poor cannot be ignored.' David Vogt presents exciting evidence of a Canadian response to this challenge in Chapter 9. Academic libraries also have opened their doors to users from off campus, and this includes provision of access to electronic resources.[5] John Feather discusses the definition and implications of 'free' access to information in Chapter 5, while John Dolan considers access to different types of library in Chapter 3 and, along with Ayub Khan, in Chapter 6. Wisniewski (2010) suggests that there is another kind of digital divide aside from the technology haves and have-nots, a divide between the physical and the online worlds, and describes technological applications that can create suitable hybrid models which combine the best of the physical and the digital. There seems to be a widespread recognition that libraries could and should be at the forefront of equalising access to information, as discussed by Jenny Craven in Chapter 7 and Jonathan Harle and John Tarrant in Chapter 8, with ICT having the potential to be an especially valuable tool to help librarians in their task (Ferro, 2010; Krebeck, 2010; Middleton and Chambers, 2010; Pateman and Vincent, 2010; Zabed Ahmed, 2010).[6]

Education and digital literacy

Libraries have long had a significant role in the support of education at all levels (Ørom, 2000). Later chapters explore the ways in which libraries can contribute to teaching and learning and the many opportunities offered by ICT,[7] with an increasing shift from lecturer to student and towards syllabus – and learner – independence (Adolphus, 2009), as David Harris concludes in Chapter 13.[8] New forms of learning environment – and hence resource provision – have particular significance in the context of distance learning, in both developed and developing countries (Jianfeng et al., 2010; Mirtz, 2010; Runfang, 2010), as Chinwe Nwezeh discusses in Chapter 12, and the concept of the 'edgeless' university is now gaining acceptance as the basis of future developments.[9] What might libraries for children and young people look like tomorrow? The future of libraries for young people is being re-visioned in exciting and innovative ways, as discussed by Judith Elkin in Chapter 16, while Sally Maynard focuses in Chapter 15 on issues relating to the developments in children's reading habits and attitudes, the effects of new technologies on these reading habits and attitudes, and the role of the children's librarian.

The ease with which information can now be accessed is, paradoxically, a disadvantage as well as an advantage. In both developing and developed countries the key issue is not ultimately the availability of information, but how best to access that information (Nijboer and Hammelburg, 2010). Speedy retrieval does not necessarily equate with quality of results. There is widespread agreement (see, for example, Hall, 2010; Meneses and Mominó, 2010) that librarians will continue to have a critical role in ensuring access to quality resources and assisting users to access, retrieve and evaluate the best information sources available, as John Feather, Biddy Fisher, José-Marie Griffiths and Donald King all conclude.

Library as physical space

Notwithstanding the significant moves towards digital provision, there is nevertheless a substantial continuing need for the library as a space – a location where certain activities, including socialising, can take place (Usherwood et al., 2005; Lippincott, 2010; Loder, 2010). Oldenburg (1989) talks of a 'third place' in his book *The Great Good Place*, somewhere that is neither work nor home but, rather, is situated in the middle. In other words, neutral territory where people can gather freely, learn and socialise; where they are encouraged and spontaneity is supported. Interestingly, the subtitle of Oldenburg's book mentions 'cafes, coffee shops, bookstores, bars, hair salons, and other hangouts at the heart of a community' but does not explicitly refer to libraries. Indeed, for him, the 'third place' combines neighbourhood and friendship networks 'comprising typically less intense relationships and making quite different demands on people'[10] to create space 'which is more predictable in its clientele at given times than most local libraries ... such an environment is best described as casual, because the elements of accident and informality are strong within it ... Without having to plan or schedule or prepare, those who move about in a familiar and casual environment have positive social experiences' (Oldenburg, 1989).

The library building is changing in the direction of Oldenburg's 'third place', and, in many ways, becoming unrecognisable from the physical space that it was only one or two decades ago, even though, at least for the time being, books can still be found on shelves (Carnegie and Abell, 2009; Darnton, 2009) in these new 'learning environments'. The best exemplars take an integrative approach that combines physical and virtual across a continuum of diverse yet complementary services and collections. David Vogt's chapter in this book looks at the social experience of information and how public libraries in Canada (along with community centres, theatres, coffee shops and so on) all form part of a community's information flow. Libraries are very much party to this development and have created comfortable, vibrant social spaces blurring the boundaries of their four walls.

The same can be said for academic libraries, where social learning spaces have been evolving over the last decade. In Chapter 10, Les

Watson discusses the creation of places as something we should be doing as part of the rebuild and refurbishment of our libraries if they are to fulfil their learning role. A case study at Loughborough University evaluated the use of a large, open-learning/social space in the library. The area, named 'Open', proved to be popular, particularly with undergraduate students, who carried out academic work and social activities simultaneously (Bryant et al., 2009). The authors also consider the difference between 'social' and 'communal' space, the social area being a space where users are engaged in social activity, where there may be 'social functions and services like cafés, art galleries, group study facilities'. In contrast, 'community activity in a library involves seeing and being seen quietly engaged in study'. The Loughborough research showed students learning and socialising simultaneously. The study also discovered independent (communal) learning in the social space. To achieve this balance the space needs to be carefully designed to accommodate the needs of both types of user. Edward Oyston reaches similar conclusions in Chapter 11.

Longer-term trends in the design of physical library space are difficult to determine, not least because of the continuing development and increasing popularity of distributed models (McNicol, 2008) that could make the large-scale physical collection a thing of the past or the very specialist only. A number of authors have explored the role of information provision in terms of helping users 'develop and sustain feelings of belonging, or a sense of place' (Moore, 2002, cited in Williamson and Roberts, 2010) by connecting to communities through information which helps people to go about their daily lives, not least because 'individuals now belong to fewer organisations, no longer know their neighbours, meet with friends less often and even socialise with family less' (Harris, 2007 commenting on Putnam, 2000). There is a danger that the Internet can leave people feeling isolated: it can be a very insular sport requiring few social skills and potentially leading to ill-health (Doraiswamy, 2010). In some places – as for example Australia – public libraries are the most heavily used buildings: 'in an era when people have become increasingly dislocated from family, friends and the traditional social structures such as churches, recreational clubs and political parties, libraries have been given the opportunity to become a community focal point'. The key role of libraries in building social capital is being recognised. As a result, new and different types of physical space – as described by a number of authors in this book – will need to be designed and created if the library as both concept and service is to remain at the heart of the community which it is intended to serve.

Value and impact

The future existence of libraries will depend to a high degree on their continued positive impact (Alwis and Fühles-Ubach, 2010) and the extent to which they create social, cultural and economic capital (Aabo and Audunson, 2002; Goulding, 2004; Chung, 2008; Goulding, 2008; Varheim, et al., 2008; Halpern, 2009), especially in the digital age (Aabo, 2005). Demonstrating value and relevance can be achieved only through effective and appropriate evaluation processes. A number of chapters in this book examine the ways in which reliable and comprehensive evidence can be obtained in order to ensure not only managing existing library services to best effect, but also enabling the creation of new ones, relevant to the future environment. Experience and achievement to date in the field of library evaluation have been mixed, making comparison especially difficult in many contexts. But in any case, and as already noted, future environments will be so changed from those that libraries, librarians and library users have previously known that new frameworks and approaches will be required that enable the key stakeholders to assess and confirm (or otherwise) the true worth of what is proposed and offered in terms of provision, both physical and virtual, and in a whole range of contexts – political, economic, social and technical – as both Claire Creaser (Chapter 3) and Stephen Town (Chapter 20) conclude.

Re-thinking the library

It is clear from the descriptions of library developments in later chapters that change is already well under way (Keiser, 2010), with a wide range of pathfinder and exemplar projects exploring new futures for libraries. Indeed, librarians have often been some of the earliest adopters of new technologies (Walter, 2010), paving the way for more widespread adoption by other public and private sector organisations, though a number of commentators have observed that progress is neither consistent nor coherent. A broadly agreed re-definition of 'the library' in 21st-century terms remains elusive (Henry, 2009), and Derek Law argues that there remains some confusion over where libraries fit within the wider context and 'where they should now interface with other parts of the organizations they serve' (Law, 2009). The services provided by a library will vary considerably, depending upon the core requirements of the key user groups, and, as digital access to a wide range of services has become ever easier, it is already often difficult to separate out individual libraries from each other, at least in the mind of the end-user. What does seem agreed, as revealed throughout this book, and especially as concluded by John Feather (Chapter 17), Biddy Fisher (Chapter 18) and – with a North American viewpoint – José-Marie Griffiths and Donald King (Chapter 19), is that where leadership is exercised by professional librarians and user wants and needs are clearly identified and satisfied, especially through the embracing of key new technologies, the centrality, vitality, relevance and value of the resulting service is not in doubt. And not only that, but such a library will be not just responding to society, but helping to re-create it (Miller and Pellen, 2006; Raber, 2007; Samek, 2007).

Re-thinking librarianship

Every chapter in this book refers to the importance of professional librarians, without whom major transformation processes will not happen. Almost inevitably, the need to update the image of 'the librarian' and to rebrand both the profession and the service is seen as an important part of the way forward (Baker and Wallace, 2002; Grant, 2010), and the core skills and key attributes long possessed by library staff are still relevant in the digital age, even though they need to be enhanced with new ones (Pinfield, 2001; Levy and Roberts, 2007; Brindley, 2009; Johnson, 2010). Harle and Tarrant make the point in Chapter 8 that information must be accessible and useable: simply being available is not enough. Librarians will always have an important role here in recognising and understanding 'searching' behaviours (Brettle, 2008), and as new technologies emerge, so too will the skills, knowledge and attitudes of the librarians of the future (Partridge et al., 2010).

Professional associations have long played a significant role in furthering the common good through effective, relevant and openly available information, as stressed by Biddy Fisher in Chapter 18. There is much evidence from later chapters in this book that such associations – as for example the Charted Institute of Library and Information Professionals and the International Federation of Library Associations – are in the lead when it comes to the future of information provision as a fundamental part of society. The challenge of re-invention and re-affirmation, underpinned by the maintenance of core professional standards and ethics (McMenemy et al., 2007), has already been taken up (Brophy, 2007), but needs to be continued and developed, not least in the context of Library 2.0 (Casey and Savastinuk, 2007), as Sarah Porter describes and discusses in her review of key future challenges in Chapter 24. Librarians still have a voice, but it has to be used confidently to best effect in political advocacy as much as in macro-level strategic planning to ensure future sustainability of library services.

Conclusion

The future for libraries of all types, then, will be a challenging one, as evinced by the many forecasts within this book. Will it be a case of 'surviving or thriving', as the National Library of Scotland puts it?[11] There are many exciting possible scenarios described in every chapter, culminating in Chris Batt's long-term forward look that concludes this book. 'Rather than a facility with four walls, the Library of the Future has no borders. Its staff works to reduce barriers to information access and to apply its expertise to information activities conducted throughout the organization ... Tomorrow's libraries will be built around the needs of people, and the success of libraries will be measured in how flexible they can be as those needs evolve' (Keiser, 2010). The landscape will inevitably be dominated by the Internet and the new types of provision and modes of communication described elsewhere in this book. Libraries will need to develop resources and services for this changed and changing environment that best meet users' needs, and in particular to develop and focus upon online provision while continuing to be organisations rooted in their user communities (Woodward, 2005; Morrone and Friedman, 2009). As discussed by Sarah Porter in Chapter 24, partnerships with other relevant service and academic organisations institutionally, locally, nationally and internationally will be of considerable importance (Yu, 2006). Libraries will be aided in this by the existence of strong professional associations that are continually rethinking the role and responsibilities of library staff. Above all, librarians will have to exercise strategic leadership in novel and agile ways in order not only to secure a bright future for libraries, but also to ensure that democratic societies survive, develop and flourish worldwide.

Notes

1. See, for example, http://www.splq.info/issues/vol43_2/02.htm; http://splq.info/issues/vol43_2/01.htm; http://splq.info/issues/vol43_2/ 03.htm.
2. See, for example, http://www.infotoday.com/cilmag/oct10/Krebeck.shtml; http://www.inthelibrarywiththeleadpipe.org/2010/vision-and-visionaries-a-whole-bunch-of-questions-to-start-off-2010-as-if-you-didnt-have-enough-of-those-already/; http://www.mla.gov.uk/news_and_views/press_releases/2010/digital_participation.
3. See, for example, http://www.mla.gov.uk/news_and_views/press_releases/2010/digital_participation.
4. http://raceonline2012.org/manifesto.
5. http://www.ucisa.ac.uk/haervi/haervi.aspx.
6. http://www.mla.gov.uk/news_and_views/press_releases/2010/uk_online_funding.
7. http://www.jisc.ac.uk/aboutus/strategy/strategy1012.aspx.
8. http://www.jisc.ac.uk/learnerexperience; http://wp.nmc.org/horizon2010/.
9. http://www.demos.co.uk/files/Edgeless_University_-_web.pdf?1245715615.
10. K. Harris (2003) 'Your third place or mine? Public libraries and local communities', http://www.local-level.org.uk/uploads/your_third_place.pdf.
11. http://www.nls.uk/media/808985/future-national-libraries.pdf.

References

Aabo, S. (2005) 'The role and value of public libraries in the age of digital technologies'. *Journal of Librarianship and Information Science*, 37 (4), 205–11.

Aabo, S. and Audunson, R. (2002) 'Rational choice and valuation of public libraries: can economic models for evaluating non-market goods be applied to public libraries?' *Journal of Librarianship and Information Science*, 34 (1), 5–16.

Adolphus, M. (2009) 'When "e" is the whole deal'. *Library and Information Update*, September, 38–41.

Alwis, R.S. and Fühles-Ubach, S. (2010) 'Success factors for the future of information centres, commercial and public libraries: a study from Germany'. *Interlending and Document Supply*, 38 (3), 183–8.

Ashraf T., Sharma, J. and Gulati, P. (eds) (2010) *Developing Sustainable Digital Libraries: socio-technological perspectives*. Hershey, PA: Information Science Reference.

Baker, S. and Wallace, L. (2002) *The Responsive Public Library: how to develop and market a winning collection*, 2nd edn. Englewood, CO: Libraries Unlimited.

Bishop, A., Van House, N. and Butterfield, B. (2003) *Digital Library Use: social practice in design and evaluation*. Cambridge, MA: MIT Press.

Brettle, A. (2008) 'Current status and future prospects'. *Health Information and Libraries Journal*, 25 (Supp. 1), 32–4.

Brindley, L. (2009) 'The digital paradoxes we face'. *Library and Information Update*, September, 21.

Brophy, P. (2007) *The Library in the 21st Century*, 2nd edn. London: Facet.

Bryant J., Matthews, G. and Walton, G. (2009) 'Academic libraries and social and learning space: a case study of Loughborough University Library'. *Journal of Librarianship and Information Science*, 41 (1), 7–18.

Carnegie, T.A.M. and Abell, J. (2009) 'Information, architecture, and hybridity: the changing discourse of the public library'. *Technical Communication Quarterly*, 18 (3), 242–58.

Casey, M. and Savastinuk, L. (2007) *Library 2.0: a guide to participatory library service*. Medford, NJ: Information Today.

Choudrie, J., Grey, S. and Tsitsianis, N. (2010) 'Evaluating the digital divide: the Silver Surfer's perspective'. *Electronic Government: an International Journal*, 7 (2), 148–67.

Chung, H.-K. (2008) 'The contingent valuation method in public libraries'. *Journal of Librarianship and Information Science*, 40 (2), 71–80.

Darnton, R. (2009) *The Case for Books: past, present and future*. New York: Public Affairs.

Doraiswamy, U. (2010) 'The role of public libraries and their future'. *Kentucky Libraries*, 74 (2), 22–5.

Ellcessor, E. (2010) 'Bridging disability divides'. *Information, Communication and Society*, 13 (3), 289–308.

Feather, J. (2004) *The Information Society: a study of continuity and change*, 4th edn. London: Facet.

Ferro, F. (ed.) (2010) *Handbook of Research on Overcoming Digital Divides: constructing an equitable and competitive information society*. Hershey, PA: Information Science Reference.

Frakas, M. (2008) *Social Software in Libraries: building collaboration, communication and community online*. Medford: Information Today.

Goulding, A. (2004) 'Libraries and social capital'. *Journal of Librarianship and Information Science*, 36 (1), 3–6.

Goulding, A. (2006) 'Public libraries in England: a valuable public service or a service in distress?' *Journal of Librarianship and Information Science*, 38 (1), 3–5.

Goulding, A. (2008) 'Libraries and cultural capital'. *Journal of Librarianship and Information Science*, 40 (4), 235–7.

Grant, C. (2010) 'How librarians can shape the future'. *Public Library Quarterly*, 29 (2), 95–103.

Hall, R. (2010) 'Public praxis: a vision for critical information literacy in public libraries'. *Public Library Quarterly*, 29 (2), 162–75.

Halpern, D. (2009) 'Capital gains'. *RSA Journal*, Autumn, 10–14.

Harris, C. (2007) 'Libraries with lattes: the new third place'. *Australasian Public Libraries and Information Services*, 1 December. Online at http://www.highbeam.com/doc/1G1–172010485.html.

Henry, R. (2009) 'Have we lost our way? Examining the purpose of libraries in a post-literate society'. *Library Media Connection*, 28 (1), 30–1.

Hyams, E. (2010) 'Where next for the serials crisis?' *Library and Information Gazette*, 4 June.

Ivey, B. (2010) 'Freedom of expression'. *RSA Journal*, Spring, 10–16.

Jaeger, P.T. et al. (2010) 'Diversity, inclusion and underrepresented populations in LIS research'. *Library Quarterly*, 80 (2), 175–81.

Jianfeng, W., Solan, D., and Ghods, A. (2010) 'Distance learning success: a perspective from socio-technical systems theory'. *Behaviour and Information Technology*, 29 (3), 321–9.

Johnson, M. (2010) *This Book is Overdue! How librarians and cybrarians can save us all*. New York: Harper.

Keiser, B.E. (2010) 'Library of the future – today!' *Searcher*, 18 (8), 18–54.

King Whyte, M. (ed.) (2010) *One Country Two Societies: rural–urban inequality in contemporary China*. London: Harvard University Press.

Kinney, B. (2010) 'The Internet, public libraries, and the digital divide'. *Public Library Quarterly*, 29 (2), 104–61.

Krebeck, A. (2010) 'Closing the digital divide'. *Computers in Libraries*, 30 (8), 12–15.

Law, D. (2009) 'An awfully big adventure: Strathclyde's digital library plan'. *Ariadne*, 58. Online at http://www.ariadne.ac.uk/issue58/law/.

Levy, P. and Roberts, S. (2007) *Developing the New Learning Environment: the changing role of the academic librarian*. London: Facet.

Lippincott, J.K. (2010) 'A mobile future for academic libraries'. *Reference Services Review*, 38 (2), 205–13.

Loder, M.W. (2010) 'Libraries with a future: how are academic library usage and green demands changing building designs?' *College and Research Libraries*, 71 (4), 348–60.

Lucas, E. (2010) 'Time to get savvy about social media'. *Professional Manager*, 19 (6), 22–5.

McMenemy, D., Poulter, A. and Burton, P. (2007) *An Ethical Practice Handbook: a practical guide to dealing with ethical issues in information and library work*. Oxford: Chandos.

McNicol, S. (2004) 'Investigating non-use of libraries in the UK using the mass-observation archive'. *Journal of Librarianship and Information Science*, 36 (2), 79–87.

McNicol, S. (2008) *Joint-use Libraries: libraries for the future*. Oxford: Chandos.

Malnig, A. (2008) 'Libraries march toward a digital future'. *The Seybold Report*, 8, 8–12.

Meneses, J. and Mominó, J.M. (2010) 'Putting digital literacy in practice: how schools contribute to digital inclusion in the network society'. *Information Society*, 26 (3), 197–208.

Middleton, K.L. and Chambers, V. (2010) 'Approaching digital equity: is wifi the new leveler?' *Information Technology and People*, 23 (1), 4–22.

Miller, W. and Pellen, R. (2006) *Libraries beyond Their Institutions; partnerships that work*. Binghampton: Haworth Information Press.

Min, S.-J. (2010) 'From the digital divide to the democratic divide: Internet skills, political interest, and the second-level digital divide in political Internet use'. *Journal of Information Technology and Politics*, 7 (1), 22–35.

Mirtz, R. (2010) 'Spatial metaphors and distance learning library services: why "where" makes a difference'. *Journal of Library Administration*, 50 (7/8), 857–66.

Morozow, E. (2009) 'Censoring cyberspace'. *RSA Journal*, Autumn, 20–2.

Morrone, M. and Friedman, L. (2009) 'Radical reference: socially responsible librarianship collaborating with community'. *Reference Librarian*, 50 (4), 371–96.

Nijboer, J. and Hammelburg, E. (2010) 'Extending media literacy: a new direction for libraries'. *New Library World*, 111 (1/2), 36–45.

Oldenburg, R. (1989) *The Great Good Place*. New York: Marlowe.

Ormerod, P. (2010) 'Nudge plus networks'. *RSA Journal*, Autumn, 11–15.

Ørom, A. (2000) 'Information science, historical changes and social aspects: a Nordic outlook'. *Journal of Documentation*, 56 (1), 12–26.

Partridge, H. et al. (2010) 'The contemporary librarian: skills, knowledge and attributes required in a world of emerging technologies'. *Library and Information Science Research*, 32 (4), 265–71.

Pateman, J. and Vincent, J. (2010) *Public Libraries and Social Justice*. Aldershot: Ashgate.

Pinfield, S. (2001) 'The changing role of subject librarians in academic libraries'. *Journal of Librarianship and Information Science*, 33 (1), 32–8.

Putnam, R.D. (2000). *Bowling Alone: the collapse and revival of American community*. New York: Simon and Schuster.

Raber, D. (2007) 'ACONDA and ANACONDA: social change, social responsibility and librarianship'. *Library Trends*, 55 (3), 675–97.

Rasmussen, C.H. and Jochumsen, H. (2003) 'Strategies for public libraries in the 21st century'. *International Journal of Cultural Policy*, 9 (1), 83–93.

Research Information Network (2009) *E-journals: their use, value and impact*. Online at http://www.rin.ac.uk/our-work/communicating-and-disseminating-research/e-journals-their-use-value-and-impact.

Rowlands, I. et al. (2009) 'Does e-journal investment lead to greater academic productivity?' *Library and Information Update*, July/August, 45–7.

Runfang, W. (2010) 'China's radio and TV universities: reflections on theory and practice of open and distance learning'. *Open Learning*, 25 (1), 45–56.

Samek, T. (2007) *Librarianship and Human Rights: a 21st century guide*. Oxford: Chandos.

Tanner, S. (2010) *Inspiring Research, Inspiring Scholarship – the value and benefits of digitised resources for learning, teaching, research and enjoyment*. JISC Report. Online at http://www.jisc.ac.uk/media/documents/programmes/elearning/elearningcommsevaluation/12pagefinaldocumentbenefitssynthesis.pdf.

Usherwood, B. (2007) *Equity and Excellence in the Public Library: why ignorance is not our heritage*. Aldershot: Ashgate.

Usherwood, B. and Linley, R. (2000) 'Evaluating equity in public library services'. *Journal of Librarianship and Information Science*, 32 (2), 72–81.

Usherwood, B. et al. (2005) 'Relevant repositories of public knowledge? Libraries, museums and archives in "the information age"'. *Journal of Librarianship and Information Science*, 37 (2), 89–98.

Varheim, A. et al. (2008) 'Do libraries matter? Public libraries and the creation of social capital'. *Journal of Documentation*, 64 (6), 877–92.

Vicente, M.R. and López, A.J. (2010) 'A multidimensional analysis of the disability digital divide: some evidence for Internet use'. *Information Society*, 26 (1), 48–64.

Walter, V. (2010) *Twenty First Century Kids, Twenty First Century Librarians*. Chicago: American Library Association.

Williamson, K. and Roberts, J. (2010) 'Developing and sustaining a sense of place: the role of social information'. *Library and Information Science Research*, 32 (4), 281–7.

Wisniewski, J. (2010) 'Bridging the other digital divide'. *Online*, 34 (5), 55–7.

Woodward, J. (2005) *Creating the Customer-Driven Library: building on the bookstore model*. Chicago: ALA Editions.

Yu, L. (2006) 'Understanding information inequality: making sense of the literature of the information and digital divides'. *Journal of Librarianship and Information Science*, 38 (4), 229–52.

Zabed Ahmed, S.M. (2010) 'Measuring performance and impact of rural community-led library initiatives in Thailand'. *Information Development*, 26 (1), 17–35.

I wouldn't start from here …
provision and use of UK libraries

Claire Creaser

Introduction

The question 'How many libraries are there in the UK?' is, on the surface, a simple one. It is not simple to answer, however, as there is no simple definition of what is a 'library'. The *Oxford English Dictionary* definition begins, 'a place set apart to contain books for reading, study, or reference',[1] but goes on for several paragraphs to incorporate the collection itself, circulation functions and materials other than books. This is perhaps a necessary definition, but may not be a sufficient one, as the concept of the 'library' has become much wider than this in the digital age, with virtual libraries and provision of information of all kinds increasingly seen as part of what the 'library' is and does. The international standard definition is rather broader: an 'organization, or part of an organization, the main aims of which are to build and maintain a collection and to facilitate the use of such information resources and facilities as are required to meet the informational, research, educational, cultural or recreational needs of its users' (ISO, 2006), and again, much more detail is provided as to the different types of library that are included.

Some types of library are easier to count than others. In the UK, in 2008–9, there were three national libraries, 4,517 public libraries, and over 900 academic libraries in universities and colleges of higher education. Beyond these sectors, numbers are harder to obtain. There are an estimated 500 libraries in colleges of further education, and an estimated 2,000 in schools. There are some 500 National Health Service libraries and perhaps 100 libraries in government departments and agencies. In the private sector, there is no current information available on the numbers of special libraries, in voluntary organisations, professional associations, workplaces and so on. Indeed, in some organisations the very existence of a library or information centre may be regarded as commercially confidential; and the historical data are known to be incomplete. There are libraries in churches, in museums, in private collections – where does a library end and an archive begin? – and they hold all kinds of material.

This chapter concentrates on the public and academic library sectors. UK public and academic libraries collect – and publish – a wealth of data about their activities, and these data form the starting point for this summary of current library provision in the UK (CIPFA, 2010; SCONUL, 2010). The chapter goes on to place this in a historical perspective and to relate it to provision elsewhere in the world and to the broader information landscape.

Library provision

Public libraries

As of 31 March 2009, there were 208 public library authorities in the UK operating a total of 4,517 libraries, including 553 mobile libraries, equivalent to one library for every 13,589 people. There were 4,966 professional librarians, supported by 20,683 other staff (full-time equivalents) and almost 16,000 volunteers. Over 75 million books were available for borrowing, with a further 13.1 million reference books and 11.5 million in reserve stocks, giving a total book stock of 99.7 million, or 1.6 books per person. Of these, 12.6 million were newly acquired during the year. Libraries also stocked 8.4 million audiovisual items – 90% of which could be borrowed. There were almost 89,000[2] newspapers, magazines and serials available, and 45,523 terminals offering Internet access to members of the public. The UK's public libraries spent over £1,181 million in 2008–9, or £19.24 per person. Most of this was on staff (54%), with 11.9% spent on premises and 10.9% on books and other materials. UK public libraries are funded by the local authorities, although they do generate some income, from a variety of sources. In 2007–8 this amounted to almost £100 million, or £1.63 per person.

Increasingly, public libraries provide more than can be described by the dry statistics available from the Chartered Institute of Public Funding and Accountancy (CIPFA).[3] They offer material in a variety of languages to meet the needs of their local communities; run reading groups, homework clubs and story times for children, and provide services for the visually impaired and the housebound. They are involved in a wide range of outreach activities, including with refugee communities, the homeless and local authority facilities. They operate the Books on Prescription service,[4] and a wide range of reading promotion schemes for both children and adults. These activities have a significant impact on the lives of individual members of the community and on society as a whole, but attempts to draw all this together on a national scale have met with little success.

Academic libraries

All UK publicly funded universities and colleges of higher education have libraries, with a total of more than 900 service points in 2008–9. All but a handful are members of the Society of College, National and University Libraries (SCONUL).[5] The user base for academic libraries is commonly taken as the number of full-time equivalent (FTE) students, and this has been used here. Data relate to the academic year, August to July.

UK academic libraries employed almost 10,200 library staff in 2008–9, of whom almost 3,800 were professionally qualified librarians. They provided their users with 188,000 study places, 51,000 of them having computers for student use. Academic libraries were open for an average of 93 hours per week during term time. A wide range of information resources were provided, with a total of 116 million books and pamphlets on the shelves, equivalent to 65 per FTE student, of which 2.7 million were newly acquired during the year. Libraries subscribed to a total of 1.5 million current serials, with 1.2 million of these available in electronic format.

Academic library spending includes staff, information resources, equipment and other operating costs, which may include an element of premises' re-charge within the institution. Overall, UK academic libraries spent over £680 million in 2008–9, equivalent to £378 per FTE student. As with public libraries, the greatest part of this was on staff (47%), with 36% being spent on information provision. Total spending on academic libraries currently represents around 2.7% of total institutional expenditure.

Academic libraries are not just providers of books and serials for research and learning. They also provide user training in a wide range of information skills, many provide copyright advice to their staff and students, and they may be responsible for the e-learning environment, the institutional web pages and the institutional repository. There are diverse arrangements in place for the management of such varied services, ranging from the self-contained library, via the converged information technology/library service, to much broader coalitions encompassing the full range of academic and student support services.

Library use

Public libraries

There are around 12.3 million people (adults and children) in the UK who actively borrow from their public library – 20% of the population. In 2008–9, 311 million books and 28 million other items were loaned – equivalent to an average of one loan every two weeks for each active borrower. There were some 103,000 housebound readers. Over 13.6 million requests were made for specific items, and more than 95% were supplied – two-thirds within seven days of the request.

Not everyone who uses a library borrows books or other materials. Results from the CIPFA PLUS library user surveys for 2006–7 (CIPFA, 2009) showed that 55% of visitors borrowed books. The same survey showed that 34% of visitors came for information, while 24% used a computer. The Department for Culture, Media and Sport's *Taking Part* survey (DCMS, 2009) found that almost 40% of adults in England (aged 16+) had visited a public library at least once in the last year. Overall, there were a total of 325 million visits to library premises in 2008–9, or 5.3 visits per head of population. All public libraries have websites providing information and, often, access to their catalogues. In 2008–9, it is estimated that more than 113 million virtual visits were made to UK public library websites.

Academic libraries

Academic libraries support 2.29 million FTE users, of which 1.8 million are students, 143,000 are academic staff and the remainder are other institutional staff and external users. These users made almost 122 million visits to libraries in 2008–9, and borrowed more than 104 million books.

Electronic resources are increasingly important to academic libraries, taking up an increasing proportion of their budgets and becoming the first place users now look for information, as discussed further in Chapter 4 and also in *Digital Library Economics: an academic perspective* (Baker and Evans, 2009). However, measuring use of such resources remains problematic, as libraries are generally dependent on the resource providers to furnish such information, and this is not always in a standard format. The Project COUNTER (Counting Online Usage of Networked Electronic Resources)[6] codes of practice are providing a standard so that usage can be compared between resources and collated across them, but they have not been universally adopted. The figures available suggest a broad total of 143 million journal articles downloaded and 24 million accesses of e-books in 2008–9; these figures are likely to be lower bounds for the true level of usage of electronic resources.

Academic libraries do not collate the results of their user surveys, not least because a variety of different survey formats and questionnaires are currently in use. The closest to a general rating for user satisfaction with academic libraries comes from the question in the National Student Survey (NSS)[7] which asks respondents to indicate their level of agreement with the statement 'The library resources and services are good enough for my needs'. Overall, in 2008, 85% of students who responded to the NSS agreed with this statement.

Trends over time

Public libraries

Data have been collected and published by public libraries since the 1960s. Here we look at some of the trends in both provision and use over the last 20 years. Key to library provision is the amount spent on the service. Over the last 20 years, total UK public library spending has more than doubled, from £584 million to £1,181 million. Even taking the population increase into account, spending has risen from £10.22 to £19.24 per head of population. However, this investment has merely kept pace with inflation – when adjusted for the change in the Retail Price Index, spending of £19.24 in 2008–9 was equivalent to £9.84 at 1988–89 prices. How the budget has been spent has changed, however. Figure 2.1 shows the proportions of expenditure on each of staffing, premises, materials and other costs at 5-year intervals. It is clear that the proportion spent on materials has fallen over the period, from 19% in 1987–88 to 11% in 2007–8.

With the proportion of spending on materials having declined over the last 20 years, it is not surprising that the number of books has also fallen. Total book stock has declined from 141 million items in March 1989 (2.5 per head of population) to 100 million in March 2009 (1.5 per head of population). Stock of other items, such as music and video materials, has increased from 5.3 to 8.4 million items over the same period. The number of new books bought has also fallen, but reached a low point in 1997–98, and has been rising since then (Figure 2.2). Public libraries are clearly adept at getting value for money when it comes to purchase of materials for use by the public, with the average price paid for books increasing only a little in cash terms, from £6.85 in 1988–89 to £7.03 in 2008–9. Paired with the reductions in overall stock levels, the rate at which the book stock is replaced has increased from 10% per year in 1988–89 to 12.7% per year in 2008–9. To put it another way, at the replacement rate of 20 years ago, it would have taken 10 years to replace the entire book stock, whereas now this could be accomplished in 8 years.

In 1998 the UK government introduced Annual Library Plans for the monitoring of library performance, with formal Public Library

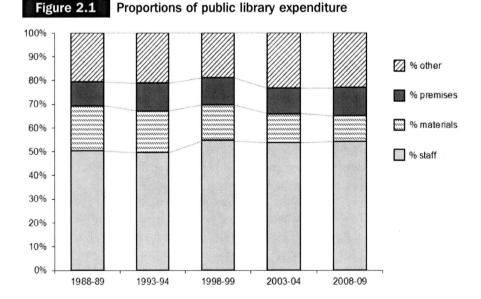

Figure 2.1 Proportions of public library expenditure

Figure 2.2 Total book acquisitions UK public libraries

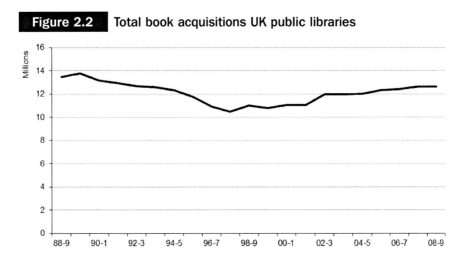

Standards being launched in April 2001. It is perhaps no coincidence that the two largest increases in book acquisitions, as shown in Figure 2.2, immediately followed these two initiatives. Another area covered by the public library standards was numbers of service points and their opening hours. While the total number of service points has fallen, the proportion open for 45 hours per week or more has increased to 26% in 2008–9 (Figure 2.3).

Figure 2.3 Public library service points

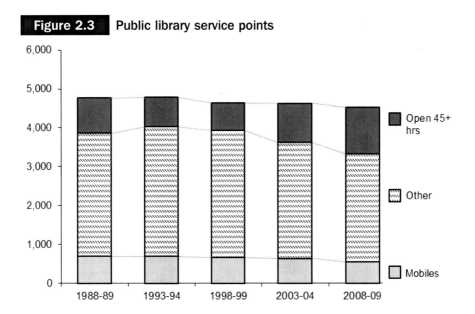

Grindlay and Morris (2004) analysed trends in public library book issues between 1980 and 1999 and found that the number of libraries open for 45 hours per week was closely associated with book issues throughout that period. If this was a causal relationship, it would be expected that book issues would have increased as the number of libraries open for 45 hours increased, but this has not been the case. The level of use of public libraries, traditionally measured by book issues, has continued to fall (Figure 2.4). Since 1992–93, data on numbers of visits made to libraries have provided an alternative measure of use, which does not present such a poor picture. Although there have been falls in numbers of visits, these have not been as dramatic as in the figures for issues, and the additional services offered by libraries are likely to be responsible. As noted above, in 2006–7, 45% of library visitors did not borrow a book during their visit, whereas in 1999–2000 (the first year for which national averages are available), just 24% of visitors did not borrow a book.

Academic libraries

There have been many changes over the last 20 years in the academic library sector within the UK, most dramatically in 1992, when the

Figure 2.4　**Use of public libraries per head of population**

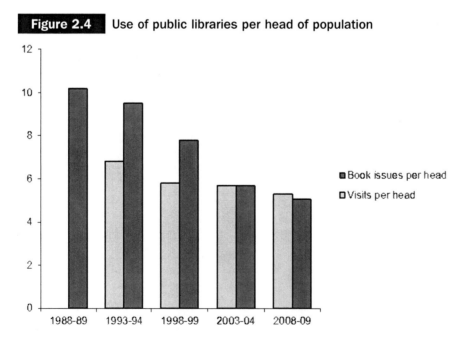

former polytechnics became independent of local authorities and gained university status. This and other organisational changes have affected the bodies collecting data about academic libraries, so that UK-wide data for the earliest years are not available. Some of these changes are described in the *LISU Annual Library Statistics 2003* (Creaser et al., 2003). This section therefore discusses trends from 1994–95 – the earliest year for which aggregated data for the whole of UK publicly funded higher education libraries are available. Universities have grown over this period, with the number of FTE students increasing from 1.31 million to 1.80 million.

A key trend has been the move towards electronic provision of information resources and services. The proportion of study spaces with computers has increased from 11% to 27% since 1994–95, while the proportion of journal titles available electronically has risen from 46% in 2000–1 (the first year for which reliable estimates are available) to 85% in 2008–9. Increasing desktop access to electronic resources and to services such as reservations and enquiry services has resulted in the number of visits to library premises falling, from 84 per FTE student to 68 per FTE student over the period (Figure 2.5). Figure 2.5 also shows that use of the print collection has not diminished, however, with the number of loans per FTE student increasing over the same period, from 50 to 58.

Total spending on academic libraries has increased by 53% between 1994–95 and 2008–9, from £246 to £378 per FTE student. This is broadly in line with general inflation, with the increase in the Retail Price

Figure 2.5 Use of academic libraries per FTE student

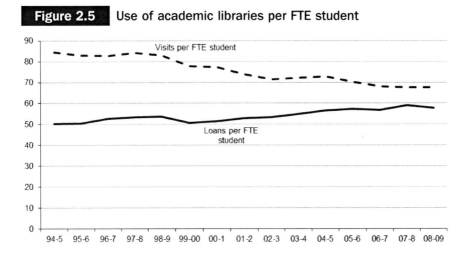

Index (RPI) being at 45% over the same period. The balance between staff, information provision and other expenditure has remained relatively constant, although within the figures for information provision there have been changes (Figure 2.6). Note that the figures for periodicals spend in Figure 2.6 include spending on e-journals, while the figures for 'other' electronic resources include e-books, databases and other digital documents. The remainder of information provision expenditure (less than 10%, and falling) is largely on inter-library lending and on binding.

The wider world

Library statistics are available for a variety of countries around the world and may be freely available on the Web. Comparisons of such data between countries must be treated with care, however, as different regulatory regimes affect the services provided, and different definitions and currencies apply to the various statistics available. The International Organization for Standardization (ISO) TC46/SC8 publishes and maintains several standards in the area of library statistics[8] which provide definitions and guidance for the collection and calculation of a wide range of management statistics and performance indicators for all types of library, but these are not universally applied to data collection in practice.

Figure 2.6 Academic library spending on information provision

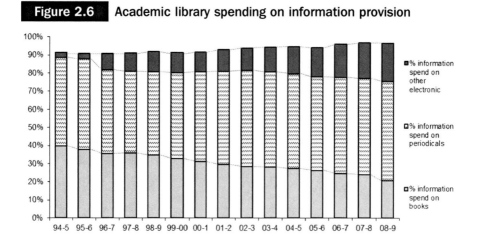

There have been a number of attempts to collect comparable national-level data on both a worldwide and a European scale, but none, as yet, has provided an ongoing and stable set of statistics describing library operations. The most ambitious was, arguably, the EU-funded LIBECON project,[9] which sought to obtain comprehensive data on library provision and use from across Europe relating to all library sectors. The most recent data available are in respect of 2001, and the project has now finished. The most recent initiative is currently being undertaken by the International Federation of Library Associations (IFLA) in collaboration with the United Nations Educational, Scientific and Cultural Organisation Institute for Statistics and the ISO, to collect a set of 23 measures for public and academic libraries around the world (Heaney, 2009). A pilot survey was carried out in Latin America and the Caribbean in 2007 (Akpabie, 2009), and the work is being taken forward by the IFLA section on Statistics and Evaluation.

The following does not attempt to be comprehensive in its presentation of international library statistics, but picks out readily available data from a few selected countries to give a flavour of what might be possible if the IFLA initiative is successful.

Public libraries

Recent public library data have been sourced for five countries.[10] In order to give meaningful comparisons, data have been presented relative to the resident population of each country. Note, however, that all comparisons must be treated with care, as the cultures, customs and regulatory frameworks in each country will vary. Note also that the data for Canada are in respect of the largest cities only, accounting for just over half of the total population. Financial data have been converted to sterling at the rate in force at the end of the year, or the first calendar year where the fiscal year spans two calendar years (i.e. 2007 for 2007–8).[11]

Figure 2.7 shows book stock per capita, issues per capita and visits per capita (not reported for Ireland). Figure 2.8 shows the population per staff member for both professional staff and total staff. Figure 2.9 shows summary financial data, for spending on stock, staff and other expenditure, per head of population, converted to sterling for ease of comparison. Note that for Figure 2.9 Australian statistics did not give separate figures for staff spending.

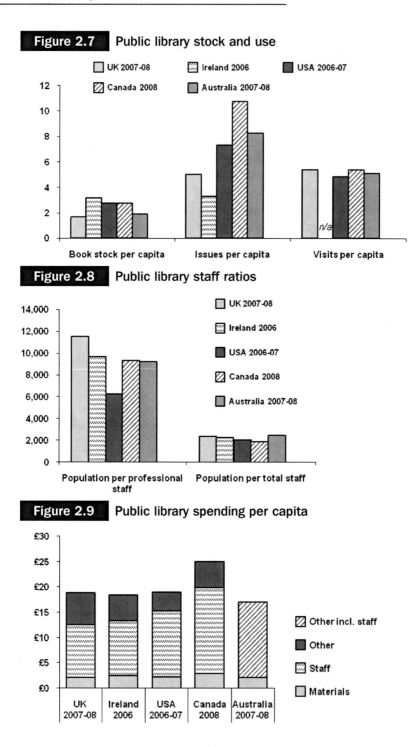

Figure 2.7 Public library stock and use

UK 2007-08 Ireland 2006 USA 2006-07
Canada 2008 Australia 2007-08

Book stock per capita   Issues per capita   Visits per capita

Figure 2.8 Public library staff ratios

UK 2007-08
Ireland 2006
USA 2006-07
Canada 2008
Australia 2007-08

Population per professional staff   Population per total staff

Figure 2.9 Public library spending per capita

Other incl. staff
Other
Staff
Materials

UK 2007-08   Ireland 2006   USA 2006-07   Canada 2008   Australia 2007-08

Academic libraries

Recent academic library data have been sourced for four countries.[12] In order to give meaningful comparisons, data have been presented relative to the total FTE student population in higher education in each country. Note, however, that all comparisons must be treated with care, as the education landscape and culture, as well as regulatory frameworks, in each country will differ. Financial data have been converted to sterling at the rate in force at the end of the year, or the first calendar year where the fiscal year spans two calendar years (i.e. 2007 for 2007–8).[13] Again, the Canadian statistics do not cover the whole country, but only those institutions which are members of the Association of Research Libraries.

Figure 2.10 shows print stock, loans and visits per FTE student, and book acquisitions and current serials per 100 FTE students. Figure 2.11 shows the FTE student population per staff member for both professional staff and total staff. Figure 2.12 shows summary financial data for spending on information resources, staff and other expenditure, per FTE student, converted to sterling for ease of comparison. Financial data were not available for the USA.

The wider context

The library and information services available in the UK are not limited to those provided by public and academic libraries, and increasingly individuals seeking information or entertainment are looking to alternatives to satisfy their needs. National libraries provide additional and specialist resources for scholars; workplace libraries target their facilities to employees; and schools provide a whole range of resources for information and reading for pleasure for children and young people. The Internet, rather than the library, is becoming the first port of call for those seeking information, and, with increasing broadband access within the home, this is set to continue.

Grindlay and Morris (2004) found a close relationship between public library book issues and the number of libraries open for 45 hours per week or more. However, the number of such libraries has increased since they carried out their analyses but book issues have not, so breaking the link. The decline in public library visitors is also dramatic – in England, 48% of adults visited a library at least once in 2005–6, while only 40% did so just three years later, in 2008–9 (DCMS, 2007). Based on their

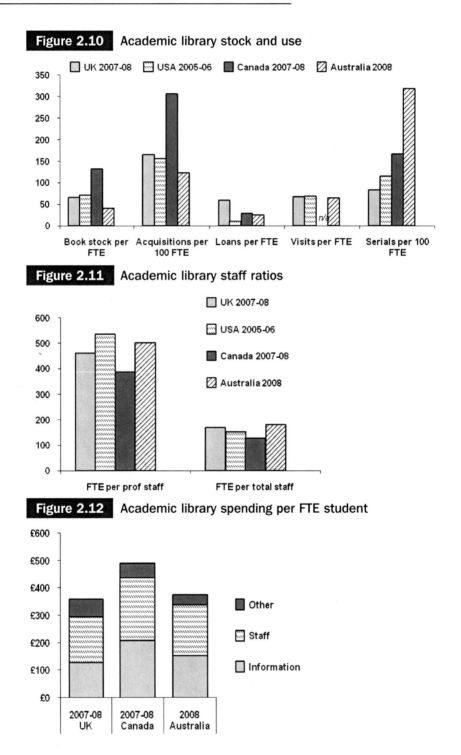

Figure 2.10 Academic library stock and use

Figure 2.11 Academic library staff ratios

Figure 2.12 Academic library spending per FTE student

analyses, Grindlay and Morris (2004) suggested that the primary cause of falling book issues was likely to be increasing affluence, which is beyond the control of libraries. Government statistics do not suggest any decline in interest in reading as a leisure activity, with 56% of men and 73% of women doing this in 2006–7 (Office for National Statistics, 2009). Ten years before, 56% of men and 71% of women read books (Office for National Statistics, 2000). In contrast, household spending on books increased by 88% between 1997 and 2007,[14] as compared to an increase in the RPI of 31% over the same period. The economic recession from 2008 has had an impact on such spending, however, with a fall of 10% in that year. It remains to be seen what effect, if any, the recession will have on public library use.

Conclusion

In the UK, there is an extensive and diverse network of libraries, serving the information and leisure needs of the population. Core services are generally free at the point of use and levels of provision appear to be on a par with those in other countries for which comparative data are readily available.

Reliable and robust evidence is key to libraries' proving their value and impact to stakeholders. Data are needed for effective management of existing services and for sound development of new ones. National, and international, comparisons can be used to advocate for better services, which will bring increased use, but the evidence to make such comparisons is lacking in some sectors.

Quantifying UK-wide levels of library provision and use is not always easy, with only the public and higher education sectors having reliable and consistent data available over time. These data show that spending on libraries is generally keeping pace with inflation, and with the increasing population, although in public libraries the proportion being spent on books and other library materials has fallen. In academic libraries, the balance of spending is also changing, with the proportion going on electronic resources increasing, whilst the proportion spent on print is falling.

The challenge for libraries in moving forward is to be found in meeting the increasingly diverse expectations of potential users familiar with all the technological solutions available in the information and leisure environment, whilst maintaining their core values and meeting the needs of their existing customer base, all to a tight budget.

Notes

1. *Oxford English Dictionary Online*, 2nd edn, 1989.
2. As at 31 March 2008 – data were not collected in respect of 2008–9.
3. See http://www.cipfa.org.uk/ and http://www.cipfastats.net/.
4. http://www.cambridgeshire.gov.uk/leisure/libraries/reference/ health_information.htm.
5. http://www.sconul.ac.uk.
6. http://www.projectcounter.org/about.html.
7. http://www.thestudentsurvey.com/.
8. See http://www.iso.org/iso/iso_catalogue/catalogue_tc/catalogue_tc_browse. htm?commid=48826 for a list of current standards.
9. http://www.libecon.org.
10. Data sources: UK and Ireland: *Public Library Statistics 2007–08*, London: CIPFA; USA: *Public Libraries in the United States: Fiscal Year 2007* (2009), IMLS, http://harvester.census.gov/imls/pubs/pls/pub_detail.asp?id=122; Canada: *2008 Canadian Public Library Statistics*, http://www. mississauga.ca/file/COM/2008_CULC_Public_Library_Survey_Report_Rev2 .pdf; Australia: *Australian Public Libraries Statistical Report 2007–2008*, http://www.nsla.org.au/publications/statistics/2009/pdf/NSLA.Statistics-20090924-Australian.Public.Library.Statistics..2007.2008.pdf.
11. £1 = €1.48; $1.96 US; $1.77 Can; $2.27 Aus.
12. Data sources: UK: *SCONUL Annual Library Statistics*, London: SCONUL; USA: *Academic Library Statistics 2006 First Look* (2008) NCES, http://nces.ed.gov/pubsearch/pubsinfo.asp?pubid=2008337; Canada: http://fisher.lib.virginia.edu/cgi-local/arlbin/arl.cgi?task= setupsubset; Australia: *CAUL Online Statistics*, http://statistics.caul.edu.au/.
13. £1 = $1.97 Can; $2.06 Aus.
14. Office for National Statistics, *Consumer Trends* Q4 2009 and Q4 2001, http://www.statistics.gov.uk/StatBase/Product.asp?vlnk=14277.

References

Akpabie, C. (2009) 'The 2007 international library survey in Latin America and the Caribbean'. In Heaney, M. (ed.) *Library Statistics for the Twenty-first Century World*. Munich: K.G. Saur.

Baker, D. and Evans, W. (2009) *Digital Library Economics: an academic perspective*. Oxford: Chandos.

CIPFA (Chartered Institute of Public Finance and Accountancy). (2009) *Social Research: 2009*. PLUS National Report Extract (personal communication from Jonathan Gordon, IPF Ltd).

CIPFA. (2010) *Public Library Statistics*. London: Chartered Institute of Public Finance and Accounting.

Creaser, C., Maynard, S. and White, S. (2003) *LISU Annual Library Statistics 2003*. Loughborough: LISU.

DCMS (Department for Culture, Media and Sport). (2007) *Taking Part: the national survey of culture, leisure and sport. Annual Report 2005/2006*. London: Department for Culture, Media and Sport. Online at http://webarchive.nationalarchives.gov.uk/+/http://www.culture.gov.uk/reference_library/publications/3682.aspx.

DCMS (Department for Culture, Media and Sport). (2009) *Taking Part: the national survey of culture, leisure and sport: PSA21: Indicator 6 – Final baseline results from the 2008/09 Taking Part survey*. London: Department for Culture, Media and Sport. Online at http://www.culture.gov.uk/images/research/PSA21-FinalBaselinereport.pdf.

Grindlay, D.J.C. and Morris, A. (2004) 'The decline in adult book lending in UK public libraries and its possible causes: II Statistical Analysis'. *Journal of Documentation*, 60 (6), 632–57.

Heaney, M. (2009) 'Global library statistics for the twenty-first century'. In Heaney, M. (ed.) (2009) *Library Statistics for the Twenty-first Century World*. Munich: K.G. Saur.

ISO (International Organization for Standardization). (2006) *ISO 2789:2006 – Information and Documentation: international library statistics*.

Office for National Statistics. (2000) *Social Trends 30*. London: HMSO. Online at http://www.statistics.gov.uk/downloads/theme_social/st30v8.pdf.

Office for National Statistics. (2009) *Social Trends 39*. London: HMSO. Online at http://www.statistics.gov.uk/downloads/theme_social/Social_Trends39/Social_Trends_39.pdf.

SCONUL. (2010) *Annual Library Statistics: 2008–09*. London: Society of College, National and University Libraries.

3

From people flows to knowledge flows

John Dolan

Introduction: a brief review of *People Flows*

In a volume about libraries and society, it seems right to ask how much libraries are serving the community rather than the institution. Research published in March 2000 as *People Flows* was undertaken in the late 1990s by a team led by Clare Nankivell at the School of Information Studies at the then University of Central England (now known as Birmingham City University). The report observed that 'most UK library cooperation has been led by practitioners' views rather than by defined user needs. This has led to a "defensive" attitude to cooperation in some areas and in some library sectors. Similarly, many public librarians have expressed concerns about it not being their role to support students with multiple copies of text books or specific course material for local learners' (Nankivell, Foster and Elkin, 2000).

People Flows was the 'first attempt to assess the uses people made of libraries across sectors and the reasons behind these uses. However, the focus was people engaged in learning ... learners were a significant group of library users across all three sectors in the survey, around seven in ten library users in university and college libraries and around one sixth of those in public libraries was a full time student. A further 13% of all those surveyed across the libraries was engaged in learning but not a full-time student – a "lifelong learner" ... variety of levels from those studying at home for pleasure to those on day release college courses to part time PhD students at university. Most lifelong learners surveyed in universities and colleges were part-time students of the institution ... full-time students and lifelong learners, with the third group of non-learners all had distinct patterns of library use' (Nankivell, Foster and Elkin, 2000).

The study accepted that 'learning' was evident in different kinds of library use. People used libraries in association with full- or part-time learning, linked directly to all manner of courses; learners 'could even be people who were studying at home for pleasure'. Since the 19th century's mechanics institutes, learning was seen as motivated by self-improvement. By the end of the 20th century, the growth of mass education, its strong association with party-political disagreement and the requirement to demonstrate success – of the individual and of the system or curriculum in place at any one time – reinforced the distinct characters of school, further and higher education and isolated them from the less tangible purpose, qualities and outputs of what is now known as 'informal learning'. Latterly, adult education was subject to cuts from budgets focused on applied learning, core skills and – more recently – information and communications technology (ICT).

Unsurprisingly, *People Flows* found that 'full-time students were more likely than lifelong learners to be frequent library users in the university and college sectors. Lifelong learners were more likely than full-time students to be frequent users in the public [library] sector. This suggests reliance by lifelong learners on the public library to meet their library needs.' However, 'public libraries were heavily used by learners altogether, with three out of every ten people surveyed in public libraries being engaged in learning at some level.' The report reveals that 'data show a large amount of library cross-use, particularly of public libraries by university and college library users. Overall, two thirds of university and college respondents and half of public library respondents had used at least one other library in the past year.'

The report describes other nuances, like learners in public libraries favouring central rather than branch libraries for their location and greater amount of study space; and, it might also be assumed, for the greater range and depth of resources, as in the 'six key reasons' that 'emerged as crucial to the choice of library':

1. Where the library is – location, transport routes to it, parking facilities, proximity to home, work or place of study.

2. The resources within the library – books, journals, IT facilities and study space – and their quality, range and appropriateness.

3. When the library is open.

4. Who staffs the library – their knowledge, helpfulness and approachability.

5. How the resources within the library are organised – catalogues, classification systems, signposting etc.

6. The library environment – how comfortable people find it, the lighting and heating, and provision of such facilities as toilets, phones and a café. (Nankivell, Foster and Elkin, 2000)

Significantly, 'across all sectors, lifelong learners were significantly more likely than full-time students or non-learners to use a particular library for the staff within it. This suggests a greater need for advice and help.' The research also identified barriers: 'the main barriers to library use were opening hours, the facility to borrow items, access to information technology and gaining entry to the library itself ... these four barriers are real to library users and create difficulties for them in accessing the resources and materials they need' (Nankivell, Foster and Elkin, 2000).

The *People Flows* conclusions

This is a selective summary of the research outcomes, but chosen to point to an informed potential for today's library provision across the whole spectrum of learning. Importantly, the report despaired: 'the solutions to the problems of cross-use of libraries and of meeting the learning needs of communities within a region would be found in library cooperation, increased use of electronic resources and networked library and resource developments', but 'whilst these solutions sounded wonderful, they were not likely in the short or medium term to be viable, without significant funds being provided'. This comes from Appendix E to the *People Flows* report, 'Possible Ways Forward: cross-sectoral use of libraries'. Sarah Ormes, Public Library Networking Research Officer at UKOLN,[1] describes scenarios in which users' needs would be more efficiently and effectively met by networking solutions, the technology for which would now be largely taken for granted – except that the cross-sectoral collaboration it could provide is only selectively on offer. *People Flows* demonstrated how people were moving between libraries to reach information and knowledge resources, seek help or find an environment in which they could work comfortably. What it also indicated was that the time was near when information and knowledge would flow to people. In that context a reconfiguring of library provision would be, at least, desirable.

Today's learning context

People Flows was researched over the later 1990s, being published on the brink of an information and learning revolution. The flood of technological innovation that began around this time continues and accelerates as technology renews itself with increasing rapidity, complexity and opportunity. More widely, technological change has delivered change in the infrastructure that underpins our economy and every aspect of our way of life. It is a matter for research and speculation whether the technology has created the change or other scientific, social and economic drivers have made the changes that drive modern life.

The excitement lies in the fact that change is accelerating and innovation is needed at a faster pace than ever before. Adaptability – in a kind of Darwinian survival struggle to be fittest – sees 'old Europe' economies facing the shifting patterns of industrial production, compounded now by a recession that will put a break on real-terms growth for some years. The emerging economies look to take on the role of global economic powers, while the USA and Europe explore innovation and creativity as a means of restoring their prowess. Some patterns are predictable. The demographic shift will have its impact: the UK's ageing population, supported by a smaller economically active workforce, must place new expectations of productivity on a reduced but more sophisticated workforce fighting to preserve hard-earned norms of protection and remuneration.

In a fascinating contrast to the UK, India aims to capture a 'demographic dividend', capitalising on a 30-year window of opportunity during which time it will be the only major nation with a growing active workforce. 'The demographic dividend is only as good as the investment in your human capital ... if people have education, they have good health, they have infrastructure, they have roads to go to work, they have lights to study at night, only in those cases can you really get the benefits of the demographic dividend ... India is at that critical point where either it can leverage its demographic dividend or it can lead to a demographic disaster' (Nilekani, 2009). Between 2010 and 2011, India will undertake a comprehensive census of its 1.2 billion population. As well as the usual measures, it will identify levels of computer and mobile phone ownership and Internet access. The country is anticipating needs and opportunities for education, production and the consumer market.

In Britain, without a large economically active population, the challenge to maintain and improve the material quality of life will be even greater. Government policy has swung between sustaining a declining manufacturing industry and investing in digital and creative economies. Both kinds of prosperity require investment in skills, but the ensuing debate will inform future politics and the character of education, training and informal learning for the decade ahead. Britain is set to extend participation in compulsory education to 18 by 2015; funding and commissioning of learning provision has moved to local authorities from a dissolved Learning and Skills Council; apprenticeships are due for expansion. Adult functional illiteracy remains high, with one in six people in the UK struggling to read and write. Their literacy is below the level expected of an 11-year-old (DfES, 2003, cited in Jama and Dugdale, 2010). Digital and information illiteracy – no longer new phenomena – compound the challenge; meanwhile, 895,000 16- to 24-year-olds in England are 'not in education, employment or training' (NEET) (DCSF, 2010). In higher education (HE), universities are about to face budget cuts on an unfamiliar scale, with commercialisation and new charging regimes. Usually vigorous in advocacy, will university vice chancellors confront a government that wants more for less?

Working out alternatives

In this environment, progress requires economies and innovation at the same time. Partnership and collaboration characterise how organisations and services will work in the future. For public libraries, current thinking reflects coping strategies as much as the pursuit of improvement, but the aspiration is for *better* as well as *cheaper*. Strategies include:

- **Shared services:** for economies in back-office support, library management systems and cross-council joint working. Not-so-new Libraries West[2] has successfully reduced costs and created innovative systems in joint acquisition, converged catalogues and a shared reservation scheme.

- **Governance:** little experienced, but tempting in its difference, is the contracting out of library service management. It failed to materialise in Margaret Thatcher's Compulsory Competitive Tendering programme[3] but has advocates and commercial players; Wigan and Luton are early adopters.[4]

In spite of renewed investment (in infrastructure, buildings, opening hours for example), the focus is more on costs, inputs and outputs and less on outcomes or innovation. Hounslow Libraries are managed privately and received much-needed council funding for infrastructure repair.[5]

People Flows pointed towards the potential for libraries in different sectors to work to similar ends because institutions' objectives are similar, could be more economically met through collaboration and could increase their impact.

Collaboration for access

In HE, the convention has been to focus on the institution, its identity and independence. In recent years, higher education institutions (HEIs) have competed to attract students, to win research grants and to achieve a better research assessment score, thus gaining students, funding and kudos. This still allows university libraries to develop coherent national strategies, models and guidelines for each institution or group to apply to their own interests: something the public library sector has only rarely achieved.

Increasing access for students, academics and the visitor

A number of projects in higher and further education explored ways to respond to the needs of students and academics who, for a variety of reasons, need access to resources in settings other than their home institution. Over time, schemes progressed incrementally from enabling access to print, then electronic, resources. UK Libraries Plus allowed exceptional access to people from other institutions; borrowing rights for researchers and distance learners, with reference access for undergraduates and staff. UK Computing Plus (2002–3) piloting in six university libraries observed student comments: 'I hope [my university] supports it reciprocally', 'why not all universities?' and 'I am all for university facilities being seen collectively as a national resource'.[6] SCONUL Access (Society of College, National and University Libraries) has rounded up and coordinated various such initiatives into a coherent offer.[7] The HAERVI (HE Access to e-Resources in Visited Institutions) project[8] was promoted by SCONUL and UCISA (the Universities and Colleges Information Systems Association) to improve the service offered by HEIs to visiting students and researchers from other HEIs wishing to access licensed e-resources. As well as evaluation and its best practice guide (2007),[9] the project was important in encouraging and enabling flexibility in the provision of e-resources for library users that would still sustain the interests of publishers and aggregators. This mutual understanding and willingness to collaborate will be of value in the coming times of reducing budgets.

Inspire 'supports libraries in working together to improve access to information and learning for all'. Led by a partnership of SCONUL and the Society of Chief Librarians, Inspire[10] has persuaded, led and supported university, public, national – initially – and other libraries to open up access to and use of their resources. Even with a national partnership, impetus and funding from the Museums, Libraries and Archives Council (MLA), Inspire was adopted unevenly across the UK but ultimately achieved almost 100% support and is a boon to learners seeking specific resources and support. Pioneering work in Sunderland in the 1990s – leading to the Libraries Access Sunderland Scheme – set the scene for the North-East region's commitment to the concept. Inspire North East[11] is among the most advanced of the English Inspire regional partnerships, involving nearly 50 diverse libraries and institutions. In the UK Home Counties cultural and strategic proximity and scale have enabled further extensive cooperation. There is still not a single UK-wide plan or market offer.

Collaboration in designing learning spaces

In the last decade, there has been a radical change in the concept of the academic library space, with similar ideas being adopted in public library and other learning settings. The balance of space and facilities varies according to subject, institution and learners; more or less room for physical resources and ICT or for research, quiet study and social learning space; the new learning environment allows for immediate staff support and spaces designed and equipped for different approaches and learner needs. The importance of the library is determined by the quality of the space, and facilities are critical to successful discovery and educational attainment.

Manchester

The city strategy for public libraries leans heavily towards collaboration and co-location. Especially in education, it features both new library buildings and strong partnerships where the public library service, homework support for pupils and school students and then further education are seen as a continuum that can be delivered by the public library, working in contractual partnership with education providers. 'New libraries will be co-located and preferably integrated with other service providers ensuring libraries are at the heart of every neighbourhood delivering a wide range of local services. Co-location means that the public library can also provide services for partners including schools and colleges, while library customers can benefit from the convenience of joined-up services.'[12]

Southend

In Southend the local authority has worked with the University of Essex and South East Essex College and also engaged the Southend Community College in conceiving a single – 'combined' – library serving each institution and the wider public, with the aims of physical and economic regeneration. A study during 2008–9 goes to the feasibility and first public consultation stages. Economies of scale, extended and improved services for all, town-centre regeneration and increased support for local business, employment and growth are seen as key benefits. As architects are selected, the term 'combined library' reflects a concern to ensure that each user group will be well served, taking account of the risk indicators associated with seamless integration. Concerns mirror the apprehensions more widely held about such a rare move. They include numbers of visitors, each group crowding out another, irreconcilable uses, limited physical materials and e-licensing restrictions, and different staffing regimes, terms and conditions. The University, in its Albert Sloman Library at the Colchester campus, already admits almost 2,000 external user-learners. There is a liberal application process. Users are not registered students or academics; they are mostly from special interest societies. Interests are subject focused, but such unobtrusive openness still indicates that a bigger but not overwhelming learner community beckons in the future, as was found by the Inspire experience.

Worcester

The most adventurous collaborative UK project is the Worcester Library and History Centre (WLHC).[13] The vision is:

- learning that people need to follow
- to bring together staff, resources and users in a single shared operation
- to give users access to all resources, physical and digital, according to need and entitlement, calculated through a holistic authentication process and following the ongoing negotiations with publishers and providers
- staff will work with all users; while specialists may concentrate in certain areas, all staff will be there to respond at least initially, to all users.

Planning is embedded in the local and regional community. It is conceived around uses and users rather than collections or institutions; some 60% of students are part time, reflecting a continuing trend in patterns of study, many being mature students, at work and/or otherwise occupied. The focus is 'not on who you are but on what you want to do'.[14] Outputs and outcomes are set against social, community, academic, learning and cultural aspirations. They will observe public library targets for participation and social and learning outcomes and the library's contribution to academic achievement; design has involved users and stakeholders.

The WLHC is challenging accepted but sometimes unreasonable barriers and traditional apprehensions:

- moving away from given systems, infrastructures and governance methods
- crafting new workforce culture and practices
- learning how to manage integrated staffing and organisation
- new models of leadership, management and delivery that take users to the resources and support they need.

The WLHC will be tested for its economic impact – in both direct and indirect benefits: job creation, skills development, tourism spend as well as qualitative benefits in its social and cultural impact on Worcester and its attractiveness as a place to study, stay, live and work.

Birmingham

The Library of Birmingham is a multi-million pound replacement Central Library. In this diverse and youthful city (in the 2001 census, 44% of the population were under 30 years old) the challenges of making a library relevant in the 21st century are considerable.[15] Although the current library has one of the biggest footfalls of any library in Europe, an investment of £193 million requires considerable justification. Anticipated partnership here points in a different direction; the public library is not only partnering with other libraries, academic or otherwise. The linkages to be developed are with the educational, cultural and informational institutions themselves. In the current library, Health Exchange[16] is a social enterprise delivering free and confidential information and lifestyle choice services. Originally a partnership between Heart of Birmingham Teaching Primary Care Trust and Birmingham City Council in 2006, this has reconfigured the library with a new user-led, community-based learning and information service. The Library of Birmingham will negotiate further such partnerships with institutions in education, lifelong learning, culture, health, public service and third sector organisations representing a further new model for the evolution of the library idea.

Collaboration in network and content

New cross-sectoral projects have been recently initiated that may connect strategies.

- **Joining JANET:** JANET (Joint Academic Network) – the UK's education and research network – and MLA have announced the option now open to public library services to transfer from their conventional connectivity via the local authority website and link to the JANET network. This allows libraries to evade the restrictions of local authority IT protocols. Moreover, it will potentially help to build further collaboration around content and user access/authentication.

- **JISC (Joint Information Systems Committee) Collections Licensing Service:** JISC Collections has begun to undertake the role developed by MLA in purchasing Reference Online.[17] This MLA success story provides a tangible modernisation of public library provision and represents a good shared interest agreement with publishers. Now JISC Collections can bring their expertise to securing licence agreements for the future public library e-library acquisitions.

- **JISC BCE:** Moving to service and provision, the JISC Business and Community Engagement (BCE) programme may identify a way forward for service content. This is a relatively new agenda for JISC, developed in response to the strategic aim #5 of the 2007–9 strategy – 'developing and implementing a programme to support institutions' engagement with the wider community' (JISC, 2007). The BCE programme is designed to support institutions in their strategic management of relationships with commercial, public sector (including charities and trusts), cultural, social and civic organisations, in order to deliver services which benefit the economy and community. It will trial innovative business and cultural partnerships to extend the reach and impact of HEIs into the community.

Knowledge flows – the lifelong library

A contextual reprise: the UK will shortly experience a complete shift in the economic balance of its population; a successful economy demands new skills and a capacity to learn and innovate; technology will define economic growth; education becomes lifelong learning, serving a continuous need to increase and improve from basic literacies and core skills to new skills and competencies; community engagement and democracy require access to information and the capacity to evaluate messages and opinions; people want to research their past as well as inform judgements about the future; people require re-learning provision on a continual basis; those who are 'not in education, employment or training' must cease to be so; learning is creative, flexible, ongoing, linked to work and fun, family life, community life and personal health and well-being.

In the *lifelong library*, service and knowledge flow to the user. This may seem unreal, but all libraries together form a matrix *lifelong library*:

- **Just in time:** Independent learning provision is there 'just in time', at the moment of need – in early years, for family and community information, for study, education and research, in work and for the enthusiast-learner and motivated active citizen. To achieve this a continuum of consistent library provision is needed – resources, guidance and support – linking public libraries, early years' settings, school, college and university libraries.

- **Just in case:** Always there – a national information and learning service – all libraries open to all on a 'just in case' basis, when circumstances require, for informal learning or research, personal, health and community needs, for citizenship and community engagement. To achieve this, a range of publicly accessible library services each opens to those who need it when they need it, in which each institution knows the others and refers people accordingly.

Both dimensions of this matrix should be built on shared vision, strategy and market awareness. Any service must refer the user to the resource and support they need in the best place to source it. It makes sense therefore to begin to develop shared policy and the strategic planning for libraries – public, academic and others – to connect their management and development, delivery and marketing as a national collaborative project, resulting in a federated 'one service' that progressively shares common characteristics across all sectors:

- **Spatial design:** In public, academic, school and community library, learning spaces are becoming more alike. Notwithstanding the different balance of books and digital resources in each type of library, the kind of place that informal learners, students and researchers require is an increasingly similar combination of flexible spaces for group learning, secluded spaces for solo study and research and social space for community cultural activity.[18]

- **Resources management:** Shared selection, acquisition, licensing and use of e-publications, negotiated partnerships with publishers, a further shift to open source and creative commons, Web 2.0 dialogues, mobile apps and services and, according to need and context, the printed book and journal.

- **Partnership programmes:** Library-to-library, but also the partnership opportunities between libraries' parent institutions, mean that the libraries within them need to be more contiguous, sharing strategy, planning and performance measures.

- **Staff learning and development:** The emerging roles of staff share increasingly common features in management, community leadership, user support, resource discovery, evaluation, promotion and performance review.

- **User communications and management:** Sharing the management of library and information research, user consultation and engagement, understanding changing patterns of learning and pedagogy, market research, performance and value-for-money studies.

Library evolution in uncertain times

Since the Coalition government came into power in the UK in 2010 both sectors are experiencing the challenge of making huge reductions in expenditure. Already under way in the academic/national library sector, the Library of the Future[19] programme is exploring future library provision through scenario planning,[20] anticipating global and national needs in learning, education and research to devise a library response unlikely to be predicated on traditional models of learning space, resources and support. Partners[21] leading the project – which concludes in 2011 – operate within the sector but a key phase at the end of the project, having written the stories that set library provision within the envisaged scenarios, will be to achieve buy-in both within the sector and with external stakeholders.

For public libraries, the 2010 government policy is more mixed. Ed Vaizey's first policy speech as Culture Minister was encouraging:

> Public libraries have a unique status in the nation's consciousness as places where anyone can go without judgement in order to learn, read, access information, get online, find entertainment. They are spaces for the individual alone or as part of a community ... During economic challenges people need the library service more than ever – to help get back to work, to access learning and entertainment and to provide community cohesion.[22]

Within the month, he announced the demise of the Minister's Advisory Council and the MLA, and public speculation was that Arts Council England would assume responsibility for library programmes. This may mean a weighting towards the literary dimension of the public library, pleasing some lobbyists, but such a change need not prevent the *lifelong library* being led by a cross-sectoral partnership between public and academic library leaders. The subsequent Department for Culture, Media and Sport (DCMS) focus was on 'improvement'. The premise, driven by the economic deficit, is the need to cut costs. The MLA/Local Government Association (LGA) Future Libraries[23] programme will 'spread learning between library authorities to achieve cost savings, new partnerships and governance models, and to take advantage of digital opportunities. Central to the programme is the vision for library services to have greater connection with other local services and an ambition for services to be designed around the needs of the public, rather than based on organisational boundaries.' So 'improvement' equals 'cost savings';

'partnerships and governance models' are local authority mergers to save money. It is conceivable that cross-sector collaboration is still advantageous, even within a narrow policy that isolates public libraries, and reduces innovation to savings. So how might a library service that is really cross-sectoral and genuinely innovative be promoted?

Conclusion: how might this happen?

There is significant economic potential in strategically connecting libraries across different sectors, bringing a critical mass of knowledge resources and staff expertise to bear on all stages of education, cultural and community life. Academic institutions connect with local communities, while local authority libraries connect with the learning and research of academic enterprise. Libraries as a whole extend their influence and relevance to the widest community. Partnership work between institutions, local authorities and other agencies is enhanced.

This is an idea that will require a powerful leadership drive from within one or other library sector, followed by supportive partners from the rest. It might seem secondary to current challenging targets, but it would create a critical mass and enlarge the capacity of each to bring huge benefits to users and parent bodies. Each user could access a continuum of learning spaces and knowledge resources and support which they could then turn to at any stage in their life; literature and reading would be open to all from early years, information skills and literacy in all media would increase alongside a capacity to source and evaluate information, ideas and knowledge and to understand how they are formed and re-invented for each age.

Is this conceivable? How might it happen? All of this can become a reality by adopting the practices rehearsed in the projects and programmes described earlier:

- **Leadership**: Without the MLA, other leaders with *lifelong library* provision are:
  - **DCMS**: should advocate with other government departments to share responsibility. Together they can facilitate and assist the collaboration that would deliver a connected library service for lifelong learning, education and research.
  - **The JISC**: shares the discoveries of the Library of the Future programme and brokers a broader lifelong learning purpose of the education and research library sector.

- The Society of Chief Librarians: adopts, in a national collaboration, the principle that libraries in different sectors will increasingly learn from each other (or not at all) and can evolve in tandem and commit to collaboration.

- The Chartered Institute of Library and Information Professionals: can adopt a cross-sectoral stance on library development that mirrors and draws on the matrix of experience and expertise of its membership.

- The LGA: can support collaboration, urging local authorities to capitalise on the opportunity for local economies and enhanced services.

- The Third Sector: will be an even bigger player in the future, but hopefully not in the tokenistic way proposed with volunteer-run libraries. The community in partnership with library providers can support users, not displace skilled staff, extending accessibility and helping diversify the library service.

- ■ Communications: A shared message, language, communications programme and timetable are devised to promote the areas of collaboration – spaces, resources access, staff development, community and user engagement.

- ■ Funding: All parties contribute to a pool of funding for innovation and roll-out.

- ■ Workforce: Training for workforce awareness and staff engagement is undertaken by each sector according to agreed programmes.

Hardly any reference to public libraries has been made in any recent strategic plan from government in the UK,[24] while local authorities' reactions to cuts, steered by alleged local decision, lack consistency and rationale. Instead, here is an achievable response to a national need, to overcome duplication, spark innovation, reach people and communities, support education and facilitate learners' progression. Education libraries have shown how a large group of often competing organisations can work together on national strategy. Under the Higher Education Funding Council for England and JISC umbrellas, they are articulating a coherent vision and have the independence to provide the leadership to initiate this process. The public library sector, supported by a tighter group of fewer national players, would coordinate a consistent response across library authorities, demonstrating the benefits of focused purpose and national leadership.

Notes

1. United Kingdom Office for Library and Information Networking (UKOLN) – see http://www.ukoln.ac.uk/.
2. http://www.librarieswest.org.uk/.
3. For background see Serco and related references at http://www.serco.com/about/index.asp.
4. See case study descriptions on the MLA Research Resources website, http://research.mla.gov.uk/case-studies/.
5. See '£5m investment to upgrade Hounslow's libraries', *Richmond and Twickenham Times*, 28 June 2009.
6. See http://www.uklibrariesplus.ac.uk/ukcp/reports.htm.
7. See http://www.sconul.ac.uk/groups/access/operatingprinciples.pdf.
8. See http://www.ucisa.ac.uk/haervi/haervi.aspx.
9. See http://www.ucisa.ac.uk/publications/haervi_guide.aspx.
10. http://sconul.ac.uk/using_other_libraries/inspire.html.
11. http://lis.tees.ac.uk/inspire/default.cfm.
12. See *Renewal: New libraries for Manchester*, Manchester Library and Information Service, Manchester City Council, http://www.manchester.gov.uk/downloads/download/3425/renewal_new_libraries_for_manchester.
13. See http://www.wlhc.org.uk/. The WLHC is a partnership between Worcestershire County Council, Worcester City Council and the University of Worcester with Advantage West Midlands (the regional development agency).
14. Interview with managers, 7 December 2009.
15. See the business case, http://www.birmingham.gov.uk/libraryofbirmingham.
16. http://www.healthexchange.org.uk/.
17. Reference Online – http://www.mla.gov.uk/what/support/online.
18. Designing Libraries, http://www.designinglibraries.org.uk/ could share more experience, design resources and ideas, tools for evaluation, user and stakeholder reactions and value-for-money observations.
19. http://www.futurelibraries.info/content/.
20. http://www.futurelibraries.info/content/page/published-outputs.
21. The British Library, JISC, Research Information Network, Research Libraries UK and SCONUL. Academic Libraries of the Future is an 18-month project and is being undertaken by Curtis+Cartwright Consulting Ltd.
22. http://www.culture.gov.uk/news/news_stories/7215.aspx.
23. See http://www.mla.gov.uk/news_and_views/press_releases/2010/future_libraries_programme.
24. Apart from, under the Labour government, in the *Learning Revolution* (DfIUS, 2009), and that as the result of a particularly energetic participation by the MLA.

References

DCSF. (2010) *NEET Statistics – Quarterly Brief February 2010.* Department for Children, Schools and Families. Online at http://www.dcsf.gov.uk/rsgateway/DB/STR/d000913/NEETQBQ4200 9final.pdf.

Jama, D. and Dugdale, G. (2010) *Literacy: State of the Nation. A picture of literacy in the UK today.* National Literacy Trust. Online at http://www.literacytrust.org.uk/assets/0000/3816/FINAL_Literacy_ State_of_the_Nation_-_30_March_2010.pdf.

DfIUS. (2009) *The Learning Revolution.* The Government White Paper on Informal Adult Learning. Department for Innovation, Universities and Skills. Online at http://www.bis.gov.uk/policies/further-education-skills/learners/learning-revolution-white-paper.

JISC (Joint Information Systems Committee). (2007) *2007–2009 Strategy.* Online at http://www.jisc.ac.uk/media/documents/aboutus/ strategy/jisc_strategy_20072009.pdf.

Nankivell, C., Foster, W. and Elkin, J. (2000) *People Flows: investigation of cross-use and development of transferable strategies for co-operation between publicly-funded libraries.* British Library Research and Innovation Report 167. London: Library and Information Commission.

Nilekani, N. (2009) 'Ideas for India's future'. Lecture at *TED: 2009.* 3–7 February 2009, Long Beach and Palm Springs, California. Online at http://www.ted.com/talks/nandan_nilekani_s_ideas_for_india_s_ future.html.

4

Scholarly communication and access to research outputs

Claire Creaser

Introduction

Scholarly communication covers a wide spectrum of activity, broadly in two areas – publishing and disseminating the results of research, and providing access to the published material. These activities have been the focus of much research in recent years, particularly in relation to academic journal articles and the movement for open access to journal articles, made possible by the increasing availability of content in electronic formats. Academic and other research libraries clearly have a significant role in the scholarly communication process as information providers and access facilitators. This role is sometimes undervalued and misunderstood, as researchers seek – and obtain – access to the resources they require from their desktops without apparent intervention from the library.

Recent years have seen a proliferation of research resources, particularly in the electronic environment, with a corresponding increase in the provision of e-resources by research libraries. Access to resources has become harder to manage, as compared to the position some 15 years ago, when almost all research material was available in print. This has been coupled with a change in attitudes and expectations, with most researchers now expecting immediate access on their desktops to all kinds of materials relevant to their research, free at the point of use. Researchers of the future are expected to have even higher demands – a recent Centre for Information Behaviour and the Evaluation of Research (CIBER) report notes that 'any barrier to access: be that additional log-ins, payment or hard copy, are too high for most consumers and information behind those barriers will increasingly be ignored' (CIBER, 2008).

Academic libraries in the UK typically spend around one third of their budgets on information resources, a proportion which has not changed significantly over time. However, the relative spending on different types of resources has changed, as illustrated in Figure 4.1, with a greater share of the budget now going on serials and electronic resources and less on books and inter-library loans. The changes have been driven, at least in part, by the increasing availability of electronic information resources and the increasing price of journals (see below). Changes in teaching practice, for example the widespread adoption of virtual learning environments as collections of, and pointers to, resources, have also played a part.

Journal prices

One key influence in the changing pattern of academic library spending on information resources is the rate of increase in journal prices. Over the 10 years from 1999, journal prices in the UK more than doubled, to an average of £607 per title in 2009. There is variation between subjects,

Figure 4.1 Breakdown of UK academic library expenditure on information provision

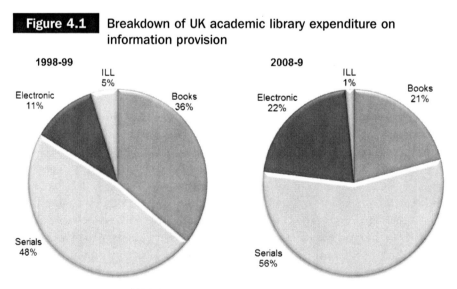

1998-99

ILL 5%
Electronic 11%
Books 36%
Serials 48%

2008-9

ILL 1%
Electronic 22%
Books 21%
Serials 56%

Note: Total expenditure in 1998-99 was £142 million; in 2008-9 it was £239 million.
Source: Society of College, National and University Libraries (SCONUL).

with the greatest increases in social sciences titles and the least in medicine (Figure 4.2). In contrast, the Retail Price Index in the UK increased by 29% between January 1999 and January 2009.

A detailed study carried out in 2007 for Oxford Journals investigated trends in the prices of biomedical and social science journals for a selection of publishers (Creaser and White, 2008). It found considerable variation between publishers, both in their overall levels of price and in the rates of increase observed over the period. There was some evidence that not-for-profit publishers may, on average, offer better value for money in terms of price per page and price per point of impact factor, but this was far from conclusive. There was little consistent evidence of any associations between price, impact factor and number of pages, although some evidence of limited associations between price and number of pages was found. However, academic library journal collection development is not driven solely by price.

Academic library journal provision

The increasing availability of electronic journals, and the various publisher 'deals' and pricing packages, have also influenced provision. While journal expenditure more than doubled over 10 years, the number of journal titles available in UK academic libraries rose by 142%, from

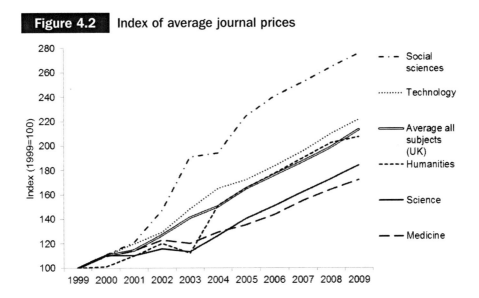

Figure 4.2 Index of average journal prices

an average of 3,650 per institution in 1998–99 to over 9,200 in 2008–9 (the most recent year for which figures are available). Much of this growth has been driven by the less research-intensive universities and colleges – members of Research Libraries UK have recorded an increase of just under 40%, compared to over 200% for the post-1992 universities (Figure 4.3).

A doubling of both the number of titles provided and the average cost per title would be expected to lead to a four-fold increase in spending. However, this has not been the case. As noted above, total spending on serials by UK higher education libraries has doubled, having increased from £65.5 million in 1998–99 to £131.5 million in 2008–9. This has been achieved largely by the growth in the availability of titles electronically, and the 'deals' offered by publishers whereby large numbers of electronic titles are included in packages at marginal additional cost, so that the average price paid per title has fallen from £105 in 1998–99 to £87 in 2008–9.

Electronic information

It is estimated that 96% of science, technology and medicine journal titles and 86% of arts, humanities and social science journal titles are now available online. In a joint study undertaken by the Research Information Network (RIN) and the Consortium of University Research

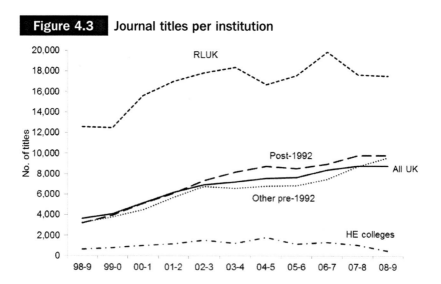

Figure 4.3 Journal titles per institution

Libraries in 2007, the increasing availability of digital information was found to be the biggest driver in promoting change in the delivery of library services. Electronic journal provision in UK academic libraries rose rapidly from about 2000, so that more than three-quarters of titles were available only in electronic format in 2008–9, with a further 8% available in both print and electronic formats. This undoubtedly improves access to research outputs for researchers affiliated to academic institutions, but creates increasing problems for others, or indeed for academics whose institution does not subscribe to the title they seek. Electronic resources are not confined to journals. Figure 4.1 showed that library spending on electronic resources (other than e-journals) has almost doubled over the past 10 years. In 2008–9, SCONUL member libraries reported a median of 78 databases (of all types) per library and over 2,900 e-books per library.

The availability of electronic resources might be expected to have a further impact on the library, in terms of the use made of the library buildings. Although opening hours have been broadly increasing in UK academic libraries, the number of visits made fell dramatically over the 10-year period, from 71 to 52 per full-time equivalent user per year. There is little evidence available concerning what users actually do in academic libraries and how long they spend there, although there is clear evidence that researchers, particularly in science disciplines, no longer visit the library regularly, choosing to access resources from their desktop or home. A majority of arts and humanities researchers still value the services provided in library buildings, however, and just over a third visit libraries other than their own on a regular basis (RIN, 2006).

Issues of access

A recent series of studies funded by RIN examined the issue of access to research resources from a range of viewpoints (RIN 2009a). The synthesis of those studies showed that researchers often encounter difficulties in accessing the information they seek, for a variety of reasons, not all of them within the remit of libraries. A majority of the research libraries included in the study reported that a lack of material available locally was 'frequently' or 'sometimes' an issue for their members. In such circumstances, three-quarters of higher education (HE) libraries might offer inter-library loans, with 70% promoting access schemes, such as SCONUL Access,[1] and the same proportion suggesting specific alternative libraries. Non-HE libraries were more likely to purchase the requested resources, with 82% indicating that they did this. Not surprisingly, such libraries were less likely to promote access schemes, as three-quarters do not belong to such schemes. Less than half the libraries would suggest Open Access (OA) resources as an alternative (RIN, 2009c). Researchers themselves reported being unable to access the content they required from their institution's library on either a weekly (30%) or monthly (26%) basis. Almost 11% reported encountering problems on a daily basis; at the other end of the scale, 17% experienced problems only two or three times each year (RIN, 2009b). This survey found that inter-library loans or document supply services were the most-cited methods used to obtain licensed content not immediately available; other surveys, however, have indicated that such services are less popular than alternatives such as seeking OA sources or asking the author for a copy, and it is likely that there are disciplinary differences in behaviour.

Recommendations from the RIN study included work to improve online catalogues and discovery services, additional training for researchers and a range of suggestions for removing administrative and technical barriers, including the implementation of the recommendations in the report *HE Access to e-Resources in Visited Institutions* (HAERVI) (UCISA, 2007). HAERVI aimed to improve access to e-resources for visiting researchers in UK academic institutions and the report provides a snapshot of that provision in 2007. It concluded that while the Joint Information Systems Committee (JISC) and Eduserv Chest had changed the terms of their model licences to allow authorised walk-in users to access e-resources (and these licences were thought to cover 50–70% of HE e-resources), two key challenges remained: ensuring that the process of gaining access is simple for visitors to use and for library staff to administer; and ensuring that the technology is in place to limit access to only those resources which are permitted under the terms of their licence. The RIN studies found that these issues remained a barrier in many institutions (RIN, 2009c).

An international library survey carried out in 2008 suggests that printed materials, including journals and monographs, are particularly vulnerable to cuts as a result of the economic downturn (CIBER, 2009). Further, pressures on space may lead libraries to dispose of printed materials or place them in storage. Although the UK Research Reserve Project[2] aims to ensure that print copies of journals no longer needed by academic libraries are retained by the British Library, the disposal of print collections led the Inspire evaluation report (Curry, 2007) to conclude that 'those academic libraries that have a history of opening library access to the public are now offering external visitors ... a level of access which is significantly limited in comparison to what was on offer ten or even five years ago'.

Library access for external users

Much of the RIN (2009a) study was concerned with issues of access to research library resources for external users – those who are not members of the relevant institution. Reference access to print resources is generally allowed free of charge for visitors to research libraries, although a small number may charge some visitors, and access to short-loan collections in HE libraries may be restricted. Access with borrowing rights usually incurs a charge for external users, and charges may vary greatly from one institution to another. Membership of an institution participating in the SCONUL Access[3] scheme confers considerable advantage within HE libraries, in terms of both borrowing from the main collections and access to short-loan material. It is, of course, ultimately the libraries' decision to specify the number of items external users may borrow and for how long; there is considerable variation in this, as there is in the loan arrangements for 'home' users.

Access to electronic resources raises rather different issues. Two key factors determine the extent of such access – the licences the institution has negotiated for its e-resources, and the level of information technology (IT) facilities available to external users within the library. The second of these is often outside the scope of the library to resolve, and the lack of suitable IT facilities and the complexity of managing different levels of access to electronic resources for different categories of users were often reported as a barrier preventing access to licensed electronic resources. Only around one third of UK HE libraries had the necessary infrastructure to allow such access by external visitors.

Licensing issues are also perceived as a barrier. While the JISC model licence for e-journals now provides for access by external 'walk-in' users, this does not apply to all electronic resources. Setting up walk-in users' access to electronic resources is a developing area and there are currently no well-developed standards and practices in the sector to help libraries manage this process. Librarians perceive that the complexity of publishers' licences (and the legal language in which they are written) precludes allowing access to external users. Under time pressures, they prefer not to risk misinterpreting licence terms but stay on the safe side of the law by refusing access to all external users. The UK Computing Plus scheme,[4] initiated in 2002–3, the HAERVI report (UCISA, 2007) and the more recent Registry of Electronic Licences[5] project have all proposed solutions to mitigate such issues.

Open access

Making research outputs freely available to all – Open Access – is clearly one way to overcome the issues surrounding access to research material. However, it raises questions which are fundamental to the process of research dissemination. The principle, outlined in the Budapest Open Access Initiative,[6] is to remove all access barriers to scholarly material so as to improve education and research for rich and poor alike. The practice, given the current starting point of an established academic publishing industry, is not straightforward, and OA has become the focus of much research and debate, prompting investigations into publishing models and researcher behaviours, although much is focused on scholarly communication within the HE sector in developed countries. The 2006 Baseline Study report (Electronic Publishing Services, 2006) examined the scholarly communication landscape in six key areas, including the economics of publishing and access, and scholars' perceptions, attitudes and behaviours.

Open access journals

The 'gold' route to OA is via OA journals. There are an increasing number of OA journals available – the Directory of Open Access Journals[7] lists more than 4,500 worldwide. A recent survey of publishers (Cox and Cox, 2008) found that almost one quarter offered at least one fully OA title. Despite the fact that it is just one of the numerous ways OA can be achieved, many commentators mistakenly equate OA journals with OA itself (Oppenheim, 2008). Open access journals are closest to the traditional route, in that papers are submitted, peer reviewed and published. The added-value role of the publisher remains, and so do the associated costs. There is no single funding mechanism, however – the commonly used phrase 'author pays' to describe such journals does not apply to all, and they may be run by volunteers, receive grants, or rely on subsidies. Commercial publishers, however, will usually require payment by or on behalf of authors when manuscripts are accepted for OA journals. In some cases, the entire journal is freely available from the date of publication; in others – the 'hybrid' model – authors may choose whether or not to have their article made freely available. Thirty per cent of journal publishers offer hybrid titles, where payment can be made for an article in a subscription journal to be made available on OA, with more than half offering this option for all their titles (Cox and Cox, 2008).

Self-archiving

The main alternative to OA journals is self-archiving by authors, called the 'green' route to OA. Authors place copies of their papers in a subject-based repository, in an institutional repository, or on their own website, generally in addition to publication in a peer-reviewed journal. There is no (financial) cost to authors, although publishers impose a variety of restrictions on which version of the paper can be deposited and may embargo any deposit until a set time has elapsed after formal publication in the subscription journal.

In some academic disciplines, self-archiving is an established and accepted practice, with highly regarded subject repositories (for example arXiv in physics;[8] RePEc in economics[9]). In others, funder mandates are driving the process (for example medical research funders requiring deposit to PubMed Central[10]). Publishers are becoming more accepting of this practice and may make the deposit on behalf of their authors. PEER (Publishing and the Ecology of European Research) has set up an Observatory to investigate the effects of publisher deposit of research papers on a large scale across Europe. Three models of publisher intervention – do nothing, invite the author to deposit, and deposit on behalf of the author – are being compared with respect to article usage, researcher behaviour and the economic consequences.[11]

Despite an established advantage, in terms of citations, in making journal articles available on OA, there remains considerable reluctance on the part of authors to self-archive their published papers. A variety of barriers have been suggested in author surveys, including lack of knowledge as to how to deposit a paper, lack of understanding of publisher policies and permissions, and insufficient time. Authors are also reluctant to cite OA material and prefer to identify the published paper to cite in their own work, if possible (Fry et al., 2010).

Mandated deposit

Increasingly, researchers are being mandated to make the results of their research freely available. The public good argument (that research paid for with public money should be freely available to all), as well as research indicating that OA could bring economic benefits to the research cycle (Houghton et al., 2009), has brought the issue to the fore in many countries. Since late 2006, major funding bodies such as the UK Research Councils, the Wellcome Trust, and the National Institute for Health in the US, have developed and published policies on OA to the outputs of research they have funded. SHERPA/JULIET[12] provides summary information for researchers on funders' current policies regarding OA archiving and publication. Academic institutions may require deposit in the institutional repository in order to raise the profile of the institution and its research. Such mandates are not yet a key driver for researchers to deposit material or publish in OA journals, however. Many researchers are unaware of self-archiving mandates, and co-authors have the greatest influence on whether or not authors self-archive their papers (Creaser, 2010).

Impact on libraries

Not surprisingly, librarians favour self-archiving of peer-reviewed post-prints, and a recent survey found some evidence that they would consider cancelling subscriptions if papers provided in repositories were peer reviewed (Beckett and Inger, 2007). However, OA appears to have made little impact as yet on academic library budgets. A recent survey of UK academic libraries found that libraries had not cancelled subscriptions and that the main effect was to allow the library to make more material available, with two-thirds including OA publications in their catalogues (Creaser, 2010).

One, indirect, impact on the library of increasing OA may be the reduction seen in spending on inter-library loans (see Figure 4.1). While such spending is influenced by many factors, including departmental and library policy decisions and the breadth of the library collections, the option of first seeking an OA copy of a resource not available through the library is one which is increasingly taken by scholars. There was concern for the future, however, and whether libraries will be expected to 'pay twice' – funding pay-to-publish charges alongside traditional subscriptions during any transitional period (Creaser, 2010). A 2009 international library survey found that print materials, including monographs and print journals, were 'highly vulnerable targets for cost saving' as a consequence of the economic downturn (CIBER, 2009).

Conclusion

Libraries face a number of challenges in providing services in this changing information environment. As providers of research resources – whether print or electronic, serial or monograph, or other research outputs such as data files, creative works and so on – academic and research libraries generally make their provision for a specified constituency of researchers. There are issues concerned with licensing and library capacity (staff resources and physical space) which may influence how libraries allow, or do not allow, access to resources for researchers outside their constituency. The technology has moved on since the eLib programme[13] produced early research in this field. Then, authentication and off-campus access to resources were key issues – issues which have since largely been resolved. Now the concern is more with the legal aspects of licensing access to intellectual property and how these can be managed without detriment to either the libraries purchasing content or the publishers and aggregators selling it.

Research undertaken by CIBER on behalf of the JISC (CIBER, 2008) predicted the nature of the research environment in 2017. The report discusses the recent phenomenon of 'power browsing', whereby researchers skim titles, abstracts and contents pages to find the information they require. In this shift from physical to virtual resources, the report argues, libraries 'have no option but to understand and design systems around the behaviour of today's virtual scholar' (CIBER, 2008). The alternative is presented in discouraging terms: 'without addressing these issues now, librarians will continue to become even more marginal players in the digital scholarly consumer marketplace' (CIBER, 2008). It is clear that immediate, seamless access to electronic resources is paramount to students and researchers, and that libraries must strive to meet this expectation.

There remains much uncertainty about the future of scholarly communication, perhaps less about what the landscape will look like, but more about how the transition will be effected. It is clear that, eventually, most scholarly articles will be available to all readers, free at the point of use. The balance between OA journals, paid for by authors (or their funders); self-archiving, whether in subject-based or institutional repositories or on open web pages; and subscription-controlled content will continue to change, with the associated uncertainties over funding. The importance of the peer-review process and copyright issues remain significant barriers in the minds of scholars. The library position might be seen as vulnerable – if content is free, library budgets may be cut. The transition from a reader-pays landscape to an author-pays landscape promises a rough ride for all.

Much of the current debate is concerned only with journal articles. While these are important in all scholarly disciplines, other forms of research output, for example conference proceedings or monographs, are also significant, in some disciplines more than in others. These forms of output are also moving to electronic formats, although relatively little is freely available at present. In the traditional model, institutions pay to give access to the research of the world for their researchers. In an OA model, payment is made to give the world access to the output of researchers. This is a fundamental difference in approach which will require a culture change on the part of researchers, institutions and publishers. The evidence so far is that this culture change is happening, but slowly. The commercial scholarly publishing industry has ample time to adjust its business models to accommodate the OA cuckoo in its nest.

Notes

1. http://www.access.sconul.ac.uk/.
2. http://www.rluk.ac.uk/node/85.
3. http://www.access.sconul.ac.uk/index_html.
4. http://www.uklibrariesplus.ac.uk/ukcp/index.htm.
5. http://www.jisc.ac.uk/whatwedo/programmes/reppres/sharedservices/licence.aspx.
6. http://www.soros.org/openaccess/read.shtml.
7. http://www.doaj.org/.
8. http://arxiv.org/.
9. http://repec.org/.
10. http://www.ncbi.nlm.nih.gov/pmc/.
11. http://www.peerproject.eu/.

12. http://www.sherpa.ac.uk/juliet/.
13. http://www.ukoln.ac.uk/services/elib/.

References

Beckett, C. and Inger, S. (2007) *Self-Archiving and Journal Subscriptions: co-existence or competition? An international survey of librarian preferences.* Report prepared for the Publishing Research Consortium by Scholarly Information Strategies Ltd, 2007. Online at http://www.publishingresearch.net/documents/Self-archiving_report.pdf.

CIBER (Centre for Information Behaviour and the Evaluation of Research). (2008) *Information Behaviour of the Researcher of the Future.* Online at http://www.jisc.ac.uk/media/documents/programmes/reppres/gg_final_keynote_11012008.pdf.

CIBER. (2009) *The Economic Downturn and Libraries: survey findings.* Online at http://www.ucl.ac.uk/infostudies/research/ciber/charleston-survey.pdf.

Cox, J. and Cox, L. (2008) *Scholarly Publishing Practice: academic journal publishers' policies and practices in online publishing: third survey 2008.* Worthing: ALPSP.

Creaser, C. (2010) 'Open access to research outputs – institutional policies and researchers' views: results from two complementary surveys'. *New Review of Academic Librarianship,* 16 (1), 1–22.

Creaser, C. and White, S. (2008) 'Trends in journal prices: an analysis of selected journals, 2000–2006'. *Learned Publishing,* 21 (3), 214–24. Online at http://hdl.handle.net/2134/3210.

Curry, S. (2007) *Opening Ours: inspiring libraries to open access for all.* Inspire Evaluation Report. Online at http://www.inspire2.org.uk/pdf/openinghours.pdf.

Electronic Publishing Services. (2006) *UK Scholarly Journals: 2006 baseline report: an evidence-based analysis of data concerning scholarly publishing.* Report for the Research Information Network, Research Councils UK and the Department of Trade and Industry. Online at http://www.rin.ac.uk/our-work/communicating-and-disseminating-research/uk-scholarly-journals-2006-baseline-report.

Fry, J., Oppenheim, C., Probets, S., Creaser, C., Greenwood, H., Spezi, V. and White, S. (2010) *PEER Behavioural Research: authors and users vis-a-vis journals and repositories baseline report.* Report to the

Publishing and the Ecology of European Research project. Online at http://www.peerproject.eu/fileadmin/media/reports/Final_revision_-_behavioural_baseline_report_-_20_01_10.pdf.

Houghton, J. et al. (2009) *Economic Implications of Alternative Scholarly Publishing Models: exploring the costs and benefits.* JISC report. Online at http://www.jisc.ac.uk/publications/reports/2009/economicpublishingmodelsfinalreport.aspx.

Oppenheim, C. (2008) 'Electronic scholarly publishing and Open Access'. *Journal of Information Science,* 34 (4), 577–90.

RIN (Research Information Network). (2006) *Researchers' Use of Academic Libraries and Their Services.* Online at http://www.rin.ac.uk/our-work/using-and-accessing-information-resources/researchers-use-academic-libraries-and-their-serv.

RIN. (2009a) *Overcoming Barriers: access to research information content.* Online at http://www.rin.ac.uk/our-work/using-and-accessing-information-resources/overcoming-barriers-access-research-information.

RIN. (2009b) *Research Report 1: How researchers secure access to licensed content not immediately available to them.* Online at http://www.rin.ac.uk/system/files/attachments/Sarah/ALC-Researchers-access-licensed-content-Outsell.doc.

RIN. (2009c) *Research Report 2: Perspectives from libraries.* Online at http://www.rin.ac.uk/system/files/attachments/Sarah/PFL-Perspectives-libraries-LISU.doc.

SCONUL (Society of College, National, and University Libraries). (2000) *SCONUL Annual Statistics 1998–99.*

SCONUL. (2010) *SCONUL Annual Statistics 2008–09.*

UCISA (Universities and Colleges Information Systems Association). (2007) *HAERVI: HE access to e-resources in visited institutions.* Online at http://www.ucisa.ac.uk/haervi/haervi.aspx.

5

Free and equal access: a conundrum for the information society

John Feather

Introduction

It is a cliché to say that access to information has never been easier. And like many clichés it is also a half-truth. For the relatively well-educated and relatively prosperous living in places with an effective infrastructure of electricity and telecommunications, access to information is cheap, simple and all but invulnerable. For others it is less certain. The digital divide – between the haves and have-nots of the network society – is social, economic and geographical on scales which vary from local to global. Pockets of poverty exist in rich countries just as peaks of wealth can be seen even in the poorest of nations. While Internet access has been a fact of daily life for millions in the United States or Western Europe for the better part of 20 years, there are still large numbers of people – numbered in millions on both sides of the north Atlantic – who lack equipment, knowledge and support to achieve access. Public policy in many developed countries has tried to find economically viable ways of overcoming the digital divide. There have been many success stories, but there have also been failures. Moreover, with every success – with every extension of the number or variety of people who can participate fully in the network society – the problem of exclusion is exacerbated in social terms even as it statistically diminishes. The Information Superhighway[1] and the People's Network[2] – genuinely imaginative political ideas at the turn of the millennium – have achieved enough of their objectives to have fallen down the political agenda. It is assumed that everyone has access to the Web; that everyone can use online systems; that everyone wants to live and work in an electronic environment. It is becoming increasingly difficult (and disproportionately expensive) to conduct certain transactions in any other way, transactions from making a tax return to buying a ticket for a train journey. At every stage and at every turn the disadvantaged are further disadvantaged.

This chapter tries to address some of these issues. It will consider:

- the historical context of our assumptions about the public good derived from public access to knowledge and information
- the real cost of regarding such access as a free good
- the limits of freedom of access
- the capacity of the Internet to facilitate and inhibit equitable access.

Free libraries – for those who can afford them

Public libraries are essentially a product of a combination of 19th-century liberal philanthropy and 19th-century social engineering. The British and American experiences, which profoundly influenced the rest of the world, particularly in Asia and Africa, were different, but in some ways similar. There was a widely shared perception that public good was to be derived from developing a better-educated population which would be socially cohesive and provide a more skilled workforce. It was argued – in various ways – that public libraries would help both to underpin education and to provide 'acceptable' forms of leisure for the working class. In Britain, and later in other European countries, and in some cities and states in the United States, this was seen – albeit sometimes reluctantly – as an appropriate call on the resources of the public purse. The public library 'movement', as it soon came to be called, gathered momentum throughout the second half of the 19th century. The pioneering public librarians were the first real leaders of the library profession, with their intimate involvement in the foundation and promotion of professional associations in both Britain and North America. There was an almost evangelical fervour about their commitment to libraries and to the benefits which libraries brought to those communities which supported them.

These benefits were often assumed rather than analysed. Moreover, there was significant opposition to the provision and expansion of public library services. There were citizens as well as politicians to whom public expenditure was anathema, the very opposite of the free-trade economics of 19th-century liberalism. There were those on the right to whom the very idea of working-class education and self-improvement was undesirable. There was little more than reluctant acquiescence from a much larger number of people who saw the provision of libraries as a useful tool for providing some counterbalance to other forms of popular entertainment such as public houses and places of ill repute. As in any public political discourse of this kind, arguments were exaggerated on both sides and exceptional incidents were treated as generally applicable cases, as they sometimes have been by historians. Gradually, however, it came to be accepted that the provision of access to information and perhaps to reading matter for improvement and even entertainment was an appropriate function for local or central government. By the end of the 19th century, some municipalities in both Europe and North America were actually taking a certain pride in the library provision they made for their citizens.

An associated assumption was that access to this provision was free. 'Free' is a word with several meanings, and a multitude of implications. In 20th-century librarianship, particularly in public libraries, it was, in practice, a simple way of expressing the idea that the service was not charged to the user at the point of delivery. In fact, of course, the costs were substantial, and were borne by both users and non-users through their taxes. In 19th-century Britain this connection between the taxpayer and the public library was explicit. Libraries were funded from a designated income stream from local taxation, and the municipal authority was under no obligation to raise this tax or to provide a service, a position which extended into the 20th century. This was even more the case in the United States, where there was some library provision at state level, but the public library as it is normally understood was provided by the city (or county) and funded out of tax revenues at that level. In other words, public libraries existed only for so long as local politicians were convinced that there was sufficient support for them to be able to justify the use of taxpayers' money; there was such support. Indeed, public libraries became, and have remained, one of the most popular and one of the most widely used of all non-compulsory public services in almost every western country. In the second half of the 20th century, particularly during periods of relative prosperity such as the 1950s and 1960s and from the mid 1990s onwards, resources were poured into them to provide better facilities, better services and better stock. The cost of the 'free' service was, however, huge and growing.

These costs were partly met by private philanthropy. Perhaps the best-remembered of the benefactors is Andrew Carnegie, a Scottish-American steel millionaire and quite possibly one of the worst employers in industrial history. He spent millions of dollars on buildings, equipment and stock for public libraries both in the United States and in his native Scotland and elsewhere in Britain and Europe. 'Carnegie libraries' became a common feature of towns – perhaps especially smaller and less prosperous towns – at the turn of the 20th century. Carnegie was exceptional in the scale of his work, but not unique in undertaking it. Many public libraries, especially in the United States, benefited from philanthropy. Often the donations were in kind – collections of books and other objects – so that the long-term effect was to create special collections of valuable and rare books, manuscripts and archives. Many collections had a local relevance and were intended to boost the self-image and the self-awareness of the communities to which they were donated.

The free public library service, however, has to be seen in a wider context. Unlike the cases of healthcare and education, there was no serious private alternative. There were, of course, commercial and subscription libraries which continued to operate until the early 1960s in some cases, and survive vestigially even in the 21st century. They are historically interesting and not without importance as cultural signifiers, but have not been major players in competition with the public libraries since at least 1945. There is, however, another domain of private sector providers which is sometimes forgotten in examining public provision of libraries and information – the book trade itself. Libraries, publishers and booksellers are in many ways interdependent, but they are also, up to a point, in competition. The competitive environment in which publishers and booksellers operate, both in their own spheres and in relation to each other's domains, is familiar and obvious. The competitive dimension of their relationship with libraries is perhaps less obvious, but consideration of it casts further light on the concept of the 'free' library. This in turn will suggest some lines of thought about contemporary developments which provide some significant challenges to the traditional concept of free access.

The price of free goods

From the very early days of tax-supported public libraries, the voices of opposition have been heard. Why should taxpayers support the information needs – and even more the leisure activities – of their fellow citizens? The answer lies at least in part in an understanding of the cultural iconography represented by the book in Judeo-Christian-Islamic culture. The 'peoples of the Book', as they call themselves, have a peculiar relationship with books because their religious beliefs derive from one which they consider to be of divine origin, and their religious practices are based on written (or printed) interpretations as well as on oral exposition. The book is seen as a fundamental cultural object, and is also seen, particularly in the western Christian tradition, as the basic instrument of education.[3] The attainment of universal literacy was one of the primary goals of 18th- and 19th-century reformers and evangelists; its attainment, or near attainment, was one of the signifiers of modernity. The modern public library grew out of this ethos and has never entirely moved away from it.

The great political achievement of the public library pioneers was to gain political support for their fundamental proposition that libraries were a socially desirable good while, at the same time, generally avoiding the concomitant danger of overt political control of their operations. Public libraries are consequently exposed, however, to two great dangers which can impact on their capacity to provide free access in the broadest sense.

First and foremost, any activity which is publicly funded is exposed to the vagaries of public funding regimes. When times are good, libraries do well; when the bad times come, there are those who see them as an obvious target for schemes intended to save money. At times and places where libraries have been genuinely popular, it has proved difficult for politicians to make too deep an inroad into their provision, but if they have moved too far away from popular provision they expose themselves to danger. The temptation to be conservative (in a non-political sense) and to resist or fear real change is often very great, if only as a defence mechanism. As a consequence, libraries close, opening hours are restricted, stock becomes out of date in content and unattractive in appearance, staffing levels are reduced and the professionalism of staff is diluted by the extensive employment of non-professional staff to do professional work. There is a cycle of decline. At the beginning of the 1990s, there were many places in the western world where that cycle seemed to be well advanced and perhaps even irreversible.

Recognising that free libraries are expensive, and that someone has to pay for them, inevitably means that there are pressures from paymasters. In the past – and sometimes occasionally even now – this has led directly or indirectly to overt or de facto censorship. There is always a danger of citing the exceptions as if they were typical, but we cannot ignore the fact that there have been public libraries where books on abortion (or evolution, or sex, or communism) have been banned. Library committees – sometimes with the active engagement of librarians – have sought to make the public library a mirror of the society which they would like to see. In other words, the library becomes an instrument of social engineering in the hands of groups with their own political, social or moral agendas. The professional bodies which represent librarians have typically protested against such censorship and have codes of practice and ethical codes, as well as practical advice, which try to address the issues. Recognising the limits of freedom is part of the price which librarians and library users have paid for their free good. This brings us to a consideration of another dimension of the free availability of books, documents and information, regardless of whether or not there is a charge at the point of delivery.

Freedom of access: rights and limits

Even in the least regimented and controlled societies, there are limits on freedom of access to information. The problem lies not in acknowledging the desirability of limits, but in defining them. At one level, we can construct an argument (which is itself perfectly logical and valid) around the balance between the right to know and the right to conceal. At the outer edges, this argument becomes complex and perhaps political (how do we balance the right to a private life against the claim that parents should be told a former sex offender lives in their vicinity?), but in most circumstances the balance is clear enough for all practical purposes. There is, however, another level at which the debate becomes more complex.

One aspect of the public good derived from public libraries is the provision of access to a common inherited culture. The same is true of all public cultural heritage institutions – archives, museums, galleries, historic sites and buildings and so on. It can be credibly argued that this heritage is common property, that it belongs to everyone and that therefore everyone should have a right of access to it. In a general sense, this is true, but it is nevertheless the case that individual heritage assets (including information) are actually owned by particular organisations or even individuals. How do we reconcile ownership with rights of access? The question even in this form is complex, but made the more so when we consider that the nature of the assets varies so much that generalised answers are not necessarily meaningful. It is one of the characteristics of information, as information theorists have generally understood it, that it is not damaged by use, unlike – say – a book or a piece of furniture. But it may nevertheless lose its value or even damage its owner by being disseminated. Where there is demonstrable and serious risk of financial or commercial damage, it would be generally agreed that some form of protection is appropriate. But when the damage itself is intangible the proposition perhaps becomes harder to sustain.

It seems reasonable to assume that there is general agreement that public right of access to a tangible but physically vulnerable asset should be protected by regulating the extent, place and method of consultation and use, by providing appropriate conditions for storage and display and so on. Public ownership of such assets does not change this fundamental proposition, but it does raise questions about the nature of ownership. A public sector library or museum is the legal owner of the objects in its custody, but this 'ownership' is really more akin to trusteeship on behalf of the nation at large. This is indeed the great difference between public and private ownership of heritage assets, and is clearly reflected in practice. The private owner of a house – Chatsworth,[4] for example – is completely free to decide whether or not to admit anyone to the house and, if so, under what circumstances and conditions. The public 'owner' of a comparable asset – say Kenwood House, owned by English Heritage[5] – is in a quite different position, with a moral and sometimes legal obligation to make it accessible to the general public while having a balancing obligation to ensure that it is not damaged by the way in which it is used or even by the number of people taking advantage of the access which is provided. The same general principles can be applied to books and documents owned by public libraries and museums. A library can meet at least part of its obligation to the collective owners of its contents by putting some of them on public display, selecting those likely to be of greatest interest to the largest number of visitors. The balance of rights and limitations is relatively clear, or at least sufficiently so to form the basis of a meaningful argument about how the balance should be adjusted.

For libraries, however, the ownership of physical assets is only the first stage. The majority of those assets are of interest for their content rather than for their physical form or manifestation. What users want is access to information which happens to be contained in the books. That information – or at least the precise expression of it in any given case –

is protected by copyright law in a way which means that the library has to impose some limits on how its assets can be used. Moreover, the use is subject to similar constraints; free access to information is not the same as uninhibited freedom to use a particular form of the information without the consent of the owner, who would normally not be the owner of the asset through which it was acquired. Copyright owners – and indeed the owners of other forms of intellectual property rights – are thus potentially in a very powerful position in the information chain which links originator and consumer. They can inhibit distribution as well as reproduction, or they can gain financial benefit from permitting or even facilitating it. That is the fundamental legal and economic basis of the whole publishing industry and the wider knowledge industries associated with it.

Access: equity and equality

Public libraries are quintessentially democratic institutions. They are open to all citizens and only in well-defined and special circumstances are distinctions made between one group of users and another. Those distinctions, however, are important, and need to be considered carefully, first in terms of costs and charges, and second in terms of access to information assets.

It is seen as a basic principle of public libraries that they are free at the point of use, but it is necessary to unpick this perception in a little more detail. It is true that there is no subscription, although there may be some charge made to certain categories of users who live outside the area which the library primarily serves. Although library systems are now adopting interchangeable membership, this has been a problem for many years, especially for those who find it easier to use libraries in the locality where they work rather than the locality where they live. This typically puts pressure on the resources of libraries in town and city centres and perhaps leaves suburban and rural libraries under-used. That having been said, however, borrowing books is normally free. But libraries are not – and have not been for many decades – merely places from which books are borrowed. Non-book materials began to be introduced into public library loan stocks in the mid 20th century. This started with gramophone records, and was extended to video as well as audio and to computer software and other media and formats in the 1970s and 1980s. Under British law, libraries could and did charge for the loan of these materials; although this was legally sound, it was logically indefensible. It had the effect, however, of giving both libraries and their users the experience of charges at the point of delivery for borrowing from stock.

Other charging regimes became common in the last quarter of the 20th century and related to circumstances under which the user took advantage of services for which the library itself had incurred direct costs. The earliest example was inter-library loans, where the cost is typically passed on to the user, with or without a service charge. By the 1980s, however, libraries were providing access to online information services and databases at a time when these were still very difficult to use, when many fewer people had the necessary skills and when access charges were extremely high. The consequence was that libraries typically offered mediated searches, passing on the direct costs, and sometimes the overheads as well, to the end-user. Practices varied, but in some libraries – particularly in major urban centres where the demand for such services was greatest – there were differential charging systems, which typically meant that business and corporate users paid more than individuals. Urban public libraries had long provided services for their business clients, but these traditionally consisted of a stock of specialised reference materials and staff with the knowledge and expertise to give appropriate advice to business users. The rapid growth of online information services in the 1980s, before Internet access became all but universal in the business world, fundamentally changed the way in which public library leaders thought about the provision of services to this client group.

It was not only public libraries which had to address this problem. In college and university libraries there were similar issues. While it was long-established practice in many institutions that the direct costs of inter-library loans would be passed on to academic departments or research groups, the use of the library for all other purposes was normally uncharged. But again, the advent of the Internet, and the arrival of the first generation of databases for which mediated searches were more or less a necessity, forced librarians to rethink their economic relationships with both their suppliers and their clients. As new practices evolved, these relationships subtly changed. An even greater change, however, came about in the 1990s when Internet access became a normal part of academic life, and indeed of professional and business life outside the academic sector, and in a domestic context. As access became more of a necessity than a luxury (or an amusement), governments throughout the West turned their attention to issues of equitable access.

It is a problem which can be addressed in many ways. Physical access – the availability of appropriate equipment – is only one aspect of this. Governments and private sector telecommunications providers invested heavily in hard-wired networks which could carry data as well as voice signals. This was the infrastructure of the 'information superhighway' which was a policy priority for the Clinton administration in the United States in the mid 1990s.[6] In Britain too, the telecommunications providers were encouraged to develop broadband networks and the principal provider – British Telecom[7] – indeed did so, and became a major Internet service provider in its own right. In effect, the telecoms companies became common carriers, charging for access and usage; the analogy was with the owner of a railway network charging operating companies to run trains over its tracks, with the operating companies passing on the costs and generating profits from passengers and the consignors of goods. Networks, however, are only one dimension of the physical aspect of Internet access. There is also the issue of the 'last mile' – the availability of connections to the high-speed network – and, perhaps even more importantly, that of the availability of appropriate equipment through which to gain access.

The British solution to this problem was embodied in the People's Network, New Labour's equivalent of the information superhighway programme at the end of the 1990s. Public libraries had a key role to play here, and were encouraged to provide large suites of networked computers for use by their clients. By the time this became common, the World Wide Web was fully functional, and this provided a plethora of sites for which no charge was made. Only when the client came to a site or database for which there was a charge was there any significant limitation on access.

Physical access, however, is not the whole problem. There is also the issue of skills. Early assumptions that older people would be disadvantaged rapidly proved to be untrue. In fact, funding from the People's Network, and other initiatives across the whole spectrum of publicly funded lifelong learning provision (such as additional support for further and adult education), made training widely available to people whose schooldays were decades behind them. The 'silver surfers' soon caught up with their children and grandchildren,[8] such that the generation gap between users and non-users will soon disappear. Even when skills have been acquired, however, there are socio-economic issues remaining. In particular, the less well-educated and the relatively poor (groups which tend to overlap in all western countries) were disproportionately deprived of their capacity to have domestic access to the Web and the skills and culture to make use of public access. It is people in these groups – already disadvantaged, in some cases multiply so – who have suffered most as libraries have developed into information services points and many goods and services from both the public and the private sectors either are only available online or can be obtained much more cheaply electronically than they can through traditional means.

The Internet has the potential to be an even greater tool for democratisation than public libraries were during the decades when they were at the height of their influence. There is some evidence that this is happening, especially with the development of Web 2.0 and its associated phenomena of interactivity and 'social' interaction. Combined with the near-universal coverage of mobile communications networks and the astonishing expansion in the ownership of mobile devices, which have long since outgrown their original functions as devices for voice communications, the network revolution really does have the capacity to reach all levels of society, and all social and economic strata, and is virtually without geographical limits. In other words, accessibility is massively increased.

These developments have massive implications for the public provision of library and information services. Is the library service destined to become a Cinderella, providing facilities only for those who cannot afford to provide their own? Will it become the place of last resort, a sort of information safety-net with a comparable function to that of social security benefits? Historical precedent suggests that although that is a possibility – and one which should not be unthinkingly dismissed – it is improbable. The growth of public libraries after 1945 did not destroy the publishing industry or the bookselling trade. Indeed, it significantly helped both of them by providing a massive market as well as a display case for their wares. Libraries could provide more than all but the most affluent readers could provide for themselves (even if they had wanted to), as well as the range of professional skills that could be offered by librarians. Fundamentally, this remains the case. First, it is important to remember that the book-lending function remains a significant part of what public libraries do, and there are already indications that librarians are successfully exploring ways in which they can make e-books available to their clients. Second, as long as libraries are staffed by properly trained and qualified information professionals, they can continue to add value to information searching by making it more efficient and more productive. Biddy Fisher, Donald King and José-Marie Griffiths and the present author, in their respective chapters, consider future requirements of and for library and informational professionals and how the profession – and education for librarianship – needs to change in order to accommodate the challenges ahead. Life has become easier for the library user, and the skills needed have somewhat changed, but the provision of information through designated service points (which may be virtual) remains an essential characteristic both in the community at large and in specialist institutions such as colleges, universities and organisations of many kinds in all sectors. Far from being the service of last resort, a well-managed information-providing institution remains the most cost-effective way of offering high-quality access to information.

Conclusion

Change is a process, not an objective; it develops of its own dynamic. The evolution of the so-called information society over the last 20 years exemplifies this. There has never before been so much information so readily available. There have never before been so many people seeking information and able to find it for themselves. Access to information has become almost as important as access to food and shelter – it is a fundamental condition of economic and social life. These changes have brought about great improvements in the quality of life for billions of people, yet there is the potential for exacerbating the problems which confront some people while addressing those which formerly confronted others. Exclusion from the benefits of the information society can have its roots in educational attainment, economic capacity or social disadvantage. Western governments have tried to overcome this, and have to some extent made use of the existing network of information institutions – libraries and other information agencies. In the process, the libraries themselves are being transformed in both form and function.

To say that libraries are in a period of transition is a statement that can be credibly made for almost any decade since the middle of the 19th century. There is, however, some evidence that this transition is different – more radical, more fundamental, more long lasting. The inclusive vision of the modern public library is exemplified in its provision of access to the networked world and its capacity to help clients not merely by providing equipment but by helping to enhance their skills. At the same time, new areas of information provision and service can be opened up at relatively little expense. Even at the most specialised end of the spectrum, full-text databases or digitised collections of books and archives can give scholars desktop access to rare materials which were previously available only in a handful of libraries in the world, and not all together in any of them. At a less esoteric level, access to specialised secondary literature – both books and journals – becomes easier and (for the user) cheaper day by day as libraries buy access to e-books and e-journals. For many library users, the problem is no longer what is available, but whether so much is available that they do not have time to make proper use of it. All of this suggests that in many different ways the Internet can and does provide equitable (although rarely equal) access to the ever-increasing store of information and knowledge which the human race has generated and preserved.

Notes

1. A route or network for the high-speed transfer of information; especially (a) a proposed national fiber-optic network in the United States; (b) the Internet (from the *Oxford English Dictionary*).
2. http://www.peoplesnetwork.gov.uk/.
3. For the cultural significance of books, see Brian Cummings, 'The book as symbol', in Michael F. Suarez and H.R. Woudhuysen (eds) *The Oxford Companion to the Book* (Oxford: Oxford University Press, 2010), Volume 1, pp. 63–5.
4. http://www.chatsworth.org/.
5. http://www.english-heritage.org.uk/server/show/nav.12783.
6. The phrase 'information superhighway' was used by U.S. President Bill Clinton and (more particularly) by Vice President Al Gore between 1992 and 2000 to describe the sort of Internet connectivity they wanted to achieve in the United States. Essentially, it was a dramatic way of describing the development of a nationwide broadband network to which citizens would have relatively easy (and cheap) access.
7. British Telecom (now known as BT) was formerly the national telecommunications provider in the UK and was the principal supplier of fixed-line and Internet communications. The telecommunications network has now been privatised.
8. 'Silver surfer' is the slightly patronising phrase used to describe older people who become regular and skilled Internet users. The reference is, of course, to the greying of their hair.

6

The more they change, the more they stay the same: public libraries and social inclusion

John Dolan and Ayub Khan

Introduction

In 1981, the Association of Assistant Librarians published Patricia Coleman's *Whose Problem? The Public Library and the Disadvantaged*. There was an outcry. *Whose Problem?* followed an earlier report of the Library Advisory Council (England), *The Libraries' Choice* (Library Advisory Council, 1978), and Coleman's secondment to the British Library's Research and Development Department from April 1979 to March 1980 as Research Officer in Library Services for Disadvantaged Groups. 'What I have done is to look at developments in the light of what I know from my own experience … I have also sought to illustrate those areas in which I feel the library service is failing and to suggest reasons for the failure' (Coleman, 1981). In a highly personal presentation, Coleman suggested solutions, actions and changes that would take the library service forward. This chapter looks at how (and if) libraries have changed in response to this and other commentaries and to new circumstances and shifting policy.

What problem?

Whose Problem? concluded that 'the failure of public libraries to provide an adequate service to the disadvantaged sections of society is the result of problems within libraries and librarians rather than within the people who are described as disadvantaged. If libraries were serving the whole community, as they are legally bound to do, their provision would automatically encompass the disadvantaged' (Coleman, 1981).

Libraries do not serve the disadvantaged effectively. Little is done to address the needs of this group as part of a wider society; most effort is directed at the provision within the library; some individual librarians place materials in centres of community activity, while a few reach out to people in the places where they live or work. There is little partnership, and the concept of 'engagement' – sharing decisions with local people – has not even entered the language.

What has changed?

Two prime ministers have dominated the period from 1979 to 2010, leading Britain from a battle to reconfigure trade union and class structures to costly and resented wars in Iraq and Afghanistan. Global economics and shifts in economic capacity herald new economic leaders in China and India, while Britain redefines its role in the world. Britain has become a more diverse society, with new facets of disadvantage, exclusion, social justice and mobility. Poverty and exclusion remain prevalent in different forms and degrees (MacInnes et al., 2009), while recent research shows that inequality of opportunity has widened (Hills et al., 2010). Emerging white-minority cities in Leicester and Birmingham illustrate the 21st-century potential of an imperial past. Britain can celebrate its diversity – a plank in the case for winning the competition to host the 2012 Olympic Games – while concerns shift to social immobility in white urban areas. The tragedies of Stephen Lawrence[1] and Victoria Climbié[2] lead to new public service responses to racism, disadvantage and children's well-being and protection. On the one hand, we have mixed reviews of the effect on tolerance and opportunity of policies on multiculturalism; on the other hand, there is increased intolerance towards migrant workers, refugees and asylum seekers. Votes for right-wing local and European politicians are attributed to resentment of immigration from Eastern Europe and Africa[3] (Goodwin et al., 2010).

High unemployment and low attainment compound the problems of many communities; the limited prospects for improvement are worse in a time of recession and further economic decline. An ageing population, while healthier, more mobile and more articulate than in the past, combines with a reduction in the size of the economically active population to put unprecedented pressures on older people's services. New technology's early challenge to information literacy defines a new 'digital divide'. Culturally, Britain has been magnified and enriched in recent decades; while commercial drivers extend experience but increase conformity, growth of funding for the arts, heritage and culture has meant unprecedented creativity. New social and economic divides, though partial and never absolute, are thus digital, cultural, generational and geographical.

Increased expectations are placed on local government services, with frequent restructuring, performance evaluations and continual budget reviews. Education is a matter of daily debate under headings such as: children's education and welfare; the quality of secondary education; and the cost of and payment for higher education. Lifelong learning struggles from neglect ('it's only leisure') to a recognition that it underpins the economy by refreshing the capacity to learn in a technology-based economy where lifelong learning and re-skilling will be ever necessary (DfIUS, 2009). The coming decade will be defined by the response to the financial crisis of 2008 and the ensuing recession. Cuts in public services are already in train, with workforce downsizing; and some services sure to be marginalised, if not abandoned. This is a time of dilemma for many, when library services could prove to be invaluable or dispensable.

What has influenced libraries?

Community libraries, rooted in their locality, emerged in the late 1970s, taking their direction from the needs of the local community. In some London boroughs and provincial cities this characterised change (albeit with some resistance) that addressed the needs of inner-city estates, multiracial, multi-faith communities and declining, late 20th-century outer-city estates. In 2003 the Department for Culture, Media and Sport's (DCMS) report *Framework for the Future* set out a 'modern mission' in three strands:

- books, reading and learning
- digital citizenship
- community and civic values.

Funding was invested in a change programme. The subsequent evaluation was positive, but the public library community remained in a state of flux as exploratory thinking about the library's role continued and the DCMS ceased to ring-fence funding in 2008. By 2009, consultation for a further DCMS review led only to the publication of a set of 'essays' and a further invitation to respond (DCMS, 2009).

During this time, probably the greatest opportunity for modernisation was at once both grasped and lost. The People's Network strategy set out a vision for a modernised, networked library service giving access to a new generation of services and resources. Lottery funding[4] of £170 million was invested in infrastructure, staff training and content. In spite of a remarkable impact on usage – more and different users for 60 million annual hours of Internet access, associated courses, staff support and web content – several authorities failed to see the digital change as integral and to build sustainability into their plans. Local authorities, nervous corporate information technology (IT) teams and libraries with inextricable loyalty to a slow-to-change literary arm of the publishing industry meant that public libraries failed to realise their destiny as drivers of digital change. This was evidenced by the failure to build the necessary skills to enable access and alleviate the awesome 'digital divide'. Public library advocates failed to define the agenda, following instead one driven by government, Ofcom (the independent regulator and competition authority for the UK communications industries) and the telecommunications industry. In contrast, the Museums Libraries and Archives Council's (MLA) Reference Online[5] and the Enquire[6] services illustrate how a national intervention can underpin and enable local difference.

Action, research and experimentation in several areas have disseminated ideas of good practice for others to emulate. Research has identified new ways of working and rehearsed the means to achieve excellence. Both have illustrated how a targeted approach to service development and delivery can impact hugely on individuals' lives. *Start with the Child*[7] is among the most valuable recent reports on children's library provision. Backed up by authoritative research, it highlights good practice but insists that evaluation, identifying best practice and embedding it in core provision are essential to sustainable impact. This, however, is not the norm.

Bookstart[8] was established to introduce babies to books and, more importantly, to support parenting and early years literacy and learning. Since Birmingham's pilot research in the early 1990s, Bookstart has evolved, survived different funding and management regimes and been emulated around the world. Most library authorities run associated activities for families, though only reaching a fraction of the population for such a labour-intensive service. Related programmes aimed at 'dads and lads', young people and emergent readers have also made their mark.

The Summer Reading Challenge,[9] led by the Reading Agency's passion for reading, attracted over 700,000 participants during 2009. The impact study for 2009, however, acknowledges that investment is needed to reverse an ongoing general decline in reading and to restore children's enjoyment – if only to halt the reversal of reading attainment through the long school summer holiday. The study references an earlier Programme for International Student Assessment (PISA) study (Kennedy and Bearne, 2009): crucially, 'the PISA international study of 2000 indicated that finding ways to engage more young people in reading was likely to be the most effective way of creating social change' (OECD, 2002 cited in Kennedy and Bearne, 2009). It has been a strongly held belief that reading skills are a route to social mobility, and that literacy is a prerequisite of personal and community prosperity. Yet, while library providers and advocates see book lending as the heart of their business, it is outreach, partnership and activities that effect change in children's lives; however, the former remains the norm, while reading development is the add-on.

From the same stable as the Summer Reading Challenge came the National Year of Reading (NYR). First staged in 1998–99, it was re-run in 2008–9. Involving many partners and, significantly, more than one government department, it gave libraries a bigger stage on which to perform. A key measure of success was to increase library membership – well exceeded at 2.3 million; yet the impact of libraries on people's reading itself – the skill and thrill – remains elusive.[10] Even so, with ventures like the NYR, reading promotion is at its most sophisticated ever; and children's services are at last at the heart of – probably – all library services.

The Libraries Change Lives award, managed by the Chartered Institute of Library and Information Professionals (CILIP), 'highlights and rewards good practice in any innovative library and information projects which:

- change lives
- bring people together
- involve user communities

- demonstrate innovation and creativity
- develop staff and services.'[11]

The competition attracts projects that illustrate and inform diversity in librarianship. In most instances, a development may be embedded in its service of origin; it may generate other, parallel activity elsewhere; but, by and large, outcomes are evidenced by description and anecdote, focused as they are on small or localised communities. Only gentle osmosis will see such innovation become the norm. However, the evidence is too inconclusive to support the presumption that libraries play a central role in associated strategies of national or local government that resist all but the most powerful advocacy. Thus, again, community librarianship sits alongside mainstream library provision, but not really within it.

More durable is Welcome to Your Library (WTYL), 'a project to increase opportunities for active engagement and participation by refugee communities ... to connect public libraries and refugee communities to nurture learning, wellbeing and a sense of belonging'.[12] The evaluation report and good practice guide for the project share the experience, but the momentum is sustained by The Network,[13] a network of organisations which 'supports libraries, museums, archives, galleries ... who are working to tackle social exclusion'.[14] Perhaps the single most thorough resource for 'tackling social exclusion in libraries, museums, archives and galleries', The Network provides information, courses and guidance, and embraces the needs of many groups who suffer from exclusion, disadvantage and injustice.

While the social and political characteristics of diversity may change, the fundamental view that the public library should *proactively support* equality of access for excluded and disadvantaged groups still requires policy justification and introductory staff training, yet the evaluation of the NYR confirmed that it 'also showed that it was more effective to promote reading through a targeted approach to specific groups such as parents, teenagers or Asian women'.[15] As if to give libraries another chance, the MLA and BIG Lottery[16] joined forces in the £80m Community Libraries programme.[17] This required funded projects to embrace community engagement, a process of giving local people a say in capital spending and programme planning.

Throughout this period there has been a struggle to distinguish the library's intrinsic and instrumental values. The performance expectations and budget pressures on local government at first demanded increased outputs (turnover in loans, increased footfall – a kind of cultural capitalism of continuous growth) and, latterly, outcomes and impact, in other words, a service delivering social and economic change for families and communities. How to fulfil the latter expectations remains elusive; to demonstrate performance in this area would require 1) investment in innovation and change at a pace that matches social, technological and commercial change in the wider world and 2) research to demonstrate outcomes and inform improvement. Neither is forthcoming while debate on the value and role of the library continues.

Before its demise, the Library and Information Commission (LIC) commissioned a policy research project, *Open to All? The public library and social exclusion.*[18] This examined public libraries' capacity to tackle exclusion and suggested how they might contribute towards a more inclusive society. A key recommendation proposed community-based approaches to library provision, incorporating consultation and partnership with local communities. Then *Libraries for All: social inclusion in public libraries* (DCMS, 1999) encouraged partnerships based around social inclusion. In his foreword to the report, then Secretary of State for Culture, Chris Smith, wrote that 'a regenerated and proactive library sector can help both individuals and communities to develop skills and confidence, and helping improve social networking'. The report described barriers that keep people away:

- institutional e.g. opening hours, staff attitudes, rules and regulations, charges, book stock policy, facilities e.g. disabled access
- personal and social e.g. lack of essential skills (reading, writing), low income and poverty, lack of permanent address
- perceptions and awareness e.g. people who are educationally disadvantaged, people who do not think libraries are relevant to their lives or needs, lack of knowledge of facilities and services, or how to use them
- environmental e.g. lack of access to buildings, poor transport links, institutional nature of buildings. (DCMS, 1999)

The report recommends that libraries should mainstream social inclusion, so as to ensure that these groups are heard through effective consultation, and identifies the need to develop new services for new communities. The report also suggests that there is a need for library services to co-locate with other services such as Citizens Advice and voluntary services. Libraries should also provide free access to ICTs, improve their opening hours so as to meet the needs of new communities, work in partnership with other agencies, e.g. a local refugee council, and be located where there is a demand, not on historical basis.

The report also sets out challenges for libraries:

- Sustainability – keeping projects and outreach activity going after external funding runs out e.g. looked after children[19] projects and People's Network.[20]

- Organisational and cultural change – taking the staff and politicians with you. Governors and trustees of organisations are very important in this process.

- ICT environment – keeping this free and replacing equipment.

- Community ownership – making sure that the community takes full ownership of what the library service is trying to achieve.

- Libraries within a wider framework – the need to work with the rest of local government to achieve your objectives.

- Demonstrating benefits of a new way of working with new groups for the survival of the service. (DCMS, 1999)

These are enormous challenges, frequently repeated, for both public and institutional libraries in universities, schools and the workplace. Looking back at these key recommendations, in can be seen that many libraries have failed to implement them.

An international perspective

In emerging and growing democracies the library may be a resource for education and lifelong learning. In the UK this would be based on an aspirational belief in the intrinsic value of the library. The best efforts to produce an evaluation framework have led to the excellent self-help resource Inspiring Learning.[21] However, elsewhere, the continuum of library provision from early years, through education and for the longer-term learning needs of the population is frequently seen as a boon for national and personal prosperity. In her essay for the DCMS review, Dame Lynne Brindley cites China's plan to create a network of '70,000 grass roots cultural centres ... digitised books collections and archives et al ... a catalyst for IT skills development' (DCMS, 2009). In India, the National Knowledge Commission[22] was a task-and-finish advisory body to the Prime Minister of India with the objective of transforming India into a knowledge society. Singapore's Libraries Online strategy[23] assumed the same agenda. Interestingly (and acknowledging the smaller national scale and lighter historical baggage), in Singapore the national and local libraries are operated as one, with a single national strategy underpinning their differentiated objectives.[24] In these nations, the library is challenged to deliver within an overall national endeavour to succeed in the knowledge society through information, skills and cultural experiences, using community-based facilities, online resources and services. The International Federation of Library Associations (IFLA) is prolific in building authoritative principles and guidelines on senior and international experience. Although UK (mostly non-public) librarians are active in authoring such resources, these seem to have little purchase among public library managers in Britain. There are parallels to CILIP's national structure in the many IFLA groups – multicultural services, special needs and so on. Ideally such resources would be drawn upon in drafting UK policy. This is rarely the case.

Although there may be cultural resistance in the UK, as a leading library nation, to adopting foreign or international sources, a notable exception was the MLA's *Guidance on the Management of Controversial Material in Public Libraries* (2009), which drew heavily on IFLA's Committee on Free Access to Information and Freedom of Expression and CILIP's own expertise. Highly pertinent to the learning purpose of libraries, the guidance came in response to criticism by the neo-conservative Centre for Social Cohesion[25] of libraries 'stocking books which preach terrorism and hatred'.[26] The MLA guidance sought to recognise the fundamental independence of the public library as a place of access to information, knowledge and ideas within the British legal framework. Perhaps declining resources will now tempt UK librarians to play a more positive part with international partners in modelling new approaches. However, 30 years after the publication of *Whose Problem?*, priorities remain unconfirmed, and while the principles of social justice and equal opportunity are frequently cited, services that reach disadvantaged communities remain fragmented, still not underpinned by national strategy.

A strategy of urgent relevance

Instead, there has been extended debate, research, experimentation and evaluation in order to assert determinedly that public libraries serve a number of key policy areas. Moreover, the public library idea can be pertinent to the needs of a diverse nation in post-empire change that is seeking a new international position, modernising its economy and renewing its values of social justice and equal opportunity. To achieve these goals the UK requires:

- a restructuring of industry to modernise manufacturing while developing excellence in knowledge and creative industries
- a reconfigured health and well-being service for an ageing population
- an education system that is able to maintain its acknowledged strength in research and learning
- support for parenting that inhibits cyclical deprivation, giving more young people the skills and confidence to survive in a modern economy
- an invasive re-skilling of the workforce for a global knowledge economy.

To meet the needs of a diverse society and a modern economy, and the outputs required of public investment, libraries must be different. The traditional model (already superseded in education) of storing physical resources in a shared meeting place can survive only as one element of a technologically innovative service that is actively delivered according to the needs and expectations of communities whose new generations are themselves moving away from traditional forms of learning and participation.

Research published in 2006[27] looked at what would motivate 14- to 35-year-olds to use libraries in the future. It concluded that the library has to become a 'destination'. This term, familiar in the wider leisure and arts environment, means that the library has to offer attractive services and programmes that make people *want* to use it. Other research (see the MLA's Research Resources[28]) makes the case that needs and attitudes themselves are changing over time and the library concept has to either adapt or fade. National and local government should work together to reconfigure it in line with a changed purpose.

This changed purpose should be centred on economic and social well-being, moving forward from the principles and strategies in *Framework for the Future* to create a service that is directly aligned with national strategies and is delivered locally. To do this:

- the library manager exercises leadership, creates partnerships and seeks new opportunities for innovation

- all library workers are community leaders performing beyond the physical library – prisons, residential centres, hospitals, community and youth centres, working with looked after children, traveller communities, ethnic minority groups and the many and more diverse groups who are all excluded and disadvantaged groups but who, together, make up the sum of people in our communities (everyone is part of something)

- the library operates in the Web environment to reach new generations and new audiences with different services – still focused on learning, ideas, information- and knowledge-handling skills, on active citizenship and on culture as part of a creative society and economy.

Not many public library authorities have adopted such survival techniques. *Whose Problem?* asserts that 'if it is possible to point to twenty library authorities in the country who are providing a high level of service to the disadvantaged, this inevitably obscures the fact that there are seven times as many authorities again who are doing either nothing or very little. The efforts of a few serve only to camouflage the inadequacies of the majority.'

If libraries are to be relevant to the needs of a diverse society and provide services that combat and compensate for disadvantage, they must be developed holistically and delivered consistently, albeit with 'local diversity'. The public library service in the UK has demonstrated that this is feasible (People's Network, Bookstart, the Summer Reading Challenge). Thirty years on from *Whose Problem?* circumstances are different:

- The rhetoric, at least, tells us that power is moving closer to the people.

- Partnerships with a voluntary, third sector have a stronger call on political attention and engage communities; the government's 'Big society' strategy could reinforce this if it is more than a mere surrogate for cost savings.

- Public sector strategists are now focused on expenditure cuts, with a reduced workforce and 'more for less' performance expectations.

- New management models, good in themselves, may obscure the need for change and deliver old services in new ways.

- Partnership, with the private, voluntary and other public sector domains, is paramount.

- Access to books is easier and more affordable, though the inquisitive child will want many books a week – more than most families can afford – while for poor families reading is expensive.

- Information is web based; people are motivated by each other's ideas and opinions as much as by facts and publications; social networking – sharing, building communities, campaigning – characterises web activity.

As adult generations pass and the 'nostalgia lobby' persists in campaigning for the traditional model, new generations will have already moved on to different lifestyles.

Systemic and cultural change

Whose Problem? criticised the 'profession' for its lack of willingness to adopt new approaches – above all, with a national momentum. The caveats and concerns – limited resources, time, capacity – are familiar. What has changed is the world around us. It is a matter of providing a service that responds to society as a whole. Recommendations for generic changes pervaded the conclusions of *Whose Problem?*, regardless of the disadvantaged group under discussion. In today's language, the following would set libraries on a coherent and exciting course:

- Cross-government strategy: DCMS in partnership with other departments leads a campaign to use investment in public libraries, in partnership with other departments, to create a national model for libraries.

- Cross-library strategy: public libraries work with education libraries in a national network of information and interactive learning.

- Without financial incentive, local authorities will not engage with costly change, so a national programme of innovation is funded.

- Implementation of a funded transformational learning and development programme for every area of the public library workforce.

Government itself would advocate the role of libraries to key partners, including national and local agencies for local government, education, health, the arts and industry.

'Cultural change' is less tangible. Even around the time of writing this chapter, there are requests on discussion lists from new or less-experienced librarians seeking help from peers. Topics include advice on undertaking outreach; library signage; services for lesbian, gay, bisexual and transgender families; and surveying black and minority ethnic groups.[29] The facility of the Web to connect the new and the experienced is a great asset. However, it also exposes the low status of diversity in local strategy, limited professional engagement with library peers and the isolation of the service from council and external partnerships already serving diverse communities. This informs the oft-cited but rarely fulfilled need for training and development with the recruitment of new staff to refresh a workforce with new attitudes and ideas. In turn, this requires a more informed understanding, among corporate management and elected politicians, of the potential for libraries to fulfil their aspirations, if and when the former strategically direct them to do so.

Political change

Early in 2010, the Labour government brought its protracted process of review to a conclusion with a policy statement and some proposed initiatives – although by then ministers would have known that its re-election was unlikely. The Conservative opposition, through the then Shadow Minister Ed Vaizey, promoted stronger leadership to the London Libraries Conference in 2009 (Vaizey, 2009). However, by late 2010 Vaizey, now Minister for Culture, Communications and Creative Industries in the Coalition government, has abolished the MLA and announced a national 'improvement' programme that is actually about the reconfiguration of structures and IT systems in order to reduce costs. Vaizey forwent the opportunity to refresh the service by giving it a constructive responsibility to contribute to the national economic recovery. By October 2010 the new government had progressed into law the Equality Act (drafted previously under Labour), but even against this background, the DCMS has neither created any new initiatives nor charged the public library system with a social role in the light of this new legislation.

In the absence of any published change programme for the public library's role and priorities, there has been some reaction in the media: the *Guardian* warns against 'improvement' that actually damages library provision for the poorest and weakest in society:

Faced with budget cuts, many councils will be tempted to retrench. They will freeze new acquisitions, cut opening hours, and perhaps charge for book clubs and children's storytimes. Some libraries will probably close altogether. The risk is that this is done as quietly as possible, in order to avoid an outcry, and without giving local people the opportunity to support their services in ways that may not have occurred to them. But a bigger risk exists: that libraries in affluent market towns are saved thanks to middle-class activism, while those in poorer areas see their book stocks shipped off to a windowless room in the supermarket on the ring road. People who know how borrowing books helped to transform their own lives now need to hold their councils to account – and not just for their own sakes.[29]

This runs counter to pre-election rhetoric; speaking to the Society of Bookmen in February 2010, Ed Vaizey said, 'Tories would introduce a voluntary Charter for Libraries and Reading for local authorities to sign up to, to commit themselves to providing a "first-class library service", as well as establishing a development agency for libraries through the MLA, with a four-year programme to inspire local authorities to invest in their library service' (Vaizey, 2010).

In the background are the fractured fortunes of disparate library services: a county that reaches out through affluent rural areas and centres of tourism to disadvantaged communities, bringing them together in creativity and skills development; a major city that disaggregates its service into localised management units with little financial viability or strategic direction; book funds and staffing that are cut, and stretched to breaking point.

The 150-year history of public libraries, though deeply rooted in working-class learning, reveals that UK library services have adopted only a weak, voluntary and inconsistent approach to social inclusion. Public libraries can and do help to tackle social exclusion. In order to make a real difference they need to change, and to work at developing meaningful, dynamic and sustainable partnerships with community organisations and groups. To be relevant and to tackle social exclusion, libraries cannot succeed alone; but in spite of some transformational accounts, they have systemically failed to engage with relevant community organisations in order to take the agenda forward.

Conclusion: or is it all a conspiracy ...?

Is tangible change only a matter of technology, performance regimes and new initiatives that ultimately just reach the same people? In many libraries you will see vibrant activity. Visit the Libraries Change Lives projects; mix with young people in Bolton's High Street Library; work the crowds in Sandwell's busy Central Library; enjoy music classes in a refurbished Handsworth Library, observe the queue for PCs in Haringey's Wood Green; feel the intensity of serious learning throughout Brixton library; take a ride with looked after children on a Shakespeare mobile for stories at Compton Verney. What characterises the people here is that they are diverse in age, class, ethnicity and gender. They are using services which they find relevant, interesting and enjoyable. In all such situations everybody, from senior manager to staff in service delivery, is working as a community librarian.

It may be that a service so closely associated with liberty and individual freedom is both out of keeping with modern public service delivery and being quietly, maybe unconsciously, nudged into decline because its philosophy is incompatible with a world that sees diversity as a threat, migrants as criminals, lone parents and the old as burdens, young people as hooded and dangerous and resists the value and validity of free information as debilitating to corporate and government control. Maybe in order to change libraries, libraries have to change society. To secure the presence and power to do so, the people who work in libraries would have to unite as a community themselves, no longer reliant on a forgotten law, a defunct national agency or a distracted government. Can they do that?

Notes

1. Stephen Lawrence was an 18-year-old student who was stabbed to death in Eltham, south London in April 1993. It soon became clear that the murder was motivated by racism. The racist murder of Stephen Lawrence was not unique – the Institute of Race Relations has documented 24 racially motivated murders in Britain since 1991, but it was the Stephen Lawrence case that caught the public eye and the media's attention. This is because the police failed to bring successful charges against five youths who were widely viewed as the prime suspects in the murder. It took two police inquiries, a public inquiry, and finally the Macpherson Report, to reveal the extent of the corruption and the conscious and unconscious racism that afflicted the

police force investigating Stephen Lawrence's murder. See http://www. guardian.co.uk/uk/1999/feb/23/lawrence.ukcrime9. The report is at http://www.archive.official-documents.co.uk/document/cm42/ 4262/4262.htm, or see a helpful summary at http://www.law.cf.ac.uk/tlru/ Lawrence.pdf.

2. Victoria Climbié was abused and murdered at 8 years by her guardians in London, in 2000. Both of her guardians were convicted of murder and sentenced to life imprisonment in January 2001. The public outrage at her death led to a public inquiry which produced major changes in child protection policies in the United Kingdom, including the formation of the *Every Child Matters* initiative; the introduction of the Children Act 2004; and the creation of the Office of the Children's Commissioner. The subsequent bifurcation of local authority services into adult and children's services had a major impact on all services.

3. 'In our study (to be published later this year by Routledge in *The New Extremism in 21st-Century Britain*), we examined a large sample of those who have voted BNP or would consider doing so. We found that the BNP is gaining new support principally from older, less educated, white working-class men – voters from Labour's historical base who feel that they have benefited little from the past decade of Labour government, and whose resentments the BNP has succeeded in articulating. These voters share the BNP's hostility to immigrants, seeing demographic change as a threat not only to socio-economic resources such as jobs and housing, but also to cultural values and the national community.' M. Goodwin and R. Ford, 'The BNP's breakthrough', *New Statesman*, 16 April 2009.

4. A UK-wide programme from the New Opportunities Fund of the National Lottery. This later became the Big Lottery Fund, which in turn was the source for the Community Libraries Programme.

5. Reference Online, a subscription-based electronic service for English public libraries brokered by the MLA, http://www.mla.gov.uk/what/support/ online.

6. Enquire, 24/7 real-time online access to a librarian, http://www. peoplesnetwork.gov.uk/enquire/about.html.

7. *Start with the Child*, CILIP Working Group on library provision for children and young people (CILIP, 2002) and the accompanying research on the library needs of children aged 4 to 17 years.

8. http://www.bookstart.org.uk/.

9. http://www.summerreadingchallenge.org.uk/.

10. National Literacy Trust, *Reading the Future*, reports on the National Year of Reading, followed through with an ongoing strategy, *Reading for Life*. See http://www.readingforlife.org.uk/.

11. http://www.cilip.org.uk/about-us/medalsandawards/libraries-change-lives/pages/lclawardintro.aspx.

12. Funded by the Paul Hamlyn Foundation and the London Libraries Development Agency. The WYTL website is at http://www. welcometoyourlibrary.org.uk/editorial.asp?page_id=23.

13. http://www.seapn.org.uk/editorial.asp?page_id=27.

14. The Network, at http://www.seapn.org.uk/.

15. MLA Press Release, http://www.mla.gov.uk/news_and_views/press_releases/2009/national_year_of_reading.

16. Big Lottery Fund is the largest distributor of money raised by the National Lottery for good causes. The money goes to community groups and to projects that improve health, education and the environment. See http://www.biglotteryfund.org.uk/index.

17. 'Open to all local authority library services in England. 58 applicants were successful at the initial application stage in October 2007, and went on to complete business plans and community engagement plans to demonstrate that communities are actively engaged in the development, delivery and management of library services', www2.biglotteryfund.org.uk/prog_community_libraries?tab=1andfromsearch=-uk.

18. D. Muddiman, S. Durrani, M. Dutch, R. Linley, J. Pateman and J. Vincent, *Open to all? The Public Library and Social Exclusion*. London: Resource (Library and Information Commission Research Report 84).

19. See 'Summary of the current outcomes', a report of the Paul Hamlyn Foundation's Reading and Libraries Challenge Fund as part of its Right to Read programme 2001–15, http://www.docstoc.com/docs/23863042/paul-hamlyn-foundation.

20. http://www.peoplesnetwork.gov.uk/.

21. Now Inspiring Learning, http://www.inspiringlearningforall.gov.uk/.

22. National Knowledge Commission, Government of India http://www.knowledgecommission.gov.in/.

23. *Knowledge, Imagination, Possibility*, National Library Board Singapore Annual report 2002/2003, http://www.nlb.gov.sg.

24. See the National Library Board's vision: 'NLB oversees both the National Library as well as the Public Libraries. By international convention, the functions of these two kinds of libraries are distinct and well-differentiated. The NLB's mission is to provide a trusted, accessible and globally connected library and information service through the National Library and a comprehensive network of Public Libraries. Also under its management are 1 community children's library and 17 libraries belonging to government agencies, schools and institutions. Through its innovative use of technology and collaboration with strategic partners, NLB ensures that library users have access to a rich array of information services and resources that are convenient, accessible and relevant', http://www.nlb.gov.sg/page/Corporate_portal_page_aboutnlb.

25. Centre for Social Cohesion, *Hate on the State*, http://www.socialcohesion.co.uk/files/1229624470_1.pdf.

26. Daily Mail Online, http://www.dailymail.co.uk/news/article-480265/Libraries-stocking-books-preach-terrorism-hatred.html.

27. *A Research Study of 14–35 year olds for the Future Development of Public Libraries*, http://research.mla.gov.uk/evidence/documents/Research_study_of_14_35_year_olds_for_the_future_development_of_public_libraries_9841.pdf.

28. MLA Research Resources website, http://research.mla.gov.uk/.

29. http://www.guardian.co.uk/commentisfree/2010/aug/31/libraries-coalition-volunteers.

References

Coleman, P. (1981) *Whose Problem? The public library and the disadvantaged.* London: Association of Assistant Librarians.

DCMS. (1999) *Libraries for All: social inclusion in public libraries.* Department for Culture, Media and Sport. Online at http://www.culture.gov.uk/images/publications/Social_Inclusion_PLibraries.pdf.

DCMS. (2003) *Framework for the Future: libraries, learning and information in the next decade.* Department for Culture, Media and Sport. Online at http://www.culture.gov.uk/reference_library/publications/4505.aspx.

DCMS. (2009) *Empower, Inform, Enrich – the modernisation review of public libraries: a consultation.* Department for Culture, Media and Sport. Online at http://www.culture.gov.uk/reference_library/consultations/6488.aspx.

DfIUS. (2009) *The Learning Revolution 2009.* Department for Innovation, Universities and Skills. Online at http://www.bis.gov.uk/policies/further-education-skills/learners/learning-revolution-white-paper.

Goodwin, M., Ford, R., Duffy, B. and Robey, R. (2010) 'Who votes extreme right in twenty-first century Britain? The social bases of support for the National Front and British National Party'. In Eatwell, R. and Goodwin, M. (eds) *The New Extremism in 21st Century Britain.* London: Routledge.

Hills, J. et al. (2010) *An Anatomy of Economic Inequality in the UK: report of the National Equality Panel.* London: Government Equalities Office. Online at http://www.equalities.gov.uk/pdf/NEP%20Report%20bookmarkedfinal.pdf.

Kennedy, R. and Bearne, E. (2009) *Summer Reading Challenge 2009: impact research report.* Online at http://www.readingagency.org.uk/children/Final_SRC_Impact_research_report_Dec_09%20v2.doc.

Library Advisory Council. (1978) *The Libraries' Choice.* London: HMSO.

MacInnes, T., Kenway, P. and Parekh, A. (2009) *Monitoring Poverty and Social Exclusion 2009.* Report for the New Policy Institute and the Joseph Rowntree Foundation. York: Joseph Rowntree Foundation. Online at http://www.jrf.org.uk/sites/files/jrf/monitoring-poverty-social-exclusion-2009-full.pdf.

MLA (Museums, Libraries and Archives Council). (2009) *Guidance on the Management of Controversial Material in Public Libraries.* Online at http://www.mla.gov.uk/what/~/media/Files/pdf/2009/Controversial MaterialReport.ashx.

Vaizey, E. (2009) Speech to the *London Libraries Conference*, 5 March 2009. Online at http://www.docstoc.com/docs/36448505/Ed-Vaizey-Speech-to-the-London-Libraries-Conference_-5-March-2009.

Vaizey, E. (2010) Speech to the Society of Bookmen. Reported in the *Bookseller.* Online at http://www.thebookseller.com/news/vaizey-libraries-we-cant-go.html.

7

Widening access to information: the haves and the have-nots?

Jenny Craven

Introduction

Societies have always been dependent on information and on how to record it, store it, retrieve it, disseminate it and control it. The principles are the same, whether it is done on a clay tablet or on a USB (universal serial bus) stick. What has changed is the ease of access to systems and widespread capacity to use them – for example, from mediated searches via an information professional, to the prolific use of search engines such as Google.

ICT (information and communications technology) has made communication faster, and increasingly people are using technology to expand their global connections – using online collaborative workspaces, social networking tools and mobile devices. The European Union firmly believes that ICTs make a positive contribution to the economy, society and personal quality of life (see *Europe's Information Society*[1]), but to achieve this, measures must be taken to ensure that equal access to information is provided for society as a whole.

The question of equitable access will be the focus of this chapter. It will begin by considering what is meant by the term 'digital divide' and then go on to discuss relevant initiatives established to help combat the divide, how technology can present barriers to accessing information and how these may be overcome. Finally, it will consider the role that libraries can play – and are playing – in widening and enhancing access and in addressing the problem of the 'haves' and 'have-nots' in the information age.

The digital divide

Much attention has been paid in recent years to addressing issues of social inclusion and combating what is often referred to as the 'digital divide'. It is perhaps helpful firstly to consider some of the definitions given to explain this term. Taking Wikipedia as a starting point, the definition given for the digital divide is 'the gap between those people with effective access to digital and information technology and those without'.[2] The Organisation for Economic Co-operation and Development (OECD), in its publication *Understanding the Digital Divide*, refers to it as 'the gap between individuals, households, businesses and geographic areas at different socio-economic levels with regard to their opportunities to access information and communication technologies (ICTs) and to their use of the Internet for a wide variety of activities' (OECD, 2001). Gurstein (2003) observes that definitions of the digital divide often do not go beyond the concept of access, and while this is 'fundamental and basic to all other developments and uses of ICT', issues related to access should be explored further to identify 'how and under what conditions ICT access can be made usable and useful' (Gurstein, 2003).

James (2008) focuses on the impact of ICT on the divide and the extent to which this impact can benefit countries, suggesting that rich countries enjoy greater benefits in terms of production – such as the availability of hardware and software – as well as take-up and use of these technologies. The concept of the 'haves' and 'have-nots' can also be used when talking about divisions within society, whether in relation to accessing community services, healthcare, education or resources such as those provided by libraries. In a study of the role of the library in equalising access to information, the digital divide is defined as 'the perceived gap between those who have access to the latest information technologies and those who do not' (Russell and Huang, 2008), and Cullen (2003) refers to the information rich and the information poor in the following terms: 'those who are "information rich" own the most powerful computers and have better Internet access to powerful streams of continuous information, whereas the "information poor" do not' (Cullen, 2003). This is a rather simplistic view, however, and requires further investigation to consider why the 'information poor' do not have equitable access.

Some assumptions about the digital divide can also be made. For example, should we assume that everyone in the developed world has access to hardware, software, and effective broadband connections? And should we assume in the UK, as a developed country, that there is no longer a digital divide in terms of technology? Or are there still members of society who cannot access technology or cannot see its benefit to them? James (2008) suggests that further divisions should be explored within countries, and this leads on to a view from Harper (2003), whereby the digital divide can be referred to as the 'social digital divide' in terms of an individual's degree of marginality to ICT and on the basis of differences in:

- perceptions
- culture
- interpersonal relationships
- operational skills (Harper, 2003).

Focusing on skills, in a study of the extent and impact of restricted access to ICT by specific groups of staff in UK further and higher education institutions, Cooke and Greenwood warn that if 'potential users are not able to develop skills … they are unable to benefit from access' (Cooke and Greenwood, 2008) (they refer to this as a 'vicious circle'). Therefore, there is a need to overcome the psychological barriers to ICT access in order to avoid what could also be referred to as a 'digital poverty trap', where uptake and use by sections of society will never be realised, due to a perceived lack of relevance of ICTs and therefore a reluctance to develop appropriate skills to engage in their use.

Digital divide initiatives

A number of national and international initiatives encourage wider use of ICTs, and accordingly seek to reduce the effect and extent of the digital divide. For example, in relation to learning and educational administration in the UK, through initiatives from the Department for Education and Skills, the British Educational Communications and Technology Agency and the Higher Education Funding Council for England; and in relation to public access, through the People's Network[3] in the UK and the Gates Program in the US. For example, the Bill and Melinda Gates Foundation sponsors the Native American Access to Technology Program, which works with 'tribal leaders, librarians and educators' on the reservations of New Mexico, Arizona, Utah and Colorado to 'increase computer access for all citizens, particularly the impoverished' (Russell and Huang, 2008). To sustain such initiatives, librarians need to forge partnerships with local communities, charitable organisations and the private sector to achieve the long-term support, training and resources which are needed 'that involve equipment, personnel, time and space' (Russell and Huang, 2008).

In 2009, the UK government (Communities and Local Government Department) funded a Digital Inclusion Task Force, the aim being to create better education, health, governmental and social opportunities for the most socially excluded people in the UK.[4] In 2009 Martha Lane Fox was appointed as Chair of the Digital Inclusion Task Force, her vision being to 'use ideas, contacts and experience from both the commercial and charitable sectors to make sure that, with the help of the Task Force, I quickly start to deliver effective projects' (Information World Review, 2009).

E-inclusion has been given a high priority on the European Commission's agenda, with actions, initiatives and strategies to address accessibility and inclusion and to achieve 'an "Information Society for All", promoting an inclusive digital society that provides opportunities for all and minimises the risk of exclusion' (European Commission, 2005). The i2010 strategy is a good example. In 2005, the Commission presented the i2010 strategy as a framework to strengthen Europe's lead in ICT and unlock the benefits of the information society for European growth and jobs. In a recent review of the main achievements of the i2010 strategy (European Commission, 2009a), the Commission outlined a list of key actions achieved between 2005 and 2009. In relation to digital libraries, recommendations were made regarding digitisation, online accessibility and digital preservation. Currently, Europe's Digital Library, Europeana, provides online access to books, maps, recordings, photographs, archival documents, paintings and films from national libraries and cultural institutions of the EU's 27 member states.[5] Digitisation clearly provides a key to widening access to information and resources; however, the continued uncertainty over the final details of the Google Book Settlement is seen as having the potential to create another divide in terms of access, due to differences between US and European copyright laws.[6]

Technological infrastructure

Many people take access to technology for granted; in the UK and other advanced global economies people enjoy access to a range of technologies and broadband provision. But, with all the excitement about engaging in Web 2.0 and Library 2.0 technologies, it is important to remember that there are still a significant number of countries that do not have the technical infrastructure to support such technologies. To take Kenya as an example, and on a more personal level, in 2008 I was involved in running a workshop on 'Improving library services for visually impaired people' for the Kenyan National Library Service; out of nearly 30 delegates from all over Kenya, less than half had access to a computer – whether in the library, at work or at home. Those who did have access described problems such as power cuts, leaking roofs and even insect infestations, as well as that of poor bandwidth connections. So, even at a basic level there are problems to be overcome before some of the new technologies that are emerging (e.g. multimedia, video streaming, etc.) can be accessed and used. Despite the situation in Kenya now looking a little brighter, with a new and faster Internet connection to the coast of East Africa, there are still concerns about cost. According to a British Broadcasting Corporation report in September 2009, the highest residential Internet speed offered by Kenya's largest Internet service provider remained capped at one megabit per second (and was available only at night and at weekends, at a then annual cost of $1,440, which exceeds the average Kenyan annual wage, estimated by the UN at about $800).[7]

In many developing countries, cyber cafés have been a popular way to provide access to technology, though this may be changing. In 2001, Dasgupta, Lall and Wheeler's report on *Policy, Reform, Economic Growth, and the Digital Divide* identified mobile phones as a 'promising new platform for Internet access'; since then, the growing use of mobile phone technology has opened up even more opportunities for access. According to an article in the *Guardian*, in 2009 developing countries accounted for about two-thirds of the mobile phones in use, compared with less than half of subscriptions in 2002, and subscriptions were rising at a faster rate than fixed-line subscriptions, 'indicating that many people in the developing world are bypassing the older technology altogether' (Tryhorn, 2009). This is a positive development and reinforces the importance of developing web content which is accessible in a mobile environment (this is explored later in this chapter under the section on e-accessibility and design for all).

It is sometimes easy to assume that countries in the 'developed world' do not have a digital divide and that the challenges faced by countries such as Africa are not relevant to them. However, in the US, a census undertaken in 2003 and 2005 revealed that 'not all geographical locations in the United States are using high-speed services to the same degree' (Russell and Huang, 2008) and that unequal access can be 'found across one city or within one school system, with the consequence that, as technology advances rapidly this will impact on those who have access and those who do not'. Similarly, a survey conducted by the Oxford Internet Survey (Oxford University)[8] in 2009 revealed that in the UK:

- Those who are most deprived socially are also least likely to have access to digital resources such as online services.

- One in 10 of the adult population (9%), amounting to four million people, suffer 'deep' social exclusion, a severe combination of social disadvantages, and have no meaningful engagement with Internet-based services.

- Three out of four of those who suffer 'deep' social exclusion, have only limited engagement with Internet-based services. This extrapolates to about 13% of the UK's population, or about six million adults.

Findings such as these were also discussed in an interview on the BBC's news programme *Hard Talk*, where the UK Digital Champion Martha Lane Fox reported that, of the 10 million adults in the UK who have *never* used and *never* had access to the Internet, she is targeting the poorest 4 million with a view to getting the majority online by 2012.[9] Therefore, it appears that much work still needs to be done to ensure equal access and uptake of ICTs so as to combat the digital divide, not only in developing countries, but throughout the world.

Uptake and use of ICT

Although digital divide initiatives such as those described above have widened access to ICTs, meeting hardware and software requirements is only part of the solution. Those who do not see the relevance of ICT will still be unlikely to take advantage of public access sites 'unwelcoming and irrelevant to their needs' (Cooke and Greenwood, 2008). It is necessary to make sure that people are aware of the relevance of ICT, and in order to enable effective uptake the user must also 'receive adequate training and educational opportunities' (Russell and Huang, 2008).

3. http://mobilemuse.ca.
4. See for example, A.J. Scott (2008) *Social Economy of the Metropolis*, Oxford: Oxford University Press.
5. http://earth.google.co.uk/.
6. http://maps.google.co.uk/.
7. http://www.google.com/intl/en_us/help/maps/streetview/.

References

Gibson, J. (1977) 'The theory of affordances'. In Shaw, R. and Bransford, J. (eds) *Perceiving, Acting, and Knowing*. Hoboken, NJ: Wiley pp. 67–82.

Hofstadter, D. (2007) *I Am a Strange Loop*. New York: Basic Books.

McLuhan, M. (1964) *Understanding Media*. New York: Mentor.

Pine, J. and Gilmore, J. (1999) *The Experience Economy*. Boston, MA: Harvard Business School Press.

Cooke and Greenwood (2008) revealed that lack of hardware and networked infrastructure is less of a barrier than lack of ICT skills and motivation to use ICTs, as well as resistance on the part of managers to providing ICT training. Their research concludes that a major challenge is to 'win the hearts and minds' of non-desk staff and their managers. However, the study identifies a lack of research into the extent to which ICTs are available and used by all personnel within an organisation (i.e. not just academic or 'desk-based' staff). They also suggest that there is a danger of a 'loss of access to key corporate and external sources of information in an increasingly "virtual" work environment ... Extending existing inequalities among personnel, creating a digital divide between the "information rich" and the "information poor"' (Cooke and Greenwood, 2008).

Digital inclusion includes efforts to address social exclusion through an emphasis on engagement with ICT (Hill et al., 2008). Engagement involves a range of behaviours which go beyond simply the 'haves' and 'have-nots'. For example, a study of the engagement of older people with technology (Hill et al., 2008) revealed that this group of people needs to be interested and motivated to engage with Internet technology and that their use is also influenced by what is personally relevant to them and of practical value. For example, e-mail was more important to them than online shopping and banking (Hill et al., 2008). A study undertaken between 2002 and 2004 to develop a longitudinal Library Networking Impact Toolkit to assess the impact of ICT provision following the implementation of the People's Network in UK public libraries also revealed that uptake of and engagement with ICT was influenced by personal relevance. Examples of engagement included keeping in touch via e-mail with grandchildren around the country and with friends who had emigrated, as well as people who had moved to the UK and who found the Internet useful for updating their knowledge about home by looking at online newspapers (Brophy and Craven, 2004).

Engagement with the Internet can create changes at societal levels – including the organisation and re-organisation of existing social, economic and political conditions and inequalities (Mason and Hacker, 2003) and can affect the digital divide. It is important to recognise, however, that engagement is multifaceted and can include:

- Internet adoption – including acceptance and rejection of ownership
- Internet access – including formal and effective access
- Internet use – including nature and quality of use.

Rapid developments in ICTs pose new challenges because basic access and take-up issues are still being addressed. For example, Web 2.0 presents a range of new access, interaction and collaborative opportunities, which could 'lead to new barriers to social inclusion for those unable to participate' (Cooke and Greenwood, 2008) and may further disengage people who are unwilling to participate. Two terms often used now are 'digital natives' and 'digital immigrants', where digital natives are 'native speakers' of the digital language of computers, video games and the Internet, and digital immigrants are those of us who were not born into the digital world but have, at some later point in our lives, adopted many or most aspects of the new technology. This notion was coined by Mark Prensky (2001) and, although somewhat criticised because of its rather simplistic view of the population, not taking individual circumstances into account (Bennett et al., 2008; Kennedy et al., 2008), it nonetheless provides an interesting point of view when considering reasons why people may or may not wish to engage with technology.

E-accessibility and design for all

Another important access issue is that of e-accessibility and design for all. The term 'accessibility' can mean many things, but in the context of this chapter it refers to ensuring that systems and interfaces can be used by all users through access to:

- different technologies, such as the operating system (such as MS Windows), application (such as Excel, Word, or a web browser) and, where necessary, assistive technology (such as screen magnification or a screen reader)
- different technologies and humans: undertaken using a combination of the above and via a user interface
- humans, technology and the context of the interaction: undertaken via a combination of the above, and within the context of the interaction (such as e-resources/materials, virtual learning environments, repositories, borrower transactions, etc) (Craven, 2008a).

The term 'design for all' refers to the accessibility issue of ensuring that information can be interpreted by the technology of choice, be it a standard PC, laptop, mobile device or used in conjunction with assistive technologies such as screen-reading or magnification software or alternative mouse and keyboard devices. An abundance of guidelines, standards and recommendations exist to implement accessibility and design-for-all principles. For example, the Web Content Accessibility Guidelines (WCAG) Version 2[10] aims to provide specific technical guidance for web design and authoring, attempting to take into account old, new and emerging technologies, and the British Standard on Web Accessibility (BSI, 2010) aims to provide a more user-friendly and flexible approach to guidelines and recommendations relating to accessible web design. However, despite legislation in many countries relating to equal access (see, for example, the Disability Discrimination Act in the UK; Section 508 of the Rehabilitation Act (29 U.S.C. 794d) in the US; and the suggestion of a European Disability Act[11]), there still appears to be a lack of awareness about web accessibility and a reluctance to implement it, as demonstrated in a number of reports. The seminal report by the UK Disability Rights Commission (DRC, now the Equality and Human Rights Commission) on *The Web: access and inclusion for disabled people* (DRC, 2004) painted a depressing picture of the accessibility of websites – in particular for access by people with disabilities. Since then, studies and reports continue to demonstrate a lack of accessibility in the design of websites across a wide variety of sectors (see, for example, Weisen et al., 2005; European Commission, 2007).

In 2008 the European Commission held an international conference on e-inclusion which included web accessibility. The conclusions of the conference were that web accessibility remained a priority of e-inclusion policies and that public authorities should have a special responsibility to deliver in this area. However, a more recent study on *The Accessibility of European Commission Websites: analysis of current status and recommendations for improvement*[12] showed that little had changed in terms of improving access to e-resources. Despite the study's findings that 'all the websites [evaluated for the study] were generally good in terms of guidelines compliance', it acknowledged that 'there is still scope for improvement'. Worryingly, the main accessibility issues identified were very similar to those identified in the DRC's 2004 report, namely:

- images with incorrect or non-existent text alternative
- section headings and lists not marked up or incorrect
- links not clearly identifying their purpose or target

- inaccessible use of technologies like PDF, Microsoft Word or PowerPoint
- inadequate page titles
- data tables marked up incorrectly
- new windows opening without informing the user.

A subsequent report, published in 2009, concluded that although some progress towards accessibility (for government websites at least) seems to be detectable, many websites fail to maintain compliance over time (European Commission, 2009b). These findings demonstrate a continued lack of awareness of some of the most fundamental accessibility requirements, and the '8 quick fixes' identified in the *Accessibility of European Commission Websites: analysis of current status and recommendations for improvement* study once again show that little has changed in the 12 years since 1999.

To try to address some of the problems associated with current standards and guidelines, a more 'holistic' approach to accessibility has been developed in recent years, initially for the creation of accessible e-learning resources. Led by experts in the field, including UKOLN,[13] the University of Dundee and the JISC TechDis service (which provides support, advice and guidance on disability and technology to the UK education sector, with the aim of increasing accessibility and inclusion),[14] this approach places the focus on what the user will get out of the learning experience, rather than just on making it accessible (Sloan and Kelly, 2008). The approach has since been presented to accessibility experts, policy makers and organisations such as the World Wide Web Consortium (W3C)[15] – and it is hoped that it has influenced the more flexible approach adopted in the *WCAG 2.0*. The *Authoring Tool Accessibility Guidelines*[16] are also seen as being highly relevant to improving web accessibility, because if authoring tool providers can build accessibility into their tools, authors need not be experts in accessibility and in web authoring. This is particularly pertinent in relation to the increase in user-generated content, where the concern is that inaccessible websites will proliferate now that 'anyone can be a web designer' and that content generators will not be aware of and therefore not adhere to standards (which help to improve accessibility and compatibility between hardware and software) such as assistive technologies. A solution to address this concern is the provision of appropriate education and training in web accessibility and design for all, which is discussed further in the next section of this chapter.

Education and training

Widening access and closing the digital divide can also be achieved through education and training of staff and end-users, as well as by ensuring that new library and information service (LIS) professionals entering the workforce are equipped with appropriate skills. For example, Manchester Metropolitan University's Department of Information and Communications is a Centre for Excellence in Teaching and Learning and specialises in information literacy as part of the LearnHigher Learner Development consortium.[17] It strives to be at the forefront in using new technologies in research and teaching and uses a range of Web 2.0 technologies in teaching undergraduate and postgraduate information and communications students (Glass, 2008).

Education and training are also key to improving awareness and encouraging implementation of accessibility in the design of websites. In 2005, during the UK presidency of the EU, the UK Cabinet Office produced a report on e-accessibility in the EU. It made a recommendation that 'all content commissioners and authors are fully trained in the importance of accessible content and in the means that are made available for them to achieve this' (Cabinet Office, 2005). This is being addressed to some extent through the Design for All Network of Excellence (D4ALLnet) (EU Information Society Technologies Programme).[18] Set up in 2001, it provides networks of excellence in Design for All across Europe to 'integrate information and identify core knowledge sets and skills for model curricula in design for all specifically for information and communication products, systems and services' (Nicolle et al., 2001). Training materials, courses and resources can be provided through the European Design for All e-Accessibility Network. For example, the web access study programme D4ALLnet has been developed to deliver an international online joint study programme in accessible web design and has been designed in a way that will enable access for as many people as possible – through formal education, continuing professional development (CPD) activities and return-to-work initiatives (Willson et al., 2010).

Good practice examples

Some excellent examples can be found of how libraries and related service providers such as museums and archives are already contributing to addressing social inclusion and digital divide issues. For example, in the UK, Leeds Library and Information Service's Across the Board project supports families with children who have autism spectrum disorder through the provision of symbol-based communication aids and visual support. The project won a Libraries Change Lives award in 2009 and an award from the Jodi Mattes Trust to promote equal access to, and equal enjoyment of, art and culture for disabled people through the use of digital media.[19] Library services also received awards for the international category of the Jodi Mattes Trust: the Regional Library of Karlovy Vary in the Czech Republic for its provision of sign language information on its website, and Dedicon in the Netherlands for the Streaming Spoken Books for People with a Reading Impairment project. Other examples include the US Making Connections programme, funded by a charitable organisation, which works with librarians and other organisations to help bring ICTs into disadvantaged neighbourhoods (Breeden, 2003).

Podcasts from the Past,[20] at the Museum of London, reaches potentially excluded people on several levels. It provides audio description podcasts that allow visually impaired visitors increased access to some of the galleries at the Museum. This is achieved through an aural route into the collections which, although designed for visually impaired visitors, are suitable for everyone, with dynamic visual content accompanying the audio description. The podcasts were created by a group of eight long-term unemployed people of different ages and social backgrounds, who were thus enabled to learn more about visually impaired people through workshops; and introduced some people to museums for the first time, helping them to realise their abilities and gain news skills and experiences which they can use in the future.

Libraries can help to ensure that users, members and visitors are able to access and interact with the content and resources provided online. Examples of good practice include Deakin University in Australia,[21] which has created an accessibility working group which meets regularly to highlight, discuss and hopefully solve website accessibility issues and provide support to academics who assist students with disabilities and encounter issues in using interactive course materials (Craven, 2008b); and the College DuPage library, USA,[22] which has undertaken user testing and testing with assistive technologies to help make pages more accessible, not just for people using assistive technologies, but also for people using devices such as handhelds – and so truly widening access for all (Craven, 2008b).

Widening access through the creation of accessible and usable resources is another important aspect of education and training. Eskins and Craven (2008) undertook a review of training and awareness of web accessibility in LIS curricula. Evidence was found of web accessibility being taught within modules and courses, such as the basic designing of usable websites (Sheffield University, UK), electronic publishing (University of Wales, Aberystwyth) and multimedia (Ionian University, Greece). At Manchester Metropolitan University's Department of Information and Communications, basic web design (which includes an introduction to accessibility) is core at both undergraduate and postgraduate levels. Accessibility is built into all web design assessments and fundamental accessibility design issues (colour contrast, accessible tables, informative title attributes) are also embedded into the ethos of the taught units.

Conclusion

This chapter has explored some of the issues that can influence the divide between the 'information rich' and the 'information poor'. It has been noted that the so-called 'digital divide' is not necessarily between richer and poorer countries, but a divide that exists within the societies of all countries throughout the world. With a particular focus on technology, the benefits of ICT can be seen as a means to combat this divide, providing access to information and communications, taking advantage of a variety of technologies available via the Internet, using online collaborative workspaces, social networking tools and mobile devices. However, technology can present barriers to accessing and engaging with information, with problems being due to a lack of adequate infrastructure to support ICTs; a lack of engagement even when the infrastructure is in place; and barriers to access, due to a poor design and structure of web-based information which can exclude access, in particular to people with disabilities and using assistive devices such as screen-reading technologies. Barriers also exist in the uptake of ICTs, where a perceived lack of relevance or a lack of appropriate skills can result in reluctance to engage with ICTs.

Libraries are well placed to contribute to closing the digital divide: they can play a role in enhancing information literacy skills and motivate people to use ICTs by introducing them to the benefits of technology in ways that are meaningful to them rather than simply providing access, and by providing appropriate support and user education. Libraries can also play an important role in widening access through the creation of accessible e-content and e-resources, and through appropriate education and training embedded into LIS curricula and programmes of CPD.

Libraries, library associations and organisations can play a role in influencing policy, as Biddy Fisher describes in Chapter 18. For example, in 2009 CILIP announced its intended involvement in government plans to tackle digital exclusion – identifying access problems such as provision for people with disabilities, a confusing range of broadband connection choices, poor rural connectivity and 'widespread poor web design and content' (CILIP, 2009). In response to the Department of Communities and Local Government paper *Delivering Digital Inclusion: an action plan for consultation*,[23] CILIP has highlighted the need to support and motivate people to engage with ICTs, suggesting a need for 'information brokers' to help people find, evaluate and use what they access. LIS workers are well placed to take on the role of supporters and motivators, and public libraries should play a pivotal role as 'they have a ready-made network and skills base' (CILIP, 2009). Looking to the future, and on an international level, the 2009–11 IFLA President, Ellen Tise, has chosen 'Libraries Driving Access to Knowledge' as her presidential theme. Tise believes that libraries and librarians must become fully engaged in their communities and societies, contributing value to society by 'providing citizens with access to knowledge and information'. It is hoped that this will help to continue to raise awareness of the benefits of widening access for all and thus reducing the gap between the 'haves' and 'have-nots' in the information society, so that 'access to information for all on equal terms is [seen as] an unchallengeable human right'.[24]

Notes

1. http://ec.europa.eu/information_society/index_en.htm.
2. http://en.wikipedia.org/wiki/Digital_divide.
3. http://www.peoplesnetwork.gov.uk/.
4. http://www.21stcenturychallenges.org/focus/the-digital-inclusion-task-force/.
5. See http://www.europeana.eu/portal/aboutus.html.
6. http://www.ifla.org/en/news/update-on-google-books-statement.
7. http://news.bbc.co.uk/1/hi/technology/8257038.stm.
8. http://www.oii.ox.ac.uk/microsites/oxis/.
9. http://news.bbc.co.uk/1/hi/technology/8302598.stm.
10. http://en.wikipedia.org/wiki/Web_Content_Accessibility_Guidelines.
11. http://europa.eu/rapid/pressReleasesAction.do?reference=SPEECH/09/429.
12. http://ec.europa.eu/information_society/activities/einclusion/policy/accessibility/web_access/commission_web_accessibility/index_en.htm.

13. http://www.ukoln.ac.uk/.
14. http://www.techdis.ac.uk/.
15. http://www.w3.org/.
16. http://www.w3.org/TR/WCAG20/.
17. http://www.learnhigher.ac.uk/.
18. Design for All Network of Excellence, http://www.d4all.gr/.
19. http://www.jodiawards.org.uk/home.
20. http://www.museumoflondon.org.uk/English/Collections/Prehistoric 1700/PodcastsfromPast.htm.
21. http://www.deakin.edu.au/dwm/accessibility/.
22. http://www.cod.edu/library/.
23. http://www.communities.gov.uk/documents/communities/pdf/1001077.pdf.
24. http://www.ifla.org/files/hq/presidents-program/acceptance-speech-et.pdf.

References

Bennett, S., Maton, K., and Kervin, L. (2008) 'The "digital natives" debate: a critical review of the evidence'. *British Journal of Educational Technology*, 39 (5), 775–86.

Breeden, L. (2003) *Connecting Families to Computers and On-line Networks*. The Annie E. Casey Foundation, Baltimore, MD. Online at http://www.aecf.org/KnowledgeCenter/Publications.aspx?pubguid={1 CF4CFD7-6A0A-4CD8-AC73-A879CABAEC78}.

Brophy, P. and Craven, J. (2004) *Longitude II: a library networking impact toolkit for a user-driven environment*. London: Museums, Libraries and Archives Council.

BSI (British Standards Institution). (2010) BS 8878:2010 *Web Accessibility. Code of practice*. London: BSI.

Cabinet Office. (2005) *eAccessibility of Public Sector Services in the European Union*. Online at http://webarchive.nationalarchives.gov.uk/ 20100405140447/archive.cabinetoffice.gov.uk/e-government/ resources/eaccessibility/.

CILIP (Chartered Institute of Library and Information Professionals). (2009) 'Digital inclusion: CILIP responds'. *Library and Information Update*, January/February, 14.

Cooke, L. and Greenwood, H. (2008) '"Cleaners don't need computers": bridging the digital divide in the workplace'. *Aslib Proceedings: New Information Perspectives*, 60 (2), 143–57.

Craven, J. (2008a) *Web Accessibility: practical advice for the library and information professional*. London: Facet.

Craven, J. (2008b) 'Web accessibility: what we have achieved and challenges ahead'. *World Library and Information Congress: 74th IFLA General Conference and Council*, 10–14 August 2008, Québec, Canada. Online at http://archive.ifla.org/IV/ifla74/papers/086-Craven-en.pdf.

Cullen, R. (2003) 'The digital divide: a global and national call to action'. *The Electronic Library*, 21 (3), 247–57.

Dasgupta, S., Lall, S. and Wheeler, D. (2001) *Policy, Reform, Economic Growth, and the Digital Divide: an econometric analysis*. World Bank. Online at http://books.google.co.uk/books?id=4v04WJ4UBEC&printsec=frontcover&source=gbs_v2_summary_r&cad=0#v=onepage&q=&f=false.

DRC. (2004) *The Web: access and inclusion for disabled people*. Disability Rights Commission. London: HMSO.

Eskins, R. and Craven, J. (2008) 'Design for all in the library and information curriculum'. In Craven, J. (ed.) *Web Accessibility: practical advice for the library and information professional*. London: Facet.

European Commission. (2005) 'Communication from the Commission to the Council, the European Parliament, the Economic and Social Committee, and the Committee of Regions: eAccessibility'. Online at http://ec.europa.eu/information_society/activities/einclusion/policy/accessibility/com_2008/index_en.htm.

European Commission. (2007) *MeAC Report: assessment of the status of eAccessibility in Europe*. Online at http://ec.europa.eu/information_society/activities/einclusion/library/studies/meac_study/index_en.htm.

European Commission. (2009a) *Europe's Digital Competitiveness Report: main achievements of the i2010 strategy 2005–2009*. Online at http://ec.europa.eu/information_society/eeurope/i2010/docs/annual_report/2009/com_2009_390_en.pdf.

European Commission. (2009b) *Web Accessibility in European Countries: level of compliance with latest international accessibility specifications, notably WCAG 2.0 and approaches or plans to implement those specifications*. Online at http://ec.europa.eu/information_society/activities/einclusion/library/studies/docs/access_comply_main.pdf.

Glass, B. (2008) 'Using Web 2.0 technologies to develop a sense of community for emerging LIS Professionals'. *World Library and Information Congress: 74th IFLA General Conference and Council*, 10–14 August 2008, Québec, Canada. Online at http://archive.ifla.org/IV/ifla74/papers/150-Glass-en.pdf.

Gurstein, M. (2003) 'Effective use: a community informatics strategy beyond the digital divide'. *First Monday*, 8 (12). Online at http://firstmonday.org/htbin/cgiwrap/bin/ojs/index.php/fm/article/view/1798/1678.

Harper, V. (2003) 'The digital divide: a reconceptualisation for educators'. *Educational Technology Review*, 11 (1), 96–103.

Hill, R., Beynon-Davies, P. and Williams, M.D. (2008) 'Older people and Internet engagement: acknowledging social moderators of Internet adoption, access and use'. *Information Technology and People*, 21 (3), 244–66.

Information World Review. (2009) 'Martha Lane Fox appointed "Champion for Digital Inclusion"'. IWR News Desk, 17 June. Online at http://www.iwr.co.uk/information-management-and-technology/3008988/Martha-Lane-Fox-appointed-%E2%80%98Champion-for-Digital-Inclusion (subscription required).

James, J. (2008) 'Digital divide complacency: misconceptions and dangers'. *The Information Society*, 24 (1), 54–61.

Kennedy, G.E., Judd, T.S., Churchward, A. and Gray, K. (2008) 'First year students' experiences with technology: are they really digital natives?' *Australasian Journal of Educational Technology*, 24 (1), 108–22.

Mason, S.M. and Hacker, K.L. (2003) 'Applying communication theory to digital divide research'. *IT and Society*, 1 (5), 40–55.

Nicolle, C.A, Rundle, C. and Graupp, H. (2001) 'Towards curricula in Design for All for information and communication products, systems and services'. *Proceedings of INCLUDE 2003, 23–26 March, London.* Online at http://hdl.handle.net/2134/1062.

OECD. (2001) *Understanding the Digital Divide*. Organization for Economic Co-operation and Development. Online at http://www.oecd.org/dataoecd/38/57/1888451.pdf.

Prensky, M. (2001) 'Digital natives, digital immigrants'. *On the Horizon*, 9 (5), 1–6.

Russell, S.E. and Huang, J. (2008) 'Libraries' role in equalizing access to information'. *Library Management*, 30 (1–2), 69–76.

Sloan, D. and Kelly, B. (2008) 'Reflections on the development of a holistic approach to web accessibility'. *Accessible Design in the Digital World. Conference Proceedings*, University of York, 22–24 September.

Tryhorn, C. (2009) 'Developing countries drive explosion in global mobile phone use'. *Guardian*, 2 March. Online at http://www.guardian.co.uk/business/2009/mar/02/mobile-phone-internet-developing-world.

Weisen, M., Petrie, H., King, N. and Hamilton, F. (2005) 'Web accessibility revealed: the Museums, Libraries and Archives Council audit'. *Ariadne*, 44. Online at http://www.ariadne.ac.uk/issue44/petrie-weisen/intro.html.

Willson, J., Craven, J. and Eskins, R. (2010) 'Education and training for accessible web design'. *ASLIB Proceedings*, 62 (1), 57–69.

8

Tackling inequalities around the globe: the challenge for libraries

Jonathan Harle and John Tarrant

Introduction

There are many inequalities in the world. The inequitable access to information is one of them, and as a result, people lack access to vital knowledge which could make significant contributions to improving and securing their health, welfare and livelihoods. This chapter reviews some of the principal challenges to improving information access in the developing world and outlines some ways in which they are being tackled. Information is today synonymous with technology, particularly Internet and mobile technologies, and it is common to talk of a 'digital divide' – as described in the previous chapter by Jenny Craven – between rich and poor nations. While recognising this divide, this chapter also outlines some of the opportunities which new technological solutions may offer to improve access to information in developing countries, and draws together a number of brief case studies to illustrate them. It argues that it is not the availability of information which will pose the greatest challenge to developing countries, particularly as connectivity and information and communications technology (ICT) provision improves, but rather how access to and use of this information requires change in ways of working in order to achieve practical and sustainable development outcomes. It concludes that, if developmental and educational opportunities are to be fully realised, library and information professionals will need to play a leading role. If they are to do so they will need to embrace new ways of working and contribute their traditional skills and expertise in new ways.

The inequalities of information

Today's world is defined by huge inequalities and exclusions. Access to good-quality education, the provision of affordable healthcare, access to safe water and secure food supplies, and the conditions of basic human security, democratic government and respect for fundamental human rights are all very unequal. While poverty is commonly defined in economic terms and with reference to absolute income levels (such as the $1 a day 'extreme poverty' line which underpins the UN Millennium Development Goals[1]), it must be understood as a complex relationship between many factors. Notions of capabilities, freedoms or rights are more useful in helping to understand the causes of extreme poverty, and ways in which it may be reduced.[2] In this context, a focus on inequality, including unequal access to information, is important in drawing attention to relative levels of wealth and social welfare between and within countries and also to the real dynamics of poverty, development and social welfare around the world, and how they are transmitted and reproduced across successive generations (Green, 2008).

In the face of many substantial development challenges, information inequality and the technology by which information is delivered and accessed may not seem to be particularly high priorities. Information is, however, essential to economic growth, to improved social welfare and to the democratic processes which underpin them. Tackling the divide between the information rich and the information poor is therefore fundamental to tackling all other inequalities. This is increasingly true as knowledge and expertise become commodities of international trade and as the challenges facing the world and its population rely on the ability to access and analyse even greater volumes of information. This is not just a matter for industrialised economies: Rwanda's president Paul Kagame has repeatedly emphasised that broadband Internet connectivity and technology are critical to his country's development. He has committed to providing every child with a laptop by 2012, and argued at a 2009 technology summit that 'in an age such as this, "poverty" goes beyond the lack of clean water, safe food, and shelter; it is also the exclusion from powerful networks of learning, production, and trade'.[3] Technology, properly attuned to needs, can in turn contribute considerably to better education, health and livelihoods, and has the potential to open up whole new ways of meeting fundamental development needs.

Overlooking libraries

Libraries have long been central to the provision of information, in a range of forms and media, to communities the world over. They have played, and continue to play, an important part in extending literacy and education, particularly where access to formal schooling is low. They offer spaces for study and learning, or simply provide a place for people to read and encounter books for pleasure. In much of the developing world the cost of building and maintaining good book collections has nevertheless proved difficult to meet, and there are few libraries outside of the major urban centres or accessible to poorer communities. Kenya has just 36 public libraries, Malawi 10 and Uganda 30 (Mchombu and Cadbury, 2006).

Libraries continue to have a vital role to play in reducing information inequalities: by supporting access to and the development of knowledge, and by bridging educational divides. Today's technology-driven world, where much information is now online and electronic, offers greater potential for libraries to develop new and innovative information services. They need to meet the needs of their existing users better and to extend their reach into communities that have not previously had access. Nevertheless, while libraries are embracing ICT, they have typically had relatively little involvement in many of the new information initiatives that have developed in poorer countries in recent years. These have more often been driven by ICT experts and development practitioners and by those with the technical skills to develop Internet- and mobile- (cell-phone) based services. Libraries' involvement has often been limited to providing computer terminals for Internet or catalogue access. As a result, not only is the considerable experience of information professionals not being used, but also the roles of the library as an information centre and of librarians as information experts, guides and facilitators increasingly risk being overlooked. Many initiatives fail because they are driven by those who lack an understanding of why and what information is needed and how it is used. There is thus an urgent need for libraries and librarians to engage, and to contribute their expertise, developed through long experience of print-based services, to the development of new mobile and online environments.

Bridging the divide: why information matters

When it comes to achieving development goals, access to high-quality information plays a critical role at many levels. Policy makers and government administrators need information that will enable them to make informed decisions and to develop the most appropriate policy responses. Scientists and scholars in research institutes and universities need access to the latest literature in their fields and to high-quality data and statistical sources. School-children need textbooks and other educational materials that present ideas in ways which are culturally and pedagogically relevant; and people at all levels of society need access to the bodies of knowledge that might help them to improve many areas of their daily lives. To cite just one example, improved access to the right information at the right time can contribute significantly to the work of farmers and farming; the ability of middlemen to exploit small producers is often dependent on the latter's ignorance of market prices and lack of alternative selling options. While the lack of selling options may be difficult to address, accurate food and crop market price information can transform farmers' negotiating power.[4]

Better access to information can also contribute to strengthening the democratic process, ensuring that institutions and governance are accountable to citizens. The importance of information in such contexts is well demonstrated when governments resort to controlling what their citizens are able to access and suppressing information (Burma, Iran, Zimbabwe, to name but a few current examples) through restrictions on reporting and publishing. The suspension of universities and other educational institutions that enable information to be disseminated and discussed is often a telling sign of the failure of democratic government. Increasingly, this is manifested in controls over the Internet, China being a case in point.[5] Of course, greater access to information and to digital networks can have negative as well as positive impacts on democracy, and care must be taken not to automatically assume an inherent good in new information technologies, as studies of Kenya's 2007 elections and ensuing violence have shown (Goldstein and Rotich, 2008).

New opportunities – but also new challenges

The Internet is awash with stories of the ways in which ICT is being creatively deployed to gather, report and disseminate information or to enable basic financial transactions. These often involve meshing computers, mobiles and the Internet to create new systems of capture, storage and dissemination. In East Africa they are assisting in disease management, enabling clinics to send treatment information alerts directly to patients' mobile phones (Lester and Karanja, 2008) and facilitating the rapid reporting of drug stocks in rural clinics.[6] They are also enabling people far from urban centres to access banking facilities, as in Kenya, where the M-PESA banking service allows users to perform basic transactions via mobile phone. For those in rural areas it not only extends banking facilities to a much wider segment of the population, but also reduces arduous and unnecessary travel[7] (Morawczynski, 2009).

Some of the most successful and widely reported applications of digital technologies to development have concerned access to up-to-date agricultural knowledge. In India and Sri Lanka, the Commonwealth of Learning has sought to enhance an over-stretched agricultural extension service by linking rural farmers to a network of universities via village Internet kiosks, allowing farmers to address questions directly to academics on such matters as how milk yields can be improved or alternative markets can be developed (Daniel and Alluri, 2008). Another example is the e-Choupal initiative, an e-commerce service, again in India, which has provided 2,700 computers to villages in five states, enabling farmers to place orders, track prices and learn about new techniques.[8] In Kenya, as in other parts of Africa, 'rural internet kiosks' are helping to deliver satellite Internet access. Kiosks are solar powered and each one hosts three computer terminals which have been specially developed to be as power-efficient as possible.[9]

Case study 8.1 Rwanda's ICT bus

Recognition of the importance of ICT to development is prominent in Rwanda's national strategy, with the government seeking to transform the country from a predominantly agricultural to a 'knowledge-based' economy. Under the e-Rwanda project, telecentres providing computing, Internet and banking facilities have been established across Rwanda. The ICT Bus project aims to bring the same facilities to currently unconnected districts, many of which lack reliable power supplies. The first two buses were launched in October 2009; in addition to Internet-connected computers, they are equipped with printers, photocopiers and scanners. The objective is for buses to serve as mobile computing centres linked to the Internet via satellite, thus enabling rural communities to access up-to-date information and to benefit from ICT training and business development services. With more than 70% of Rwanda's private sector being made up of small and medium-sized enterprises, which are predominantly rurally based, the hope is that these centres will help to stimulate and support rural entrepreneurship and encourage familiarity with and use of ICTs.[10]

Education is a particularly important area where expanding access to information through technology has the potential to make a real difference to the lives of millions of people. Sugata Mitra's work on the provision of 'hole in the wall' computers in urban slums or rural villages has shown that Indian children are able to teach themselves basic computer literacy without additional guidance or instruction (Mitra et al., 2005); Digital Doorways[11] brings a similar approach to South Africa. Mitra also suggests that 'one laptop per child' may not be the best policy, as children seem to learn better in small groups rather than working alone at a laptop. A number of research projects are similarly investigating the potential applications of technology to improving access to high-quality education across the world. These include work on computer-assisted learning in primary and secondary schools, the provision of low-cost laptops and initiatives to create banks of open educational resources (OERs) to improve the availability of teaching and 'textbook' materials. Selinger (2009) discusses further the experiences and challenges of applying ICTs in primary and secondary education.

At the tertiary level, distance learning has been around for many decades: through the University of London International Programmes,[12] as delivered by the many well-established open universities (such as the Open University in the UK, UNISA in South Africa, Athabasca University in Canada and the Open University of Sri Lanka) and through other mixed-mode programmes. But greater access to the Internet, improved connectivity and the increasing availability of OERs have combined to offer new modes of delivery, and to broaden dramatically the reach and improve the quality of formal education, and of professional training in key areas such as health, veterinary science and business. Some of the world's leading academic institutions are now contributing content freely; the Massachusetts Institute of Technology (MIT) has, for example, made materials for some 1,900 courses available through its OpenCourseWare initiative.[13] The UK Open University's Teacher Education in Sub-Saharan Africa programme combines a variety of media to provide open, modular materials which local institutions can use to create their own training programmes. The materials, provided in a range of languages, are specifically developed to help teachers to upgrade their skills through classroom practice, rather than requiring extended campus-based study (Anamuah-Mensah et al., 2008).

For academics and students, one of the major obstacles to teaching, study and research has long been the lack of books and journals, with library collections often being many years out of date. This has typically been the result of the high cost of purchasing publications from abroad, and of limited local markets which have frustrated attempts to establish domestic and regional publishing. The emergence of electronic journals has given rise to a number of valuable initiatives such as the HINARI (Health InterNetwork Access to Research Initiative),[14] AGORA (Access to Global Online Research in Agriculture)[15] and OARE (Online Access to Research in the Environment)[16] schemes of the United Nations' health, agriculture and environment agencies. There is also the International Network for the Availability of Scientific Publications (INASP) Programme for the Enhancement of Research Information,[17] supported by many major academic publishers providing free or heavily discounted access to many thousands of journals and databases. These have not only dramatically improved the availability of scholarly material but have also done much to transform the fortunes of university libraries.[18]

Common to most of these examples of how technologies are delivering critical information in new ways (with the exception of journal provision) is the absence of a library or librarian. In some instances, an information professional has no obvious role, but in others a trained and skilled information professional would have much to add. Clearly, the profession needs to find ways of engaging with such initiatives and to demonstrate the substantial additional experience that librarians can bring to bear in facilitating the processes by which users access information and process it into knowledge. That is not, of course, to overlook examples where libraries are fully engaged. Health libraries, for example, have a long tradition of working with medical professionals and are striving to develop new technology-enabled services, as is noted in a recent review of provision in Zambia (Chanda and Shaw, 2010).

The technology gap

As the examples above illustrate, access to information increasingly goes hand in hand with access to digital, networked and mobile technologies. In fact, 'information' is now synonymous with ICT and it is impossible to disassociate the provision of information from the technology through which it is delivered and accessed. Yet, while information is widely available in many forms, the tools for getting to it are outside the reach of many people. Computer access is extremely limited in many parts of the developing world and Internet penetration is low: fewer than 5% of people use the Internet in Africa, for example, and broadband penetration is just 0.2%, compared to 55% and 19% respectively in the developed economies.[19] Fixed-line telephone penetration in many countries is also limited. Typically, the cost of installing and maintaining such networks in tropical climates and in scattered rural communities, combined with the inability of many to afford their own line rentals, have pushed traditional telephony out of the reach of most people.

On the other hand, mobile networks have proved more economically viable, cheaper to install and maintain and more rapidly scalable. The dramatic growth of mobile telephony has offered many new opportunities. By the end of 2007, 64% of mobile subscribers were from developing countries, compared to 44% in 2002. Africa now has the highest mobile growth rate in the world: 32% in 2006–7.[20] Furthermore, because phones are often shared among families or communities, access to a mobile device is actually much wider than the figures for mobile accounts are able to capture. While initiatives to supply affordable and robust laptops or mobile computing facilities offer the prospect of increasing access to computing and the Internet for some, it seems clear that mobile phones, more affordable and more readily accessible by a far greater number of people, offer the greatest potential. Significantly, more mobiles with data capabilities (enabling greater Internet use) were reportedly imported into Africa in 2008 than those without, suggesting that opportunities for mobile delivery of Internet content may increase steadily in the coming years (Banks, 2009).

Whether the device is a PC or a mobile handset, unlocking their potential as information tools will depend fundamentally on good broadband connectivity. For many years, African countries – the least connected in the world – have relied principally on expensive satellite connections. While the example of the Kenyan Internet kiosks suggests that this is affordable for community use and for basic information services, it will not stand up to larger data demands or be affordable for individual connections. However, the continent is set to benefit from a series of new fibre optic cables which will ring the African coast in the coming years. In 2009 two high-speed undersea cables came onshore in East Africa, connecting Kenya, Tanzania, Mozambique, Madagascar and South Africa to Europe, the United Arab Emirates and India. A further cable entered service in July 2010, and new West African cables are scheduled for completion in 2011. New terrestrial networks will ultimately deliver this connectivity across countries and to their landlocked neighbours. Kenya has reportedly made considerable progress in developing its own terrestrial infrastructure through the National Optic Fibre Project, on which much of East Africa's connectivity will rely. Tertiary and research institutions in a number of countries have formed national research and education networks to develop dedicated high-speed academic networks. Ultimately, the hope is that these can be linked directly to the European backbone network (Gathara, 2009; Harle, 2010).

At present, however, many of these advances in connectivity are confined to major urban centres. Extending broadband networks to relatively dispersed communities means that a set of problems similar to those that have long limited fixed-line telephony will be encountered – the need for expensive underground cabling, often to places where demand is unlikely to support the substantial cost. Developments in so-called 'last mile' wireless technology, such as WiMAX (Worldwide Interoperability for Microwave Access) or BPL (Broadband over Power Line) may help to bring down the cost of extending high-speed Internet connectivity into rural areas, but the connectivity challenge remains substantial.

Managing, maintaining and keeping up

The cost of keeping pace with technological change poses a real problem. There is a tendency for a ratchet effect in hardware and software – increasingly sophisticated software requires greater hardware capabilities, which in turn enable more demanding software to be produced. Keeping up, let alone catching up, is becoming harder and harder; the development of open source software, netbooks and cloud computing offers one solution. Software is hosted on Internet servers (the 'cloud') rather than directly on a user's computer, which, as a result, can be much smaller and have less memory. One of the major obstacles that secondary and tertiary institutions face in developing countries is the lack of well-equipped science laboratories. Using a cloud approach, MIT has been able to develop remote-access laboratories, enabling African students to conduct experiments in science and engineering in real time and using actual MIT facilities (Theroux, 2006). Cloud computing nevertheless reinforces other problems because it requires fast connections and access everywhere.

The ability of people to gain access to and use the information available to them depends increasingly on how their networks and computer systems are managed. This is particularly the case in large institutions, such as universities. The volume and speed of data that can travel from the Internet to people's computers and back again depends on many things. Poor network configuration – the routing and signalling which control the traffic flow – can hamper access, as can viruses, spam, file sharing and the streaming of large audiovisual files. The problem is particularly marked where hardware is typically older and bandwidths are lower, as is the case in many developing countries.

People also use Internet connections for a wide range of purposes, from e-mail and social networking, to listening to music or following sports teams. Where these Internet connections are primarily provided for enabling access to educational information, as in libraries, schools and universities, limited bandwidth has to be carefully managed, as any other scarce resource would be. Unfortunately, skilled network administrators and technical staff are often lacking in many developing-country institutions, meaning that an institution's connection is often poorly managed. Good bandwidth management (Case study 8.2) can help to improve dramatically the volume of information that users are able to access over an existing connection, without the need to purchase expensive additional capacity or infrastructure.

Case study 8.2 The bandwidth problem

Bandwidth – the amount of data that can be pushed through a computer network in a given unit of time (usually expressed as bits per second) – is an expensive resource in many developing-country universities. In recent years, African universities have been paying up to 20, 50 and even 100 times the price per unit that users in Europe or North America pay. Bandwidth is not only expensive but also extremely restricted: many universities have a similar bandwidth available for their whole campus to that used by a single European domestic connection. Where this bandwidth is unmanaged, it will typically be consumed for low-priority and non-educational uses. The high use of external e-mail providers (Hotmail, Yahoo and Gmail) rather than internal university e-mail servers also places considerable strain on bandwidth. Upgrading infrastructure and hardware can help in the short term, and of course costs can be lowered through consortia or by pushing for greater liberalisation of the telecoms market. Bandwidth will, however, soon become limiting once again as traffic increases and as further low-priority applications or websites are loaded. INASP research in 2003 pointed to a lack of bandwidth management in 59% of African universities (INASP, 2003). Without good management, an extremely valuable resource, for which universities have paid a staggeringly high purchase price in the first place, is easily wasted.[21]

Some of the websites through which information is available have become unnecessarily bloated and are not designed to run well in low-bandwidth environments (Jackson, 2009). While many websites have long included a text-only function as part of global accessibility standards, this still requires the main site to be loaded before the lower-graphics site can be accessed. An alternative solution is the Loband application, developed by the UK-based organisation Aptivate, which simplifies sites so that they load faster over slow connections.[22] Another approach that has been implemented in a number of contexts is asynchronous access to the Internet, whereby data or e-mails are downloaded overnight, when connections are faster and access is thus cheaper; the data/e-mails are then relayed between a connected town and local villages on portable data drives or USB (universal serial bus) sticks or uploaded from a local kiosk to a bus fitted with a data storage device, and downloaded when the storage device reaches its destination (Day and Greenwood, 2009; Nightingale, 2009).

Access and use

Most access to information happens not only outside of the formal setting of a library but also without the guidance of librarians or information professionals. This is certainly true in the South,[23] where access to libraries has long been very poor, particularly in rural communities. Despite much hope and ambition to use technology to drive poverty reduction – through economic growth, improved health systems and accessible education – many projects have proved unsuccessful (Leach and Scoones, 2006). Simply delivering technological solutions – providing access to e-mail, ability to browse the Internet, or helping more people to own mobile phones – does not enable people to use new information to tackle daily challenges. Examples abound of technology-driven development projects where too great a focus on the technology and insufficient attention to the original need and the social and cultural context have led to disappointing results (Unwin, 2009). For information technologies to be useful they must support a need articulated directly by their potential users: for example, a service which gives them meteorological updates, agricultural prices or basic health information. The technology should simply be the means of fulfilling this need. Moreover, while there is a tendency to assume that rural needs are focused on the concerns of everyday livelihoods, it is important to recognise that needs and interests will include social, political and cultural affairs, world events, parliamentary politics and even the latest films and sporting events (Gunawardena, 2005, cited in Unwin, 2009).[24]

Similarly, the simple availability of information is not enough – it needs to be both accessible and useable. There is no serious shortage of information, and much of it can now be accessed without subscription or payment as open source content material. In fact, in many circumstances the challenge is not to locate information, but to be able to filter and make sense of all that is available. The principle of the World Wide Web is that anyone can make any material available to everyone. Much of this 'information' is trivial, inaccurate or wrong. The Web can provide support for any point of view – no matter how extreme. At the same time, of course, there is also much that, while contributed by non-traditional authors (often via blogs), is of considerable value. The challenge is in identifying what is useful. Search engines can help to a limited extent to order and make sense of what is available, but the sheer volume of what can be found remains daunting. As the volume of information continues to grow, so does the redundancy of much that is available and the background 'noise' that interferes with every information request. As new knowledge is developed, the 'half life' of information is shrinking. One way to measure this is to plot citations of journal articles over time. In the physical and medical sciences the decay rate is very high and the number of citations is halved in as little as two or three years (Thomson Reuters, 2009). Simple use of search engines rarely provides the date of the information sources. Access to an exploding body of information means that the traditional role of the librarian in guiding people through the information landscape and moderating what is available is ever more urgently required. Is it available?

Skilling users and skilling staff

The digital divide is commonly framed as a technological gap to be bridged by investments in computing facilities and improved broadband connectivity. But the divide is also, and critically, an issue of skills, capabilities and a willingness to change ways of working. Higher education institutions across Asia, Africa and Latin America are now entitled to free or significantly discounted access to a considerable volume of scholarly material. Many libraries have organised themselves into national consortia in order to leverage greater negotiating and purchasing power and secure national licences. Yet the *use* of the material by students and academics is often quite low[25] (Kiondo, 2008; Musoke and Kinengyere, 2008). While insufficient ICT facilities and poor bandwidth undoubtedly limit use, it is awareness, skills and teaching and learning styles which account for much of this under-use. The results of a recent study by the Association of Commonwealth Universities in conjunction with universities in eastern and southern Africa suggest that in many cases the greatest obstacle to the use of information is that students and academics are simply unaware – or poorly aware – of what is available to them. They remain unable to navigate through a complex landscape of publishers' databases to locate what they need, and lack the skills to query databases and search engines effectively. They rely on very basic Google searches that return unmanageable numbers of results, many of which are not relevant (Harle 2010). This is itself partly the result of low exposure to computers and lack of time to experiment with the Internet and digital resources. It is exacerbated by lack of guidance from teaching and library staff. Academic staff may not demand citations in assignments and are often uncertain themselves about online sources; as a result, students are not encouraged or helped to make greater use of the information to which they now potentially have access.

Many librarians are well aware of this problem – and have been for some time – and there are ongoing discussions about how the librarian's role might be redefined and the library be repositioned, and the ways in which libraries can contribute to educational, social, cultural and economic development (see for example Mcharazo and Koopman, 2008;

Adeogun, 2008). Librarians commonly point to a need for greater ICT competency amongst their own staff before they are able to assist students better; and to students who may have more experience of the Internet (if not in handling the information they find) than do the librarians to whom they turn (Parker, 2003). When asked about the principal challenges facing the university library, an East African librarian pointed without hesitation to human resources, emphasising the need to upskill staff so that they can operate effectively in an increasingly online library world, manage the library's digital materials and educate and assist users to do the same.[26]

Conclusion

The above discussion has highlighted some of the challenges of providing and developing information-based and technology-enhanced services in developing countries. Resources are constrained, infrastructure is overstretched and distances are often considerable. New information services are commonly being driven and developed by those with technical knowledge and skills, such as software engineers or Internet-savvy and entrepreneurial researchers, development professionals or educationalists. In some cases, information is being sourced in unanticipated ways. There are anecdotal and news reports discussing so-called 'human Google' services, where an ICT-literate person – but rarely an information professional – takes information requests and provides some possible answers. Librarians and information professionals appear to be much less involved in such services, and in many 'information for development' situations it is precisely their contribution that is missing. Beyond the formal education system, and as Internet connectivity slowly travels outwards from urban centres, new types of information professional will be needed if people and technologies are to be effectively brought together in ways that are people rather than technology centred. These might be within village ICT or information centres, or in a mobile capacity similar to Rwanda's ICT bus. After all, the first horse-drawn mobile library service is thought to have been developed as early as 1859 in Warrington in the UK, and there are a number of examples of mobile library services in Africa.

The 'mobile library' of the future may in reality be a library service accessed via *mobile phone*. Indeed, there are a number of emerging initiatives here, captured by papers from the first two M-Libraries conferences held in 2007 and 2009, and it is in this area that librarians may be able to regain and re-offer their leadership (Ally and Needham, 2008, 2010). Publishers are beginning to develop their content for mobile delivery and librarians are beginning to develop new services, beginning with reference requests and advice by SMS (short message service) and extending into the future delivery of content direct to mobile devices, as well as information training courses. While these services are growing in Europe and North America, there are important contributions from the South, such as those of UNISA, South Africa's distance university, and driven by the great interest in and growing access to mobile technologies highlighted above (Mbambo-Thata, 2008).

Changes are also undoubtedly required within the education sector. Commentators are often quick to suggest that the simple availability of online information on everything means that libraries, librarians and other intermediaries are no longer required. Libraries can then simply become rooms full of computer terminals. While some university libraries in developing countries are now reasonably well connected and deliver at least a partially electronic service, the ways in which they operate remain largely unchanged. As library orientation has switched to information literacy and training in electronic and online information resources, many libraries have struggled to formalise their training roles, and a lack of pedagogically skilled librarians makes delivery of training sessions difficult. There are very few cases where substantially new services have been developed to meet the changing needs of users, and which ensure that new facilities and resources are harnessed to meet new educational needs.

To be effective, librarians need not only to be familiar with sources of online information, but also to be able to communicate the value of these new sources and to be adept at tailoring what is available to the specific needs of users. The Internet means that much more information is potentially accessible than ever before, but it also means that much more disinformation is available. The need to direct students towards academic and scholarly materials is greater than ever. There is clearly a critical role for librarians, working closely with teaching staff, to ensure that students are given the understanding, skills and tools to interrogate and analyse information effectively; close academic liaison is discussed further by Edward Oyston in Chapter 11.

Librarians can play a vital role in ensuring that developing countries are producers of information and contributors to, rather than simply consumers of, academic literature and online materials. In part, this will be achieved by ensuring that researchers are helped to access the material they need in order to undertake high-quality research and write publishable articles. Librarians can also help academics to publish their own work locally. Online publishing allows for new ways of contributing, and librarians have, or are in a position to develop, the skills needed to do this successfully. Many libraries are, accordingly, developing institutional repositories to capture and make available conference papers and other unpublished work, and are indexing the journal articles produced by their researchers. Much educational material is produced in Europe and North America, and although efforts are made to ensure that some OER material is culturally appropriate, there is a great need for more locally conceived and written material to be made available to learners and teachers. In some cases this may be in languages other than English, which is the Internet's dominant language.

Much of the shift will depend on a change in teaching practices and a better understanding of the role of ICTs in education. Access to high-quality and appropriate OER material allows a shift in focus from instruction to student-centred learning. While these are not entirely issues for libraries, librarians need to help push such changes forward and to demonstrate the role they can play in facilitating online learning as well as remote research collaborations and greater university–community linkages. Of course, these challenges are not confined to developing countries. Nevertheless, it is, arguably, a more urgent task in developing-country universities and their libraries, where information access starts from a lower base, where appropriately qualified teaching staff are fewer in number and where computer and Internet access are much less widely available.

The information divide has very major technological dimensions and it is important not to underestimate the difficulties of finding the right technological solutions. However, as with so many cases in the world of economic and social development, it is the human dimension that is both critical and the most difficult to get right. Technological fixes very rarely work, and even where information and the technology to access it are both available, the skills and experience to manipulate and use this information are not present. More importantly, the paradigm shift in the *way* that professionals work has hardly begun.

Notes

1. http://www.un.org/millenniumgoals.
2. See, for example, A. Sen (1999) *Development as Freedom*, Oxford: Oxford University Press.

3. Address by Paul Kagame at the World Technology Summit, 16 July 2009, New York http://www.paulkagame.com/news16-07-2009.php.
4. For a discussion of one such project see N. Ashraf, X. Giné and D. Karlan (2008) 'Finding missing markets (and a disturbing epilogue): evidence from an export crop adoption and marketing intervention in Kenya', HBS Working Paper Number 08-065, http://www.hbs.edu/research/pdf/08-065.pdf.
5. Until plans were recently shelved, the government had been planning to mandate the installation of filtering software on all computers: http://www.guardian.co.uk/technology/2009/aug/13/china-drops-web-censorship; Google recently announced that it would no longer censor its Chinese service, a practice which it had undertaken in order to launch its Chinese service in 2006: http://www.guardian.co.uk/world/2010/jan/21/china-internet-censorship-great-firewall.
6. Such as the pilot use of the Ushahidi platform by the Stop Stockouts initiative to track medical supplies across Kenya, Uganda, Malawi and Zambia, http://stopstockouts.org/ushahidi/ (accessed 25 January 2010).
7. http://www.safaricom.co.ke/index.php?id=745.
8. http://www.scidev.net/en/new-technologies/digital-divide/opinions; http://www.itcportal.com/rural-development/echoupal.htm.
9. http://www.elearning-africa.com/newsportal/english/news212.php; http://www.ruralinternetkiosks.com.
10. http://www.independent.co.ug/index.php/news/regional-news/78-regional-news/1248-rwanda-set-to-launch-ict-buses-with-telecentres.
11. http://www.digitaldoorway.org.za.
12. http://www.londoninternational.ac.uk/renaming/index.shtml.
13. http://ocw.mit.edu.
14. http://www.who.int/hinari/en/.
15. http://www.aginternetwork.org/en/.
16. http://www.oaresciences.org/en/.
17. INASP is the International Network for the Availability of Scientific Publications, based in Oxford, UK: http://www.inasp.info/perii.
18. For further discussion of these initiatives, and the wider context of journal access in African universities, see J. Harle (2009) *Digital Resources for Research: a review of access and use in African universities*, London: Association of Commonwealth Universities, http://www.acu.ac.uk/publication/download?id=173.
19. International Telecommunications Union (2009) *Measuring the Information Society: the ICT development index*, http://www.itu.int/ITU-D/ict/publications/idi/2009/material/IDI2009_w5.pdf.
20. *Ibid.* Furthermore, this accounts only for individual mobile line subscriptions, whereas in many cases mobiles have actually become shared resources, rented out by local entrepreneurs, and it is thus possible to access a mobile without actually owning one.
21. Aptivate (2007) *Bandwidth Management Position Paper*, Cambridge: Aptivate, http://www.aptivate.org/attach/Projects.BMOPositionPaper/AptivateBMOPositionPaper.pdf.
22. http://www.aptivate.org/Projects.Loband.html.

23. http://en.wikipedia.org/wiki/Global_South.
24. See also http://www.scidev.net/en/opinions/communication-rights-and-communication-wrongs.html.
25. Data collected through interviews and observations undertaken by J. Harle, see Harle (2010).
26. Interview conducted by the author, September 2009.

References

Adeogun, M. (2008) 'Emerging university library services in an ever-changing and knowledge-intensive learning environment'. Paper presented at the Association of Commonwealth Universities Conference of Executive Heads in Hyderabad, India, 28–30 November. Online at http://hyderabad2008.acu.ac.uk/presentations/Margaret_Adeogun.pdf.

Ally, M. and Needham, G. (eds) (2008) *M-Libraries: libraries on the move to provide virtual access*, Proceedings of the First International M-Libraries Conference, London. Online at http://m-libraries2009.ubc.ca/.

Ally, M. and Needham, G. (eds) (2010) *M-Libraries 2: a virtual library in everyone's pocket*, Proceedings of the Second International M-Libraries Conference. London: Facet.

Amanuah-Mensah, J. et al. (2008) 'Building an Effective Open Education Resource (OER) Environment for Teacher Education in Sub-Saharan Africa: the TESSA experience'. Paper presented at the Fifth Pan-Commonwealth Forum on Open Learning, London, 13–17 July. Online at http://www.tessafrica.net/images/stories/static_files/tessapcf5paper.pdf.

Banks, K. (2009) 'Mobiles offer lifelines in Africa'. BBC News website. Online at http://news.bbc.co.uk/1/hi/technology/8256818.stm. Accessed 16 September 2009.

Chanda, K.L. and Shaw, J.G. (2010) 'The development of telehealth as a strategy to improve health care services in Zambia'. *Health Information and Libraries Journal*, 27 (2), 133–9.

Daniel, J. and Alluri, K. (2008) *University–Community Links for Rural Prosperity*. Association of Commonwealth Universities' Conference of Executive Heads, Hyderabad, India, 28 November. Online at http://hyderabad2008.acu.ac.uk/presentations/University_Community _Links.pdf.

Day, B. and Greenwood, P. (2009) 'Information and communication technologies for rural development'. In Unwin, T. (ed.) *ICT4D: information and communication technology for development.* Cambridge: Cambridge University Press.

Gathara, V. (2009) *Fibre Comes East ... Is Kenya Prepared? A preliminary report on the impact of the arrival of international submarine fibre on development in Kenya.* Department for International Development in Kenya and Somalia. Online at http://www.gg.rhul.ac.uk/ict4d/workingpapers/Gathero.doc.

Goldstein, J. and Rotich, J. (2008) *Digitally Networked Technology in Kenya's 2007–2008 Post-Election Crisis.* Internet and Democracy Case Study Series, Berkman Centre for Internet and Society. Online at http://cyber.law.harvard.edu/publications/2008/Digitally_Networked_Technology_Kenyas_Post-Election_Crisis.

Green, D. (2008) *From Poverty to Power: how active citizens and effective states can change the world.* Oxford: Oxfam International.

Harle, J. (2010) *Growing Knowledge: access to research in East and Southern African universities.* London: Association of Commonwealth Universities. Online at http://www.acu.ac.uk/publication/download?id=291.

INASP (International Network for the Availability of Scientific Publications). (2003) *Optimising Internet Bandwidth in Developing Country Higher Education.* Infobrief 1. Oxford: INASP. Online at http://www.inasp.info/uploaded/documents/infobrief1-bandwidth-english.pdf.

Jackson, A. (2009) *When It Comes to Websites ... Small is Beautiful: a guideline for making bandwidth friendly websites.* Oxford: INASP/Aptivate. Online at http://www.inasp.info/media/www/documents/Website-guidelines-print.pdf.

Kiondo, E. (2008) 'Monitoring and evaluation of electronic resource usage: a case study of the University of Dar es Salaam Library, Tanzania'. In Rosenberg, D. (ed.) *Evaluating Electronic Resource Programmes and Provision: Case Studies from Africa and Asia.* INASP Research and Education Case Studies: 3. Oxford: INASP. Online at http://www.inasp.info/file/c85e1f2bd439dd5aa2c350814e81c4cf/evaluating-electronic-resource-programmes-and-provision-case-studies-from-africa-and-asia.html.

Leach, M. and Scoones, I. (2006) *The Slow Race: making technology work for the poor.* London: Demos. Online at http://www.demos.co.uk/publications/theslowrace.

Lester, R. and Karanja, S. (2008) 'Mobile Phones: exceptional tools for HIV/AIDS, health, and crisis management'. *The Lancet Infectious Diseases*, 8 (12), 738–9.

Mbambo-Thata, B. (2008) 'Libraries and mobile phones in Southern Africa: possible applications at the University of South Africa Library'. In Ally, M. and Needham, G. (eds.) (2008) *M-Libraries: libraries on the move to provide virtual access*, Proceedings of the First International M-Libraries Conference, London. Online at http://m-libraries2009.ubc.ca/.

Mcharazo, A. and Koopman, S. (eds) (2007) *Librarianship as a Bridge to an Information and Knowledge Society in Africa*. IFLA Publication 124. Munich: K.G. Saur.

Mchombu, K. and Cadbury, N. (2006) *Libraries, Literacy and Poverty Reduction: a key to African development.* London: Book Aid International. Online at http://www.bookaid.org/resources/downloads/Libraries_Literacy_Poverty_Reduction.pdf.

Mitra, S. et al. (2005) 'Acquisition of computing literacy on shared public computers: children and the "hole in the wall"'. *Australasian Journal of Educational Technology*, 21 (3), 407–26. Online at http://www.ascilite.org.au/ajet/ajet21/mitra.html.

Morawczynski, O. (2009) 'Exploring the usage and impact of transformational mobile financial services: the case of M-PESA in Kenya'. *Journal of Eastern African Studies*, 3 (3), 509–25.

Musoke, G.N.M. and Kinengyere, A.A. (2008) 'Changing the strategies to enhance the use of electronic resources among the academic community in Uganda with particular reference to the Makerere University'. In Rosenberg, D. (ed.) (2008) *Evaluating Electronic Resource Programmes and Provision: case studies from Africa and Asia.* INASP Research and Education Case Studies: 3. Oxford: INASP. Online at http://www.inasp.info/file/c85e1f2bd439dd5aa2c350814 e81c4cf/evaluating-electronic-resource-programmes-and-provision-case-studies-from-africa-and-asia.html.

Nightingale, K. (2009) *Rural Internet – not online but still connected.* SciDev.Net, 13 February. Online at http://www.scidev.net/en/new-technologies/digital-divide/features/rural-internet-not-online-but-still-connected.html.

Parker, S. (2003) 'Bridging the digital divide: report on the brainstorming session hosted by Kay Raseroka, IFLA President elect, at the 68th IFLA conference in Glasgow, 21 August 2002'. *IFLA Journal*, 29 (65), 72. Online at http://archive.ifla.org/IV/ifla68/papers/brainstorming.pdf.

Selinger, M. (2009) 'ICT in education: catalyst for development'. In Unwin, T. (ed.) (2009) *ICT4D: information and communication technology for development.* Cambridge: Cambridge University Press.

Theroux, K. (2006) 'Linking African Universities with MIT iLabs'. *Carnegie Reporter*, 3 (4). Online at http://carnegie.org/publications/carnegie-reporter/single/view/article/item/153/; see also http://icampus.mit.edu/iLabs/.

Thomson Reuters. (2009) *ISI Journal Citation Report 2009.*

Unwin, T. (ed.) (2009) *ICT4D: information and communication technology for development.* Cambridge: Cambridge University Press.

9

Islands in the cloud: libraries and the social life of information

David Vogt

Introduction

Digital media continue to transform society, resulting in uncertainty about the future of traditional institutions, including libraries. Yet libraries have always thrived on servicing the social value within humanity's relationship with information, particularly as a function of community, and in regenerating the life of community. The author, an applied researcher in mobile-social technologies, predicts strong ongoing viability for this mediating role between information and community, given that libraries can become better plugged in to both. As we learn to live in information clouds, libraries will be our common ground: islands in the social life of information.

A world of experience

While most of us do not dwell on the reasons why we venture forth into the world, going to work or buying groceries is more than routine. We wear clothes and drive vehicles that express our identity, frequent trusted locations that reinforce our values, and revel when we can share our steps with friends. Yet the real joy of an everyday journey is not about familiarity, it is about feedback. We quietly but diligently seek out and process those things that are diverting and unexpected, and apply this 'news' to continuously refreshing our sense of self. Without being aware of it, we are 'strange loops' (Hofstadter, 2007): every mundane excursion is a self-referential adventure. And as we go about the world, despite all of its natural and artificial stimulations, we seem compelled to additionally clothe ourselves in our media. Traditional public media behaviours such as reading a newspaper or a book have expanded dramatically to include talking on the phone, texting, listening to music, playing games, surfing the Web, watching television, answering e-mail and doing work. While from a social perspective such 'mobile media' are partly fashion and partly armour, until very recently a shared limitation of these media was that they were all 'alien' and 'dumb' – they knew nothing about the real world you were immersed in and could not respond to it in any way. While people are therefore clearly capable of simultaneously occupying several mutually unintelligible universes (amazing when you think about it!), a reasonable question to ask is what might happen if these separate universes were to begin to communicate and cooperate on your behalf.

In 2004 the author founded the Mobile Muse Network (MUSE),[1] using Vancouver, Canada as a 'living lab' to explore the social and cultural possibilities of mobile media. MUSE collaborates with community organisations such as opera companies, film festivals, museums, art galleries, and tourist attractions to engage audiences in new ways through their mobile devices, using interactive messaging, streaming media, location services, social networks and large public displays. Similar to libraries, traditional mobile services focus on effective provision of information. In contrast, MUSE focuses on meaningful experience. MUSE aligns with Web 2.0[2] thinking that value is something co-created by users, and with the experience economy (Pine and Gilmore, 1999) theory that consumers are really seeking memorable events (products or services enhanced by experience). While there is no single path from information to experience, our journey in the real world typically involves some combination of:

- information
- communications
- context (who I am, who I'm with, my current purpose, place, time etc.)
- participation (I'm doing or contributing something).

Over the years MUSE, with its community partners, has overlaid urban streets with interactive games, created rich-media explorations that visitors can autonomously contribute to, and rallied participatory citizenship within circles of trust formed through instant messaging. A recent focus on 'Community Generated Media', building toward the 2010 Winter Olympic Games, demonstrated how communities can use video streaming, social media aggregation and public displays to collectively publish and sustain a unique identity (Figure 9.1).[3]

A current focus is youth-driven sustainability: merging sensor and network data concerning sustainability indicators with data acquired by the individuals themselves to inform hand-held, personalised sustainability dashboards that foster responsible behaviour. Common to these innovations are the development of web services that enable communities or community groups to use mobile-social media to easily launch programmes that engage particular audiences in particular places over particular times, a 'vertical' capacity that is not generally available from 'horizontal' mobile service providers.

But mobile experience is not about technology, nor is it about information. It is about people engaged in rich, evolving, self-fulfilling narratives about identity, discovery, sharing, expression and socialisation. It is a mash-up of people, places, ideas and things. There are now all kinds of smart mobile devices that can digitally blend information, communications, context and participation to expand your experience of the everyday world. But technology is the easy part. Mobile experience is a fundamentally new medium for humanity; possibly the most profound yet. There are no design guidelines: this

Figure 9.1 Mobile Muse Network 'Community Generated Media' programme

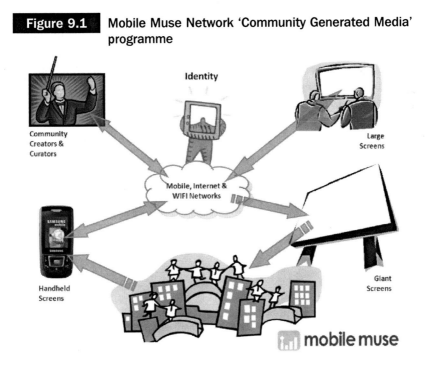

Identity

Community Creators & Curators

Large Screens

Mobile, Internet & WIFI Networks

Handheld Screens

Giant Screens

mobile muse

intimate coupling of the Web with reality creates entirely unprecedented affordances (Gibson, 1977) and potentials for the richness of human existence. The staging of context-aware mobile-social experience will emerge as a defining element of our lifestyles, and of community and economic development.

Taking apart architecture

Think of architecture as civilisation's way to overcome the natural world's incapacity to support our evolving information and communications requirements. What happens when this incapacity is resolved in a world seamlessly, invisibly augmented by media? For example, the design of the modern office building, right down to the cubicles, arose from the need to manage activities, communicate with people, access tools, share information, store documents and so on. How many of these needs still exist in the same way, with their attendant bricks-and-mortar overhead costs, in a wirelessly networked digital world?

As an overly glib thought experiment, let us deconstruct a school. Its calendar still satisfies an agrarian-lifestyle constraint that has disappeared. Curriculum and accreditation serve a workforce model that no longer exists. Classrooms are not required for their ability to contain the tools and resources for effective learning. Once the centuries of academic engineering have been undone, the crucial remaining architecture-determining requirement is that humans learn best socially. No networking environment can challenge the rich and complex social benefits generating from a community-embedded school experience. Schools may need rethinking in the digital age, but their value in the social landscape is unassailable. Deconstructing a library would reveal an equivalent social imperative. The architectural trappings of access to information may be diminished, but the community-focused necessity for open socialisation of that information is unchanged, perhaps growing.

Making Creative Cities flow

The Creative Cities[4] movement has tried to identify processes for harnessing and amplifying the creative potential of a city's human capital. If the social contexts of information are appreciating, and its technical constraints are falling away, it makes sense that the most creative spaces are those designed to serve people and information equally well. Companies have responded to this logic by expanding 'water cooler' spaces for casual meetings and sharing of ideas. But even so, increasing amounts of information-intensive and collaboration-driven 'work' are now being done in the convenient, socially amenable atmospheres of coffee shops, concourses and urban parks. Information is flowing in the streets.

Libraries have similarly responded by creating more comfortable, stimulating and socially vibrant spaces integrated with their collections. In Vancouver, for example, the new Vancouver Public Library (Figure 9.2) successfully applies bold architectural lines and a mall-like pedestrian corridor to energise its public presence, and the new Barber Learning Centre (Figure 9.3) at the University of British Columbia is enormously popular for its 24/7 blend of lounge and study hall. In these cases the collections provide a versatile set dressing and stage for flowing human–information dramas.

Figure 9.2 Vancouver Public Library

Photo: Andrew Raun. Reproduced under Creative Commons Attribution-ShareAlike 2.0 Generic license.

Figure 9.3 Barber Learning Centre, University of British Columbia

Photo: Martin Dee. Reproduced courtesy of University of British Columbia, Public Affairs.

The useful trend is that the monolithic library building is giving way to landscape architecture concepts of its value within a commons. Communities are defined by accommodation, transportation, work and clusters of amenities that continuously refine the sense and identity of the community. As libraries are less constrained by the technical management of information, they can be more strategic about being agents of identity. An 'anchor tenant' status within a cluster of community amenities is unnecessary, perhaps even risky. Becoming an equal part of any commons – which might include rubbing shoulders with community centres, theatres, coffee shops, laundries, grocers, offices and schools – offers a better ability to become actively relevant to a community's information flow, and therefore to its life and identity. In the end, as far as creative communities are concerned, the medium is the message (McLuhan, 1964). The most fertile ground for creativity is the community itself. Libraries, when well situated and integrated within community, can perform a vital catalyst role in the information creation–consumption cycles that distinguish creative communities from ordinary ones.

The social life of information

Before there were computers, or books, or clay tablets, or libraries, there were oral cultures. Individuals then were remarkably effective at conveying valued cultural information from generation to generation, often over thousands of years, via memorable experiences involving poetry and performance. A great example on the north-west coast of North America is the Raven trickster cycle, headlined by Raven's Theft of Daylight (Figure 9.4), which required many days for a full performance/recitation.

The role of the individual and of experience in the social life of information is dawning anew. This statement does not dismiss the value of books or any other medium, including those enabling us to know

Figure 9.4   *Raven and the First Men* by Bill Reid, Haida, 1980

Reproduced courtesy of University of British Columbia, Museum of Anthropology. Bill McLennan photo.

about Raven. It merely suggests that people are beginning to use, create, convey and value information in significantly different ways than ever before. A primary agent of this change is the sheer volume of information being created every moment, which has commoditised its value.

One symptom of this change relates to **trust**. Doctors, lawyers, bankers, newspapers, books and references have all lost much of the trust with which society once approved them. Trust is now being generated more locally and socially, not by authority. For example, people will readily challenge their doctor's advice with something they've read in a chat room, and a 'staff pick' recommendation in a bookstore will sell better than professional reviews on the book jacket. Street wisdom – including the wisdom of crowds – has always carried weight (deserving or not); it simply circulates better now than ever before. And individuals know that their opinions – no matter how inexpert – can have an impact.

Another symptom relates to **relevance**. Modern communities are home to a bewildering spectrum of ideas and issues that 'matter', often making strangers out of neighbours. On the one hand, individuals can more easily discover and connect with other people, both near and far, who share unique interests. On the other hand, largely impersonal digital diets make people hungrier for meaning: we feast on opportunities that make us feel relevant. This explains the extraordinary popularity of social networking sites, as well as the unusual impact of real-world encounters – such as a chance conversation with a stranger on a bus – on our opinions and beliefs.

What can a library do to respond? Step further into nearby streets, both asphalt and digital. As local agents, libraries can identify and amplify sources of wisdom resonant to social and community values. Such sources may include traditional authorities as well as local individuals or groups who have demonstrated a tempered interest in the subject at hand. It is the same function that libraries have always performed in cultivating information sources, except that more of these will now be secondary, two-legged filters. To continue being a community's information touchstone, libraries need more touch.

100-mile information diets

Humanity's relationship to information is curiously analogous to its relationship with food. Over history, we have evolved from self-reliant hunter-gatherers to collective agriculturalists to globalised processors. During that time we have largely lost our connection to the sources of our food and to its production. There are unresolved concerns about genetically modified food, processed food, packaging, nutrition and health that mirror concerns we have regarding the sources, quality and effects of the information we consume. Society as a whole is starting to realise that urban agriculture, farmers' markets, 100-mile diets and artisan products are necessary parts of a generalised response that cares about healthy, local and sustainable food systems. There is an open opportunity for libraries to more aggressively champion the healthy, local and sustainable information systems movement in their communities. For example, even though librarians were once the go-to individuals for answers to any question, they cannot compete directly with Internet search engines to satisfy appetites for high-calorie 'fast food' information requests. And perhaps they should not seek to compete there at all, except to understand and communicate the application of fast sources within balanced information lifestyles.

Conversely, there are few potential competitors at a community scale to compete with libraries in the cultivation, appreciation and delivery of socially nutritious 'slow' information. Books have traditionally been a library's staple slow offering. However, the deep, irresistible appeal of the slow food movement owes everything to a hunger for social experience, and this is true for slow information as well. While books are an experience, and book clubs (for example) can make them social, there are infinitely more informational and experiential ingredients available in a library's pantry. More bluntly, books are part of information's commodity stream; in order to survive, libraries will need to re-invent their focus on adding value to the stream, which will not be as much about controlling, storing and providing access.

Islands in the cloud

Very few bricks-and-mortar institutions are immune to the existential anxiety caused by the Internet, especially now that the Web has begun to claim-stake the real world. Municipal governments, for example, are deeply concerned about losing control of the urban narrative to applications like Google Earth,[5] Google Maps[6] and Google Street View.[7] Within the magic and global scale of these technologies and the uncertainty of their impact, it is easy for traditional institutions to undervalue their core assets, and their ability to leverage these assets successfully in a newly webbed world. With a library, for example, there is a huge operational advantage to having a real location, a real audience and a trusted community mission as a foundation for the future. The shelf-life of technology companies, their applications, their devices and even information itself is unnervingly short, relative to the evolutionary drift of a community. A search engine may be able to harvest and map a significant portion of the information contexts of a community, in any number of valuable ways, but for the imaginable future it will be a servant to the energy, ethos and experience of that community. The business objective of a library is therefore not to dance with information; it is to dance with community at the tempo of information.

In fact, as far as human communities are concerned, it is appealing to imagine that we are emerging from the dark ages of media and information into a social renaissance. For centuries, our most treasured media technologies have been deeply antisocial. Books are a fundamentally singular experience. When movies were invented, they took people off the streets, hundreds at a time, to sit in dark places without talking. Along came TV, this time invading the home to compel families to sit together in the dark, being entertained and not communicating. Then the Internet slyly removed even the togetherness, isolating us in our rooms and offices to consume media alone. And finally Web 2.0, most insidious of all, fabricated a new 'social' to make us believe we were truly connecting with one another. There is nothing deliberate in this antisocial spiral; it is a side-effect of the limitations of each of the media platforms, which can deliver experience only in an abstract sense. Now, however, with context awareness, our major media are beginning to spill back into the streets: in tune with our lives, engaged with experience and able to amplify our social opportunities. For the first time, media can be designed as a real-world social ice-breaker, and for inclusion rather than isolation. What will this feel like? How will we embrace it, given how long our media have made us inert? Are we ready? Do we know how to design it? For example, when Raven was performed in the Northwest Coast Winter Ceremonials, individuals changed families and homes for weeks to adopt new names and put on costumes to participate in a rich, collective celebration of community identity. This is unlikely to be our future, but at least nobody was starving for trust or relevance.

Libraries are perfectly placed to be islands in the cloud: proactive mobile-social media hubs to help us continuously co-create our individual and community identities. They can be a first truly 'open' realisation of the information commons. The necessary talents and tools are at hand, embedded in the community and the cloud. From a practical perspective, libraries will be doing what they have always done. All media are essentially narrative, whether they are read or watched or performed. All memorable experience is essentially narrative as well. And a community is itself a strange loop; an ongoing self-referential adventure channelled through and networked with the experiences and hopes and dreams of its citizens.

Conclusion

Seen through the lens of the social life of information, the great opportunity for the future of libraries and communities involves stewardship of the social experience of information more than social access to information. Building cultural capital with mobile-social media networks involves three simple steps:

1. **Forget information and interaction; think engagement and participation.** The hardest part of being relevant is designing information-based experiences where the information itself is enhanced and refreshed, and the experience improved, through the participation of those involved in the experience.

2. **Turn your institution inside out and outside in.** Use available technologies and resources to activate a presence for your engagement and participation efforts across your community, and to enable community, individuals and organisations to partner with you in these efforts internally.

3. **Leverage your strengths.** Your community is brilliant. Your audiences are priceless. Your mission is golden. Your location is a stage. Your collections are inspirational. Your staff are amazing.

Your institution can be the champion of a social renaissance in your community. Good luck!

Notes

1. David Vogt (2004) http://mobilemuse.ca.
2. O'Reilly (2005) http://oreilly.com/web2/archive/what-is-web-20.html.

10

From the passive library to the learning library – it's an emotional journey

Les Watson

Introduction

It is not hard to create a modern 21st-century library. Assuming that you are not constructing a completely new building (but it is likely this also applies if you are) you will need to repurpose some of the space with a sensible stock reduction strategy – and why not, with all the digital material that is available and growing by the minute? Most of the paper resources in our libraries are not used much and the British Library, being a key player in the UK Research Reserve project,[1] has a copy of everything anyway, so reducing your stock to only your most-used items (probably about two-thirds of what you have now at the most, and conceivably much less than this) is perfectly feasible, especially if you can find a way of still being able to get back some of what you throw out, when it is requested, by housing it in nearby accessible storage. Once the stock has been sorted, the recouped space in the building can be used to create some great new facilities. You will need a café, of course – no self-respecting 21st-century library could do without one – and it also seems you cannot have a modern library without creating some social space or, if you are really 'switched on', some social learning space. These types of spaces are some of the clear trends in new library space. Furnish these new spaces with some smart, new, brightly coloured furniture and put in some new computers and flat screens and your space will be 'up there with the best of them'. Or will it? And why would you want to do anything like this anyway?

Change is needed

We hear a lot about the need for change in our libraries. In her speech to the 2009 Public Library Authorities conference in Bristol,[2] Margaret Hodge, then UK Minister of State for Culture and Tourism, had some good things to say about public library services that related to their long and successful history; but she also identified some worrying issues. For example, a year-on-year fall in use of public libraries since 2005 (by 2007–8, according to Hodge, use of libraries had fallen to 45%; and it dropped a further 5% to less than 40% the year after); the closure of 63 public libraries since 1997; and book borrowing falling by 41% over the last 10 years. According to the Minister, all this had been achieved at a time when local authority library expenditures had risen by nearly 50%. This does not sound good – as Claire Creaser also notes in Chapter 2 – and it is therefore not surprising that it is time for change. The public library review launched by Margaret Hodge and, for a time, handled by the then Secretary of State for Culture, Media and Sport, Andrew Burnham (DCMS, 2009), saw public libraries as 'a welcoming and stimulating place at the heart of the community where people can come together to learn'.[3]

One of the central issues for this review, also deeply relevant to university and college libraries, is how to connect with young people in an age of powerful personal technologies – technologies that for many young people are the 'heart of the community where they come together to learn'.[4] The answer has to be about making libraries places worth visiting: and that means that the new spaces we create have to have purpose. The intention of this chapter is not to describe good or bad examples of café and social learning space seen in libraries or to provide clear rules for development (there probably aren't any), but to highlight some perspectives worth thinking about that could inform new space developments.

If libraries are to remain relevant and reverse the trends of falling use, then focusing on their role as places of learning – and this applies to both institutional and public libraries – offers some hope for the future. It is not only about creating new spaces but also about a more strategic approach that has its roots in a deeper understanding of the effects that our environments have on us as learners. At the University of Lincoln, England, Professor Mike Neary has been conducting a project over the past few years that has been researching aspects of the 'learning landscape'[5] in higher education. The concept of the learning landscape is a useful one. For a university or college it includes all of its services, facilities, processes and buildings that support learners and their learning, and it is not hard to see that we could apply this concept not just to organisations such as universities and colleges but to nations as well. And it is also clear that libraries, in whatever sphere they operate, are part of a learning landscape. Libraries have a contribution to make to learners and their learning at the organisational, local community or national level. For many libraries, this is not new ground but, if implemented rigorously, it is a new emphasis; for all libraries it presents challenges. Making such a contribution by successfully adopting this new emphasis depends on recognising the prerequisite of a clear understanding of what makes facilities effective for learners.

A new focus integrated with current facilities

> The knowledge base that guides library space planning is poorly balanced, tilted heavily toward library operations and away from systematic knowledge of how students learn. (Bennett, 2005)

With respect to learning, the traditional library has been rather 'passive', preferring, typically by default rather than intention, to concentrate on library operations such as collection management. Of course, libraries still need to manage their collections and all the other operational activities that make a library a library, and they probably even have to do that more aggressively than ever before if they are to create the space needed for new facilities, but they also need to refocus.

What does the passive library have to do to become a learning library? If the question is approached superficially, then the stereotypical 'copy-cat' changes to its use of space, described in the first paragraph of this chapter, will suffice. However, such a superficial approach that results in a set of 'bolt-on' facilities will not, in my view, produce the deep and lasting change that is needed to transform a passive library into a learning library – or to make library space a learning place. What we need to do is create facilities that mirror our vision for, beliefs about and understanding of learning.

Knowledge of some of the current thinking on learning is an essential part of developing successful learning places. At its most succinct, this is simply that 'all learning starts with conversation' (Seely and Duguid,

2000). The deep significance of this statement is best articulated in the detail in Professor Diana Laurillard's conversational framework (Figure 10.1) (Laurillard, 2009) that has been developed at the London Knowledge Lab at the Institute of Education, London, England. This framework shows how conversation plays a key role in the widest range of learning activities and interactions involving materials and resources, peers and teachers, technologies and activities. The framework shows conversation contributing to a spectrum of learning activities that include acquisition of and inquiry about knowledge and information, discussion, practice, and collaboration and production. The framework also indicates how conversation fits within a wide range of current learning theories, including social constructivism, instructionism, constructionism and situated learning. The opportunities for libraries, as learning places, to contribute to the activities identified in the conversational framework cover the whole range of activities from knowledge acquisition through discussion to practice and production.

It is commonly agreed that the current educational system, in all its age phases, pays more attention to some of these learning theories and modes of learning than to others – instruction being the theory behind the most commonly practised mode of delivery. However, instruction is

Figure 10.1 Laurillard's conversational framework

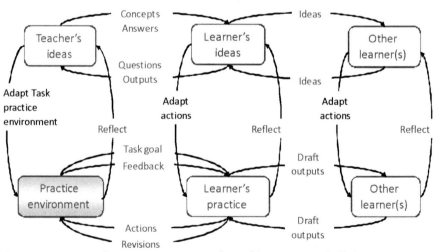

Reproduced with kind permission of Professor Diana Laurillard.

only one of the set of theories of learning, and increasingly practitioners are realising that paying attention to the full set of possibilities leads to more successful learners and learning. The conversations of social and personal constructivism and situated learning are now recognised to be as important as, if not more important than, the largely unidirectional conversations of instruction in the development of personal learning skills. Libraries, successfully reconfigured to focus on a learning role, are some of the most appropriate places for the learning conversations of discussion, practice and production, as well as being obvious places for the acquisition of information and knowledge, both analogue and digital. The strength of the library as a learning place lies in the potential for learners to combine the use of books and other information resources with access to digital information using the technology tools housed in libraries and the human support and extended hours of access they provide. Adding imaginative conversational spaces to this list of ingredients can provide learners with some of the best learning facilities possible to support the majority of modes of learning outlined in the conversational framework. However, the success of new spaces in enhancing the mix of resources that libraries already have is less likely if the spaces provided are superficial and bolted on to existing facilities. What is needed is an approach that embeds the vision for learning throughout the broader space provision within the library.

It's subtle and it's emotional

Our knowledge of learning and how it occurs has increased considerably in the past 10 years. In particular, there is now clear acknowledgement that learning has an important emotional component. Positive and negative emotions can improve or hinder learning. Jensen (2005) reminds us that not only are emotions important as drivers and barriers to learning but also they are present all the time, connected to our behaviours and transient – continuously dynamically changing. In a teacher-led setting, teacher awareness of student emotion is vital to ensuring the success of learners. The most successful teachers use a range of strategies to ensure that students have positive, motivated emotional states. With the student-led peer-group learning that we wish to encourage in our 'learning libraries' the emotional state will depend largely on the environment that we create. Interestingly, in an account of how our brains distort and deceive us, Fine (2007) tells us that 'seemingly trivial things in our environment may be influencing our behaviour; dormant goals are triggered without our even realising it'. She explains that such is our susceptibility to the environmental cues that surround us that 'if someone asks you about a good friend and then asks you for a favour, you will be more willing to help'. Such an effect relates to the ability of a stimulus to awaken other contextual factors in our subconscious that affect our conscious thoughts and emotions, hence the need to think carefully about the environments that we create in our libraries and the contexts that they set for those using them. The interiors that we create can improve or hinder learning through the subtle effects that they have on those who inhabit them.

The context – that is, the environment in which we find ourselves – has deep significance, affecting us psychologically and even physiologically, as shown by the work of Harvard psychologist Ellen Langer (Langer, 1990). Langer describes an experiment in which she took a group of elderly men (aged 75 to 80) to a retreat to see whether 'behaving' younger and reliving the past, rather than just talking about it, as a control group did, could influence ageing. Great care was taken with the experimental group to ensure that its experience was contextually authentic; environmental details, for example not just playing radio programmes of the past but playing them on old radios rather than modern ones, were key to ensuring the authenticity of the experience. The participants who 'lived' the past showed real improvement in a range of physiological factors such as height when sitting, manual dexterity and some improved vision; they also showed improved performance in some intelligence tests as compared to the control group, who merely talked about the past. This intriguing work hints at the possibility that the context in which we live and work, which in part at least is the environment(s) that we inhabit, can have deep and far-reaching effects on us beyond what we might expect. To link the emotional aspects of learning and the emotional states triggered by the learning environments in which we learn does not seem unreasonable. John Haidt's happiness equation also acknowledges the importance of context and environment through the inclusion of 'conditions' as one of its component terms (happiness = set point of personal happiness + the conditions in which we work and live + our values – H=S+C+V) (Haidt, 2006).

It's not optional: whatever space we create has emotional effects

That the places that we inhabit do have emotional effects on us has long been recognised. In his work *The Architecture of Happiness*, Alain De Botton cites Ruskin:

> John Ruskin proposed that we seek two things of our buildings. We want them to shelter us. And we want them to speak to us – to speak to us of whatever we find important and need to be reminded of. (De Botton, 2007)

The default position is that whatever environment(s) we create as we develop and refurbish our libraries as learning places, they will undoubtedly have emotional impacts on those using them, affecting their capacity to learn, their emotional state and possibly their happiness. A café with brightly coloured furniture and a corporate splash of orange across the wall will have an impact – but what will it do to the emotional state of those using it, and will it help them as learners? This example from De Botton gives us some clues as to the effects that a place can have on us:

> A few years ago, caught out by a heavy downpour, with a couple of hours to kill after being stood up for lunch by a friend, I took shelter in a smoked glass and granite block on London's Victoria Street, home to the Westminster branch of McDonald's. The mood inside the restaurant was solemn and concentrated. Customers were eating alone, reading papers or staring at the brown tiles, masticating with a sternness and brusqueness beside which the atmosphere of a feeding shed would have appeared convivial and mannered. (De Botton, 2007)

De Botton's perhaps unfair description suggests, by the behaviours he notes, a place of negative emotional impact. It is unlikely that McDonald's intentionally set out to do this – and one could speculate that if it did, then it is a good way to improve throughput of customers and enhance profitability – but rather that this is an unfortunate consequence of garish décor, commodity furniture and bad weather. What is striking is the lack of conversation, and if all learning does start with conversation then a McDonald's-style café is not the most appropriate environment to create. Contrast this absence of conversation with the range of conversations that took place in 17th-century coffee-houses, as described by Ellis:

> To scholars, both of the arts and sciences, coffee-houses became one of the most significant locations for debate and the exchange of ideas, evolving into an important research tool, somewhere between a peer review system, an encyclopaedia, a research centre and a symposium. (Ellis, 2004)

To use John Ruskin's metaphor, if our ambition is to create 21st-century libraries as places of modern learning, we should be creating libraries that speak of our aspiration for meaningful, purposeful conversations and the learning that results from this. The library café equipped with second-class furniture that exists because people need to 'get a drink' to relieve the tedium of long hours in the library is unlikely to achieve this aspiration. Such places, often run simply as a catering outlet in the library, are more akin to the McDonald's model. Ellis tells us that it was the sociability and conviviality of the 17th-century coffee-house that made it work so well, and this is what we should be striving to create when we introduce coffee into the library.

Embedding such facilities in our libraries is challenging, not least because of our expectations of user behaviour – we do like to have rules. But a successful 21st-century library does not forbid coffee near the computers, just as the successful 17th-century coffee-house had little need for rules. Ellis notes 'the subtle kinds of implicit regulation that coffee-houses created in their customers' expectations':

> When entering, a man might expect to behave in a certain manner appropriate to the setting, conducting himself differently in a tavern, a private dwelling or a church. (Ellis, 2004)

That places speak to us is clear, as is the point that different places speak to us about different things and persuade us, through this unheard conversation, to behave differently. Add to this learner individuality as, for example, identified through Gardner's multiple intelligence theory (Gardner, 1993), and it becomes clear that the design of new library space is highly complex: little wonder that when faced with such complexity we often resort to accepting the answers that our architects provide.

Conclusion: some useful types and metaphors

The message is that we need to create a range of spaces and consider both their overt purpose and their potential underlying emotional effects. Rizzo provides some useful guidance based on the expectations of users of an academic library of types of space that they seek:

1. Highly active and engaging communal places.
2. Interactive collaborative places for individual research and group work.
3. Quieter, less active places such as reading/study rooms and alcoves.
4. Out of the way contemplative places for quiet reflection and deep thought. (Rizzo, 2002)

The extent of the marketplace (or mall) (Rizzo's type 1) and the monastery (Rizzo's type 2) and the balance between all of these types of space will vary from library to library. Most often, thinking about the balance between these types of space and how any imbalance can be addressed leads to rethinking social or social learning space of types 1 and 2. But the creation of place is not merely about a range and balance of such spaces, it is about how they interrelate and flow from one space to another. It is about how a fragmented feel is avoided and the 'bolt-on' facility is integrated into the whole. According to Mikunda (2006), the creation of a third place (those places that are not work and not home but that hold special significance to those who visit and use them) needs to have a 'golden thread' running through it and to make us 'mall' and want to explore it, using the tricks of suspense and revelation; such places also have a landmark or core attraction that arouses curiosity – the 'wow' factor that is so often found in new spaces and buildings, such as a public work of art or an impressive atrium space.

Hildebrand, in exploring some of our fundamental expectations in response to architecture and interiors and their emotional effects, suggests that at a deeper level our wish to experience a place may originate from the innate human behaviours of our distant ancestors, linked, for example, to the need for survival in hostile environments (Hildebrand, 1999). These ideas include such things as our need 'to find a good home', linking perhaps to Rizzo's range of different spaces – types 3 and 4. Ideas of the need for refuge and surprise in the interior environment suggested by Hildebrand and the activity of exploration all link to Mikunda's factors in modern-day third places. How far these ideas are from the floor areas and risk registers that dominate much library planning! Considering such aspects of space development is the key to creating libraries as places and not mere spaces. Creating places – and especially third places – is what we should be doing in the rebuild and refurbishment of our libraries if they are to fulfil their learning role. According to Mikunda, third places 'used to be the Viennese coffee-houses … they recharge us with emotion' (Mikunda, 2006). They should major on the sociality of learning and have the conviviality of the 17th-century coffee-house embedded deeply in their soul. A 21st-century library should be a third place that engages the senses and that challenges, excites and entertains those that use it with surprise and fun.

If we adopt these ideas and create new spaces that engage the emotions, inspire our users and make them want to return, how will we know that they effectively support their activities as learners? Elsewhere in this book there are chapters on evaluation, but what can be said here is that logging the bald numbers using spaces designed to enhance learning will not suffice as evidence that those spaces are doing their job. More imaginative approaches are needed – for example, behavioural video analysis, social network analysis, and experience sampling (Hektner et al., 2007) that have been so successfully used to measure human experience in real time.

Endnote

Having stated earlier that I have no intention of pointing to good and bad spaces I cannot resist a short 'tale' about the toilets in the Saltire Centre at Glasgow Caledonian University as an example of playful interior design. There are two sets of toilets on each floor of the building. They are unisex – that is, they do not have urinals – so that either of the toilets can be designated male or female and these can be switched over, for example, each year. The reason for maybe wanting to reassign the male toilets as female and vice versa is that one in four of the cubicles, selected randomly at fit out, has a graphic on the back of the door that you do not see until you have entered it and closed the door. The range of graphics covers how to be a DJ, how to dress in a sari, how to sign the alphabet, guidance on recycling, how to collect water in a desert, how to play a bunker shot at golf and other topics. Students at the university could potentially use the Saltire Centre every day for the four years that it takes to gain a degree and never see one of these graphics – but one day they might. These graphics say: you can never completely know this building; it will always have something to surprise, interest and delight you. It will always be a place and never become a boring space. It speaks to those that use it of playfulness, engagement and fun.

Notes

1. http://www.ukrr.ac.uk/.
2. M. Hodge, Keynote address to the Public Library Authorities conference, Bristol, UK, 8 October 2009, http://webarchive.nationalarchives.gov.uk/+/http://www.culture.gov.uk/reference_library/minister_speeches/6372.aspx.
3. Hodge, *ibid.*
4. *Ibid.*
5. Learning Landscapes in Higher Education, http://learninglandscapes.blogs.lincoln.ac.uk/.

References

Bennett, S. (2005) 'Righting the balance'. In CLIR, *Library as Place: rethinking roles, rethinking space.* Washington, DC: Council on Library and Information Resources. Online at http://www.clir.org/pubs/abstract/pub129abst.html.

DCMS. (2009) *Modernisation Review of Public Libraries.* Department of Culture, Media and Sport. Online at http://www.culture.gov.uk/what_we_do/libraries/5583.aspx#1.

De Botton, A. (2007) *The Architecture of Happiness.* London: Penguin Books.

Ellis, M. (2004) *The Coffee House: a cultural history.* London: Orion Books.

Fine, C. (2007) *A Mind of its Own: how your brain distorts and deceives.* London: Icon Books.

Gardner, H. (1993) *Frames of Mind: the theory of multiple intelligences.* New York: Basic Books.

Haidt, J. (2006) *The Happiness Hypothesis.* London: Arrow Books.

Hektner J., Schmidt J. and Csikszentmihalyi, M. (2007) *Experience Sampling Method: measuring the quality of everyday life.* London: Sage.

Hildebrand, G. (1999) *The Origins of Architectural Pleasure*. London: University of California Press.

Jensen, E. (2005) *Teaching with the Brain in Mind*. Alexandria, VA: ASCD Books.

Langer, E. (1990) *Mindfulness*. Boulder, CO: Westview Press.

Laurillard, D. (2009) Keynote presentation to the *Learning Landscapes Conference*, 4 December, University of Lincoln, UK.

Mikunda, C. (2006) *Brand Lands, Hot Spots and Cool Spaces: welcome to the third place and the total marketing experience*. London: Kogan Page.

Rizzo, J.C. (2002) 'Finding your place in the Information Age Library'. *New Library World*, 103 (11/12), 457–66.

Seely Brown, J. and Duguid, P. (2000) *The Social Life of Information*. Cambridge, MA: Harvard Business School Press.

11

The modern academic library

Edward Oyston

Introduction

The core purpose of the academic library is not much different today than it was in the early 1990s, before the most radical changes in the use of library space took place: within the context of the institutional academic mission and priorities, it is still to provide secure, supported learning environments over extended hours, where students can learn, interact with others, access learning materials and receive help in meeting their information, learning and research needs. However, even in the context of this core purpose, someone whose last visit to an academic library was just 15 years ago might find much of what they see unrecognisable, whether this be service arrangements, study space or equipment and facilities. The familiar presence of books on shelves may give some reassurance but would now misrepresent the information environment available in the building. In some university libraries, this newness is more than skin deep, with the primary emphasis of design being on student learning, not just information provision. In others, this core purpose is being extended beyond learning and information support to encompass a broader range of student support services.

The focus of this chapter is on buildings that have been designed and developed around this new agenda. Reference will be made to the 'Information Commons' at the University of Sheffield, which addresses the new agenda from the perspective of a research-intensive university (for a detailed case study of the Information Commons see Lewis, 2010). The example of the development of the Adsetts Centre at Sheffield Hallam University over 15 years will be used as the principal case study. Perhaps the most radical expression of the new agenda is delivered in buildings like the library of the University of Huddersfield, or the learning resource centres of Liverpool John Moores University (LJMU), where an even more holistic approach is taken to the student experience, encompassing areas such as student finance, enrolment, module registration, enquiry management, guidance, careers and employability support, welfare and counselling. Reference will be made to LJMU to illustrate this development.

For some, 'academic library' may still be considered adequate to describe the new physical learning environment; for others, a new name is needed for buildings that contain many of the essential functions of an academic library but which have a different character or emphasis. For example, the Information Commons at the University of Sheffield expresses the idea of a shared space where the University's academic community can come together to access a wide variety of information and learning resources. As is common in the USA, the Information Commons represents only part of the University's overall library provision, aimed mainly at the undergraduate learning experience. The use of 'learning centre' by Sheffield Hallam University indicates that its primary focus is on the activity of learning, with resources, service provision and facilities being means to that end.

The new agenda: a focus on learning

The most distinctive characteristic of the new academic library is its focus on learning. Changes in institutional learning and teaching strategies, whether driven by resourcing pressures, the diversity of the student body, or a greater focus on effective student learning, have placed greater emphasis on learning outside the classroom and provided libraries with an unmissable opportunity to extend their role in supporting the curriculum; to do so, however, requires the will and the resources to recalibrate the physical learning environment. The greater prominence given to the development of critical, reflective and analytical skills and supporting learning strategies such as enquiry-based learning requires students to be active participants in the learning process, capable of more independent, self-directed study. The previous predominance of space and layout dedicated to supporting individual study is no longer adequate to support this more active learning style, especially when it translates into group study. Demas (2005) lists what people come to libraries for as:

- reading and relaxing in safety and quiet
- individual study
- group study
- checking e-mail and using the Web
- finding information for class assignments and academic projects
- information production
- classroom-based teaching and learning
- browsing.

He then lists what he considers to be 'non-library' uses:

- using other academic support services
- meeting and socialising
- eating and drinking
- participating in cultural events and civic discourse
- having fun
- visiting/touring
- viewing exhibitions.

Designing effective learning spaces to provide a choice of environments to meet this broad range of requirements and preferences is much more than changing the furniture or bolting on a café, as Les Watson stresses in Chapter 10. For librarians, this means a shift of thinking from a resource and service culture, which is only a means to an end, to a learning culture that needs to be reflected in library space. 'We need to understand that the success of the academic library is best measured not by the frequency and ease of library use but by the learning that results from that use' (Bennett, 2005). At a practical level, the rules governing behaviour in libraries may need to be reconsidered, going beyond an acceptance that some kinds of noise are an integral aspect of learning, to a recognition that libraries must support the social dimension to learning. Providing refreshments is undoubtedly a part of this, not just as fuel for tired brains but for its social contribution: as an aspect of creating a community among learners.

A more calibrated range of learning spaces is needed to accommodate the wide range of required and preferred learning styles. To meet this need, the University of Sheffield developed its own typology of learning spaces, encompassing: individual spaces, many of which are provided with a PC, or at least power-enabled for laptop use; a range of open-plan group facilities providing different levels of privacy; silent study space; enclosed rooms with presentational facilities; informal spaces, for individual and social use; flexible spaces with mobile furniture; classroom spaces; and cyber café spaces.

A student-centred perspective on learning spaces can challenge traditional thinking about where the balance of power lies between library staff and users of 'their' buildings. The ownership of space is at the heart of this student-centred perspective: students are more likely to regard learning space as successful if they have some control over it and can influence its design to meet their changing needs. Versatile and flexible space where students are encouraged to customise space by rearranging furniture is a good start. Going further, library staff must step back from trying to define what a space is for and the rules governing its use, giving students more freedom to decide this. Bennett (2005) suggests that study space fosters learning by:

- supporting a distinction between studying and socialising that does not deny the social dimension of study
- favouring learning functions in the space's mix of academic and social functions
- providing choices of place, ranging from personal seclusion to group study, that variously reinforce the discipline needed for study
- permitting territorial claims for study that enable students to govern the social dimension of their study space
- fostering a sense of community among students.

He argues that looking to the design of domestic space might help to neutralise some of the inequalities inherent in campus workspace. The conceptual framework for the design of learning space developed by LJMU (Melling, 2006) illustrates how these principles can be applied. It is based on:

- allowing users to own and adapt space according to their needs, with flexible spaces and furniture
- supporting different communities of users, using design to signal changing activities throughout buildings
- supporting social learning with group areas and catering facilities
- using bold design and aesthetics to create a sense of space and a recognition of centres as a place of learning

- providing embedded ICT which enables and supports a range of learning styles
- recognising convergence of space – eroding conventional boundaries between teaching/social/library space and staff/student space.

If the new library is to be credible as a learning space focused on learning outcomes and responsive to students' learning requirements, it must have a strong connection with the curriculum through close academic liaison with faculty staff and students; it must also have a close relationship with academic development more generally. Bennett (2008) makes the point that library and IT staff cannot themselves create a 'learning commons', 'as they serve but do not define institutional mission'; the design of learning space requires collaboration with those who influence institutional learning strategies more directly. For example, the academic focus of Sheffield Hallam University's Adsetts Centre, and indeed the Learning Centre department of which it was the physical embodiment, was strengthened by the inclusion of the University's Learning and Teaching Institute in both. Similarly, the location of a centre of excellence in teaching and learning, the Centre for Inquiry-based Learning in the Arts and Social Sciences, within the Information Commons at the University of Sheffield, has created an important academic partnership.

The exploitation of technology

This process began with the convergence of information and the underlying technologies that over the last two decades has transformed the scholarly information environment and in doing so has offered opportunity, rather than imminent threat, to the academic library – at least to date. The first development that has had a significant impact on the physical library environment began in the early 1990s with the application of the PC as an integrated desktop bringing together networked access to information resources, office software and Internet access. Apart from requiring robust new support mechanisms, this development did not really change the underlying role of the academic library or represent a significant change of use. Its main contribution was to add a new dimension to what students have always used libraries for: to research and write academic work. However, the lack of these facilities, whether because of the difficulty of installing the power and data infrastructure or because of the increased pressure they placed on space, did compromise the ability of some libraries to fulfil their mission in line with changing times and also added impetus to new building development.

More recent developments in the technology itself, its application to learning and the development of the digital information environment have the potential to be much more disruptive to the academic library as place. Emergent mobile technologies certainly have the potential to effect change by delivering learning materials to the devices students carry around with them everywhere; whether students will use them in this way is, of course, another matter. At the same time, the technological infrastructure available in libraries puts them in a strong position to be places of choice from which to access the virtual learning environment. This in turn offers opportunities to be engaged more broadly in the student learning experience but does depend on the willingness and ability of librarians to extend their role to provide the associated learning support. *The 2010 Horizon Report* (Johnson et al., 2010) identifies several learning technologies, such as simple augmented reality and gesture-based computing. Should these more specialist learning developments have a place and space within libraries?

A new model for service delivery

Library staff have always taken responsibility for the services, resources and facilities available within the library. The service delivery model offered within the modern library and provided virtually from it is, however, not just broader but also more complex in terms of the systems, processes and staff expertise needed to provide a layered approach to general and more specialist support. In this environment, one important question is the degree to which the functions supported by the front-line service can be integrated, first of all in terms of location and then, if they are co-located, the extent to which service delivery will be either separated by function and staff professional specialisms (information, IT, circulation) or integrated. If the latter approach is taken, further thought needs to be given to the depth of support that will be offered at the front line. At one end of the spectrum the service point can be simply a place for users to report problems with little expectation that they will receive an answer immediately – a shallow approach that receives calls, answers a few straightforward queries but logs most and refers them on to a second line of support. At the other end of the spectrum lies the expert service point where users would expect, and would receive, a first-time fix or solution for almost all queries raised – a deep approach that provides answers to a wide range of queries and does so to a great depth. This model requires a large number of knowledgeable staff committed to the front line, raising issues of cost and the appropriate use of expert staff to deal with straightforward enquiries.

The nature and extent of front-line integration will define the breadth and depth of knowledge required of first-line support staff. Any integrated approach is likely to challenge the traditional division between information, IT and, possibly, circulation functions and therefore the staff roles and professional specialisms that underpin them. Whatever service model is chosen, it needs to:

- provide help and assistance to enquirers as smoothly and seamlessly as possible
- minimise delay in getting specialist advice
- provide a robust system for transferring enquiries from the front line
- direct enquiries to the most appropriate persons.

It also needs to make provision for the various ways in which enquiries might be received – face-to-face, by e-mail, by telephone or via other technologies such as instant messaging – and enable interaction with students and staff using their media of choice. The model also needs to take into consideration the different support patterns in operation at various times of opening, especially weekends and evenings. A student-centred approach is as relevant here as it is in the design of learning spaces: the service desk is the most prominent symbol of staff authority. Redesigning it to enable staff to work alongside, rather than opposite, students or to break up its monolithic appearance should be considered.

A partnership approach to service provision is taken in the University of Sheffield's Information Commons, reflecting the joint ownership by the library and IT services of the building and its services. Library and IT staff are part of one multi-professional team, working closely together in a way that encourages the sharing of expertise but also recognises the necessity of referral between staff to exploit their particular skill sets. The service delivery model offered in the library of the University of Huddersfield and in the learning resource centres of LJMU illustrates how the accessibility and service ethos of the academic library can be extended to more generic student support. In both, the ground floor of each building provides the focus for a broad range of student support. Given the breadth and widely differentiated nature of the services provided in its learning resource centres, the approach taken by LJMU in bringing together what were five separate front-line services channels, previously delivered by four different professional and faculty service areas, is to develop a unified approach to the way customer services are managed and delivered, in order to achieve consistent standards regardless of the processes being administered. This front-line service is supported by the expertise of the specialist areas within the service and informed by robust faculty liaison.

Case study 11.1 Adsetts Centre, Sheffield Hallam University

The learning centre model developed at Sheffield Hallam University has been driven by an educational philosophy that recognises that students learn best when they are actively engaged in learning and that they are more likely to succeed when they have the maximum number of choices about how they engage in learning. The initial business case for the Adsetts Centre (which opened in 1996) was set firmly within the University's academic development priorities. Its initial brief, to create 'a stimulating building that conveys the excitement of learning and discovery to our students and staff', recognised that the design of the physical environment was an active ingredient in determining the quality of the learning experience. Space, services and facilities were designed to provide:

- accommodation for both individual and collaborative learning that encourages users to work in an integrated way with material in both conventional and digital formats
- integrated learner support
- access to information resources in all formats: print, media and digital
- extensive information technology provision as an integral part of the general study space, providing access to software, networked information and other services and learning materials
- study skills workshops where tutors and students could work together
- information production facilities.

The ongoing development and expansion of the Adsetts Centre continues to evolve to accommodate the changing learning needs of its student population. Twenty-four-hour operation of the entire building was introduced in 2000. A four-storey extension was added in 2008. Learning space, services and facilities have been reconfigured on several occasions to keep the building at the centre of the delivery of the University's Learning, Teaching and Assessment Strategy so as to ensure that it continues to provide an essential and prominent component of the learning landscape. For example, an informal social and creative learning space which contains a catering facility has been added, together with learning environments that provide a test bed for new ideas, such as an interactive games facility and a 3-D visualisation learning environment. Ground-breaking research is also being undertaken by learning centre staff to develop a clear, in-depth understanding of how students use learning centres and other campus learning spaces now, and to ascertain their future learning preferences.

The main driver for further development will continue to be the University's learning, teaching and assessment priorities. Accommodation for individual and collaborative learning will continue to encourage students and staff to work in an integrated way with material in both conventional and digital formats. As the capabilities of learning technologies develop and become increasingly important to the student experience, learning centres can develop further their role as technology-enriched learning environments, where students can choose from a range of options, both individual and collaborative, to satisfy their learning needs. The most recent phase of development has responded to a University priority relating to 'authentic' learning, which aims to support students' understanding of a professional, real-world environment. A new learning space has been designed that expresses this professional theme through furniture style and configuration and additional facilities for collaborative work and presentations. As part of an aim to encourage students to take more ownership of the building, a new initiative, 'Art in Adsetts' has also been introduced from the beginning of the 2010/11 academic year. This is an exhibition across every floor of the building that provides an excellent showcase for the best of Art and Design students' work, extends the definition of what a learning centre represents within the University and generally 'lifts' the quality of its environment.

The underlying vision for any further development is one where:

- the internal layout and design of the building is focused on its use as a learning space, accommodating a wide range of learning styles, and new technologies, rather than just as a resource centre

- students can to some degree determine what space and technology they need

- students can do much more for themselves, through increased provision of easy-to-use self-service facilities

- support is available through high-profile, visible and easily accessible staffed services

- innovation and creativity in curriculum development are reflected in the learning spaces and opportunities offered by the physical and virtual environments

- flexibility and versatility are at the heart of the buildings, to:
  - create spaces that can be adapted frequently and easily to different uses and thus facilitate innovative approaches to learning
  - extend access to resources

- layout and design recognise the requirements of extended opening, to facilitate effective supervision and to ensure staff and student safety

- information, learning and communications technologies and developments in information provision are fully exploited to enhance access to information, IT and media resources

- facilities, ambience and the allocation of space acknowledge that for many students effective learning takes place in a social environment

- accessibility of services and facilities meet the needs of all students using the facilities, including those with disabilities

- learning spaces are designed to encourage users to work productively with minimum disruption to others

- changes to the building should reflect the need, wherever possible, to improve environmental issues for all staff and users.

From the start, the integrated approach to services, resources and facilities was complemented by an integrated approach to advice, help and guidance to enable students and staff to make more effective use of information and IT services and learning resources. Learning centre staff roles were also converged, with a change of job title from Assistant Librarian to Information Adviser symbolising a new professional model. Separate IT Helpdesks, which supported IT facilities elsewhere on campus, acted as referral points for more complex IT queries that could not be dealt with by learning centre information desks. In 2005, this operational convergence was extended and deepened by organisational convergence, when the Learning Centre department was brought together with the University's central IT department, and then in 2008 their respective information desks and helpdesks were brought together, in each learning centre, to form one integrated campus-wide point of access to information and IT support, together with book circulation and audiovisual equipment lending services. This physical service is complemented by a virtual service (e-mail, telephone or any of the other emerging communication methods such as instant messaging), which provides a single point of contact for telephone callers. The key principles of this new service delivery model are to ensure:

- that services continue to be responsive to changing customer requirements and expectations rather than arranged around organisational convenience
- learner autonomy (helping them to help themselves), acknowledging both that this is part of their learning, and that services need to be available even when the service points are not staffed
- an accessible, transparent and seamless service that is viewed by students and staff as a knowledgeable and responsive 'first point of contact', not a call centre or reception point for merely logging questions and problems
- that service provision is also aimed at reinforcing and developing student skills as well as providing solutions to immediate problems and queries
- that staff working on the Helpdesk (physical or virtual) have the necessary training and support to enable them to deliver a quality service and for the staff themselves to feel a sense of fulfilment and satisfaction in being able to help
- that technology is used appropriately to support and develop services, but always keeping in mind that some customers will prefer to access services face to face
- that the aim is to remove, or at least reduce, complexity
- an efficient referral of queries from the first point of contact to the relevant specialist area to ensure that the query is dealt with effectively. The aim is to build a working body of knowledge about such queries to be used by front-line staff where this is appropriate and possible.

In terms of depth, the service therefore provides a knowledgeable and deep first line, sufficient to deal with a high percentage of enquiries (80%+) at first contact. It is based on IT, information and other services being available to all students and University staff, across all locations and through a range of delivery modes. The aim of the service model is to join up different types of services in a seamless way, supported by appropriate technology such as helpdesk software, intelligent telephony and shared IT facilities. A well-populated, user-friendly and authoritative Knowledge Base has been created for Helpdesk staff so as to support informed and consistent responses.

The key to delivering high-level satisfaction at first point of contact is a multi-skilled group of staff, with a commitment to customer service, who also bring a range of deep knowledge to the front line. These staff need to possess a 'T-shaped' skills profile, with a broad level of knowledge across several disciplines (represented by the horizontal bar), combined with deeper expertise in at least one area (the vertical bar). Both formal and informal knowledge and experience sharing amongst staff providing the first-line service is recognised as crucial to the quality of service. The first-line service is supported by a second line, and behind that a third line, that together provide access to the specialist expertise of staff across the department for queries that cannot be dealt with by the first-line service for whatever reason (e.g. time, knowledge, privacy issues). There is also an important additional element to the support model: self-help materials have a key role to play in supporting user needs and helping to fulfil the department's commitment to supporting and enabling autonomous learning.

The original intention of this service model was to move to a position of full integration, where counter services such as book circulation were incorporated into the integrated service delivery model, rather than just being co-located. However, consideration of this has been deferred for reasons of both practicality and principle. In practical terms, this would be feasible only with a significantly reduced number of counter transactions, which will not happen until a new online payment system is introduced. As a matter of principle, it may be that the addition of circulation to the already broad horizontal bar of the 'T' could dilute staff expertise and call into question the provision of a deep front line.

Conclusion

The core purpose of the academic library as outlined in the first paragraph of this chapter is sufficiently inclusive to ensure its continuing place at the heart of a University's learning and research priorities. With this as a starting point, it should not be too difficult to refocus the library in its role of supporting learning, such that it sees itself not just as a place to access academic information resources but also as a public space that is more inviting of other activities. While it may have lost some of its uniqueness to other local learning spaces elsewhere on campus and to an alternative, virtual library space, there seems to be no reason to worry about the future of the academic library as place, at least for the medium term. Librarians have been very successful in reconfiguring the physical learning environment to ensure that it continues to be aligned with institutional strategy. The success of 'the modern library' in adopting a broader perspective, with a much stronger focus on support for learning, is evident in very high levels of use.

There are undoubtedly challenges and threats on the horizon. At the moment the virtual library can be seen as complementing the physical library environment. It remains to be seen how far and how soon this will change to a position where a more sophisticated virtual learning environment, an expanding digital information environment and mobile computing combine to challenge it, both in terms of its role in the discovery and delivery of information resources and also as an environment for learning. With a reduced dependence on its big collections of print resources, the unique role of the large central library could be challenged in favour of a more distributed model that favours more local, perhaps subject-based learning communities. Whatever the future brings, anyone whose next visit to an academic library is in 2025 may well find it to be just as unrecognisable as today's library is to the visitor from 1995.

References

Bennett, S. (2005) 'Righting the balance'. In CLIR, *Library as Place: rethinking roles, rethinking space*. Washington, DC: Council on Library and Information Resources. Online at http://www.clir.org/pubs/abstract/pub129abst.html.

Bennett, S. (2008) 'The information or the Learning Commons: which will we have?' *Journal of Academic Librarianship*, 34 (3), 183–5.

Demas, S. (2005) 'From the ashes of Alexandria: what's happening in the college library?' in CLIR, *Libraries as Place: rethinking roles, rethinking space*. Washington, DC: Council on Library and Information Resources. Online at http://www.clir.org/pubs/abstract/pub129abst.html.

Johnson, L., Levine, A., Smith, R. and Stone, S. (2010) *The 2010 Horizon Report*. Austin, TX: The New Media Consortium.

Lewis, M. (2010) 'The University of Sheffield Library Information Commons: a case study'. *Journal of Library Administration*, 50 (2), 161–78.

Melling, M. (2006) *Designing Space to Support Learning: moving on from learning resource centres*. [Internal document] Liverpool John Moores University.

12

Libraries and distance education

Chinwe Nwezeh

Introduction

Distance education creates and provides access to learning when information sources and learners are separated by time or distance or both. It involves the creation of an educational experience of qualitative value for the learner that is best suited to their needs outside the classroom. Distance education is often referred to as distance learning; it is a field of education which focuses on pedagogy, andragogy, instructional systems and technology to deliver education to students who are not in a physical classroom or campus setting. Distance education is also synonymous with the terms 'open learning', 'correspondence learning' and 'external study'.

Modern distance education has been practised since Isaac Pitman taught shorthand in Britain via correspondence in the 1840s (Moore and Kearsley, 2005). The first university to offer distance learning degrees was the University of London, which established its external programme in 1854.[1] The University of South Africa has been offering correspondence education courses since 1946. In the United Kingdom, the largest distance education university is the Open University, founded in 1969. University-level distance education or extramural study began in New Zealand at Massey University in 1960. The Fern Universität in Hagen, Germany was founded in 1974. There are now many similar institutions around the world, sometimes with the name Open University (in English or in the local language). Online education is rapidly increasing, particularly in the United States, where online doctoral programmes have even developed at prestigious research institutions (Herbert, 2007). Virtually all 'open universities' use distance education technologies as methods of delivery (Moore and Kearsley, 2005). The

Sloan Consortium reported in 2006 that more than 96% of the largest colleges and universities in the United States offered online courses and that almost 3.2 million US students were taking at least one online course during the fall 2005 term (Allen and Seaman, 2006).

The *Standards of Distance Learning Library Services*[2] approved by the Association of College and Research Libraries (ACRL) Board of Directors (July 2008) states that every student, faculty member, administrator, staff member or any other member of an institution of higher education is entitled to use the library services and resources of the institution. This includes direct communication with appropriate library personnel, who will provide information in response to requesters' needs. Distance learners, no matter where they are located, are just as entitled to access library materials as are individuals on the main campus, off campus and through regional campus programmes. Online access to library resources has made it possible for both main campus online users and distance learning users to access library resources. Thus, the scope of distance learning has developed rapidly and enormously in recent years.

Distance learning: an African context

In Nigeria some institutions, such as the National Open University of Nigeria (NOUN),[3] Distance Learning Institute of the University of Lagos,[4] Center for Distance Learning of the Obafemi Awolowo University, Ile-Ife[5] and the External Studies Programme of the University of Ibadan,[6] run distance education programmes. Distance education is important in developing countries, especially in Africa, because of the lack of opportunities for many people to undertake full-time university education. It creates opportunities for those in full-time employment to pursue and further their education, thereby enhancing their prospects of career advancement. Distance education programmes in Africa are provided in two organisational models. One is the dual model, in which a university operates both the full-time on-campus programme and the distance education programme simultaneously and both sets of learners follow the same curriculum and the qualifications obtained at the end of the programme are the same. This model is common in many universities in Africa. The other is the single model, in which the distance education programme is the sole mandate of the university and the university does not offer its programme full-time on campus (Aina, 2008). This model exists in many countries. The oldest university operating it in Africa is the University of South Africa (UNISA), Pretoria, which was established in 1946. Other universities in Africa that operate this model include the Zimbabwe Open University, Harare, Zimbabwe, the Open University of Tanzania, Dar-Es-Salem, Tanzania and the National Open University, Lagos, Nigeria.

In Africa some case studies have been done on distance education and libraries (see Kavulya, 2004). Kavulya's study examines the efforts being made by Kenyan university libraries to fulfil the information needs of the distance education students in their respective institutions. It concludes that, even though efforts have been made, there is still room for improvement through adequate planning, financing and collaboration between information personnel and those who design and implement the distance education programmes. A study by Mabawonku (2004) focuses on the use of library and information resources by distance learning (part-time) students in three Nigerian universities. It was discovered that the students hardly used reference and electronic resources and that the majority of the students did not receive any guidance on using the library. Some of the students could graduate without ever having used libraries. The study recommended that universities should make provision for students to access library and information resources, and should provide training on information sourcing to their part-time distance learning students. A study by Msuya and Maro (2002) discusses the provision of library and information resources to the students of the Open University of Tanzania. Oladokun's 2002 research discovered that learners at the Open University of Tanzania depended more on the existing library stock of private and public library systems, and that this was not an adequate solution because the stock of these libraries was not sufficiently relevant. At the University of Nairobi in Kenya, students are encouraged to make their own arrangements to use other university libraries in addition to the University of Nairobi Library and the British Council libraries, theological college libraries and learning resource centres in teacher training colleges. In addition to making their own arrangements with other libraries, students were encouraged to make a contribution towards the augmentation of the available stock. Oladokun (2002) describes UNISA, which is one of the world's foremost distance learning universities and which has the latest information technology (IT) and resources in its library. These resources include a book stock of over a million volumes, many journal titles, microfilms, CD-ROMS, video and audio recordings. UNISA has branch libraries and study centres all over South Africa and also has cooperative services with other academic and public libraries, and networks of many databases and bibliographic services that the students can access.

Nwezeh (2010) examines the effort being made by Nigerian universities to meet the information needs of distance education students in their respective institutions. These students are not adequately catered for as far as the use of library resources is concerned. The study recommends that planning and financing should be adequate to enable distance learning students to make use of libraries and information resources. In a study that was carried out in order to establish the adequacy of library and information services' support for distance education learners in Africa, Aina (2008) reviews documentary studies on the provision of distance education library and information services in African universities. The review revealed that the library and information needs of distance learners are not adequately catered for. Aina examined the guidelines for distance education library services that have been adopted by library associations in other countries. Based on this analysis, a set of guidelines was formulated that could be adopted by African university libraries. Aramide and Bolarinwa (2010) presented a case study of NOUN's study centre. They investigated the availability of audiovisual and electronic resources and their use by distance learning students. The study reveals that even though NOUN has made provision for audiovisual and electronic resources for students' use, a majority of such resources are available only through the students' own personal provision. It was also discovered that the majority of distance learners make regular use of audiovisual and electronic resources in carrying out their assignments. Using computers and printed media, students are able to pursue their education without attending classes on a college or university campus. They can communicate and study at times of their own choosing, using a variety of technologies that enable them to interact in real time and in many different ways via the Internet.

Providing library services for distance education

Distance learning courses have been categorised into two formats. In the 'self-contained course', students study from pre-packaged materials and are not expected to read or consult sources beyond the supplied materials. The package is expandable, and in this second format the students use packaged materials, but in certain sections of the course they are required to engage in wider reading (Kavulya, 2004). Library services and resources are essential to the attainment of higher academic skills in post-secondary education, regardless of where students, faculty or programmes are located. The library plays an important role in the production of distance learning students who can operate as independent thinkers and researchers. Library research and information literacy are essential components of the academic learning experience: instilling lifelong learning skills through general bibliographic and information literacy instruction in academic libraries is a primary goal for the distance learning community, just as it is for students based on traditional campuses (ACRL, 2000). Libraries are charged with providing distance education students with the user-based library services and information assistance that are necessary for the successful completion of coursework, research papers and independent reading and research. Distance learning students need to be provided with the full range of library services, such as lending, inter-library loan, reference assistance, course reserves/restricted loans[7] and Internet-based resources.

Developments in telecommunications

Developments in information and communications technology (ICT) have resulted in completely new ways of disseminating information and knowledge and are changing educational methods. The importance of libraries as providers of information is evident, and technology is becoming widely used in universities and institutions around the globe. Recent technological advances have raised recognition of the potential for distance learning to provide individual attention and communication to students internationally. 'Transactional distance' is the most widely cited pedagogical theory of distance education (Holmberg, 2005), and ICT may offer a genuine opportunity for placing libraries within community development. With ICT, libraries can serve as public gateways to information highways, providing users with access, guidance and learning facilities.

Libraries and information literacy

Information literacy is defined as a set of abilities that allow individuals to recognise when information is needed and to locate the required information, evaluate it and use it effectively (ACRL, 2005). Distance learning students need to be information literate in order to access library materials and services because they are physically removed from the library while at the same time requiring access to the full range of library services. As the world of information becomes more complex, information literacy has become an increasingly important element in the education process (Smith, 2005), involving the mastering of a complex set of concepts and skills and the interplay between them. Knowledge of library and computer skills is an integral part of information literacy. These skills are tools for the realisation of higher goals that include the ability to identify, access, evaluate and interpret relevant information in order to make informed decisions. Sharma (2007) states that it takes reinforcement, sustained effort and time to develop higher-order information literacy skills. Distance education librarians need to teach students how to search databases. Knowing how to obtain and evaluate information is a lifelong skill that students need to master and that will have an impact on all areas of their lives. To ensure that distance learning stays on track, effective assessment methods are needed, because how well the students are served depends on how accurately the success of a programme is assessed.

Librarians need to work closely with course teachers to identify what is expected of the students, so that they can provide research assistance that is appropriate to the successful completion of the course. To ensure distance learners' success, the distance education librarian must work very closely with the other members of the library and academic team, and distance learners need to associate themselves with the library. Every member of the distance education team needs to have a learner focus; the duty of the librarian is to help students to navigate the library, which is the storehouse of knowledge. Distance education centres should be able to help distance learners in the following ways:

- assist distance learners to become independent in library literacy skills
- provide a quality distance learning programme
- train the students in how to access information
- enhance students' critical thinking and research skills
- enhance students' self-reliance in using online databases and the Internet for research
- accommodate the informational needs of the distance learning community

- provide a challenging environment to enable distance learners to become problem solvers and to seek their own solutions

- augment students' computer skills in order to enhance the educational process.

Staff activity needs to be coordinated, because many people must collaborate in order to produce and disseminate good-quality distance education programmes. Library services are essential to a successful distance education programme and librarians should strive to meet the information needs of students in a broad information environment. Therefore, librarians need to plan, implement, coordinate and evaluate library resources and services in order to address the information and skills needs of the distance learning community (Bryant, 2001).

What is 'information literacy'?

In a print society, 'literacy' meant the ability to read and write, and by this means one could become a fully participating member of a democratic society. Two kinds of literacy can be distinguished: general literacy and information literacy. Schamber (2003) defines literacy in general as being the ability to read, write, speak and do some mathematical computation to a certain level. Functional literacy involves the skills needed to cope at an adult level in everyday situations such as reading a newspaper or completing a job application form.

The term 'information literacy', sometimes referred to as information competence, is generally defined as the ability to access, evaluate, organise and use information from a variety of sources. Information literacy is an abstract concept, with roots in the emergence of the information society. The concept arose as a result of the rapid growth in the global availability of information through developments in ICT. Being information literate requires:

- knowing how to clearly define a subject or area of investigation

- formulating search strategies that take into consideration different sources of information and the variable ways that information is organised

- analysing the data collected for value, relevance, quality and suitability

- subsequently turning that information into knowledge.

This involves a deeper understanding of how and where to find information, the ability to judge whether that information is meaningful and, ultimately, how best to make use of the information to address the problem or issue at hand. To be information literate, a person must be able to recognise when information is needed, to locate the needed information and to evaluate and use it effectively. Although definitions of information literacy can attract different interpretations, the central focus remains that of enabling information users to acquire a broad understanding of information sources, of the proper handling of such sources and of the critical evaluation of information in various situations in which it is used in order to support effective decision making, problem solving and research.

Information literacy combines a number of literacies, such as computer literacy, library literacy, Internet literacy, media literacy, research literacy and critical thinking skills. In a real sense, information literacy is not the same as computer literacy (which requires technological know-how to manipulate computer hardware and software). Isbell and Hammond (1993) defined information literacy within the contexts of lifelong learning and a broad information continuum that ranges from data to knowledge to wisdom, and state that information literacy focuses on five broad abilities:

- to recognise the need for information
- to know how to access information
- to understand how to evaluate information
- to know how to synthesise information
- to communicate information.

Bawden (2001) states that information literacy is the adoption of appropriate information behaviour to identify, through whatever channel or medium, information that is well suited to information needs, leading to wise and ethical use of information in society. Two kinds of literacy are becoming increasingly important in the contemporary environment of rapid technological change and prolific information resources. The escalating complexity of this environment means that individuals are faced with diverse and abundant information choices in their academic studies, in the workplace and in their personal lives. Literacy is necessary first in the information that is available through libraries, community resources, special-interest organisations, media and the Internet. Increasingly, it reaches individuals in an unfiltered form, raising questions about its authenticity, validity and reliability. A second kind of literacy is related to the information that is also available through multimedia, including graphical, auditory and textual media. This poses new challenges for individuals in evaluating and understanding it. The challenge here is how to create an informed citizenry with a cluster of abilities that are necessary for effective information use (ACRL, 2005).

In fact, we are furnishing our schools, colleges, universities, libraries and homes with electronic technologies, but are we preparing our students and teachers for the onslaught of information that these technologies provide? What happens when students get more information from the Internet than was previously conveyed by a teacher or a textbook? What should a student do when faced with so many information possibilities? How do you determine which information is credible and which is not? The provision of so much more information, and more misinformation, necessitates that everyone, whether or not they are in the education system, should have not only reading and computer skills but also information skills. It is the role of libraries to provide literacy education for their users.

The implications of information literacy

Implications for libraries and librarians

The impact of moving from text-based learning to resource-based learning will involve heavier use of library materials and a demand for more, and more varied, media resources, including print and non-print. The linking of library holdings and the stepped-up demand for resource sharing among libraries increases the importance (and costs) of inter-library loans. As information specialists, librarians will be called upon more frequently to consult with teachers and learners and to provide training and guidance for the sharpening of information literacy skills, not only in schools and academic libraries but also in public and special libraries. Librarians led the way in the early 1970s in conceptualising information literacy and its relationship to lifelong learning, and the early development of the concept of information literacy frequently focused on the future role of libraries and librarians in helping with the application and use of information.

Implications for teaching

Becoming information literate is an active process that requires the seeking out of knowledge from multiple sources. The teacher's role must evolve from provider of knowledge to being more of a coach or guide. Teachers, librarians, administrators and the community must collaborate to develop ways to involve the students not only in using classroom materials, but also in using resources acquired from the broader community and mass media. Teachers and librarians must prepare to teach students to become critical thinkers, intellectually curious observers, and creators and users of information. This means shifting some of the responsibility for acquiring knowledge from the teacher/librarian to the student and allowing students to develop questions and strategies for searching, and to formulate conclusions.

Implications for schools

In order for schools to produce learners who are computer literate, they will need to integrate information literacy skills into the curriculum, across all subject areas. If schools could produce information-literate learners who could access, evaluate and use information from a variety of sources, then they would be producing pupils who would become fully participating members of a democratic society.

Implications for learning

Becoming information literate will involve a dramatic change in the ways in which many students are accustomed to learn. Students have to become more self-directed in their learning; this kind of learning prepares students for real-life problem solving. One method of developing information skills is through resource-based learning, in which the students assume more responsibility for locating the materials from which they learn. As students become competent in their use of information resource options, they become aware of their individual styles of learning and preferred ways of assimilating knowledge. In this respect, undertaking distance education has many advantages:

- completion of classes at the student's own pace
- ability to live anywhere in the world, study from anywhere in the world and pursue an independent choice of distance education courses

- gaining additional knowledge by learning computer and Internet skills, which can also be applied to other facets of the student's life

- self-paced learning environments can be used to advantage by both the quickest and the slowest of learners, increasing levels of satisfaction while reducing stress

- accessibility factors – distance education addresses the physical accessibility issues that people with mobility problems can encounter in the traditional on-campus classes

- provision of general and professional education that are useful in the application of technology to all sectors of development.

Conclusion

The role of libraries has changed since the advent of the Internet. The roles of librarians have changed, and so have their duties. Librarianship is no longer a profession for book lovers; rather, it is now for technology and information professionals as well. With the advent of the electronic age, librarians can now work in a variety of special libraries, or even for themselves. Librarianship has been of benefit to all areas of the Internet, such as web page design and maintenance, troubleshooting and expertise in Internet searching. The Internet has helped librarians not only in consultancy work but also in expanding the scope of librarianship. Machines can do so many things; nonetheless, librarians are still better at categorising and making the right information available. The advent of new technologies has created new employment opportunities for information professionals, such as with dot.coms, vendors, corporations and as information brokers or consultants. With the global information infrastructure available via the Internet, more people now have access to external learning resources. One can now have unrestricted access to the world of learning, provided that communication networks are fully in place. The new information environment makes it necessary for librarians to acquire new skills and expertise, more so in the use of ICT, electronic publishing, digital information management and knowledge management.

One of the many reasons for globalisation in distance education is the importance and necessity of taking the distance out of higher education so as to enable growth and development around the world (Falade, 2005). Globalisation and distance education are successfully conquering illiteracy and innumeracy, both of which are sources of insecurity (Jegede, 2003). The field of distance education is growing rapidly and there is an unprecedented demand for it. It is therefore vital that we, in the library profession, respond to the exciting challenge of a new learning environment.

Notes

1. http://www.londoninternational.ac.uk/about_us/facts.shtml.
2. http://www.ala.org/ala/mgrps/divs/acrl/standards/guidelinesdistance learning.cfm.
3. http://www.nou.edu.ng/.
4. http://www.unilag.edu.ng/index.php?page=about_dli.
5. http://www.oaudistancelearning.org.
6. http://www.dlcuiaudiovisualmat.com/history.php.
7. Restricted loans are used for books that are in high demand and of which there are an insufficient number of copies to go round, or when a lecturer asks for a book that is crucial to the course to be put on reserve so as to ensure that as many people as possible can access it.

References

ACRL. (2000) *Guidelines for Distance Learning Library Services.* Association of College and Research Libraries: Washington, DC. Online at http://www.ala.org/ala/mgrps/divs/acrl/standards/guidelines distancelearning.cfm.

ACRL. (2005) *Information Literacy Competency Standards for Higher Education.* Association of College and Research Libraries. Online at http://www.ala.org/ala/mgrps/divs/acrl/standards/informationliteracy competency.cfm.

Aina, L.O. (2008) 'Library and information services support for distance education programme in African universities: proposals for further development'. *Nigerian Libraries,* 41, 1–11. Online at http://www. unilorin.edu.ng/publications/aina/Prof.Aina.pdf.

Allen, E. and Seaman, J. (2006) *Making the Grade: online education in United States.* The Sloan Consortium. Online at http://sloan consortium.org/sites/default/files/Making_the_Grade.pdf.

Aramide, K.A. and Bolarinwa, O.A. (2010) 'Availability and use of audiovisual and electronic resources by distance learning students in

Nigerian universities: a case study of National Open University of Nigeria (NOUN), Ibadan study centre'. *Library Philosophy and Practice.* Online at http://www.webpages.uidaho.edu/~mbolin/aramide-bolarinwa.pdf.

Bawden, D. (2001) 'Information and digital literacies: a review of concepts'. *Journal of Documentation*, 57 (2), 218–59.

Bryant, E. (2001) 'Bridging the gap'. *Library Journal*, 126, 58–60.

Falade, G.O. (2005) 'Globalization and distance education: its effects on educational system in Nigeria'. *Journal of E-learning*, 1 (1), 14–24.

Herbert, D.G. (2007) 'Five challenges and solutions in online music teacher education'. *Research and Issues in Music Education*, 5 (1). Online at http://www.stthomas.edu/rimeonline/vol5/hebert.htm.

Holmberg, B. (2005) *The Evolution, Principles and Practices of Distance Education.* Oldenburg: BIS-Verlag der Carl von Ossietzky Universität. Online at http://www.mde.uni-oldenburg.de/download/asfvolume11_eBook.pdf.

Isbell, D. and Hammond, C. (1993) 'Information literacy competencies'. *College and Research Libraries News*, June, 325–7.

Jegede, O. (2003) 'Taking the distance out of higher education in 21st century Nigeria'. An invited Convocation lecture presented at the Federal Polytechnic, Oko, Anambra State on the occasion of the Convocation ceremony and 10th Anniversary Celebration held on 28 November 2003.

Kavulya, J. (2004) 'Library services for distance education in Kenya'. *African Journal of Library, Archives and Information Science*, 14 (1), 15–28.

Mabawonku, I. (2004) 'Library use in distance learning: a survey of undergraduates in three Nigerian universities'. *African Journal of Library, Archives and Information Science*, 14 (2), 151–65.

Moore, M. and Kearsley, G. (2005) *Distance Education: a systems view*, 2nd edn. Belmont, CA: Wadsworth.

Msuya, J. and Maro, F. (2002) 'The provision of library and information services to distance learners: the Open University of Tanzania (OUT)'. *Libri*, 52 (3), 183–91.

Nwezeh, C.M.T. (2010) 'Libraries and distance education in Nigerian universities: a revisit'. *New Review of Academic Librarianship*, 16 (1), 102–15.

Oladokun, O.S. (2002) 'The practice of distance librarianship in Africa'. *Library Review*, 51 (6), 293–300.

Schamber, L. (2003) *The Role of Libraries in Literacy Education.* Online at http://www.libraryinstruction.com/literacy-education.html.

Sharma, S. (2007) 'From chaos to clarity: using the research portfolio to teach and assess information literacy skills'. *The Journal of Academic Librarianship*, 33 (1), 127–35.

Smith, S. (2005) *Web-based Instruction: a guide for libraries*, 2nd edn. Chicago: American Library Association.

Syllabus independence and the library

David Harris

Introduction

In this chapter, I aim to illuminate and discuss the changing role played by libraries in the development of UK distance education by considering the development of the UK Open University (UKOU). After some initial failure to consider the provision of library materials, UKOU course designers attempted to provide self-sufficient packages, which would include all the necessary additional reading, and to encourage students to buy books where they could not borrow them. However, even such a full provision could not cater for a particular variant of independent learning – 'syllabus independence'. Such independence is a desirable educational goal for both students and academics, and it clearly requires access to suitable educational materials beyond what are provided in the teaching package itself. In other words, it depends on a library. Recent electronic developments have not only remedied this early deficiency, but now offer such creative possibilities that they must be considered as essential components of a modern distance education system.

The United Kingdom Open University

One of the many innovations for which the UKOU became famous from its inception in 1970 was the idea that higher education (HE) could be conducted at a distance, without continual face-to-face interchange with academics, and, even more controversially, without frequent attendance at a university library. Libraries were then primarily based around paper and print, housed in specific institutions. The UKOU had decided to offer access to its courses across the UK, and it soon became apparent that this meant there would be students in remote locations many miles away from a university library. Of course, there would be summer schools and tutorials, with negotiated library rights, at host universities, but library access emerged as a serious problem.

It is necessary at this point to go back into the history of the UKOU. The usual view (shared by the contributors to Tunstall, 1974) was that a group of idealistic politicians and academics met in Belgravia at the end of the 1960s and decided that they wanted to offer a university-level education to all adults who wanted to pursue one. They were fired by criticism of an existing education system that was seen as excessively selective and elitist, restricting opportunity mostly to upper- and middle-class males. The UKOU would break through these social barriers, offering a second chance to those who would have been able to attend a conventional university, had they not come from the wrong social background. Notions of openness included wanting to help make the occupational system itself more meritocratic by producing many graduates from unconventional backgrounds so as to meet the need for highly skilled workers that arose from early shifts towards the knowledge economy and from government policy. Apparently the then prime minister, Harold Wilson, was concerned about a shortage of skilled draftsmen holding back the expansion of manufacturing industry (Hoult, 1975). More tangibly, a major government policy in 1970 insisted that all school teachers should be graduates: this decision alone virtually guaranteed the success of the new institution, as thousands of school teachers holding certificates decided to upgrade to degree-level qualifications, partly encouraged by generous credit exemptions.

It is easy to idealise that exciting early period, although the present author's view is that the UKOU's commitment to openness was actually rather more pragmatic, commercial and political. The initiating White Paper (HMSO, 1969) had identified a pool of talent of some 300,000 people who had the ability to benefit from a university course but had been denied access before. It was those talented people – who were often teachers and other professionals – whom the UKOU wanted to target. Far from being interested in teaching those with no qualifications or educational experience at all, those establishing the UKOU actually devised an application system which could have had the effect of limiting their access. Planning for this application system took the form of circulating internally several working papers during 1969 which have never been published, although Harris (1987) has a summary of them. Applicants would be taken on a 'first come first served' basis, but certain applicants would be referred initially to a counselling system that would gather information about people's social and educational background. This information could also be used to further weight applications. Those who already had good qualifications and with what looked like standard middle-class social commitments and 'high quality leisure interests' would be awarded a weighted grade, and the 'computer [could] ... cream off "super alpha" applications coming from teachers and/or graduates etc', according to one internal document, while 'housewives', 'manual workers' and 'shopkeepers and service workers' would be offered initial counselling (Harris, 1987). Then 'the sum of the weights would be used to bring forward the date of application by an amount to be agreed ... [For example] ... someone applying on 15 January might have this date advanced after weighting to 18 December', according to another working party document (Harris, 1987). It turned out that the first applicants were mostly from conventional middle-class backgrounds anyway, and so the proposed selection system was not actually used: 'less than 2 per cent of the 42,821 applicants are, in our view, not yet ready for an Open University course', to use the terms of some materials prepared for a press conference (Harris, 1987). In this way, the UKOU was never really faced with the challenges of what might be seen as radical openness, including the problems of providing for those unable to access libraries.

There were implications for academic discourse as well. Conventional academic discourse had ossified into rigid subject compartments, for example, whereas new inter- and multidisciplinary courses were required to meet the new conditions. The UKOU response was to produce introductory undergraduate courses, in a course team composed of several specialists, including broadcasters, covering areas such as the humanities or the social sciences, which would contain elements from a range of different academic subjects. As the public soon began to notice, conventional pedagogy would be altered as well, most noticeably by embracing the new electronic media of communication, limited in those days to radio and television (and film cassettes where television coverage did not reach). There were also attractively designed correspondence packages, with excellent layout and artwork. These packages also indicated the first attempts to address the problems of missing libraries, since they contained relevant extracts from published materials. The UKOU was also able to persuade publishers to produce cheap, paperback versions of some of the more obscure academic works. Course teams also recommended particular books for purchase as set texts and, of course, students soon developed a healthy trade in second-hand course materials and texts. The inclusion of British Broadcasting Corporation producers as members of course teams also offered a particularly valuable political advantage, whatever its pedagogical limitations, connecting the UKOU in the public's mind with a prestigious institution, and also partially disguising the costs of start-up. Whether course teams really did solve problems of interdisciplinary or multimedia communication is rather more problematic (Riley, 1984).

However, there is one underlying theme which is perhaps less evident. The UKOU was committed to a conventional kind of pedagogical philosophy, despite its willing experimentation with different disciplines and media. The White Paper (HMSO, 1969) promised to square the circle of university standards and relatively unqualified applicants by putting faith in a new kind of educational technology, including the experiments noted. In practice, the UKOU was intending to address its students in a highly didactic way, to use 'telling' as a dominant form of communication. The limited radicalism of the founders assumed that this was the best, or perhaps even the only, way to address the unqualified, following a rather long tradition in educational thinking (Lewis and Cook, 1969). The 'new pedagogy' of many modern universities makes the same assumption. Non-traditional students are to be addressed clearly and firmly, with aims, objectives or outcomes clearly specified, with instructional material closely adjusted to those outcomes, and with careful planning of pace and content. They are to be guided by a range of pragmatic 'study skills' approaches that can offer rational information management techniques, almost irrespective of actual content (Arksey and Harris, 2007). Unqualified students cannot be expected to develop any independent interests in the material, so they have to be constantly engaged with a range of techniques to involve them, to encourage, almost to force 'participation', and to be driven along by frequent and pervasive assessment. Educational technology promised to offer a set of design principles, which were more or less the same as rational project management, to guide the construction of a complete package that would offer all the relevant material delivered in the approved manner. Educational technologists at the UKOU thought of this as a 'right first time' procedure. For the most hard-line advocates, face-to-face teaching would hardly be needed at all, except possibly in a kind of remedial and feedback gathering role, and nor would libraries.

It is worth pointing out that there is an open and democratic side to this development. A number of commentators, from Bentham (1983) to Bourdieu et al. (1996), have noticed that conventional academic communication is inextricably mixed with aspects of 'style' that are both inefficient and socially exclusive. It is very appealing to try to develop an alternative that is much more sparse, clear and rational. For Bentham, in 1806, the basic principles of academic subjects need to be exposed, and ordered logically. At the UKOU, starting up some 164 years later, the same principles were being offered in an extraordinary curriculum design project which aimed to recast academic discourse into unambiguous concepts, linked in a network by a limited vocabulary of logical relations, using a branched computer program as an analogy (Pask and Scott, 1973).

This clarity is achieved at the cost of reducing structured ambiguity and uncertainty and avoiding the need for justification and argument. It is fashionable again to see such qualities as mere 'noise', but in the present author's view they can lead to a kind of conceptual openness. If academics wish to develop materials that permit critical engagement on the part of the learner, they should not be concealing all the non-logical aspects of argument, but encouraging critique that ranges fully across logic and rhetoric. Habermas' 'notion of the "ideal speech act"' describes the fully open ideal case with experienced and independent learners, where any participant can raise doubts about the technical validity of the arguments in each of the main areas – truth, logical consistency, sincerity and social appropriateness (Habermas, 1979). Far from 'sanitising' an illogical structure, to use Pask's terms, academic material designed to foster critical engagement should be pointing to the inevitable ambiguities, glosses, reductions of complexity, literary tropes, slippery metaphors, decisionistic leaps, rhetorical appeals to authority, and authoritarian closures that affect all arguments (including this one). Of course, there are pedagogical implications which might mean we mediate this approach initially.

Syllabus independence

The apotheosis of the learning and teaching package means that students are told there is no need to depart from the materials provided to address the specific syllabus and to cope with assessment. It follows that any defence of libraries must refer to the kind of learning and teaching that goes on outside of the syllabus. As with many such terms, 'independent' learners have been defined in such a way as to fit in with the pre-packaged notion of learning: learners go off in their own time, and sometimes at their own expense, in order to find their own way to the outcomes teachers have specified, or to achieve the sorts of grades they seek. This sort of independence is often advocated, but from an educational technologist's point of view it just seems completely inefficient – why not just tell people what they need to learn, as clearly and as efficiently as possible, while eliminating 'irrelevant scholastic displays' (Lewis, 1971)?

We need a much richer notion of independence and participation if we are to stave off this obvious argument. There is a place for didactic teaching, in that clarified way, so that new students can find their way around a scholarly field without being overwhelmed with what looks like a morass of competing positions. However, the old notion of a university education as offering a degree of 'syllabus independence' is also valuable. The provision of useful, relevant and high-quality educational material which goes beyond the limited selection offered in the syllabus is precisely what libraries do. In paper and print libraries, many academics have talked of the benefits of serendipitous browsing, for example. More organised searches, which come from experience or from the skilled assistance of a librarian, can provide considerable critical insight for the enquiring student.

Electronic access extends these possibilities hugely, of course. Everyone knows that the Internet in the raw threatens to deliver a baffling relativism, where serious academic discourse is found next to lunatic ranting or commercialised froth, but electronic access as mediated by libraries and librarians is another matter. It becomes possible to find material that will test or challenge arguments on the syllabus. One example concerns the availability of comparative material, referring to, say, the social structure of other countries, which offers an easy way to expose any ethnocentrism, intended or not. Classic arguments can be compared to more recent developments; set texts can be pursued into recent debates, arguments and criticisms; particular authors can be put back into context by discovering earlier and later works; new arguments can be constructed on the basis of new, additional and sometimes contradictory work.

Course design – why academics need libraries

The same implications apply to the production end for distance materials. As we have seen, UKOU academics took advantage of the new conditions to produce new inter- and multidisciplinary courses, although it should be said that they were not always that willing to do so. Multi-disciplinary courses can be assembled fairly readily, especially if there is only a weak kind of integration being proposed – an administrative matter rather than an academic one. Administration did tend to dominate in the early phases of UKOU course production, as Lewis (1971) explains. Because of the need to provide printers and television studios with a smooth flow of work, often involving considerable advance planning, the components of early courses were sometimes produced simultaneously or in accordance with production schedules, and the case for any academic connections or sequences was made only afterwards.

Interdisciplinary or transdisciplinary courses are a different matter, requiring attention to be paid to the conceptual and philosophical differences between existing academic subjects. Ideally, differences and similarities should be openly discussed as a course topic itself. Genuinely inter- or transdisciplinary courses therefore require at least a working knowledge of the typical arguments and procedures found in disciplines other than one's own. Of course, some disciplines are already rather weakly 'framed' and 'classified', to use a famous typology (Bernstein, 1971), with fairly permeable boundaries between neighbouring disciplines and between real-life applications and other kinds of practical and technical expertise. It is in this context that libraries, especially the use of electronic databases, come fully into their own.

Considerable progress can be made by using the straightforward procedure of typing the name of one's own familiar concepts into a search engine and seeing what results. An early discovery in the author's case, for example, was that the term 'semiotics' was used in economics, as well as in more familiar disciplines. The same goes for terms like 'risk', used and discussed rather differently not only in sociology and leisure studies, but also in psychology and economics. Additional dimensions have been discovered when searching under each one of the concepts discussed in a 'key concepts' book (Harris, 2004). Serendipity has become much more organised.

The importance of using electronic databases in this way is also apparent in simply extending knowledge of what is available. Subject boundaries are often set in practice by practical considerations as well as by theoretical commitments: it is impossible to read everything, and very tempting to follow familiar paths through the material according to career paths and other considerations. Electronic databases play a major part in helping overcome those constraints, to a degree that was impossible before. At one stage personal visits to physical libraries were the only way to help read more widely, and this usually involved considerable travel and labour. Similarly, anyone who has pursued their apprenticeship by laboriously poring over index volumes and going off to trace the physical artefacts to which they lead, or waiting patiently while hard-pressed librarians retrieve items from stacks, will recognise the enormous gains in productivity provided by electronic access.

Conclusion

'Independence' tends to get confined to what a given system is prepared to offer students, to describe those activities which cannot be regulated tightly but which require self-disciplined and unsupervised effort on the part of students still aiming at system goals. By contrast, 'syllabus independence' opens the possibility of learners becoming much more autonomous, and being able to escape the often artificial constraints of courses offered in a formal university setting. Syllabuses are constrained by professional considerations of what counts as effective teaching and assessment, notions of 'levels' of attainment, 'quality' of provision, 'standards' of assessment and the market for credentials. Students obviously have to accept these constraints when undertaking their academic apprenticeships and acquiring their credentials, but it is right to insist that there are other purposes for education, other goals and other rewards.

The UKOU in the 1970s and 1980s marked the high point of a project to offer total design for an educational environment, and, significantly, the project involved controlled access to educational works, a kind of purpose-built partial library to support course goals and activities. Syllabus independence requires a full library, and electronic technology offers the most exciting access to educational work. However, releasing new students into a proper library, whether housed in a building or on a server, can produce confusion and dependence again unless the skills needed to find personal routes through the imaginarium are also provided.

The future of independent learning in its full sense depends on a judicious combination of new technology and the old skills of teaching, guiding and organising learners both to track down what they are seeking, and to glimpse new possibilities and expanding horizons.

References

Arksey, H. and Harris, D. (2007) *How to Succeed in Your Social Science Degree.* London: Sage.

Bentham, J. (1983) 'Essay on nomenclature and classification'. In *Chrestomathia: the collected works of Jeremy Bentham*, edited by Smith, M. and Burston, W. Oxford: Clarendon Press.

Bernstein, B. (1971) 'On the classification and framing of educational knowledge'. In Young, M. (ed.) *Knowledge and Control: new directions for the sociology of education.* London: Heinemann.

Bourdieu, P., Passeron, J.-C. and Saint Martin, M. (1996) *Academic Discourse: linguistic misunderstanding and professorial power.* Cambridge: Polity Press.

Habermas, J. (1979) *Communication and the Evolution of Society.* London: Heinemann.

Harris, D. (1987) *Openness and Closure in Distance Education.* Barcombe: The Falmer Press.

Harris, D. (2004) *Key Concepts in Leisure Studies.* London: Sage.

HMSO (1969) *The Open University.* Report of the Planning Committee to the Secretary of State for Education and Science. London: HMSO.

Hoult, D. (1975) 'The Open University: its origins and establishment September 1967–June 1969'. Unpublished MEd thesis, University of Hull.

Lewis, B. (1971) 'Course production at the Open University 1: Some basic problems'. *British Journal of Educational Technology*, 2 (1), 4–13.

Lewis, B. and Cook, J. (1969) 'Towards a theory of telling'. *International Journal of Man–Machine Studies*, 1 (2), 129–76.

Pask, G. and Scott, B. (1973) 'CASTE: a system for exhibiting iLearning strategies and regulating uncertainties'. *International Journal of Man–Machine Studies*, 5 (1), 17–52.

Riley, J. (1984) 'The problem of drafting distance education materials'. *British Journal of Educational Technology*, 15 (3), 205–26.

Tunstall, J. (ed.) (1974) *The Open University Opens*. London: Routledge.

Libraries in the information society: cooperation and identity

Bas Savenije

Introduction

Like most European countries, the Netherlands has ambitious targets for the knowledge society. In a knowledge-based society, economic growth, instead of being generated by the traditional production factor of labour, is generated by knowledge. Three elements are of fundamental importance within this development: the (financial) investment in knowledge; education and training standards; and innovative capabilities. A further essential aspect is that knowledge must be entrenched in society in the broadest sense. Libraries and information professionals traditionally play an important role in this respect. Currently, the Netherlands faces significant challenges in meeting its formulated objectives for the knowledge society. Likewise, there are considerable gaps in terms of the availability and sharing of knowledge for society at large.

Culture, as much as knowledge, makes an important contribution to the process of innovating society. Digitisation enables new forms of cultural participation. Information literacy and media savvy are an important requirement for citizens to function purposefully in the new reality that is created by digitisation and in which media have become ubiquitous and intertwined. A national culture policy is needed to ensure that all citizens are included as cultural participants in society. Key elements include participation in amateur arts, anchoring culture in the education system and improving the accessibility of the arts (Ministerie van Onderwijs, Cultuur & Wetenschap, 2007). Libraries have a role to play in this.

As in many countries, the Dutch library system is very much decentralised, in the sense that it is funded by various agencies and there is limited cooperation. The present situation is seen as an impediment in terms of the library system's ability to fulfil the role one would expect it to have in an information society. This chapter explains why it is necessary to strengthen cooperation and describes how this is currently being pursued within the Dutch library system through the creation of a national infrastructure.

The Dutch library system

In the Netherlands, there are three categories of libraries that are available to the public: public libraries, the Koninklijke Bibliotheek (KB) (National Library of the Netherlands) and the university libraries. A description of these three categories is given below.

Public libraries

The first public libraries in the Netherlands were established by private initiatives at the beginning of the 20th century. At that time the majority of public libraries were in the cities. However, after the Second World War large regional libraries known as *Provinciale Bibliotheekcentrales* were set up to support the smaller municipalities in the provision of library services. Traditionally, the social function of the public libraries was to support the fundamental values of constitutional democracy: freedom and equality. It is the duty of government to encourage diversity (of information supply, reflecting a range of opinions and interests), independence (objective and independent service provision) and accessibility (physically accessible and affordable services) and to safeguard the quality of the public library system (cohesion and effectiveness of the library system). The social significance of the public library extends to the following domains (WRR, 2005):

- **democracy**: providing opportunity for citizens to become acquainted with a range of viewpoints to encourage individual opinion and social participation
- **education**: supporting lifelong learning, with ample attention to the development of reading, language and media education

- **culture**: stimulating cultural participation by actively presenting cultural heritage material and other cultural expressions, in conjunction with other cultural institutions
- **the economy**: providing working people with access to professional, academic or scientific knowledge and information
- **leisure time**: providing opportunities for people in their own time and own environment to read, listen to or view media, for example, by being able to borrow or digitally access books and other reference materials.

In many cases the administration of Dutch libraries is organised under a foundation structure. However, libraries are funded primarily by the public purse, while also raising contributions for the use of their services. Since 1987, the funding of public libraries has been fully decentralised and the municipalities and provinces are now responsible for all library funding and planning policy. Central government continues to be responsible for the cohesion, effectiveness and quality of the public library system. Because the national government does not earmark the funds that it allocates to the provinces and municipalities there is a degree of variation in terms of the resources available to libraries. As a result, there are notable differences with respect to the quality of the services provided. Among the public libraries, a handful are so-called 'Plus libraries': libraries that offer academic services to all regional libraries and their customers. For some years now, the government has used an additional stimulus subsidy to stimulate the libraries' innovation process on two levels:

- **restructuring**: creating basic services – libraries to serve the needs of multiple municipalities and provincial networks, and introducing a nationwide quality assurance system
- **library innovation and social (re)positioning**: improving and broadening the social scope of library services.

An important area of focus is the building of a digital public library. This facility is being developed jointly by a network of public libraries in order to establish a synchronised collective of national, regional and local digital services.

The provincial library organisations have been transformed into provincial library service organisations based within each province. These organisations are funded provincially, and quality can vary from one province to another.

The KB, National Library of the Netherlands

The KB was founded in 1798. Since 31 August 1993 it has been an autonomous administrative body, financed by the Ministry of Education, Culture and Science.

The main functions of the KB are:

- preservation, management, documentation and accessibility of the national cultural heritage
- deposit library for Dutch printed and electronic publications and the national bibliography
- research library for the history, language and culture of the Netherlands
- stimulating and coordinating a common information infrastructure for Dutch libraries
- centre of expertise for digitisation, preservation and digital preservation.

In contrast to most other national libraries, the KB archives Dutch publications on a voluntary basis; publishers are free to decide whether to donate publications to the KB. In many other countries, this deposit function is a mandatory one. This notwithstanding, some 95% of all Dutch publications are deposited in the KB. Between now and 2013, the KB will be working intensively to create a digital library that will offer everyone access to all digital and printed publications appearing in the Netherlands. This implies the increasing acquisition of digital-born publications, in parallel with the digitisation of the existing print collection. Another priority is the long-term archiving of digital information. Since 2002 the KB has had a depository (e-depot) for digital publications, and ensuring long-term archiving and access is one of its priorities. Also archived in the digital depository of the KB are digital periodicals from the large academic publishers, ensuring permanent access to international academic publications. In its role of national library, the KB, together with the public libraries and the university libraries, will work intensively in the years ahead on the improvement of the national infrastructure. In the area of cultural heritage material, the KB is working closely with other cultural institutions to build a shared infrastructure for digital cultural heritage.

University libraries

There are 13 universities in the Netherlands, each with its own university library. The purpose of the university libraries is to support the universities' primary processes: education and research. Thus, primarily they serve their own staff and students. The populations of the Dutch universities vary from 29,000 students and 2,800 academic staff (Utrecht) to 5,000 students and 1,200 academic staff (Wageningen). There are three technical universities and one agricultural university. The 13 university libraries work together in an informal consortium, UKB, which also includes the KB. Although negotiations take place on behalf of the consortium, none of its members can commit or sign on behalf of the consortium. Each university library is financed by its parent organisation, which, in turn, is financed by the Ministry of Education, Culture and Research.

There are differences in the ways that the libraries are organised and financed within the universities. The older and more comprehensive, more conventional universities had a decentralised library organisation during the last decades of the 20th century. As well as a central library, there were faculty libraries reporting not to the university librarian but to faculty management. All the conventional university libraries are currently involved, or have recently been involved, in a process of organisational centralisation. There are also differences in the ways that the universities finance their library services. Some libraries do not receive any budget allocations directly from university management, but have to 'collect' their resources in yearly negotiations with the faculties. Others are entirely centrally financed, and several hybrid forms of financing also exist. In most of the universities, however, funding for the acquisition of information resources (books, journals, databases etc.) is provided by the faculties, rather than directly by university management (Savenije, 2009). Unlike the public libraries, university libraries fulfil an archiving role: information resources, once acquired, remain available. The premises of the Dutch university libraries are accessible to non-members of the university community, who can apply for a library pass at a cost comparable to that of membership in a public library.

The need for cooperation

As is the case in other European countries, the Netherlands is facing considerable challenges in achieving its ambitions for the knowledge economy, for a variety of reasons. A precondition for the successful creation of a knowledge economy is a proper information infrastructure, providing educational institutions, companies and individuals with adequate access to available information sources. The present information infrastructure in the Netherlands is inadequate, and a citizen seeking reliable information will meet with various barriers. The infrastructure is very fragmented, and lack of cooperation between the different organisations means that a fee must be paid even for something as basic as merely consulting the national catalogue. Not only individuals, but also journalists, patients' organisations, educational institutions and medium and small businesses face similar obstacles.

The Dutch library system suffers from the fairly rigid distinctions that exist between the public libraries, on the one hand, and the university libraries, on the other. There is little central direction and cooperation. For information seekers who know little about how the library system works, it appears to be either a maze (it is not clear where information can be found) or a fortress (users feel that information is not available to them). The result is that people resort to Google. Googling is free and easy; however, it is often not possible to determine the quality of the information that is found. Libraries, on the other hand, select relevant information resources on behalf of their target groups and make them accessible. Nevertheless, it is difficult to gain an understanding of the actual totality of certified information, that is, information that one or more libraries have established to be reliable on the basis of source, author or creation procedure. And accessing those documents is usually even more difficult.

An additional obstacle is that certified information – in particular, information published in academic journals and periodicals – is expensive. Likewise, the 'marketing' of information, for example, by university libraries to external groups (non-academics), is hampered by the publishers, who restrict access to their own target groups and will not (or only very occasionally) cooperate with other groups, whereby a licence granted for payment may be extended to include externals (affiliated institutes, alumni). Electronic inter-library loan traffic is also resisted by the publishing industry. Furthermore, few people are aware that it is possible to request academic publications from a university library via a public library. The academic population appears to be well catered for by the university libraries, and usually knows where to find (and get) the required information. Others, however, face considerable problems in finding the information they need, and many are ill-served. This situation has been identified by the Dutch Council for Culture:

Public libraries in the Netherlands are currently working on ... the construction of a collective, multilayered network collection uniting text, imagery and sound from a number of sub-collections. However, the public libraries have very limited digital *content* and in that respect are largely reliant on cooperation between the university libraries, the libraries of cultural heritage institutions, the National Library (KB) and many other, related institutions, such as the National Archives, the Dutch Literature Museum, and the Digital Library for Dutch Literature. As more digital material becomes available, greater synergy between institutions not only becomes *possible*, but, moreover, is *necessary*. Especially in the digital domain, there is a need to integrate services, so that people no longer have to go door-knocking to many different institutions ... (Raad voor Cultuur, 2007)

The Council for Culture considers the establishment of a broad, primary infrastructure offering free public access to all available resources of culture and information as both a logical and a necessary step in the process of library innovation. To build a 'collection infrastructure' of this nature will require intra- and inter-sector synergy and harmonisation, both between public libraries and between the various library groups (Raad voor Cultuur, 2007). Lorcan Dempsey (2006) has described a comparable situation in the United States: lack of integration increases transaction costs. By integration, Dempsey means integration within processes (there are many discovery options, for example) and between processes (the processes are not always seamlessly connected):

- **Discover:** the discovery experience is a fragmented one. A user has a range of discovery tools available and may not always know which is the most suitable.

- **Locate:** having identified an item of interest, a user needs to find a service that will supply it.

- **Request:** this is another transaction, which may involve one or more steps.

- **Deliver:** again, several potential options exist for resource delivery, which may involve more or less difficulty depending on how the delivery options are presented and on the disposition of supplier and user. (Dempsey, 2006)

The picture outlined above contrasts sharply with the ambitions of the Dutch government in the context of the knowledge economy. Knowledge should be easily accessible to the entire Dutch community, and that includes individuals as well as organisations. Information professionals, who want to work on the basis of a demand-focused approach, find themselves faced with a daunting task. People are unaware of what information is available, or where it can be found: the full array of the information supply is so fragmented that the obstacles for users are simply too many. Once a full view has been created of the totality of the information supply, a better articulated information demand will develop and this will create a basis for interaction between information requesters and providers (Savenije, 2008).

With regard to books, some significant progress has already been made. The Dutch university libraries have a tradition of cooperation in infrastructure. PICA (Project for Integrated Catalogue Automation) was formed in 1969 and soon became a foundation for academic libraries in the Netherlands, but is now part of the Online Computer Library Center (OCLC). As the Dutch organisation for library automation, PICA was responsible for a national catalogue in which most of the university libraries and also the larger public libraries participated. Connected with this catalogue was a system for inter-library loans (Bossers, 2005).

These efforts are not enough, however. The need for access to up-to-the-minute information and the speed of communication drives the demand for digital information at ever higher speeds. Clearly, the current infrastructure falls short of meeting that demand. Recently there has been an improvement in this situation. At the initiative of the Ministry of Education, Culture and Science, an innovation process has been set in motion within the public library system that relies on central direction. In this context, the necessary cooperation with university libraries is a matter that requires attention. Also, the university libraries and the KB (united in the UKB) have emphasised the necessity of increased cooperation between libraries in planning longer-term policies.

With respect to digital information, the following current status can be observed:

- The public libraries offer a minimum of content that is accessible from the private home.

- All university libraries are increasingly making the same information available.

- Public library members, the secondary education system, professional education and the business community all want to access academic publications, but the average Dutch person is not aware of how he/she can access the information.

- Essentially, we all want access to all information, but we accept that the conditions of access may be different for different target groups.

The conclusion is very clear: the creation of a common digital library in the Netherlands must be pursued – the question being how to design it in the most efficient, customer-oriented manner. For this, it will be necessary to work together closely, across the traditional boundaries.

Towards a digital library of the Netherlands

It is an illusion to think that libraries could become *the* information portal for the Dutch population, the website everybody would use as the starting point of any information search. But why would the libraries even wish to pursue that ambition? Booking a holiday or a flight, finding a hotel, checking the opening hours of a museum or the match schedule of your favourite football club are all quite basic actions and one would hardly expect the libraries to offer such services. However, it becomes a little more complicated when, for example, you are searching for certain medical information. Family doctors and even specialists are increasingly advising their patients to check the Internet to find out more about their illness. Clearly, this type of information must be reliable. The family doctors themselves would probably find it helpful to have access to scientific publications, as would organised patients' groups. When looking for information – historical information, for example – it is important to have an understanding of the reliability of that information. Google cannot deliver here, because it does not select information. Libraries, on the other hand, do select, and this is where they provide added value. Anyone seeking information would benefit from a collective and integrated library and archives information resource that would enable the user, in a single search, to search the totality of information that has been selected by the Dutch libraries and archiving institutions as being relevant and of sufficient quality. A collective, integrated information supply needs to be presented in a user-friendly manner, with a clear overview of all the available information: a one-stop search, in other words, and one that matches a Google-style service in terms of user convenience. Various services are currently available that provide certified information selection in specific fields. However, these cover particular, limited areas only and, unless they are provided by a library, in most cases charge a fee. Many libraries select and certify their information resources, but do so only for their own target groups.

It is not difficult to imagine how the sub-processes 'discover' and 'locate' could be improved. By providing integrated public access to all publicly funded library services, anyone could obtain an overview (at no cost) of the availability in any area of information of a reputable quality. Once the searcher decided that he or she wished to obtain the information, there would normally be a charge. Such a system would need to provide an indication of the various options for acquiring information (such as 'Go to the library nearest to you'; 'Register with your public library for inter-library loans', along with advice of anticipated delivery time and cost; 'Use enclosed form to request direct digital delivery', again, specifying delivery time and cost.) The customer would choose the relevant option. It might not always be very easy actually to obtain the information. In such cases a 'Help' function should be available (for consultation either digitally or by telephone), referring the user, for example, to the local public library.

This type of service could be realised even within the business models currently existing in the information sector. It may be noted that, once the public develops a clear view of the information supply, this will start to generate requests, possibly leading to comments on the efficiency (or lack thereof) of the manner in which the requested information is made available. Associated costs are also likely to invite criticism. However, if we are to achieve substantial improvement in the subsequent processes of 'request' and 'deliver', it will be necessary to create a new, joint infrastructure. As described above, for printed materials a national catalogue has been available for many years in which the National Library, the university libraries and the large public libraries disclose their collections. This national catalogue is also linked to a system of inter-library traffic and it could be extended to include the collections of those public libraries not currently participating in it. The network of public libraries is currently working on this, with financial support from central government. The intention is to create a new structure that will not only include the catalogue but will also offer possibilities for providing additional services, such as user-generated content, book cover scans, and so on.

With respect to digital information resources, the challenge is greater. Currently, the public libraries have only limited digital content available to their users. The university libraries, on the other hand, have substantial digital collections, notably of academic periodicals. The licences under which this content is accessible are often contracted in the form of 'Big Deals': agreements covering all digital content of a particular publisher, whereby termination of parts of the content is discouraged by pricing. Direct digital supply to persons not covered under the licence is not permitted: the requested article must, in such cases, be printed first and then scanned in order to be forwarded digitally. With national standard rates of, on average, around €10 per article, this is a highly cumbersome procedure that does not recover its costs and is consequently discouraged. Negotiations are currently taking place with several large publishers with a view to allowing one or more libraries to make digital delivery direct, on the proviso that commercial customers are excluded from the service.

In order to build a national infrastructure, it is necessary to create a publicly accessible database of all digital content offered to users by publicly accessible libraries. This database must also be accessible via all current search engines. Negotiations are currently in progress between the public libraries, the university libraries and the KB to discuss this. The discussions are organised by a steering group in which all the relevant parties are participants. In this context, it is relevant to note that the KB owns and operates a digital depository for the archiving of all current and future digital content published in the Netherlands. In addition, the KB archives digital articles from a large number of publishers of academic journals and periodicals in its digital depository. Thus, the KB has assured the future availability of all the digital information resources that are relevant to Dutch libraries.

With respect to the database containing the metadata, connection to the KB's digital depository is already possible. This provision could be used in the near future for delivery of material to those who are not covered under a licence agreement and who can access the websites of the various publishers only upon payment of a relatively high fee (e.g. €30). The KB plans to conduct a pilot for this in the near future, including a large number of journals and periodicals from Elsevier Science. Thus, two databases will be created for metadata: one for printed material, and another for digital material. The intention is to create a single search function that will enable users to simultaneously search either type of file. An important requirement of this search function is that it must be able to select and organise results on relevance and within a particular context. The search function could be enhanced by adding specific parameters based on the user's personal interests profile to generate a personalised search outcome. It is conceivable that a number of libraries will decide to use a shared search system. This is actually already envisaged by the public libraries, and similar joint initiatives are currently being undertaken by university libraries. It is, however, not a precondition. The infrastructure can be represented schematically as in Figure 14.1. Once a structure as outlined in Figure 14.1 is operational, cooperation can be further extended.

The common catalogue will effectively render redundant the need for every library to maintain its own catalogue. Furthermore, it will make it possible to create a common subscribers' file, e.g. one for the public library system and one for the university libraries. Similarly, a collective library pass can be introduced. A possible next step is replacing the existing management systems within the libraries (cataloguing, acquisition, circulation) with a central system, with resulting significant cost savings. Within such a central system it would still be possible for the individual libraries to set or maintain their own presentation to their target groups, or to include specific additional services. However, an efficiency change of this magnitude is not to be expected in the short term. A second area in which expansion is possible is content. At present, the public libraries are jointly purchasing digital content to only a limited extent. The university libraries are doing this on a much larger scale. As

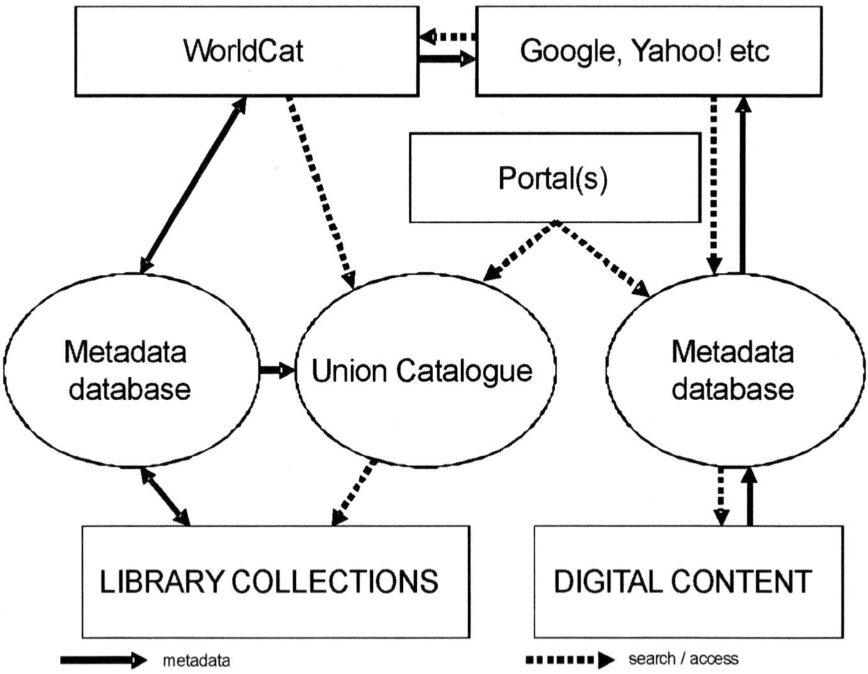

Figure 14.1 Schematic infrastructure of a shared search system

noted above, the current broad licensing agreements of the universities could be extended to include digital document delivery or pay-per-view for those not directly covered under the licence agreement. This would effectively create a national licence: an information supply accessible to all, possibly on varying terms (direct access, pay-per-view, and at different rates, e.g. profit versus not-for-profit).

It is important, furthermore, that the new infrastructure should also provide access to all freely available content. First, this concerns Open Access information resources: journals and periodicals published via the Directory of Open Access Journals, as well as repositories containing the freely accessible publications of academic institutions. Second, there is digitised heritage material: scans of printed works, at least those covering all materials not subject to copyright. Over time, links could be established between the holdings of different heritage institutions: archives, photos, films and museum materials. Thus, it would be possible to meet the ever-increasing expectations of users, which are placing such a significant demand on libraries' investment capabilities, and to achieve the following aims: improved availability, stronger cooperation and interoperability, reduced overlap and assured long-term availability of heritage material. The result, for many libraries, would be reflected in improvements over the current situation in terms of service provision, and in cost reductions for all parties concerned, as compared to the current situation.

Conclusion: changing roles in a network of organisations

The previous section outlined the development of a single digital library for the Netherlands to which every Dutch citizen would have access, either from home or from work, albeit under varying conditions. Realising such a joint information infrastructure will require effort on the part of all the parties involved (public libraries, academic libraries, the KB) in the areas of expertise, content (including cultural heritage), technology and administration. Some type of management structure will have to be designed for the joint infrastructure. This does not, however, mean that we are heading for a system in which every user gets identical services. Libraries will have to take into account the fact that there are different user communities, such as:

- scholars, differentiated by discipline
- students and lecturers, differentiated by education level and branch of studies
- professionals, such as doctors, pharmacists, lawyers, management consultants
- interest groups, such as patients' associations and political groups
- local communities, such as community committees.

The services and activities of the libraries may well differ. Academic and public libraries may present themselves by adjusting their services to specific target groups: by offering additional content relevant exclusively to these groups (for instance semi-finished products), by offering their own presentation of the content (depending on the online behaviour of the target group) and by adapting their services to the wishes and working methods of the target group. In addition, some activities will be location based, aimed at the institution's own target groups. Successful examples include the Amsterdam Public Library, with its wealth of cultural activities, and the Utrecht University Library at the Uithof, which has developed into a cultural centre on that campus. It is evident that the KB is well placed to play a coordinating and facilitating role, and in doing so could carry out an essential part of its task under the law:

> As the national library, the Koninklijke Bibliotheek is active in the areas of the library system and information provision ...
>
> At any rate ... it promotes the creation and maintenance of national facilities in the areas mentioned above. (Article 1.5 of the Higher Education and Research Act)

Through its digital repository, the KB could play an important role in the national infrastructure. This does not however, imply that every citizen should approach the KB to find the information he or she required. Local libraries have their own target groups, and the members of these target groups will have easier access to their own libraries. Thus, the digital repository of the KB would be part of the common back office and each library would serve as a front office to its own target group. Public libraries might serve as helpdesks, making research information accessible to their members. Of course, they will have to meet their local responsibilities as well, by offering differentiated services and location-based activities to their specific target groups. The integration of services relating to education and research processes will pose an important challenge to academic libraries. Since the differences between disciplines are more substantial than those between individual institutions, a more discipline-oriented cooperation between the library institutions will be required. This might be achieved through provision of additional services for local target groups, whether location based or not.

At the moment, the quality of a library is determined to a large extent by the content it makes available and by the infrastructure of its services. Since these elements are increasingly shared, content and infrastructure will hardly be discriminating factors in the future. The manner in which libraries succeed in targeting services to their own groups will be of vital importance. In the future, the quality of a library's staff and its facilities will determine the quality differences, and libraries will have to stress their distinctive features in this respect. But this is not all. As a consequence of developments in the areas of information and communications technology, many traditional boundaries will either blur or disappear. This applies, for instance, to the traditional demarcation lines in the information chain, such as those between libraries and publishers. The same applies to the relationships among libraries, and between libraries and other institutions in the cultural sector. All over the sector, the boundaries between the active institutions will fade, and cooperation within the network will become essential (Raad voor Cultuur, 2010). The identity and the significance of an institution will be determined less and less by its mission alone, as long as this mission is restricted to the institution's core business and focuses on its own identity. Increasingly, an institution's identity within a network of relevant institutions will be determined by the number and type of partners to which it is connected.

References

Bossers, A. (2005) *Samenwerkende bibliothecarissen en technische innovaties*. Leiden: OCLC PICA.

Dempsey, L. (2006) 'Libraries and the Long Tail: some thoughts about libraries in a network age'. *D-Lib Magazine*, 12 (4). Online at http://www.dlib.org/dlib/april06/dempsey/04dempsey.html.

Ministerie van Onderwijs, Cultuur & Wetenschap. (2007). *Kunst van Leven. Hoofdlijnen Cultuurbeleid*. Online at http://www. rijksoverheid.nl/documenten-en-publicaties/kamerstukken/2007/07/ 13/bijlage-kunst-van-leven-hoofdlijnen-cultuurbeleid.html.

Raad voor Cultuur. (2007) *Innoveren, Participeren!* Online at http://www.agendacultuurbeleid.nl.

Raad voor Cultuur. (2010) *Netwerken van Betekenis. Netwerktaken in digitale cultuur en media.* Online at http://www.cultuur.nl/adviezen_vervolg.php?id=4andadvies=6662.

Savenije, B. (2008) 'Panorama, een vergezicht met perspectief'. *Informatieprofessional*, 12 (10), 34–7.

Savenije, B. (2009) 'Digital library economics: the Dutch perspective'. In Baker, D. and Evans, W. (eds) *Digital Library Economics: an academic perspective.* Oxford: Chandos.

WRR (Wetenschappelijke Raad voor het Regeringsbeleid) (2005) *Focus op Functies: Uitdageingen voor een toekomstbestendig mediabeleid.* Den Haag, 2005.

Children's reading habits and attitudes

Sally Maynard

Introduction

The importance of reading undertaken in childhood cannot be overestimated; it provides a foundation for the acquisition of knowledge as well as for a love of reading for pleasure. The strength of this foundation depends not only on the encouragement children receive from parents and teachers, but also on the efforts of those who work in children's libraries. Indeed, the role played by libraries and librarians in providing access to reading material cannot be over-emphasised.

The significance of literacy and the development of reading skills are issues which have been reinforced by their becoming a priority at government level. Initiatives such as a second government-funded Year of Reading in 2008 and Reading for Life[1] are among those bringing the matter to the fore. Indeed, in the decade since 1999 there have been a number of high-profile, government-funded initiatives to promote reading and to improve literacy (see, for example Boys into Books,[2] Reading the Game,[3] Reading Connects[4] and the Summer Reading Challenge.[5] The importance of libraries and librarians in children's reading is clear in the last example; an impact research report on the Summer Reading Challenge 2009 (Kennedy and Bearne, 2009) found that children undertaking the challenge saw it 'as an overwhelmingly positive experience', although those who took part tended to be committed readers already. The report also showed that the Challenge helps to prevent the 'summer holiday dip' in reading motivation and attainment and 'boosts children's inclination to read at home ... of the children who participate'. Interestingly, the 'children who undertook the Summer Reading Challenge read far more books over the summer than those who are keen readers but who did not undertake the Challenge'. Evidence that the Summer Reading Challenge can help all children was found in the fact that children eligible for free school meals gained in motivation to read after the challenge, showing that practical help should be given to all children whose family circumstances make it difficult for them to participate.

The Summer Reading Challenge is, of course, delivered via public libraries and is most successful in cases where there are strong links between schools, teachers, librarians and children's and youth services. The impact research report found that librarians 'appreciate what the Summer Reading Challenge offers' (Kennedy and Bearne, 2009) and that 'they value the ways it encourages links between libraries and schools and provides an opportunity to engage with children and their reading'. This is a very important way in which libraries, and thus, children's librarians, are playing a significant part in children's reading.

Furthermore, it is clear that literacy and the development of reading skills amongst children is not just a national concern, but is also of significance in other countries, as evidenced in initiatives such as Reading All Over the World, 'a comparative study of reading achievement of ten-year-olds in 2001' (Twist et al., 2003). The study was conducted around the world under the auspices of the International Association for the Evaluation of Educational Achievement. In addition, studies of children's reading habits and opinions about reading have been carried out in several countries other than the UK. Examples include *Opening Doors to Children: Reading, Media and Public Library Use by Children in Six Canadian Cities* (Fasick et al., 2005); *What's the Story: the reading choices of young people in Ireland* (Children's Books Ireland, 2002); *Young Australians Reading: from keen to reluctant readers* (Woolcott Research Pty Ltd, 2002); and, emanating from Denmark, *The Precious Time* (Centre for Children's Literature, 2001) and *Children Read Books. Reading habits, reading ability, reading aloud* (Steffenson and Weinreich, 2000).

This chapter aims to discuss issues relating to the developments in children's reading habits and attitudes, the effects of new technologies on these reading habits and attitudes, and the role of the children's librarian.

Children's reading habits and attitudes

As a result of the importance of children developing reading skills, there is continuing interest in the UK in young people's views about reading and in their current reading habits. Consequently, there have been various attempts to investigate these issues, and reports of studies of children's reading often appear in the media. It is often suggested that children's interest in reading is in decline, and so a number of studies investigating children's reading have recently been undertaken, to explore such questions as:

- young people's 'attitudes towards reading, their reading preferences, and what would motivate them to read more' (Clark, Torsi and Strong, 2005)

- why some pupils choose to read and others do not (Clark and Foster, 2005)

- the resources for supporting literacy available to young people at home and how these relate to reading enjoyment, attitudes and attainment (Clark and Hawkins, 2010).

The research concurs in finding that, as suitably expressed by Clark, Torsi and Strong (2005), young people's reading is 'rich and diverse, but that the particulars vary according to gender or age'. These studies have drawn conclusions about various aspects related to the subject, including children's reading habits and attitudes, their perceptions of themselves as readers, their preferences for reading material and the involvement of their parents and other concerned adults in children's reading. Some of the results of these studies are discussed below, in an attempt to describe the current patterns evident in children's reading habits and attitudes.

Research has found that a love of reading is more important for children's educational success than is the socio-economic status or wealth of their family (Clark, Torsi and Strong, 2005). The general picture is of a majority of young people claiming to enjoy reading. For example, Clark, Osborne and Akerman (2008) found that 58% of their 1,600 Key Stage 2 and Key Stage 3 participants enjoyed reading 'either very much or quite a lot and rate themselves as proficient readers'. Around half of the 8,000 primary and secondary school participants in Clark and Foster's (2005) study claimed to enjoy reading 'either very much or quite a lot and rated themselves as proficient readers'. Furthermore, in a study for the Reading Champions Initiative, 61.2% of the 1,512 respondents enjoyed reading 'quite a lot or very much' (Clark, Torsi and Strong, 2005).

In the main, young people have positive attitudes towards reading, agreeing with statements suggesting that reading is important and disagreeing with statements that reading is boring or hard (Clark and

Foster, 2005; Clark, Torsi and Strong, 2005). Unsurprisingly, pupils with positive attitudes towards reading tend to report greater reading enjoyment and higher reading proficiency (Clark, Torsi and Strong, 2005; Clark, Osborne and Akerman, 2008). In addition, 'enthusiastic' readers are more likely to rate themselves as more proficient readers, and hold more positive attitudes towards reading. They also report reading outside school more frequently than do reluctant readers (Clark and Foster, 2005).

The generally accepted idea that girls are more likely to enjoy reading than boys has also been borne out (Clark, Osborne and Akerman, 2008; Clark, Torsi and Strong, 2005). Clark, Osborne and Akerman (2008) found that a higher proportion of girls than boys said that reading makes them feel calm and happy, and Clark and Foster (2005) concluded that, in line with the findings of previous studies, girls reported greater enjoyment of reading than boys and boys tended to hold more negative attitudes towards reading than girls. In addition, boys were more likely to believe that reading is boring, that they find it hard to find interesting books and that they only read at school. Boys were also more likely than girls to believe that reading is for girls (Clark, Torsi and Strong, 2005).

Studies continue to highlight the importance of the affective aspects of reading, such as motivation and attitudes, and the reader's self-concept. For example, Clark, Osborne and Akerman (2008) found that a great majority (71%) of participants in their study defined themselves as readers, although they also discovered that more girls than boys saw themselves as readers. In addition, the authors found that reading habits were greatly impacted on by whether or not the participants saw themselves as readers – those who rated themselves as more proficient and indicated reading more frequently outside of school. Furthermore, self-defined readers endorsed a wider variety of texts, with magazines, fiction books and websites being the more frequently read types of reading material.

With regard to the frequency of their reading, it seems that most young people read on a weekly basis, either every day or once/twice a week (Clark, Osborne and Akerman, 2008; Clark and Foster, 2005). They generally believe that this is a sufficient amount of reading (Clark and Foster, 2005). It is also clear that reading enjoyment declines with age, with indications that secondary pupils are more likely to believe that reading is boring, to claim that they have problems finding interesting books and to suggest that they read only at school (Clark, Torsi and Strong, 2005). More primary than secondary school pupils read outside school every day and they hold more positive attitudes towards reading, rating themselves to be more proficient readers than the secondary pupils (Clark and Foster, 2005). Another survey (Maynard et al., 2007) found that the proportion of children rating themselves as 'enthusiastic' readers (reading a lot, with pleasure) decreased as the children got older, although the proportion rating themselves as 'average' (reading an ordinary amount) did in fact increase with age.

The involvement of parents in children's reading

The importance of the home environment and of the level of support for reading that is received from the family is widely acknowledged. Parents are generally willing to encourage their children to read, being prepared to pay for any reading matter which might interest their offspring, for example, comics and magazines (Maynard et al., 2007). The great importance of parents and other family members has been reinforced by several studies and is highlighted in a National Literacy Trust report entitled *Young People's Reading: The importance of the home environment and family support* (Clark and Hawkins, 2010). This research found that those young readers who receive 'a lot of encouragement to read' from either parent are 'more likely to enjoy reading, to read frequently, to have positive attitudes towards reading and to believe that reading is important to succeed in life than young people who do not get any encouragement to read from their mother or father'. In addition, half of the participants who read above the expected level for their age noted that their parents read a lot, while only around a third who read below their expected level said that their parents read a lot (Clark and Hawkins, 2010). This is also related to actually seeing a parent reading and talking about reading. That is, young people who see their parents read a lot and who talk with their family about what they are reading are more likely to enjoy reading, to read frequently, to have positive attitudes towards reading and to believe that reading is important to success in life than are young people who do not see their mother or father read at all or who never talk with their family about reading (Clark and Hawkins, 2010). Another study found that most respondents 'would like to read to or discuss reading with their mothers, followed by their fathers and a friend'. Perhaps unsurprisingly, female participants were more likely to want to discuss books with their mothers and friends, while boys prefer to discuss books and reading with their father (Clark, Torsi and Strong, 2005). Disappointingly, Clark and Foster (2005) have found that more boys than girls never talk about reading with their family – this seems to concur with other findings relating to boys and reading, as compared to the experiences of girls. Female parents and carers are particularly important, with pupils stating that their mother encourages them to read more frequently than does their father (Clark and Foster). In another study, most of the pupils indicated that their mother encouraged them to read; considerably fewer claimed that their father did so (Clark, Osborne and Akerman, 2008). The situation with older children is less clear cut, since parents and others are more likely to read with younger children and, it seems, more likely to talk about reading with children of primary school age. Indeed, more primary than secondary pupils 'not only reported being encouraged to read by their mother and father but they also reported that their mother and father spend a lot of time reading' (Clark and Foster, 2005).

Preferences for reading materials

It has been found that children and young people enjoy reading a wide range of materials, with magazines, text messages and websites being particularly popular (Clark, Torsi and Strong, 2005), especially for reading outside school (Clark, Osborne and Akerman, 2008; Clark and Foster, 2005). Girls and boys preferred reading different types of materials and different types of fiction; findings which confirm those of earlier research (Clark and Foster, 2005). More girls than boys read magazines, e-mails, blogs/networking websites and poetry, while more boys than girls read newspapers, comics/graphic novels, websites and manuals/instructions (Clark, Osborne and Akerman, 2008; Clark, Torsi and Strong, 2005).

Although it is clear that new forms of reading (particularly via electronic means) are becoming increasingly popular, many children still claim to enjoy reading fiction. The specific types of fiction preferred are adventure, comedy and horror/ghost stories (Clark and Foster, 2005; Clark, Torsi and Strong, 2005). Girls are generally more likely than boys to read romance books, animal-related stories and poetry, while boys are more likely than girls to read science fiction, comedy and crime/detective stories (Clark, Torsi and Strong, 2005). A particular interest in series books has also been found, reflecting the success of examples such as the

Harry Potter books, Lemony Snicket's *Series of Unfortunate Events* and the Alex Rider books (Maynard et al., 2007). This same survey of reading found that series books were relatively popular with children of all ages, but that they increased in popularity with age.

Not surprisingly, children and young people of varying ages (and therefore differing developmental stages) like different reading materials; these partly reflect their age differences and their access to various electronic resources, such as computers (Clark and Foster, 2005). Furthermore, as the interests and experience of young people change with age, so do their preferences for reading matter (Maynard et al., 2007). For example, Clark, Torsi and Strong (2005) found that secondary pupils were significantly more likely than primary children to read websites, newspapers and magazines, while primary pupils were more likely to read jokes, non-fiction books and fiction. From the wealth of research investigating children's reading habits and attitudes, it is apparent that reading is one of many activities enjoyed by the children involved. It is perhaps fighting for its place amongst these other activities, and in some cases it is being usurped by the more visual technologies, particularly for the boys.

Effect of new technologies

It can therefore be seen that the current reading habits, and opinions towards reading, of young people are rich and diverse, a situation which has historically always been the case. However, concerns continue to be voiced relating to whether the increasing dominance of new technologies is having an effect. Such an effect might be felt either in the sense that children are more interested in activities undertaken on the new technologies than in reading, or that reading increasingly involves the use of electronic sources (UKLA, 2007). With 85% of respondents to Clark and Hawkins's study (2010) claiming to own a mobile phone or have access to one at home, and 84% also either owning a computer or having access to one at home, it is clear that new technologies are of increasing prominence. This can also be seen in the fact that children watch an average of 2.8 hours of television per day, and seven in ten 5- to 16-year-olds have their own television (Childwise, 2010). The very suggestion that reading is decreasing in popularity amongst young people has been tested by various surveys of reading in the last few years, often taking an earlier study by Whitehead et al. (1977), 'a comprehensive study of children's voluntary reading' (Benton, 1995), as a benchmark. Whitehead's study has been described as the 'first survey of children's voluntary reading using a stratified random sample so selected that its findings can justifiably be generalized to the total relevant populations of children in England and Wales' (Whitehead et al., 1977), and is therefore an influential research source. An example of the study's use as a benchmark can be found in Benton (1995), whose research involved surveying a representative sample of 789 Year 8 pupils (aged 12–13 years). The findings suggest that, among the participants in the study, there was no great decline in the reading of fiction overall, although a downward trend is noted between 1977 and 1995 in the amount of fiction being read by boys, and a slight increase in the amount being read by girls.

Similarly, Hall and Coles (1999) set out to investigate children's choices of leisure-reading matter, also intending to repeat the work carried out by Whitehead et al. (1977). They wished explicitly to investigate the reputed link between the rise of new technologies and the perceived decrease in reading, through the suggestion that watching television displaces time spent doing something else, and that reading was the activity being superseded. The authors found that children generally reported spending significantly more time watching television than reading. Furthermore, 'heavy' readers were more likely than others to have watched no television the previous evening, and an inverse relationship between the amount of television viewing and the amount of book reading was generally the case in this survey. However, the authors found that this relationship is not as simple as it may appear, and some children 'manage to accommodate a considerable amount of television viewing and a considerable amount of reading in their leisure time activities'. In addition, from the data obtained about the number of books that had been read by participants in their leisure time during the four weeks previous to the survey, it did not seem that the many other distractions on offer to children in the 1990s (but not in the 1970s) had led to an overall decline in the amount of book reading achieved since the Whitehead study. In addition, approximately 65% of participants viewed reading in a positive light, and around 96% owned their own books. With regard to the relationship between reading and computers, Hall and Coles (1999) asked participants about their computer use on the evening prior to the survey and 44.5% reported some such use. No significant relationship was found between the participants' reported use of a computer and whether or not they had been reading that same evening. The findings did not suggest that using a computer has any notably adverse effects on children's reading.

These studies are not particularly recent, however, and other, more current studies show conflicting results. For example, a study of the reading habits and attitudes of both adults and children (Book Marketing Ltd, 2000) involved a postal survey among a nationally representative sample of approximately 1,000 British households (2,500 adults and children). Among many other issues, the survey investigated the reasons why respondents either did not read books or did so only occasionally. The survey found that 17% of the children (aged up to 16 years) who answered the question gave the reason that they used electronic media instead. Notably, this was twice as many as the number of adults who mentioned using electronic media instead of reading books. In a study investigating which factors influence a child to read, McKool found that children who watch more television and take part in 'organised activities' do less voluntary reading. This supports the argument that activities such as watching television displace time that could be spent reading (McKool, 2007) and, as more advanced technologies appear, many may view the 'old fashioned' book increasingly negatively. Young people nowadays are often more comfortable sitting in front of a computer surfing the Web than they are sitting reading a book, with the suggestion being made that readers no longer have the concentration to read articles through to their conclusion (Kingsley, 2010).

These studies present a mixed picture of whether the distractions of new technologies are having a widespread effect on children's reading. As has been discussed above, although many children themselves are aware of the benefits of reading, they may not necessarily be motivated to read as a result. There is always a minority of pupils who believe that reading is boring and that they cannot find books that interest them (see, for example, Clark, Torsi and Strong, 2005). According to the National Literacy Trust, while self-defined 'non-readers' saw 'readers' as people who are likely to 'do well' and people who are 'intelligent', conversely they also thought that 'readers' are 'geeky' and 'boring' (National Literacy Trust, 2007). Since the majority of children do not start out with a reluctance to read, it seems that this attitude develops as children progress through school. There is plenty of evidence that children's attitudes towards reading become more negative with age (Stauffer, 2007), and even with the advantage of a home environment that is positive about reading a child may still become a reluctant reader at some stage in their life.

It has been suggested that the electronic environment is becoming more important to the growing number of children who do not respond well to traditional print media and who are reluctant to read. New technologies are now in existence which could change the way children (and indeed the rest of us) read. Electronic books (e-books) can potentially bridge the gap between printed media and other, more interactive forms of media. Indeed, with devices such as the Nintendo DS-Lite offering interactive books in the form of 'Flips',[6] it is clear that the difference between books and computer games is becoming increasingly blurred. Recent research shows that books read on electronic devices, such as the Kindle and the iPad, satisfy users as much as do printed books, despite reading speeds being generally slower (Nielsen, 2010). It seems that an increasing number of people are embracing e-readers and e-books; perhaps the biggest indication yet that a shift has taken place is the fact that Amazon's e-books began to outsell their hardback equivalents in 2010 (Teather, 2010). The recent release of the iPad is likely to see the further promotion of e-books, as has the launch of Amazon's new Kindle device and its recent availability on Amazon's UK website (Cellan-Jones, 2010). This has led to new and renewed predictions of 'traditional texts' eventually being 'superseded by electronic books'.[7]

The e-book represents the combination of the advantages of the printed book with the capabilities of the computer. As a result, the e-book is likely to be quite similar to a printed one in that it will have pages incorporating text and pictures, but it offers an extra dimension in that it has the potential to include additional media. Thus, the electronic book can add more to the text and pictures in terms of animation, sounds and a narrator (Maynard and McKnight, 2001), which may render it attractive to children, in particular those for whom visual literacy has become very significant. E-books may, therefore, have the power to bridge the gap between print and other media, and thereby encourage reading in those children who are reluctant readers (Maynard and McKnight, 1999). In fact, it can be argued that e-books allow users to do more than simply read the book because they offer increased levels of interactivity through features such as being able to check the meaning of a word simply by highlighting it.

Interactivity is one of the areas in which children might benefit from e-books. Warren (2010) discusses 'digital novels', which can combine 'text, audio, video, special effects and gaming'. Such a combination of media allows users to be involved in the story they are reading, which is likely to appeal to many children. Another study investigated whether an interactive e-book could improve literacy amongst kindergarten children and found that the book had the potential to improve the children's literacy as well as to amuse and motivate them. It is noteworthy that this research showed that further research investigating e-books and educational e-books is needed (Shamir and Korat, 2007). It is also clear that the interactivity of e-books is continually developing, as is the market for e-books and e-readers. Indeed, recent research in the USA has suggested that about a quarter of the children surveyed (all kinds of readers) had 'already read a book on a digital device, including computers and e-readers' and, interestingly, 57% aged between 9 and 17 years said they 'were interested in doing so' (Bosman, 2010). Conversely, however, there is evidence that screens are not replacing the book, and in fact reading on screen may often boost the reading of paper-based texts (Bearne, 2009). It can therefore be suggested that print and electronic media are likely to exist alongside one another, at least for the time being.

Role of children's librarians

It can thus be seen that the reading habits and attitudes of children and young people are in a state of flux. As mentioned above, the role played by libraries and librarians in providing access to reading material cannot be overemphasised, and this applies to all kinds of material, not just books. The current position of children's librarians, in both public and school libraries, seems to be to ensure that young readers use their libraries. Encouraging for librarians is the fact that, although figures show that issues of children's books (fiction and non-fiction) from public libraries in the UK fell by 20.4m (from 110.3m to 89.9m) between 1995/96 and 2005/6, the trend has been upward since 2003/4, with a 5.6% rise in issues of children's books in the past five years (from 88.6m in 2004/5 to 95.4m in 2008/9) (Creaser et al., 2006 and CIPFA, 2010a). Indeed, CIPFA has been moved to claim that children's fiction is a 'major growth area for UK libraries', with the number of issues of children's fiction books having risen 'significantly' in the UK (CIPFA, 2010b). This is a trend in the right direction for librarians, especially given the perceived decline in the importance of the library as a part of daily life, and in the light of predictions that public libraries will become obsolete within the next 20 years.[8] Considering the fact that children who use the library regularly are more likely to continue using it as adults, they are potentially both current and future users of public libraries; it is therefore reasonable to suggest that children and young people represent the public library's best hope for the future.

In addition, a large-scale survey undertaken in 2005 (Maynard et al., 2007) asked young people about where and from whom they borrowed books. The most popular option for all groups of respondents was the school classroom or library, followed by the local library; these results demonstrate that libraries remain the prime sources for book borrowing. This research was intended as a follow-up study to a survey undertaken nine years earlier, and the figures for 2005 were higher than for 1996 (Children's Literature Research Centre, 1996), with 76.1% of the girls and 78.6% of the boys often borrowing books from school and 46.9% of the girls and 42.4% of the boys often borrowing from the local library. This therefore suggests a general increase in borrowing from local libraries, and the authors note it to be difficult to state with any certainty why this should be the case. However, they also cite the initiatives that have been undertaken in an attempt to encourage young readers into public libraries, noting in particular the Bookstart scheme.[9] The scheme involved young babies across the UK receiving a free bag of books on or around their eight-month health check, usually accompanied by an invitation to join the local library. As noted by Maynard et al. (2007), the first babies to benefit from the scheme may now be beginning to show in the reading survey, and at the same time older siblings may well have been unwitting beneficiaries of this scheme, joining the library in the company of their baby brothers or sisters.

It is, of course, important for librarians to keep children and young people interested in continuing to use their services. Indeed, research undertaken on behalf of the Museums, Libraries and Archives Council (MLA), the Department for Culture, Media and Sport and the Laser Foundation has attempted to investigate how to 'develop full understanding and provide evidence for potential future strategies for the public library service that will result in increased usage amongst the 14–35 age group' (MLA, 2006). The study found that many libraries need to be 'modernised', a term which is notably difficult to define, but which refers to the quality of the stock and services. Perhaps most notably, the report notes the significance of a transformation in the range and quality of stock in terms of media, as well as in subject matter and currency. Additionally, modernisation is required in terms of increased accessibility via electronic means – both of these requirements reflect young people's interest in the new technologies. It seems that children's libraries will succeed if librarians attempt to keep the new technologies in mind (perhaps in the form of e-books), together with alternative reading material in the form of, for example, graphic novels, comics and magazines, as well as the more traditional printed forms of children's literature.

Conclusion

It can be seen that the importance of literacy and the development of reading skills is widely accepted, as is the involvement and encouragement of parents, teachers and children's librarians. This chapter has aimed to provide a picture of children's current reading habits and attitudes and the effects of new technologies on them, together with the importance and potential role of children's libraries.

Notes

1. http://www.summerreadingchallenge.org.uk/.
2. http://www.sla.org.uk/boys-into-books-overview.php.
3. http://www.literacytrust.org.uk/reading_the_game.
4. http://www.literacytrust.org.uk/reading_connects.
5. http://www.summerreadingchallenge.org.uk/.
6. http://nintendodsflips.com/.
7. http://www.bbc.co.uk/news/uk-scotland-edinburgh-east-fife-10652613.
8. http://news.bbc.co.uk/go/pr/fr/-/1/hi/uk/3661831.stm.
9. http://www.bookstart.co.uk.

References

Bearne, E. (2009) 'And what do you think happened next?' In Styles, M. and Arizpe, E. (eds) *Acts of Reading: teachers, text and childhood.* Stoke on Trent: Trentham Books.

Benton, P. (1995) 'Recipe fictions … literary fast food? Reading interests in Year 8,' *Oxford Review of Education*, 21 (1), 99–111.

Book Marketing Ltd. (2000) *Reading the Situation: book reading, buying and borrowing habits in Britain.* London: Book Marketing.

Bosman, J. (2010) 'In study, children cite appeal of digital reading', *New York Times*, 29 September. Online at http://www.nytimes.com/2010/09/29/books/29kids.html?_r=1andhp.

Cellan-Jones, R. (2010) 'E-books: Amazon bites back'. Online at http://www.bbc.co.uk/blogs/thereporters/rorycellanjones/2010/07/ebooks_amazon_bites_back.html.

Centre for Children's Literature. (2001) *Precious Time*. Copenhagen: Centre for Children's Literature.

CIPFA. (2010a) *Public Library Statistics 2008–09 Actuals*. London: Chartered Institute of Public Finance and Accountancy.

CIPFA. (2010b) 'Children's fiction is major growth area for UK libraries'. Chartered Institute of Public Finance and Accountancy. Online at http://www.cipfastats.net/.

Children's Books Ireland. (2002) *What's the Story: the reading choices of young people in Ireland*. Dublin: Children's Books Ireland.

Children's Literature Research Centre. (1996) *Young People's Reading at the End of the Century*. London: Roehampton Institute.

Childwise. (2010) 'Childwise monitor trends report 2010'. Online at http://www.childwise.co.uk/childwise-published-research-detail.asp?PUBLISH=53.

Clark, C. and Foster, A. (2005) *Children's and Young People's Reading Habits and Preferences: the who, what, why, where and when*. London: National Literacy Trust.

Clark, C. and Hawkins, L. (2010) *Young People's Reading: the importance of the home environment and family support*. London: National Literacy Trust.

Clark, C., Osborne, S. and Akerman, R. (2008) *Young People's Self-perceptions as Readers: an investigation including family, peer and school influences*. London: National Literacy Trust.

Clark, C., Torsi, S. and Strong, J. (2005) *Young People and Reading*. London: National Literacy Trust.

Creaser, C., Maynard, S. and White, S. (2006) *LISU Annual Library Statistics 2006*. Loughborough: LISU.

Fasick, A., Gagnon, A., Howarth, L. and Setterington, K. (2005) *Opening Doors to Children: reading, media and public library use by children in six Canadian cities*. Regina, SK: Regina Public Library.

Hall, C. and Coles, M. (1999) *Children's Reading Choices*. London: Routledge.

Kennedy, R. and Bearne, E. (2009) *Summer Reading Challenge 2009: impact research report*. London: UKLA. Online at http://www.readingagency.org.uk/children/summer-reading-challenge/.

Kingsley, P. (2010) 'The art of slow reading', *Guardian*, 15 July. Online at http://www.guardian.co.uk/books/2010/jul/15/slow-reading.

McKool, S. (2007) 'Factors that influence the decision to read: an investigation of fifth grade students' out-of-school reading habits'. *Reading Improvement*, 44 (3), 111–31.

Maynard, S. and McKnight, C. (1999) 'Children's classics in the electronic medium', *The Lion and the Unicorn*, 23 (2), 184–201.

Maynard, S. and McKnight, C. (2001) 'Children's comprehension of electronic books: an empirical study', *New Review of Children's Literature and Librarianship*, 7, 29–53.

Maynard S., MacKay, S., Smyth, F. and Reynolds, K. (2007) *Young People's Reading in 2005: the second study of young people's reading habits*. London: Roehampton University.

MLA. (2006) *A Research Study of 14–35 Year Olds for the Future Development of Public Libraries*. London: Museums, Libraries and Archives Council.

National Literacy Trust. (2007) *Demystifying the Reluctant Reader*. London: National Literacy Trust. Online at http://www.literacytrust. org.uk/research/nlt_research/269_demystifying_the_reluctant_reader.

Nielsen, J. (2010) 'iPad and Kindle reading speeds'. Online at http://www.useit.com/alertbox/ipad-kindle-reading.html.

Shamir, A. and Korat, O. (2007) 'Developing an educational e-book for fostering kindergarten children's emergent literacy', *Computers in the Schools*, 24 (1), 125–43.

Stauffer, S. (2007) 'Developing children's interest in reading', *Library Trends*, 56 (2), 402–22.

Steffenson, A. and Weinreich, T. (2000) *Children Read Books. Reading habits, reading ability, reading aloud*. Copenhagen: Centre for Children's Literature.

Teather, D. (2010) 'Amazon's eBook milestone: digital sales outstrip hardbacks for the first time in US'. *Guardian*, 20 July. Online at http://www.guardian.co.uk/books/2010/jul/20/amazon-ebook-digital-sales-hardbacks-us?INTCMP=SRCH.

Twist, L., Sainsbury, M., Woodthorpe, A. and Whetton, C. (2003) *Reading All Over the World*. London: NFER.

UKLA. (2007) *Reading on Screen*. Leicester: United Kingdom Literacy Association.

Warren, J. (2010) 'The progression of digital publishing: innovation and the e-volution of e-books', *The International Journal of the Book*, 7 (4), 37–53.

Whitehead, F., Capey, A.C., Maddren, W. and Wellings, A. (1977) *Children and Their Books*. London: Macmillan.

Woolcott Research Pty Ltd (2002) *Young Australians Reading: from keen to reluctant readers*. Prepared for the Australian Centre for Youth Literature and the Audience and Market Development Division of the Australia Council. Online at http://www.australiacouncil.gov.au/research/literature/reports_and_publications/young_australians_reading.

16

The user of tomorrow: young people and the future of library provision

Judith Elkin

Introduction

The debate about the future of libraries in an era of sophisticated technology is well covered elsewhere in this volume. But what are the implications for children? What traditional or new literacy skills might they require for the future? What might libraries for children and young people look like tomorrow? This chapter attempts to crystal-gaze, with the child in mind. It will look at the importance of reading and literacy in a future society where the child will need every opportunity to help it survive in an ever more demanding technological environment. It will look at how libraries might cater for the many and varied future needs of the child and will conclude by looking at recent examples of new public libraries in the UK to see how they are planning to serve the needs of children and young people. The focus will be on the recently opened Newcastle Public Library and two forthcoming libraries, currently under construction: Worcester Library and History Centre and the Library of Birmingham, also referred to in Chapter 3 by John Dolan.

Reading and literacy

Many eloquent writers have considered why reading is important:

> Reading is not necessary to our survival, if by survival we mean eating and staying warm. It is necessary to our larger survival, however, to an enriched, aware life in which we exercise some

measure of control over our well-being, our creativity and our connection to everything around us. (Gold, 1990)

We read to understand, or to begin to understand. ... Reading, almost as much as breathing, is our essential function. (Manguel, 1996)

Reading still has a transformational power. For the older generation, this will largely mean reading in printed form. For them, the digital world will never sound the death knell of books, particularly for leisure reading. At the time of writing, there is no doubt that the Internet has revolutionised access to information. However, the jury is still out on the value of e-books, particularly to replace adult and children's books. The Kindle, the Sony Reader and others appear to have had little impact on the children's book market. The number of children's authors opting out of the proposed Google Book Settlement may well prove to be significant (Davies, 2010).

What impact will the digital future have on reading and literacy? Will the unfettered growth of texting and Twittering amongst (particularly) the young affect how children need to learn to read, or will such innovations just require different ways of communicating, with new languages, as part of a broader spectrum of communication skills? The Organisation for Economic Cooperation and Development (OECD) report *Reading for Change* forefronts the importance of literacy in a global context:

Reading literacy is a dynamic rather than a static concept that needs to parallel changes in society and culture. The reading literacy needed for individual growth, economic participation and citizenship 20 years ago was different from what is expected today. ... Literacy is no longer considered an ability only acquired in childhood during the early years of schooling. Instead, it is viewed as an expanding set of knowledge, skills and strategies which individuals build on throughout life in various situations and through interaction with their peers and with the larger communities in which they participate. (OECD, 2002)

Writers have begun to explore the need for a more sophisticated approach to literacy, citing 'multiliteracies' as a requirement of the future:

The changes in work, public and private lives indicate that during our working lives we will be required to change tasks, 'multiskill' or change occupations, and each of these changes will require us to acquire new literacy skills and interact in different ways ... the changing technologies of our work, public and private lives mean the acquisition of literacies associated with these new technologies. ... Multiliteracies focus on the many modes of representation and forms of text that have been made available through multimedia and technological change. Therefore, being multiliterate requires not only the mastery of communication, but an ability to critically analyse, deconstruct, and re-construct a range of texts and other representational forms. (Anstey, 2002)

The Director of the Harvard University Library explores the case for books and libraries in today's digital environment:

A generation 'born digital' is 'always on', conversing everywhere on cell phones, tapping out instant messages, and networking in actual or virtual realities. The younger people you pass on the street or sit next to on the bus are simultaneously there and not there. They shake their shoulders and tap their feet to music audible only to them inside the cocoon of their digital systems. They seem to be wired differently from their elders, whose orientation to machines comes from another zone of the subconscious. ... And the library? It can look like the most archaic institution of all. Yet its past bodes well for its future, because libraries were never warehouses of books. They have always been and always will be centers of learning. Their central position in the world of learning makes them ideally suited to mediate between the printed and the digital modes of communication. Books, too, can accommodate both modes. Whether printed on paper or stored in servers, they embody knowledge and their authority derives a great deal more than the technology that went into them. (Darnton, 2009)

It would appear that, in a future technological world, people will require ever more effective and flexible reading skills. The fundamental skills of wide, effective reading and early literacy acquisition will remain paramount.

Children's reading and early literacy

Less attention has been given to future literacy skills acquisition and how teaching in schools might need to change. Bettina Hurlimann, writing 40 years ago, is much quoted for her view that:

> In this restless age of technology, when the emphasis is always on records of attainment and productivity, there is some danger of forgetting that a child does not require too much in the way of books. ... What he does need are the right books at the right time so that he may find in literature a true point of balance in an often disordered world. It is for us as parents or teachers, librarians or publishers, to recognize this need and to know how best, how most imaginatively, to fulfil it. (Hurlimann, 1967)

Prophetic in the late 1960s, this in many ways still holds good today, particularly for very young children and children on the threshold of learning to read. This view places children's literature as ever more critical in the child's educational, social, cultural and emotional development, with wide, diverse reading a critical part of the child's early life. Arts Council England reflects this view in the 21st century, while recognising the changing global context:

> We see children's literature as the touchstone for a healthy and sustainable literary culture. ... It affords the means by which children can dialogue with their futures, not only through the printed word, but also through children's literature's intimate connections with the visual arts and design, film and television, theatre and new technologies. Its value is private and public, cultural and artistic, and also social and economic. (Arts Council England, 2003)

The recent *1001 Children's Books You Must Read before You Grow Up* reinforces this:

> There is little that is more influential than the stories we read in childhood. From their meaning and their language come a welter of emotional experiences – and the words with which to express them that cannot easily be reached in any other way. Stories are places of enchantment, mystery, surprise, dread, and – above all –

consolation, and nowhere can they be found in richer abundance than in children's books. (Eccleshare, 2009).

Baroness Blackstone, in the preface for *Start with the Child*, the Chartered Institute of Library and Information Professionals' (CILIP) report on the future of library services for young people, emphasised the importance of good literacy skills:

> Society today is changing rapidly. Children and young people need to be equipped with the right skills to take up the opportunities, which are open to them and to deal with the challenges they face ... By making sure that our children and young people have good literacy skills, we are providing them with the foundations for future learning, enabling them to develop their own talents to lead fulfilling lives. (Blackstone, 2002)

Michael Rosen, former Children's Laureate, is passionate about the subject. He is outspoken about the need for reading and real books to be taken more seriously in schools and accepted as a priority by politicians:

> Children who read widely and often are school achievers. And they can get hold of abstract and complex ideas. Politicians know this. And they know that many children are not reading widely and often. But they do very little about it. (Rosen, 2009)

> At the heart of reading, writing, listening, speaking (and they're all interconnected, not discrete) are books. Books should be at the centre of the primary curriculum; real books produced by people with the sole intent to engage the interest, involvement and excitement of children ... ICT is not separate but should be integrated and used properly as part of reading, writing, thinking, speaking. (Rosen, 2010)

Story-teller Alec Williams is equally passionate about children's books and story-telling, particularly in today's context of texting and social networking:

> Stories ... grab and hold attention; they illuminate any subject; they play with language; they stir the emotions; they lift words off the page; they celebrate listening – and they're inside all of us, waiting to get out. ... In a world of texting and social networking sites,

speaking face-to-face can take second place to words and pictures, but all of us need to encounter good speech ... Storytelling is a basic human need. (Williams, 2009)

Acknowledging the political sensitivity of the topic, the National Literacy Trust has recently launched a Manifesto, to emphasise the importance of literacy, with four literacy challenges to government:

- ensure that every child develops the speaking and listening skills they need

- enable every parent to be their child's first and best teacher

- ensure that every pupil is a motivated reader, and uses their skills to interact in a digital age

- ensure every individual knows that literacy can change their life and bring new opportunities. (CILIP, 2009)

Libraries for children and young people

Such considerations continue to place libraries, both children's and school libraries, at the heart of education, with a focus on literacy and communication at the centre of learning. Early access to stories and to books remains essential to the child's pre-reading experience and needs reinforcing as they become sophisticated readers, learners and thinkers. The role of libraries is paramount in supporting this and ensuring equitable access to all, regardless of age, gender, race, wealth, physical or intellectual ability or geographical location.

Ten years ago, the UK Library and Information Commission (LIC) celebrated libraries as symbols of accessibility, neutrality, shared community and family values, discovery, opportunity and choice. It saw libraries as places of sanctuary, secure, risk-free social places welcoming to all; caring, helpful, supportive places where people met on equal terms. It viewed libraries as non-judgemental, non-competitive, non-accrediting places, gateways to knowledge; places to discover and delight in diversity (LIC, 2000). These sentiments were evidenced, with respect to libraries for children, by research for *A Place for Children* (Elkin and Kinnell, 2000). It found that libraries contributed to the child's reading development in many of the ways suggested above; they supported children's development, improved their reading skills and helped them to grow intellectually, socially, emotionally and culturally. They offered a welcoming, safe, socially inclusive place in which to read and a neutral ground for those disaffected from school. As well as providing access to books and other facilities, they were active in promoting reader development, supporting family reading and literacy groups, giving advice to parents, helping with home-educated children and encouraging love of books and reading.

The concept of libraries as safe, nurturing spaces for children has remained central to library thinking, particularly in areas of particular deprivation. It is also worth being reminded that children have a right to information under the 1989 UN Convention on the Rights of the Child:

> Wilful failure to respond to children's search for knowledge by states, churches, schools and libraries – even parent and community groups – effectively constitutes a violation of a major international agreement … the Convention provides a solid endorsement for libraries for children, when their choice of materials put on shelves or their unwillingness to apply powerful filtering software to Internet resources is challenged. The library as a browsable set of resources and access facilities has been used by children in many times and cultures as a kind of secret garden for the mind. Behind the walls of protection provided by librarians they have been able to pursue their personal quest for knowledge with little or no interference. The justification for the protection is stronger when we realize that it can be argued through from rights arising from the basic characteristics of the developing human mind. … By this reasoning, libraries and librarianship for children are not mere matters of resources and techniques, but a response to the very strongest human needs. (Sturges, 2009)

Professional children's and schools librarians

In parallel to providing some of the services mentioned above, children's and schools librarians have responded to the challenges brought about by the information age. Media and technology impact inevitably on the development of the child. Provision of multimedia, audiovisual and computer technology, in addition to the printed word, are the prerequisites for developing library services to children of the 21st century. Libraries now and in the future will continue to respond to established media and the emergence of new technologies through their collections and services.

The 2009 Public Libraries Authorities Conference looked at the future role of libraries and books for the child. Delegates widely endorsed the future role of library services for children and the need for librarians with an understanding of the child's reading and information needs. Miranda McKearney, Chief Executive of The Reading Agency, gave a rallying call to librarians:

> Children's librarians are people who believe in the power of literature to transform lives ... the nation needs what you, and you alone, can do. (McKearney, 2009)

The *Youth Library Review* in 2009 took as its theme the importance of children and young people's librarians in a changing world. The Chief Executive of CILIP, the late Bob McKee, was fulsome in his praise:

> Professional Librarians are an important part of the schools and children's workforce. Librarians help give children a love of reading and also help develop their information skills. ... This helps their educational attainment and stands them in good stead throughout their lives. ... More than any other sub-set of our profession, children's librarians engage with the literature and with authors, illustrators and publishers. ... We say that 'libraries change lives' but actually they don't. Libraries are brought to life by librarians and the interaction between librarians and users. It's the librarians who can change lives for the children and young people with whom they work. ... Ted Hughes wrote compellingly about the value of a library for a child. But the child needs a librarian to help them turn that key. (McKee, 2009)

At the time of writing (December 2010), the demand for statutory school libraries is gaining momentum, with a campaign to make the provision of school libraries (run by properly qualified staff) a statutory requirement.[1] It has drafted a set of entitlements that every school pupil should enjoy throughout their primary and secondary education. These entitlements encompass the fostering of a reading and information culture, promotion of independent learning and instilling the information literacy skills necessary for negotiating an increasingly complex information society:

Every child, at every stage, is entitled to:

- designated library staff able to encourage 'wider reading and reading for pleasure

- a 'skilled library practitioner' to teach pupils to handle 'information overload', lifelong learning and employers' demand for 'problem-solvers and independent thinkers'

- a safe library environment inside and outside school hours, with help, resources and advice

- high quality, wide-ranging, easily accessible resources to support the curriculum, carefully selected to suit their age, learning style and ability

- be valued as an individual, with reading materials 'exploited by a knowledgeable person' to support the whole person.

Every teaching team is entitled to a designated library professional who:

- understands the curriculum and their pastoral needs

- collaborates on curriculum planning and teaching

- works with other organizations within and beyond the school. (CILIP, 2010)

New libraries for children

Bearing all the above in mind, how are public libraries anticipating the future needs of children and young people? This section will look at how libraries for children and young people have featured in recent library developments, taking three innovative examples. The first, in Newcastle, was opened by the Queen in November 2009, to great acclaim. The other two, both under construction, in Worcester and Birmingham, have been welcomed as imaginative models for the future, not least in terms of high city-centre profiles, but also for overt partnership working. Worcester Library and History Centre is a public and academic partnership between the University of Worcester and Worcestershire County Council. Due to open in 2012, it will be the first joint public and university library to be designed and built from scratch in the UK. The Library of Birmingham is a partnership between the public library and a major city-centre theatre, Birmingham Repertory Theatre. It is due to open in 2013.

All three libraries have led a strong re-thinking and re-visioning of the role of libraries in the 21st century, in their respective cities and regions and following public consultation. Fascinatingly, all three, despite starting from different places, have focused on accessibility, transparency, flexibility, community, regeneration and partnership, melding new and traditional technologies throughout the service. All of them have placed a priority on children, families and education. They are all looking for new and efficient ways of working, to maximise the professionalisation of staff. They are all seen as significant economic regeneration drivers.

Newcastle City Library[2]

Newcastle's state-of-the-art public library was hailed by Andrew Motion as:

> A shining light and a beacon of what a library should be doing in the 21st century, a magnificent reminder of everything that libraries can offer their communities. (Motion, 2009 cited in Fay and Forster, 2010)

The library opened to the public on a Sunday in June 2009, as a symbolic statement emphasising the city's commitment to providing excellent, easily accessible and customer-focused services. Accessibility means being open outside traditional hours – as public libraries, in their early days, used to be! There were a number of design principles, which have all been well effected in the final building. These were:

- visibility, to ensure that the library had a high-profile street presence with two clearly visible entrances
- transparency, to ensure that the building, unlike its predecessor, should be transparent, with passers-by able to see into the building and be attracted by facilities and activities
- self-service, with 100% self-service, to free up staff for more supportive duties
- delight and inspiration, to put emphasis on a building that delighted and inspired everyone.

It was built as a private finance initiative (PFI), on time and on budget, by the Kajima Consortium, which included Ryder Architecture and

Tolent Construction. The result is a stunning six-storey, temperature-controlled glass-and-steel structure with a soaring atrium full of light, built on the site of the former 1960s building. It has been designed to take into account all of the prescribed priorities and enables a completely different way in which people can meet, study and work. The council and library staff's vision was that it should be the virtual living-room of the city. It has a large, colourful, vibrant children's library, as well as a 180-seat performance space, a café and a crèche. The whole building is self-service, with self-issue and self-return facilities.

It was also very clear that the new library should be a driver in developing a new type of library service across the city and the impetus for further service modification. One of the key features of the new library is the requirement for staff to work across all floors and services. This required a major programme of customer-service training and new staff roles and responsibilities. All staff are expected to be approachable, friendly and attentive and to have an awareness of the resources, range and types of material available and how to use them (Fay and Forster, 2010). The library has already won a number of building awards for accessibility and innovation. In the time since its opening, library use has doubled.

Worcester Library and History Centre[3]

Worcester Library and History Centre will be a landmark building, with a combination of indoor and outdoor spaces. It is situated adjacent to the River Severn and on the edge of the University of Worcester's new city-centre campus, with links (via a pedestrian bridge) to the city centre. It is being built by Galliford Try Investment consortium as a PFI project in a partnership between the University of Worcester and Worcestershire County Council. The library will be the symbol of shared learning, culture and information in a way that contributes uniquely to the regeneration of Worcester.

From early discussions, it was clear that the public and university libraries shared a vision, albeit often differently expressed, that could revitalise what is meant by lifelong learning for an entire community. Re-imagining the traditional view of libraries offered a way of welcoming the entire community, student or not, into a building that would offer experiences, access and services relevant and useful to them at different times of their lives. The concept of the library is that everyone, from babies and toddlers to teenagers, research students, those in need of information, community groups, undergraduates, people who want to experiment with media and those who just like reading, will find what they want under one roof, in a way that makes it accessible and appealing. For families who do not have computers or books and newspapers at home, the public library has always been a gateway to opportunity. But in this concept, it will literally be a step away from the university – it will draw people in to the 'university in the city'.

The design ensures that no one feels intimidated by what might otherwise be seen as an elitist structure. The building will be organised so that finding one's way is easy and intuitive, to make access to the enormous range of opportunities feel smooth. In addition to conventional services, the building will incorporate:

- a business library, leading-edge technology
- a place to experiment with media, research collections and archives
- exhibition space, rooms for seminars and community group meetings
- Business Advice Centre
- the city's Hub Customer Service Centre
- County Record Office
- County Historic Environment and Archaeology Service.

The site will include restaurants and retail outlets which complement the ethos of the building. Uniquely, it will all be shared, through a carefully developed partnership agreement.

It is in the area of children and young people that the shared expertise and commitment of the joint library is paramount. Worcestershire's Library Service has specialist children's librarians and an exciting range of children's activities, particularly in the field of reader development. The University works with professionals in delivering education and services to children across a number of areas: teaching, social care, health and creative development. The collections and services of the public and academic libraries will be entirely integrated, with the synergy and energy from both offering an unmatched opportunity to enrich the service to children. The children's zone will be bright and inviting, with space for quiet work, space for noisy and creative activity, space for story-telling, performance, computers, as well as space for study, school groups and clubs. Having the Record Office and History Centre as well as the Archaeological Services in the same building will provide a huge potential for multidisciplinary work and creative opportunities. Working with students from different disciplines will be a further, unusual opportunity for trainee teachers, nurses, social workers and play leaders. Teachers, parents and carers will have access to the print and electronic resources from the University. Vice Chancellor Professor David Green is fulsome in his approval:

> It will be a wonderful, transformative facility for students and staff at the University as well as the wider community. ... It will be a true engine of educational inclusion and an inspiring bridge to the world of culture and learning. At its heart will be the first class children's library in which our students training to be teachers and educationalists will work and study purposefully alongside children, their teachers and parents. The library will provide much enhanced facilities for study, scholarship and research and will be a magnet for our students and their potential successors from local schools, colleges and the community as a whole. Colleagues with interests in history and cultural and social development will gain considerable new resources thanks to the accessibility and proximity of the archive. (Green, 2009)

Library of Birmingham[4]

The new Library of Birmingham, to be built in the city's Centenary Square, is also viewed as a flagship regeneration project. Reflecting a new opportunity for a cultural partnership, the library will be joined to Birmingham Repertory Theatre at ground and mezzanine levels and will share the foyer, bars, restaurants and a new 300-seat studio theatre. The strategic agenda for the library has three distinct themes, which resonate with the city's strategic vision: building the knowledge economy; investing in children, young people and families; promoting community culture and heritage. The library aims to set new standards for libraries in the 21st century, creating an exceptional resource for learning, information and culture. It will be a community hub, reaching out to all parts of the city in an exchange of knowledge and ideas: a place to interact, a place to learn and study, and a place to meet and take part in activities and events for families, businesses, groups and individuals of all ages.

The library will be child and family friendly, inspire children and young people as future participants in the world economy; promote a love of reading and a need for literacy; encourage children and young people to develop skills and gain qualifications and foster lifelong learning. It is being designed to appeal to children, young people and families throughout, not, as with the current library, confined to a specific area. It will offer a flexible choice of learning settings and styles, with safe and welcoming spaces; stimulating, inviting and accessible learning environments with a range of resources across all media, including the latest interactive technologies; opportunities to explore and learn by discovery and opportunities to learn in different ways. The library will support parents and carers in helping their children, by providing an informal environment where they can share and learn together. A specialist children's library will provide reading for enjoyment, activity spaces, literacy support and a stimulating learning environment for children and young people. It will be a safe and welcoming space to go, a place to develop personal skills, with a wide range of fun and interesting things to do. A dedicated area for teenagers will be designed to include improved individual study space, areas for group working and discussion, more informal seating and the creation of an environment that is welcoming and inclusive and which encourages young people to follow their interests and achieve their full potential; greater provision of new interactive and immersive technologies to stimulate and attract new users. Birmingham's Assistant Director of Culture extols its virtues:

> Birmingham City Council has approved investment in a new Central Library: the Library of Birmingham. Such an exceptional corporate commitment to the value of culture in delivering physical, social and economic regeneration demands an ambition of the highest order. ... We aim to create the best library in the world. For such an investment the people of Birmingham deserve nothing less ... Integrated with Birmingham Repertory Theatre, the Library of Birmingham will be a unique centre for learning, information and culture. An enduring beacon for Birmingham, it will raise the City's international profile and deliver excellence to local communities. Accessible and welcoming to all, it will reach out to the most disadvantaged citizens. It will be a universal meeting place, a hub for the region, an engine for the knowledge economy. Through written, printed, audio, visual and interactive resources and technologies, the Library of Birmingham will link the people of Birmingham to the world. It will bring the world to the people of Birmingham. ... The Library is universal, accessible and inclusive. It will offer something to everyone in the community.

This cannot be said of traditional city-centre reference libraries, even the great ones. This will be a library both for the learned, and the learner. (Gambles 2009a)

Conclusion

Three new and very different libraries provide clear evidence that the future of libraries for children and young people is being re-visioned in exciting and innovative ways which fully integrate resources across all media with traditional, print-based resources. As Library of Birmingham champion Brian Gambles says:

> The book is and always will be central to the 'library experience', but it is not the book as commodity that interests me, but what we do with books. ... I want to continue to promote reading and literacy, but I also want the library to be a true 'knowledge centre'. Increasingly the raw material for this process is to be found in many media, not just books. (Gambles, 2009b)

Notes

1. http://www.thebookseller.com/news/gibbons-calls-school-libraries-be-made-statutory.html.
2. http://www.newcastle.gov.uk/core.nsf/a/librariesnewcitylibrary.
3. http://www.wlhc.org.uk.
4. http://www.birmingham.gov.uk/libraryofbirmingham.

References

Anstey, M. (2002) 'It's not all black and white: postmodern picture books and new literacies'. *Journal of Adolescent and Adult Literacy*, 45 (6), 444–57.

Arts Council England. (2003) *From Looking Glass to Spyglass: a consultation paper on children's literature*. London: Arts Council England.

Blackstone, T. (2002) 'Preface'. In *Start with the Child: report of the CILIP Working Group on library provision for children and young people*. London: CILIP.

CILIP (Chartered Institute of Library and Information Professionals). (2009) 'Importance of literacy still undersold, says Trust'. *Library and Information Update*, November, 7.

CILIP. (2010) 'CILIP: schools manifesto'. *Library and Information Update*, January/February, 9.

Darnton, R. (2009) *The Case for Books: past, present and future*. New York: Public Affairs.

Davies, C. (2010) 'Authors cry foul over rights grab'. *Guardian*, 1 February. Online at http://www.guardian.co.uk/books/2010/feb/01/authors-google-rights-grab-books.

Eccleshare, J. (2009) *1001 Children's Books You Must Read before You Grow Up*. London: Cassell Illustrated.

Elkin, J. and Kinnell, M. (2000) *A Place for Children: public libraries as a major force in children's reading*. British Library Research and Innovation Report 117. London: Library Association.

Fay, D. and Forster, A. (2010) 'Newcastle's shining light'. *Public Library Journal*, 25 (1), 2–4.

Gambles, B. (2009a) 'Aiming high: the Library of Birmingham 2013'. *Open Access* (newsletter of the West Midlands branch of CILIP), 52 (2).

Gambles, B. (2009b) 'The vision takes shape'. *Library and Information Gazette*, 24 April–7 May.

Gold, J. (1990) *Read for Your Life: literature as a life support system*. Ontario: Fitzhenry and Whiteside.

Green, D. (2009) *Vice Chancellor's Report to the University of Worcester Academic Board*, February 2009.

Hurlimann, B. (1967) *Three Centuries of Children's Books in Europe*. Translated and edited by B. Alderson. London: Oxford University Press.

LIC. (2000) *Libraries: the essence of inclusion*. London: Library and Information Commission.

Manguel, A. (1996) *A History of Reading*. London: Viking.

McKearney, M. (2009) 'A manifesto for change'. *Public Library Journal*, 24 (4), 7–8. Online at http://www.cilip.org.uk/get-involved/special-interest-groups/public/journal/24/Documents/PLJWinter09PLAForgan McKearneypp5–8.pdf.

McKee, B. (2009) 'Why we *are* important – children and young people's librarians in a changing world: turning the key'. *Youth Library Review*, 39 (5), 5–7. Online at http://www.cilip.org.uk/filedownloads library/groups/ylg/ylr%202009.pdf.

OECD. (2002) *Reading for Change: performance and engagement across countries, results from PISA 2000.* Paris: Organization for Economic Co-operation and Development.

Rosen, M. (2009) *Library and Information Update*, December, 5.

Rosen, M. (2010) Keynote Address at the *Children's Literature and Its Impact on Improving Writing Skills Conference*, Courtyard Theatre, Hereford, 26 January.

Sturges, P. (2009) 'Why is poo brown?' *Public Library Journal*, 24 (4), 15–18. Online at http://www.cilip.org.uk/get-involved/special-interest-groups/public/journal/24/Documents/PLJWinter09Sturgespp15–18.pdf.

Williams, A. (2009) 'The tell tale library'. *Public Library Journal*, 24 (4), 19–20.

17

Redefining the librarian

John Feather

Introduction

> Without knowing Mr Larkin, what do [you] call him? ... *Philip* he plainly is not, though *Larkin* is over-familiar too, suggesting a certain fellow footing. Being a librarian doesn't help; I've always found them close relatives of the walking dead. (Bennett, 1982)

No doubt Alan Bennett's tongue was firmly in his cheek when he wrote these lines – he has been and is a good friend to libraries – but his readers would have known exactly what he meant. Indeed, Larkin's carefully cultivated public persona of being distant and brusque, as well as the superficial respectability of his life and his shabby-genteel appearance, re-enforced the stereotype. He was certainly not gregarious; he could be charming when he chose to be, as he was to the present author when we met at a conference – he a world-famous literary figure and I a very junior assistant librarian – where both of us would have preferred not to be. And the lifestyle – known only to a few before his death – is now a matter of public knowledge. In Larkin's case the appearance was deceptive, but the image is real enough. Yet libraries themselves, as is apparent in every chapter of this book, are undergoing radical and unparalleled changes. Some of these have indeed been imposed from the outside, but far more have been driven from within the profession by imaginative, innovative and passionately committed librarians. Why has this disconnect developed? What are its consequences? And how can it be rectified? These are some of the questions addressed in this chapter.

Historically, the word 'librarian' is first found in English in the 18th century, replacing the older term 'library keeper'. This phrase, a translation of the Latin *bibliothecarius*, emphasised the function of the librarian as a custodian of books and documents, an emphasis which continued long after the modern word came into common parlance. Indeed, it was only in the second half of the 20th century that the great majority of librarians began to see themselves as having a service function that was focused on readers and other library users rather than on the institution itself and the materials which it contained. In practice, librarians are engaged in a wide range of activities, including the management of large and complex institutions, providing support for education and for programmes to develop literacy and to promote reading, and engaging in public service activities such as the provision of community information. It is precisely because the public image of the librarian has not changed as quickly as the reality that there developed the tendency to avoid the word as much as possible.

The library profession: a historical perspective

As an organised profession, librarianship is a product of the 19th century, although the custodianship of formal collections of books and documents can be traced back for millennia, to the ancient civilisations of the Middle East and China. It was, however, in Britain and the United States that librarians came together to acquire the characteristics of a profession from the 1870s onwards. After a meeting of librarians called to coincide with the US Centennial Exhibition of 1876, a group of librarians from urban public libraries and some academic libraries agreed to form the American Library Association; a few British librarians followed suit in the following year to form the Library Association (LA) (now the Chartered Institute of Library and Information Professionals (CILIP)).

Both associations, and the professional bodies founded subsequently in most other countries, had the same broad objectives:

- to promote the interests of the profession and its clients
- to regulate entry into the profession
- to develop appropriate standards and ethical codes for professional practice.

It could be argued that a profession is defined by having a publicly recognised body with this or a broadly similar remit. In that sense, the library profession is heading towards its 125th birthday.

The 19th-century model of a profession, which survived throughout the 20th century and is still vastly influential today, does, however, have some negative connotations. When the professions were formalised, and their representative bodies came to be recognised by public authorities and sometimes even by the law (as in the case of the powers given to the professional bodies in medicine and indeed in law itself), the power to regulate standards – and particularly standards for new entrants – meant that they began to acquire some of the characteristics of a monopolistic guild or even a trade union. This was particularly marked in the case of what have come to be known as the 'statutory professions', that is, those in which the professional body has a regulatory role underpinned by the law. The register of practitioners maintained by the professional body then becomes a record of licences to practice, from which people can be removed, in the event of misconduct, through the process normally called 'striking off'. Generally speaking, these are professions where the recipients of the professional service are endangered rather than merely inconvenienced by malpractice – most obviously medicine and the law, but also including, for example, nursing and dentistry. Librarianship obviously did not fall into that category, so that attaining qualification for enrolment on the professional register was merely a public statement of commitment to the profession and of having attained certain standards of practice and levels of knowledge.

This situation presents both challenges and opportunities to the information profession at the present time. The challenge is perhaps exemplified by the failure of the LA and CILIP over many decades to persuade employers that chartered membership (i.e. being in possession of a full professional qualification) should be a precondition of employment in a professional post in a library or information service. While some local authorities did adopt this position for their public libraries during the middle decades of the 20th century, it was never more than a self-imposed voluntary agreement. A handful of academic libraries did the same thing, but this usually reflected the personal professional commitment and engagement of the university librarian rather than an institutional requirement dictated and supported from a higher level. Librarianship was a very open profession, with all the good and bad consequences which flow from that. Although by the end of the last century the vast majority of those in professional posts had at least some sort of professional qualification (usually in the form of a degree or postgraduate diploma in Library and Information Studies), relatively few, at least outside the public libraries, bothered to obtain chartered status and even fewer were active in the LA or CILIP. The challenge for the professional bodies, therefore, is to speak for a profession that they do not wholly encompass and perhaps do not even fully represent.

Promoting the profession

The phrase 'promoting a profession' can have several meanings and nuances, some of them contradictory of each other. At one level, it can refer to encouraging people to consider entering the profession; in other words, it is a mechanism for recruitment. It can also mean enhancing the public profile of the profession and seeking to achieve a higher level of public recognition of the existence and singularity of the profession. At a more complex level, this begins to merge into promoting not merely awareness but respect: the recognition of the profession's unique contribution to society. It can also mean promoting the best interests of the profession's beneficiaries or clients by setting, maintaining and enforcing standards of professional practice and conduct. And it is at this point that the complications really begin. When a profession claims to speak for its clients as well as for itself, there is always a suggestion of *d'haut en bas*, perhaps best described as the 'doctor-knows-best' syndrome. In turn, this has sometimes led to a deferential attitude to professionals which has left them immune to challenge. In the long term, this has not always been in the best interests of clients. The professional bodies in librarianship have always seen the promotion of libraries and the services they offer as an integral, indeed central, aspect of their role. The historic name symbolises that – it was the *Library* Association, not the *Librarians'* Association. The full name of CILIP, incorporating the phrase *Library and Information Professionals*, was actually adopted in order to include the word 'information', but the underlying implication is that this is a body representing practitioners, rather than one representing the interests of the institutions in which some of them work. Although this is a line of argument which could be pursued too far, the implications of the words should not be wholly ignored.

During a period of fundamental change in information service provision, how has the information profession promoted itself? And how successful has it been? Concerns about the 'image' of the librarian have worried contributors to the professional press – not to mention conversations in library staff rooms and at conferences – for almost as long as the profession has existed. The fact that the stereotyped image is misconceived and perverse is largely irrelevant; what matters is perception. It is perhaps not too optimistic to argue that, over the last 20 years or so, the perception has indeed begun to change. Fundamental to that change has been the different perception of the library itself. It is ironic that, in the longer term, the sometimes dangerously close identification of the institution with the individuals who work in it has proved to be advantageous to both. Public and academic libraries alike have changed profoundly. From the user's point of view – which is central to the perceptual issue – the visible manifestations are everywhere, from the banks of computer screens which now dominate much library space, to the furnishings and decoration of the library, or the very name of the building and the service. The public library has become not merely a place for borrowing books – although that remains both a popular and important service which it offers – but a place to seek and find information, whether through an intermediary or directly through the use of electronic resources beyond those that are domestically available. Similarly, in the academic sector, the institutional library is the centre from which a college or university provides information services to its staff and students, while also providing study space and learning materials, of which some are in the form of print on paper. The lay user can actually *see* that a contemporary library is not merely an integral part of the information society, but actually a gateway through which it can be accessed.

It may seem self-evident to say that the role of a librarian in such a service is very different from that of his or her predecessor in a 'traditional' library, but we need to avoid the danger of taking an introspective view. In some respects, librarians have become less visible even as the visibility of their services has been enhanced. Partly for practical reasons – not least the cost of employing staff – users are becoming, and indeed are required to become, more self-sufficient. This is true, whether we look at self-service issue systems – which have eliminated one of the principal points of contact between staff and users, albeit one which created a misleading image of what a 'librarian' is and does – or the displacement of much traditional reference and enquiry work by the provision of facilities for users to undertake their own electronic searches. These changes raise some critical issues about what constitutes the corpus of knowledge and skills which defines an information professional, and how it is acquired and validated.

Redefining the librarian

The increasing self-sufficiency of users and the general availability of information through channels which do not necessitate any intervention in a library or from a librarian at the point of search are driving the redefinition of the knowledge base and skill set of the profession. The knowledge base is perhaps the easier of the two to define. CILIP's *Body of Professional Knowledge* (BPK),[1] which underlies its scheme for professional qualifications, was developed with the intention of providing a conceptual framework within which information professionals could develop their practical skills. In achieving this, the BPK defines the intellectual context of professional information work and thus allows those who are developing and delivering professional education programmes, particularly at entry level, to ensure that such programmes include the basic requirements for effective professional practice.

The knowledge base (the 'Core Schema' in the language of the BPK) is built around understanding information itself, the documentation and recording of knowledge and information, the management of information resources (including institutions in which it is generated and stored, and through which it is disseminated) and the communication of information in the context of working with users. Taken as a whole, this encompasses the essence of what a contemporary information professional does. The skill set built on this understanding of the intellectual foundation of the profession is wide enough to describe the work of any manager of information resources. It also – and crucially – provides a framework within which a professional practitioner can identify his or her own training needs and the profession as a whole can recognise and exploit opportunities for development and change.

There is, however, no room for either complacency or inflexibility in contemplating these generally welcome changes. The development of the profession is driven essentially by the changing needs, perceptions and capacities of users, but it must also be responsive to the changing social, economic and political context. This is not merely a matter of responding to temporary factors – important as they are – such as current public policies or the state of the public finances. Whether in the public or the private sector, the professional providers of information increasingly have to justify their very existence, and the existence of the institutions and organisations through which they have historically provided their services. In the academic sector, for example, university libraries are increasingly presenting themselves as the institution's centre of expertise in information provision rather than merely as a source of information. At the same time, actual visits to the library are declining. Desktop access to the Internet, all but universal in the academic sector throughout the developed world, has profoundly impacted on what librarians do and what services libraries need to offer. For students, the library is perhaps most important as a well-provided study space with high-quality facilities for information access. For researchers and teachers it is probably most important as the provider of access to external information resources and advice on how best to make use of them.

Even this highly simplified version of the changes in academic libraries suggests the need for significant revisions in the role of the librarian, much of which has indeed taken place over a period of several years. At a more strategic level, however, the role of the 'library' in the university also needs to be reconceptualised to recognise contemporary reality. Above all, library leaders have had to become more than merely the managers of services. The information professional of the 21st century is working not only with fellow professionals and with users, but with professionals in other disciplines and in the wider context of an organisation. This is as true of public librarians as it is of academic librarians. There is some evidence that many librarians are ill equipped for the quasi-political roles which are now being thrust upon them. The merger of historically separate directorates in many British local authorities cruelly highlighted these deficiencies. As libraries found themselves in large organisational units which might include services as diverse as leisure facilities and education as well as the whole spectrum of cultural services, it was rare indeed to find that a librarian was appointed at the highest level of management. Academic librarians perhaps fared a little better when many universities began to reconfigure their library and information technology services in the 1990s, but there was not always room for self-congratulation in how such convergences were achieved.

Looking forward

The information professional of the future will need a greater breadth of vision than all but a handful have achieved in the past. The visions will need to include not merely what *is* changing or *has* changed, but a view of the changes yet to come. The 'Google generation' has already been indirectly responsible for the recent transformations in academic libraries, but there is much more to come. The profound social and economic change – some of it driven by the very developments in information storage and communication which are fundamental to libraries – that characterised the decades on either side of the turn of the century is far from complete. Perhaps this is most obvious when we look at the issues not from the viewpoint of the provider, but from that of the user. Tens of millions of people around the world search for information every day. We still know very little about how many of those searches are successful, and even less about how many of them are optimal in producing the highest quality of results. The fact is, however, that this is the way of the future, and the future of the information profession needs to be built around this fact. Users want efficient, comprehensive and relatively easy-to-use systems which will satisfy their information needs. That much at least is obvious to them.

Less obviously, users also need skills. Many of those skills are those which have been traditionally associated with the library and information professions. There is little point in bemoaning the inefficiency of non-expert users if the experts do not use their expertise to help users to help themselves. This raises some culturally difficult issues for librarians. All professions have always defined themselves in part by exclusion – the unique ability to do what lay people cannot. Librarianship was never able to go down the whole length of this road, but the very idea of a body of professional knowledge, or indeed of a profession, is built upon the assumption that there is a distinctive role, some parts of which are indeed unique. The issue which librarians have to acknowledge and perhaps address is that the boundaries of the unique parts of this domain are rapidly contracting. Arguably, the best service that information professionals can provide is to enable those who would once have been their clients to do the job for themselves.

This is far from being either a frivolous suggestion or a remote possibility. The skills of information literacy are becoming fundamental to pedagogy at every level, from early years education to doctoral research and beyond. It can credibly be argued that the central objective of education should be to enable children to acquire the skills which will allow them to acquire knowledge. This can be taken too far; to make sense, education needs content to be learned as well as the skills to learn and interpret, but educators can no longer simply assume that these skills will be acquired through some kind of osmotic process as a consequence of learning. The information profession is a repository of a vast store of understanding of learning processes as well as of effective techniques for resource discovery and information retrieval. A reconfigured curriculum for the 21st century will be built around the acquisition of skills for learning as well as the achievement of knowledge and understanding. Moreover, it is not merely the technical skills of effective searching which need to be universalised. The self-providers of information will also need to learn how to assess what they have found. The ability to evaluate information and, by implication, sources of information – another of the key skills of the information professional – will of necessity have to be more widely disseminated if best use is to be made of the systems and facilities which are now so readily available. This may be seen by some as a challenge to professional distinctiveness, but it is actually perhaps the greatest opportunity in the history of the information profession. All the fine words about the central significance of information can now be translated into reality.

Even so, it remains a challenge to the profession. But it is more than that – it is a challenge to professionalism itself, and that is not unique to the library and information domain. Quite apart from the social phenomenon of the rapid decline in the deference traditionally shown towards 'professionals' – significant as that is – the widespread availability of information may be thought to call into question the need for a profession at all. In fact, as has been implied, what is being offered here is a challenge to which there can be a positive and exciting response. Nor should this be thought of as an issue for the future. It is an issue for the here and now. The contemporary and future information professionals – leaders and potential leaders alike – need political and pedagogic skills in addition to those more traditionally associated with the profession. An expanded knowledge base will have to take account of this (the BPK implies it up to a point but needs to be revisited), and the skill set will need to include an extended emphasis on the absolute necessity of flexibility and continuous as well as continuing professional development. The providers of professional education and training – another distinction which is perhaps more blurred now than it has been since the early years of the 20th century – are also re-examining how they interpret and present the knowledge and skills which the new professionals will need. The information profession of the future will be defined by what it does and the public perception of how well it does it, rather than by membership of a particular organisation or having obtained a predefined qualification. Librarians and information workers, like everyone else, need to understand what they do and to contextualise it (which is why the knowledge base remains important), but they also need to ensure that what they build around the context is relevant and forward looking, rather than merely unique.

Conclusion

It is a cliché to say that this is a time of great opportunities for both libraries and librarians, but it is also true. However, great opportunities only arise at a time of change, and change embodies threats as well as promises. All professions are threatened to some extent by the changing attitude of the public towards the providers of services – the demand for greater accountability, the challenge to unique authority and the need to demonstrate qualitative value for money. The provision of information is neither uniquely endangered by societal change nor uniquely placed to benefit from it. Nevertheless, it can benefit. After several decades of sometimes obsessive self-examination, the profession is at last beginning to develop a new vision and broader horizons. Recognising that access to information is beyond the control of any group – even states, let alone the members of one small profession – it is reorienting itself so that it can provide the services that are actually needed to clients who recognise their benefits. This will need a greater focus on helping users to help themselves, while retaining the essential elements of the traditional library. The focus, however, is on content, not medium and not on the means of transmission. The profession will, at least for the immediately foreseeable future, be called upon to provide people who can manage institutions, with all that that implies for the acquisition and exercise of a wide range of personal, financial and political skills. But it will also have to continue to adapt itself, with enthusiasm and energy, to the changed circumstances in which it operates.

Note

1. http://www.cilip.org.uk/sitecollectiondocuments/PDFs/qualifications chartership/BPK.pdf.

Reference

Bennett, A. (1982) 'Instead of a present.' In Thwaite, A. (ed.) *Larkin at Sixty*. London: Faber and Faber.

18

Redefining librarianship

Biddy Fisher

Introduction

Can the library and information profession make the necessary changes to fit itself for a 21st century existence? This chapter recognises the traditional foundations on which the current paradigm is based and explores their potential for constraining continuing recognition of the profession within contemporary society. It acknowledges the context within which any organisation advocating for a specific area of professional practice has to operate; and speculates about future professional practice, the potential for professional organisations in a new regime of public service, and of the influence the profession could exert were steps taken to develop a new model.

Background

In the United Kingdom, the library profession was founded in the Victorian age, at a time when notions of public service were being formed. The Public Libraries Act of 1850 was followed by the recognition of the Library Association by Royal Charter in 1898. During the 20th century, the development of other state-funded public services reached a zenith. Education, health and the police were all the subject of nation-wide developments to provide service to society. Following the 1964 Public Libraries Act, libraries were developed in a role aligned to education, perhaps in recognition of the critical function of libraries within universities for several centuries previously. In their communities, libraries were to become recognised as an icon of cultural maturity.

Within libraries, specialist posts were created to deal with the complexities of organising and creating accessible routes to information held within that service. The practice of library experts was shared and gradually became organised and formalised. The development of a set of roles for professional librarians was a response to the need for such services to be recognised, and in creating an organisation with royal recognition, it afforded members a status which could be understood by the communities they served.

At the century's mid-point, information science emerged as a distinct and different discipline. This was a consequence of the growth in scientific and technological literature, recognised in 1948 by the Royal Society at its first conference dealing with scientific information. Further developments met the need for industry and commerce to have dedicated systems for the organisation and dissemination of such information. In 1958, the Institute of Information Scientists was established to act in the interests of this new group of 'information scientists'.

The present day

The 21st century is emerging as a notable time for reviewing and restating consensual values of 'public good' in terms of moral and ethical aspects of our citizenship. This review should also embrace notions of professionalism. Significantly for library and information services (LIS), this is as a result of altered ways of working and the technological impacts on the tools of our work. In the 16 years since the author reviewed the role of the professional body in continuing professional development (Fisher, 1994), workplace and employment practices have changed dramatically. In 2006, Black and Hoare observed that 'most library activity of the past century and a half ... can be viewed in the context of the changing contours of modernity'. To appraise library activity, and particularly professionalism (as applied to library and information work), in the 21st century, it is necessary to look at some major global and national issues. Several disparate strands force this review:

- Democratic idealism is a cause of global warfare.
- The UK's mainstream political parties are eroding their previous differences.
- Western society has lost its implicit trust in financial and business ethics.

- Technological advances have reached areas beyond the laboratory and into domestic and workplace settings, and normal modes of communication are mobile.

- Society views 'the Internet' as an enormous information resource but the veracity of sources is not always questioned.

- Selective truth, invisible censorship and market forces often lie behind media reporting of the issues that affect our society and community.

A society that once relied on professionals to provide authority is now in possession of the technology to access a vast information resource. The opportunity to acquire personal skills to find, use and analyse that information has replaced dependence on the professional skill set of others. This situation could ultimately dispense with any need for professionals to act as intermediaries, those whose practice is governed by the structures and compliance of a professional organisation. However, it should be remembered that the professional skill set also includes the application of professional judgement and the ongoing development of expertise. The received wisdom is that additional authority is given to the expert if they are a member of a recognised body, a professional association or chartered institute. It is not at all clear that this is seen as a benefit to the individual or to society.

Professional status and membership

The status of being a professional association or institute is granted to those organisations that include a code of ethics and a code of professional practice in their guiding principles. Members of that profession are trusted to adhere to these or be subject to disciplinary action. However, in the United Kingdom there are many librarians who may have had the education and training but who exercise a personal choice not to belong to a professional organisation. If the public expectation is that only a professional has, as a duty, to put public good above private views, opinions and personal power, then perhaps it is time to undertake a very public review of the profession and notions of professionalism.

The reasons individuals cite for opting out of membership of any formal organisation are beyond the remit of this chapter. There is, however, a similarity in the decline in membership of a formal body for the LIS profession and in the decline of commitment to participation in the formal political system that relies on the electorate voting (Park et al., 2010). Having mislaid the guiding moral and improving passion of the early stages of the development of the profession, members have become stalled on a notion of the technical management of information. This point is well made by Ian Cornelius (2006). The new challenges for libraries, librarians and information professionals, and any associated professional organisations, are wrapped up in both the political and social context of the age. Libraries now compete with a seemingly boundary-less online information store. Librarians have had their expertise in understanding and manipulating information eroded by new players. These recent arrivals see no barriers to their adoption of a skills base and a body of professional knowledge and assume equality in the 'information society' (Moore and Steele, 1991). At the same time, the professional's skills base has been further diluted by the availability of technology-based search engines on proprietary and freely accessed software. In addition, the concept of a professional body has undergone government examination (House of Lords, 2000) and been found wanting (BIS, 2009) in a time of social inclusion in the workplace. Yet there are lacunae evident in the achievements of school pupils, the skills of those presenting themselves for all levels of employment and the knowledge that members of our society have about the 'way things work'.

Reviewing the profession

If a profession that 'professes' to collect, preserve, organise and promote information has any role in society, it is to ensure that it contributes to the gaps identified above, to be recognised for that contribution, and for its formal institutions to be represented and featured at the highest level of social decision making. It is a big challenge that needs to be answered by future professionals. It is this group which has the responsibility to keep up the momentum within an organised body that has responsibility for the quality and capability of its members and is answerable to the public or other consumers of library and information services. Re-appraisals of what attributes and activities an organisation representing library and information professionals should possess have occurred at regular intervals in the past. Douglas Foskett (1962) proposed a strengthening of professional practice but indicated that librarians should remain above ethical and political persuasion, while Hovecamp

(1997) explored the difference between the legitimate activities of a trades union and those of a professional association. Members of the Chartered Institute of Library and Information Professionals (CILIP) and its predecessors may be critical of the way it approaches advocacy for the profession. They recognise the stance it takes regarding direct member representation as different from the position allowed to a trade union. Situations such as that which occurred in the Wirral, in the UK, whereby a public inquiry in 2009 deemed that a planned closure of public libraries was contrary to the Public Libraries Act 1964, illustrate that difference and are explored later in this chapter. Blaise Cronin is a regular poser of the 'whither LIS professionalism?' question. His 2004 article could serve as a model for a regular review (Cronin, 2004).

In order to ensure recognition of members' professionalism, Oppenheim argues that the UK's CILIP should introduce more robust professional education on ethical issues (Oppenheim and Pollecutt, 2000). He believes that by CILIP's taking an informed position on, for example, intellectual freedom, society will be better served by its information professionals, as access to information would be improved. On the other hand, a pessimistic note is struck by Bill Crowley in his challenge to the future of the profession. Not only does he consider the state of education for librarianship and information science lacking in relevance, but he also cites CILIP as having created a process for recognising professional achievement that militates against any modern application of what is occurring in the information world. He is equally critical of the American Library Association, stating that the organisation is missing an opportunity to provide essential pointers to members to engage in 'lifecycle librarianship' for the public to enjoy all that libraries offer across all ages (Crowley, 2008).

Four dimensions of future professional practice

The authors quoted above offer pointers that should be given high priority when defining an information profession suitable to operate in the 21st century. The issues can be summarised as:

- the application of ethical competence
- the reassertion of a political stance in professional practice

- knowing when and where advocacy or representation is the appropriate position to adopt
- using current social analysis and evidence to identify and act upon opportunity for the betterment of society through the evidence of professional LIS contributions.

These are the issues in front of the author and reader.

Ethical competence and public good

Ethical competence may be viewed as the additional value that a professional brings to a task. This value is quantitatively above that offered by any similar service provider and is measured by the extent of knowledge, advice and guidance offered within a framework of professional practice. This additional value can be guaranteed only if the professional engages in improving their practice through continuous professional development as required by their professional or regulatory body. The other essentials to assure ethical competence are that the professional body has a knowledge base, a standard of professional practice and a regulatory framework for all awards, standards and achievements of the membership. The ethical route to competence is more altruistic than the 'market path', a subject elegantly discussed by Michael Sandel in his series of 2009 BBC *Reith Lectures* (Sandel, 2009). The inherent values of the majority of the LIS profession are based on concepts of equality and a belief that all members of society, irrespective of their background, race, class, age, gender or sexual orientation, should have equal rights of access to the resources and benefits of a service offered in the interest of public good. Working within a chartered institute, LIS professionals are perceived to embody the basic tenets of social justice. It is likely that in the future members will need to apply these to their work within new communications media, specifically Web 2.0.[1]

A future LIS professional will be required to prove public good in their professional practice more overtly than in previous generations. In the current LIS environment, an individual's professionalism is invisible to most because information is offered freely and becomes accessible to anyone who seeks it. Members of contemporary society may choose to bypass the authority of a professional information provider. They can arm themselves with the wealth of information readily available through the Internet and, in the wake of the scandal that brought about a near-breakdown of western society's financial system, they are more critical of professions than ever before. Many information resources available via current media are no more than 'sound-bites' or clichés. Individuals using such short cuts for arguments on issues may be deluding themselves on the strength of any argument they proffer. Similarly, without the skills for formulating an evidence-based defence against personally hurtful or seemingly discriminatory situations, a worse situation may arise.

LIS professionals understand their responsibilities in relation to the provision of information-based services. Services under their management are set against benchmarks of good practice and with full knowledge of the implications of unethical conduct. In the ethically competent scenario of the future, professionals will have to operate more along the lines of social justice. They will need to engage at the highest level of persuasion to overcome the damage done by professionals who have not worked in the public good but are perceived to have put personal gain first. To re-engage with society and regain trust will mean committing to a refreshed set of ethical and professional standards written in accessible language, taking collective responsibility for putting public interest before personal gain and accepting personal responsibility for continuing professional growth through education and training.

Political involvement

To guarantee a meaningful future, the LIS profession needs to seek more political involvement in important social issues, as John Feather also stresses. In the United Kingdom, for example, government ministers in Northern Ireland, Scotland and Wales take advantage of a greater ease of access to senior professionals that can rarely be obtained by their English equivalents. This brings a higher profile to those librarians who manage large tranches of the public purse. National librarians are of specific interest to policy makers and are entrusted with the responsibility of ensuring that the national library truly reflects, amongst other things, the culture, knowledge and history of its home nation. This is achieved by the expert acquisition, development, preservation and promotion of collections. Intervention in strategic issues concerning the national collection offers ministers an opportunity to gain an awareness of other professional issues related to information, including intellectual property, the knowledge economy, communication with the community and other matters of relevance. Equally, it is important that a national library develops its strategy to reflect the strategic priorities of its government. The National Library of Scotland, for example, recognised the potential of a 'political strategy' by instituting a continuing 'horizon scanning' exercise using a PEST (political, economic, scientific and technological) analysis.[2]

There is a question about whether the social and political idealism and values of public good that informed the development of libraries in the 19th and 20th centuries can be supported by a new generation of information professionals. Public disillusionment with the 'big politics' of Westminster government has never been higher. The 2009 British Social Attitudes survey (Park et al., 2009) saw an 8% drop in the number of people believing in a public duty to vote. Interim local elections are seen as an opportunity to express dissatisfaction with the performance of the national government. In a similar way, dismay at a local council's decisions to circumvent democracy or ignore statutory obligations can provide good opportunities for professional bodies to show leadership. Such timely interventions can be beneficial to the public's notion of the role of a professional body. In 2008, the announcement by Wirral Council that it was to close public libraries within its area caused ripples that resulted in a public inquiry being held in June 2009. Responding to the need for the public good to be at the forefront of any such decision, CILIP was called upon to provide evidence of any contravention of the Wirral Council's statutory duty under the 1964 Public Libraries Act. The evidence presented by the late Dr Bob McKee, CILIP's then Chief Executive, was clear:

> Wirral Council sought to implement a library closure programme:
> 1. Without carrying out a library service review or an impact assessment or a proper assessment of local community need;
> 2. Without any confirmed arrangements for replacement or alternative provision in place;
> 3. With no logic to the proposed closures;
> 4. And with no sense of a strategic vision for the library service and its contribution to the wider Council policy agenda. (McKee, 2009)

Public good in this example was obtained by ensuring that the existing national legislation was adhered to at a local level. The argument was precise and indicated that the local authority had not acted with evidence or forethought before announcing the intention to close libraries. It is situations such as this that offer future professionals opportunities to refresh their collective political appetite. With the duty to vote being questioned (Park et al., 2009), professionals will be much more involved in politics at a local level. Regional and local differences will be as important to those running public services as will be national agendas, and this will require a high degree of involvement in local needs analysis and service developments. LIS professionals, who are part of an international network, must be provided with skills that enable them to enact appropriate national policy at a local level. Recognition of this will become part of a professional's education and ongoing development.

The structures within a professional body and its activities in the political arena must reflect devolved legislatures. During 2009, CILIP undertook extensive consultation to identify how matters relating to the nature of business within the 'devolved nations' were progressing. It is expressed simply in the advocacy strategy that they will work within their own political contexts and to their national agendas. The existing Devolved Nations Forum of CILIP announces its remit as being 'to enable the development of relevant and different strategies and advocacy routes in the light of devolution within a broad agreed framework of policies, principles and accountabilities; and to assist Ridgmount Street [CILIP's headquarters address in London, England] in moving away from an Anglo-centric approach to policy development and practice' (CILIP, 2009). This situation is to be formalised within the regulations pertaining to the governance of CILIP in 2010.

Advocacy, leadership and representation

The Wirral case (McKee, 2009) serves as an example of advocacy. A professional body is bound to safeguard public interest and thus will advocate the best result for society or the community. This is in contrast to the position that can be taken by a trade union, where members can expect personal advocacy and workplace representation. Taking a stance on advocacy includes representing professional self-interest. This requires the organisation to have a democratic governance structure that includes member participation in policy formulation and implementation. The adopted policies should be accessible as well as meaningful to a majority of members. The inclusive nature of its governance will lend legitimacy and authority to public statements, whether they relate to matters of professional practice or the wider social applications of information access and use, or to legal issues of copyright, intellectual property or other statutory requirements. Society will judge the authority of an organisation by its ability to be heard, seen in print and other media, and by the influence it has with local, regional and national government. The organisation must lead on issues that illustrate the benefit of that profession to society and communities. At best, this will be achieved by persuasive arguments based upon a body of evidence that is centrally maintained and updated.

Members must believe in some tangible benefit if they are to belong to a professional body. From their perspective, the critical functions include the provision of network opportunities, advocacy of their work and the provision or validation of qualifications and accreditation of educational courses. The Professional Associations Research Network[3] in the UK has initiated a project to explore the expectations of potential members and their attitude to professional bodies. CILIP has commenced a review of its future,[4] while other international library and information associations have also investigated what members believe is at the heart of a modern professional association for the 21st century.

Earlier work by Ashcroft (2003) indicated that the CILIP membership could not envisage any issue as more important for their professional body to focus on than pay and conditions. However, acceding to this view will impede the organisation in moving on a larger stage and in particular making political partnerships and leading on policy and advocacy issues. The role of the professional body should be to collect the evidence and data needed for members to use in their representation. Visibly working in partnership with the organisations that have the bargaining power in the workplace, and primarily the trade unions, could bring greater understanding of the difference in their respective roles.

Social analysis and the evidence base

The use of research methods to determine planning imperatives must become commonplace. There has been a conscious effort to introduce project methodologies, including target setting for time and resources, to improve the achievement of planning and implementation. The profession uses such tools in daily professional practice, but it is rare to find them applied to the creation of a robust evidence base to be used in advocacy for the impact of professional practice on major social issues. Data sets identifying the outputs of a service and anecdotal evidence are the traditional responses to enquiries and government-led reviews. Many, including Johnson (2004), have advocated the need for research that identifies the impact of services and facilities. Initiatives in benchmarking and impact analysis have been well received, but as yet a core evidence base has not emerged. Leading this work in the UK are Sharon Markless and David Streatfield, whose many publications and professional activities in the field of impact are well received by the profession at large (see for example, Markless and Streatfield, 2009). The difficulty of turning such theory into practice is articulated by John Feather, who correctly points to tensions between the practitioners and the academics that stifle the emergence of a practice-informed research agenda and a research-informed model of professional practice (Feather, 2009). Leading the movement for the creation of the evidence-based library and information practice are Andrew Booth and Jonathan Eldredge (see, for example, Booth and Eldredge, 2002; Booth and Eldredge, 2003; Brice et al., 2004). In a paper delivered to the FOLIO-EBLIP Gloss course in March 2007, Booth stated that 'as librarians we don't often interrogate our own evidence base' (Booth, 2007).

Context and environment

Irrespective of the core functions of a professional body, it is necessary that they are conducted in accordance with any overarching set of principles governing those who hold employment or office within the sphere of public life. In the UK these are known as the 'Nolan Principles', the name taken from the Chair of the Committee that produced the *First Report on the Committee on Standards in Public Life* (Nolan, 1995). The seven principles of selflessness, integrity, objectivity, accountability, openness, honesty and leadership are aligned with the common ethical principles adopted in the 30 Organisation for Economic Co-operation and Development countries. In Scotland, the Scotland Act of 2000 prescribed for ethical standards in public life.[5] In addition, there is a set of nine criteria that are applied to distinguish a group as a profession. These criteria were quoted in the UK's House of Lords *Science and Technology Sixth Report* (2000) when determining issues of those professionals allied to medicine. They relate to the determination of an organisation's:

- governance
- educational standards
- ethics and professional standards
- benefit to the public
- protection to the public
- disciplinary process
- competent, capable experienced members
- independence in thought and outlook
- professional leadership to the public.

Conclusion

In order to continue to lead with the authority vested in them on behalf of society, professional bodies will have to continue in their ethical and professional standard setting. An era of change, and of change management, has led to continuous reviews of services and facilities in all LIS sectors. In the UK, two professional organisations have become one. The role of professional organisations in representing their area of expertise to society is more important than ever.

Political and social partnerships will emerge as the chosen way of progressing issues. Single voices will not be strong enough to carry weight and win arguments. The work of the professional body will encompass the forging of alliances with organisations that share beliefs and value sets. The emphasis will be on local or regional agendas, thus creating a locus of action away from heavily centralised and perhaps ponderous decision making.

There will be significant change in the methods used to carry out the functions of a professional organisation. The culture of more traditional organisations will alter, so that formal structures will be a last resort rather than the normal way of agreeing procedures. The post-war reliance on committee and consensual agreement to change will move towards a more flexible model that will employ lighter control mechanisms. The post-modern influence that social media currently exert indicates that they will emerge as the major channel used to convey views, ideas and responses, as well as in initiating discussion and setting agendas.

The creativity of individuals will become more obvious as social media give voice to a wider community of information workers. These informal conversations will be used to provide a reality check or temperature of the profession. They will provide the indications that will lead to further investigation and analysis. Ultimately, though, they will not replace the established and proven truth sought by society. Opinion-based professional philosophy can only be accepted when the evidence for any professional statement has been established, acknowledged and integrated into practice.

The future LIS professional will rely on his or her professional organisation for its consistent use of current social and economic analysis. Once evidence is identified, they will expect influential action that will lead to opportunity for professional LIS contributions to improve society. The international platform for professional networks will become increasingly important in providing opportunity for sharing practice. Future generations of professionals will expect their voices to be more easily accessible, using media of their choice rather than traditional representative bureaucracy. Once the new leaders of the profession have taken these major steps, we will surely have arrived at a modern, responsive, reflective and securely founded organisational environment for our future professional practice.

Notes

1. See http://www.onlinesocialjustice.com.
2. www.nls.uk/about-us/horizon-scanning.
3. http://www.parnglobal.com.
4. http://www.cilip.org.uk/get-involved/cilipfuture/Pages/default.aspx.
5. http://www.legislation.gov.uk/asp/2000/7/contents.

Further reading

Booth, A. and Brice, A. (2004) *Evidence Based Practice for Information Professionals: a handbook*. London: Facet.

Brewerton, A. and Corrall, S. (2005) *New Professional's Handbook*, 2nd edn. London: Facet.

Broady-Preston, J. (2006) 'CILIP: a twenty-first century association for the information profession?' *Library Management*, 27 (1/2), 48–65.

Chartered Insurance Institute. (2009) *Twenty-First Century Professionalism: raising standards and building trust.* Papers in Professionalism series, paper 1. Online at http://www.cii.co.uk/downloaddata/PP1_21st_Century_Profm_27April2009.pdf.

ESRC. (2009) *Conceptualising the Contemporary Professions.* Seminar series held 2009–10. Economic and Social Research Council. Online at http://www.contemporaryprofessions.com.

Feather, J. (2003) 'Libraries and politics: where two worlds meet', *Journal of Librarianship and Information Science*, 35 (1), 1–3.

Friedman, A. (2006) 'Strengthening professionalism: ethical competence as an alternative to the market path towards the public good'. In Craig, J. (ed.) *Production Values: futures for professionalism.* London: Demos.

Library and Information Research. (2005) *Special Issue on the 'Impact Implementation Programme'*, 29 (91), 10–19.

Markless, S. and Streatfield, D.R. (2006), *Evaluating the Impact of Your Library.* London: Facet.

Sandel, M. (2009) *Justice: what's the right thing to do?* London: Allen Lane.

References

Ashcroft, L. (2003) 'Raising issues of salaries and status for library/information professionals'. *New Library World*, 104 (1187/1188), 164–70.

BIS. (2009) *Unleashing Aspiration – the final report of the panel on Fair Access to the Professions.* Department for Business, Innovation and Skills. London: HMSO.

Black, A. and Hoare, P. (eds) (2006) *The Cambridge History of Libraries in Britain and Ireland: Volume 3, 1850–2000.* New York: Cambridge University Press.

Booth, A. (2007) *The Evidence Based Practice Process.* FOLIO EBLIP-Gloss course. Online at http://eblip-gloss.pbworks.com/f/transcript.doc.

Booth, A. and Eldredge, J.D. (2002) 'Evidence-based librarianship: a Socratic dialogue'. *Bibliotheca Medica Canadiana*, 23 (4), 136–40.

Booth, A. and Eldredge, J.D. (2003) 'Editorial … evidence-based librarianship?' *Health Information and Libraries Journal*, 20 (1), 1–2.

Brice, A., Booth, A., Crumley, E., Koufogiannakis, D. and Eldredge J. (2004) 'A future for evidence-based information practice?' In Booth, A. and Brice, A. (eds) *Evidence Based Practice for Information Professionals: a handbook*. London: Facet.

CILIP (Chartered Institute of Library and Information Professional). (2009) Committee papers of the CILIP *Devolved Nations Forum*, meeting of 1 June.

Cornelius, I. (2006) 'The interpretation of professional development in librarianship since 1850'. In Black, A. and Hoare, P. (eds) *The Cambridge History of Libraries in Britain and Ireland: Volume 3, 1850–2000*. New York: Cambridge University Press.

Cronin B. (2004) 'Pierce Butler's *An Introduction to Library Science*: a tract for our times?' Review article. *Journal of Librarianship and Information Science*, 36 (4), 183–8.

Crowley, B. (2008) *Renewing Professional Librarianship: a fundamental rethinking*. Westport, CT: Libraries Unlimited.

Feather, J. (2009) 'LIS research in the United Kingdom: reflections and prospects'. *Journal of Librarianship and Information Science*, 41 (3), 73–181.

Fisher, B. (1994) 'Professional organisations and professional development'. *British Journal of Academic Librarianship*, 9 (3), 167–78.

Foskett, D. (1962) *The Creed of a Librarian – no politics, no religion, no morals*. Library Association Reference, Special and Information section, North Western Group occasional papers. No 3. London: Library Association.

House of Lords. (2000) *Science and Technology Sixth Report*. London: HMSO. Online at http://www.publications.parliament.uk/pa/ld199900/ldselect/ldsctech/123/12301.htm.

Hovecamp, T.M. (1997) 'Professional associations or unions? A comparative look'. *Library Trends*, 46 (2), 232–44.

Johnson, I.M. (2004) 'Are you making any impact?' *Library and Information Impact*, 3 (6), 34–5.

Markless, S. and Streatfield, D.R. (2009) 'Reconceptualising information literacy for the Web 2.0 environment?' In Hatzipangos, S. and Warburton, S. (eds) *Handbook of Research on Social Software and Developing Community Ontologies*. Hershey, PA: Information Science Reference.

McKee, R. (2009) *Bob's Blog*. Online at http://communities. cilip.org.uk/blogs/cesdesk/archive/2009/06/11/on-the-wirral.aspx.

Moore, N. and Steele, J. (1991) *Information Intensive Britain.* British Library Research and Development Report number 6038. London: Policy Studies Institute.

Nolan, Lord. (1995) *Standards in Public Life: First Report of the Committee on Standards in Public Life.* London: HMSO.

Oppenheim, C. and Pollecutt, N. (2000) 'Professional associations and information science'. *Journal of Librarianship and Information Science,* 32 (4), 187–203.

Park, A., Curtice, J., Thomson, K., Phillips, M. and Clery, E. (2009) *British Social Attitudes: the 25th report.* National Centre for Social Research. London: Sage.

Park, A., Curtice, J., Thomson, K., Phillips, M., Clery, E. and Butt, S. (2010) *British Social Attitudes: the 26th report.* National Centre for Social Research. London: Sage.

Sandel, M. (2009) *A New Citizenship: new politics of the common good.* BBC *Reith Lectures.* Online at http://www.open2.net/reith2009/index.html.

Streatfield, D.R. and Markless, S. (2008) 'Evaluating the impact of information literacy in higher education: progress and prospects'. *Libri: International Journal of Libraries and Information Services,* 58 (2), 102–9.

19

The future of librarians in the workforce: a US perspective

José-Marie Griffiths and Donald W. King

Introduction

The future of libraries and librarians has been the subject of a great deal of speculation, mostly resulting from the tremendous technological change that has occurred over the past 30 years or so. However, other changes such as demographic trends towards multicultural societies, economic fluctuations, and the changing roles and perceptions of government and other institutions in society are emerging as significant additional drivers of change. Consequently, not only are there implications for the numbers of librarians and information professionals that will be needed in this changing world, but the nature of their roles and the institutional contexts within which they operate could alter the information services landscape quite dramatically. In turn, the educational preparation of librarians and information professionals must adapt to the changing landscape. This chapter discusses the future of librarians in the United States (US).

Projections of supply and demand for librarians

Over the past decade, concerns have been expressed about the impending loss of 'ageing/greying' workers to death, disability or retirement and the resulting labour shortages for many occupations (see for example St Lifer, 2000; Berry, 2002; Lenzini, 2002; Lynch, 2002; Lipscomb, 2003).

In 2000, the US Bureau of Labor Statistics (BLS) placed librarians seventh among occupations with the highest percentage of workers aged 45 years and older in 1998 (Dohm, 2000). The same article estimated that 46.4% of librarians would leave the workforce during the period 1998–2008, resulting in anticipated replacement needs for 50,000 librarians.

The library workforce did, in fact, experience a decline in the number of librarians employed, with a drop of almost 29% from 209,000 in 1998 to 149,000 in 2000, followed by an increase of 12% to 167,000 from 2000 to 2002. In addition to replacement of departing librarians, the number of librarians was expected to grow as new jobs were created. BLS projections (Hecker, 2001) anticipated a total of 41,000 job openings from new job creation and net replacements from 2000 to 2010. The BLS produced projections of the number of librarians from 2006 to 2016 where librarians (occupational code 25-4021) were characterised as 'administering libraries and performing related library services' and detailed task descriptions ranged from cataloguing to strategic research and working with databases. The BLS projections were for 158,000 librarians in 2006, projected to 164,000 in 2016, a 3.8 % increase.

IMLS-sponsored study on the future of librarians in the workforce

As a result of these projected changes in the library workforce, the Institute for Museum and Library Services (IMLS) commissioned a study in 2005,[1] *The Future of Librarians in the Workforce* (Griffiths and King, 2009) to:

- identify the nature of anticipated labour shortages in the library and information studies (LIS)[2] field resulting from retirement of current workers over the next decade
- assess the numbers and types of LIS jobs that will become available in the US from retirements or new job creation through the year 2016
- determine the skills required to fill such vacancies
- assess the current and potential capacity of graduate LIS schools to meet future demand for LIS professionals
- develop effective approaches to recruiting, educating and retaining workers to fill these positions.

The study involved 21 surveys of libraries and library staff conducted with public, academic, special and school libraries. Each type of library was sent a web-based survey which had a section common to all surveyed libraries. However, four surveys included a second part dealing with operations, services, functions or competencies. A fifth survey asked the libraries to forward a staff survey to their staff members. A survey was also sent to US LIS schools with American Library Association (ALA) accredited programmes. Altogether, we received responses from 6,733 out of 21,544 libraries, from 5,742 library staff including 2,207 accredited Master of Library Science (MLS) librarians and from 47 of the 51 LIS schools with accredited programmes.

Demand for librarians

The study determined that from 2008 through 2017 the demand for librarians to work in public, academic, school and special libraries is expected to significantly outpace the current supply of graduates from ALA-accredited programmes in the US.[3] In 2007–8 there were approximately 101,000 librarians employed in 119,207 libraries. Over the following decade, more than 62,300 librarians will need to be hired by libraries to fill vacancies and newly established positions (Table 19.1).

At the start of the projection period, there were over 3,764 positions vacant. During the next 10 years an additional 47,809 vacancies will result from current librarians dropping out of the library workforce for a number of reasons. Over the same time period, an estimated 4,762 new librarian positions will be created, mostly in public libraries, as the population increases. Thus, there is an estimated 4.71% increase in MLS

Table 19.1 Demand for accredited MLS librarians (2007–8 to 2016–17)

	Public	Academic	Special	School	Total
Current MLS Librarians	36,169	29,278	17,719	17,797	100,963
Current vacancies	1,408	401	850	1,105	3,764
Anticipated vacancies	21,165	14,502	7,540	10,587	53,791
New positions	3,745	168	377	472	4,762
Total demand	26,318	15,071	8,767	12,164	62,320

Source: University of North Carolina at Chapel Hill, School of Information and Library Science for the Institute of Museum and Library Services (IMLS).

librarians over the years, which is the same order of magnitude as the 3.8% increase forecast by BLS for all librarians. Finally, of newly filled positions during the decade, 5,985 will need to be refilled as more librarians leave the workforce. The annual demand decreases steadily from 11,374 vacancies in 2007–8 to 4,333 in 2016–17 (Table 19.2).

Reasons for librarians leaving the library workforce

Librarians drop out of the library workforce for a variety of reasons, including death, illness or disability; retirement; employment in another occupation; family obligations, education or military reasons; downsizing or being laid off, among others. In 2007–8, the patterns of librarian departures from the library workforce varied somewhat by type of library (Table 19.3). While the patterns are similar for public and academic libraries, special librarians experienced significantly more downsizing and lay-offs (22% of librarians leaving the workforce compared with 2–3%) and fewer retirements (24% compared with 45–50%).

Table 19.2 Total MLS librarian demand by source of demand, by years (2007–8 to 2016–17)

Year	Total attrition	Current vacancies	Expected new positions	Total demand
2007–8	6,925	3,764	685	11,374
2008–9	6,408	–	643	7,051
2009–10	6,102	–	599	6,701
2010–11	5,723	–	555	6,278
2011–12	5,438	–	507	5,945
2012–13	5,160	–	460	5,620
2013–14	4,861	–	406	5,267
2014–15	4,778	–	355	5,133
2015–16	4,314	–	304	4,618
2016–17	4,085	–	248	4,333
Total	53,794	3,764	4,762	62,320

Source: University of North Carolina at Chapel Hill, School of Information and Library Science for the Institute of Museum and Library Services (IMLS).

| Table 19.3 | Proportion of accredited MLS librarians leaving the library workforce, by reason for leaving (2007–8) |

	Public (%)	Academic (%)	Special (%)	School (%)
Death, illness, disability	9	14	15	9
Retirement	45	50	24	46
Employed in another occupation	10	9	13	n/a
Downsized or laid off	3	2	22	n/a
Other	32	25	26	47

Source: University of North Carolina at Chapel Hill, School of Information and Library Science for the Institute of Museum and Library Services (IMLS).

The number of librarians working outside libraries is also expected to grow. Currently an estimated 20–25% of qualified librarians take positions outside libraries, mostly performing librarian-like duties.

Supply of librarians

The total number of Master's degrees awarded from US programmes accredited by the ALA has grown somewhat since 1980, but remained relatively flat through the 1990s and then experienced a burst of growth from 2003 onwards (Davis and Hall, 2006). The IMLS study's 2009 survey of ALA-accredited programmes in the US determined that approximately 5,850 Master's degrees were awarded in 2008–9. Much of this recent growth has been attributed to the emergence of web-based distance education programmes and expansion of ALA accreditation to include a handful of additional Master's programmes in Information Science, Information Management and so on. However, the library workplace faces increasing competition for those graduates, especially from the growing information industry. Individual academic programmes estimated that between 49% and 96% of their graduates take jobs in libraries, resulting in an overall average of 77%. This yields an effective supply of approximately 4,500 graduates moving into library positions in 2008–9.

The library staff survey yielded an estimate of 3,437 graduating in 2006 taking jobs in academic (1,380), public (1,260) and special (797) libraries. The school librarian survey results had too few responses to make an estimate. However, the other results appear to confirm the number of graduates going into the library workforce.

Very few programmes are anticipating growth over the next several years: some are experiencing a slight decline attributed to the economy; a handful are anticipating small increases.[4] We can assume that the supply of qualified librarians will remain steady during the decade. Thus, the anticipated demand for 62,320 librarians to work in libraries over the next decade cannot be met by the 45,000 graduates expected to take library positions during that time. The unmet demand of 17,320 librarians is the equivalent of almost four times the total annual US supply of librarians into libraries. Two factors exacerbate this deficit in supply: the age at which librarians graduate with their Master's degrees, and increasing competition for librarians.

Age of graduating librarians

The IMLS study determined the average age at graduation for librarians to be 30.6 years. In a complementary study, Marshall et al. (2009) found that the average age of graduates from all library science programmes in the state of North Carolina during the period 1964 to 2007 was 32.7 years. Not all of the programmes were/are accredited by the ALA. Just under half (47%) of currently employed librarians earned their MLS degrees after they turned 30 years old, while 29% were over 35 years old. The significance of the older graduation age is that individuals tend to spend less time in the profession and the replacement cycle is shorter than for some other professions. On the other hand, one reason for this phenomenon is that MLS librarians have had considerable experience in previous jobs, often have additional advanced degrees and are more mature and better able to assimilate into the library workforce.

Just over one third (36%) of librarians had prior full-time work experience in a library, while almost the same proportion (37%) had worked as a professional in another occupation prior to acquiring their MLS degrees. Not only did they have prior work experience, but many had spent substantial time working elsewhere. Nearly half of those with prior work experience had 10 or more years of experience in these capacities. Those working in another occupation had lengthier experience than those working in a library (31% versus 17% respectively with 10 or more years of prior work experience). Public librarians had the lengthiest prior work experience in a library, but all types of librarian had extensive experience in another occupation.

Academic and special librarians are much more likely to have other advanced degrees than are public librarians. Approximately 37% of academic librarians and 29% of special librarians have other degrees (Master's and doctorates), as compared with 17% of public librarians. This difference could, in part, contribute to the fact that public librarian salaries are much lower on average ($39,730) than academic ($53,770) and special ($59,300) librarian salaries.

Increased competition for librarians

The second factor exacerbating the librarian supply deficit is increased competition for librarians, especially from the growing information industry. The IMLS study projects a growth in demand for librarians (current librarians plus current vacancies plus new positions created) over the decade of 3.8%. This is similar to the BLS projection of 3.6% (Dohm and Shniper, 2007) for librarians. The same BLS report projected increases of between 16% and 29% for some competing occupations in the information industry: computer systems analysts, database administrators, management analysts, computer and information systems managers, and computer and information scientists engaged in research. Over the decade, the total projected demand for these competing occupations is 796,000 jobs, as compared with 62,320 for librarians in libraries. Furthermore, these competing occupations have much higher average salaries (Liming and Wolf, 2008). The average librarian salary is $49,110; the average salary for the competing occupations is $73,840 (ranging from $69,760 to $100,104). Thus the competition for librarians is very high in terms of both demand and salary in alternative but related occupations.

Yet another source of competition for librarians is the increasing number of educational programmes preparing graduates in a variety of information-related disciplines. In 2007, the American Society for Information Science and Technology's then president, Nancy Roderer, launched the Information Professionals Task Force to study trends in the evolving information professions, the educational programmes that prepare information professionals and the processes aimed at ensuring the quality of those programmes. As part of its efforts the Task Force, in partnership with the Council on Library and Information Resources, commissioned a review – *Graduate Information Programs and Accreditation: landscape analysis and survey* (Becker and Kinney, 2008). The study identified Master's level programmes and accreditation practices associated with US and Canadian programmes related to information disciplines. In all, over 900 distinct information-related Master's programmes in 468 institutions were identified. To put this volume of programmes and institutions into context, there are currently 62 ALA-accredited Master's programmes in Library and Information Studies and related information disciplines in 57 institutions in the US and Canada. Of the 900 programmes identified, some are designated as majors and others as concentrations within a major. A total of 220 distinct majors or concentration areas were found in 500 academic units. Slightly more than one third of the programmes are located in four core disciplinary domains: engineering, computer science, information science and applied information science/informatics. Of the remaining programmes, half were found within the business domain. Most of the remaining programmes are distributed among biological and health sciences, library science, public administration, communications and education. Some 60% of the programmes have majors or concentrations in the four categories: information systems (305 programmes), informatics (106 programmes), information technology (118 programmes) and information science (98 programmes). Almost all programmes, regardless of the specific degree title, arrange their curricula around three or four overlapping areas which include aspects related to:

- **information content:** information organisation, retrieval, analysis, design, architecture
- **technology:** computer infrastructure, networks, database design, programming
- **management:** managing information organisations, project management
- **people:** information behaviour, human–computer interaction, information policy.

Given the large number of alternative programmes to the MLS and the growing demand for information professionals in the expanding information industry, the traditional markets for librarians and their educational preparation account for a small and decreasing share of the total landscape. Responses to the changing landscape have varied. The ALA has for decades engaged in lively discussion and debate on the future of library education. These activities have engaged other professional associations and organisations that work with libraries, such as the American Library and Information Science Educators, American Society for Information Science and Technology (ASIS&T),

Medical Library Association, Special Libraries Association, OCLC etc. Now, after more than a decade of a broadening of both LIS curricula and interpretation of accreditation standards, there appears to be a refocusing on the professional librarian working in libraries and library-like information organisations. Under his presidential initiative, Michael Gorman invited discussion of reform for library education, including 'how librarianship could reclaim its turf from the invading computer geeks, informationists and alien PhD holders from other disciplines who have conquered faculty posts and deanships at many schools' (Berry, 2006). This met with strong resistance from the younger, more technologically adept librarians. Burnett and Bonnici (2006) argue, on the other hand, that the division between librarianship and the information technology professions is based on whether the professional perspective is to be retained in LIS education or whether it should be abandoned in favour of a purely academic discipline. While no specific changes emerged from the Gorman initiative, it did stir up the debate and led to his successor Leslie Gorman's establishment of a Library Education Task Force which recommended adoption of *Core Competencies of Librarianship* (ALA, 2009b), and *2008 Standards for Accreditation of Masters Programs in Library and Information Studies* (ALA, 2008). These documents aim to 're-orient both library education and the relationships between practicing librarians and library educators in a positive direction to ensure the supply of a new generation of knowledgeable, well-educated librarians to staff the libraries and information agencies of today and tomorrow' (Hayden, 2009). The Task Force also recommended the establishment of a special task force on library education outside the ALA-accredited Master's programmes.

At the same time, others sought to expand the view of the information profession. ASIS&T responded by looking broadly at the total information professional landscape and seeks to engage collaboratively with other professional groups and leverage its role as a bridging organisation. Perhaps the most comprehensive review of professional groups and the underlying disciplinary arenas has been developed by Marcia Bates (2007). In designing the new, third edition of the *Encyclopaedia of Library and Information Sciences* she convened a large number of collaborators to help define the intellectual territory that should be covered, from which developed a model of the disciplinary areas and their interrelationships. What emerged was a confirmation that there are a number of information disciplines and that they belong to the category of meta-disciplines, along with communications/journalism and education.

Meanwhile, a group of deans of schools offering multiple information-related academic programmes started to identify themselves as information schools or 'iSchools' and established the 'iCaucus', to increase the recognition of the information field and its importance to society and to provide a forum for collaboration (Larsen, 2009). While initially a small group of institutions took the lead in establishing the iCaucus organisation,[5] the defining characteristics of iSchools include:

- an interest in the relationship between information, technology and people

- a commitment to learning and understanding the role of information in human endeavours

- a recognition that expertise in all forms of information is required for progress in science, business, education and culture

- a belief that this expertise must include understanding of the uses and users of information, as well as information technologies and their applications (Larsen, 2009).

King (2006) observed that iSchools 'straddle the academy's ancient engagement with information and the contemporary challenges of ubiquitous information affecting all aspects of society. ... The [iSchool] movement is emergent; its equilibrium can only be found in an essential tension among competing visions in a world of rapid technical and social change. [iSchool] identity is elusive and will remain so for the foreseeable future.'

Academic institutions are also facing significant retirement of faculty (Harrison and Hargrove, 2006). This phenomenon is prevalent in LIS programs with ALA accredited programmes in North America. In 2005, one-third (34%) of the full-time faculty and just over one-fifth (22%) of tenure-track faculty (i.e. those in more senior academic positions or widely published) were over 60 years of age; 58% of full-time and 61% of tenure-track faculty were aged over 50 years.

US librarians and libraries during recessions

Today's economic situation calls into question and increases uncertainty about the future employment prospects and opportunities for librarians. Recessions in the US seem to coincide with the turn of decades. The past three recessions include:

- the early 1980s, when there were two economic troughs, in January 1980 and November 1982, and average unemployment rates ranged from 5.8% in 1979 to 9.7% in 1982

- the early 1990s, when the trough was in March 1991 and unemployment went from 5.6% in 1990 to 7.5% in 1992 and back to 6.1 in 1994

- the early 2000s, when the trough was in November 2001 and unemployment went from 4.0% in 2000 to 6.0% in 2003 and down to 5.5% in 2004.

The current recession began in earnest in 2008 and continues at the time of writing. We examined evidence of the effects of these recessions on librarians, visits to libraries, library services and library operations. Our most in-depth information relates to public libraries, but we also provide some evidence for academic, school and special libraries. The size of public, academic, special and school library staff was obtained by surveys conducted in 1982 for the National Center for Educational Statistics (Cooper et al., 1983). Estimates of staff size were obtained for the years 1978 (when unemployment was 6.1%) to 1982 (when unemployment was 9.7%, the peak year). Observations were made for full-time equivalent librarians, other paid professionals, and technical, clerical and other support staff. The results indicate that the number of public librarians increased by 3.5%, academic by 6.6%, special by 18.9% and school by 7.2%.

Generally, all types of library staff increased during this recession, even though overall unemployment during this period increased from 6.1% to 9.7%. Non-librarian staff showed a much greater growth, particularly in terms of other professionals during a time in which considerable library technology was being introduced. One reason for the slower growth in librarians as compared with other staff is that the supply of graduates of library education programmes decreased substantially during this time. The number of MLS librarian graduates decreased from 5,500 in 1978 to 4,200 in 1981 and was expected to drop to 3,700 in 1982. By 1983, the number of graduates had fallen to 3,494 (Myers, 1986). Furthermore, during this time, librarian graduates were increasingly hired in non-traditional work, even though starting salaries of librarians increased by 8.0% in constant dollars from 1978 to 1981. Library expenditures increased from $1.25 per capita in 1978 to $1.50 in 1980, suggesting that this did not appreciably affect employment during the early three years of the recession.

The National Center for Education Statistics had begun collecting detailed public library statistics by 1990, and through the last two recessions (and now up to 2007, maintained by the IMLS). The unemployment rate changed from 5.6% in 1990 to 7.5% in 1992 and back down to 6.1% in 1994. Staff sizes varied somewhat between the two recessions, although the number of librarians (MLS and other) increased during both recessions (11.4% in the 1990s and 4.4% in the early 2000s). Adjusted by population size, the changes were +5.7% and -1.3%, respectively. The size of other paid staff was up 2.2% (or -4.2% when adjusted by population) in the early 1990s and up 4.6% (or -1.2% when adjusted). During the 2000s recession, the total number of full-time equivalent academic librarians increased from 25,170 to 26,469 (a 5.2% increase), although the average per library decreased 2.2% because the number of academic libraries increased by 8.3% during this period. The number of 'other professionals' increased by 10.4%, but non-professional staff actually decreased by 1.2%. There is little evidence of how the current recession has affected or will affect library staff, other than a BLS estimate that the number of librarians decreased by 4.2% from 2007 to 2009 and library technicians decreased 3.8%, although both show an increase from 2008 to 2009 (4.6% for librarians and 13.6% for library technicians).

A worldwide survey of libraries was conducted by the Centre for Information Behaviour and the Evaluation of Research (CIBER), University College London (CIBER, 2009) to examine the effects of the current global recession. These results mirror US results in that 71.7% of institutions indicate no plans yet to cut staffing levels. Of the 23.8% of institutions that were planning cuts, academic libraries were most likely to cut, and corporate libraries least likely. Most libraries that plan cuts say they would do so through a freeze on recruitment and/or not filling vacant posts.

Generally, the library workforce seems to hold up during recessions even though income and expenses are cut substantially. Perhaps the workforce size is retained because library visits and services are generally increased substantially during economic downturns. Below we discuss such use trends for public libraries for which data are more prevalent. In the US the number of public libraries has increased steadily over the years, although not at the same pace as the population. During the early 1990s recession, the population increased 5.4% but the number of public libraries decreased slightly (-0.6%), but during the 2000s recession population increased 5.8% while public libraries increased by 1.5%. During both recessions the number of mobile libraries declined, probably as a cost-cutting measure. The starkest consequence of recessions was cuts in revenue and expenditures. As an indicator of these cuts, results are provided in constant dollars per capita. Funding, measured this way, was up slightly in the 1990s recession (+1.8%), but down in the 2000s recession (-1.9%). In both instances, increased local sources of funding made up for drastic cuts in state, federal and other sources (+5.1% and +3.8% increases in local resources, respectively). The ALA (2009a) reports a decline in public library funding between financial year (FY) 2009 and FY 2010, where 24 states (of 50 states and the District of Columbia) report cuts in state funding and half of these were greater than 11%. Another ALA report (Davis, 2010) suggests a substantial departure from previous recession sources of funding from FY 2008 to FY 2009: local/county down -2.7% in constant dollars, state (-4.7%), federal (+22.0%) and other (+16.9%), with an overall increase of 3.1%.

Expenditures of public libraries in constant dollars per capita reflect funding sources. The 1990s recession showed an increase in expenditure per capita of +4.5% and +1.8% in the 2000s recession. Salaries increased during both recessions (14.4% and 4.3%, respectively) and the ALA reports that salaries increased +5.7% from FY 2008 to FY 2009 (Davis, 2010). Thus, salaries do not appear to suffer, partially due to local government policies, but also because service demand also increases during recessions. Generally, salaries tend to be about two-thirds of overall expenditures. The CIBER (2009) study shows that 37.4% of institutions expect to cut spending over the next two years. Of these institutions, 28.3% are reported to be cutting staffing budgets and relatively few (18.1%) indicate they plan to cut services over the next two years. Relatively few (18.1%) indicate that they plan to cut library services over the next two years. In US public libraries both visits and services increase during recessions, as shown below in Table 19.4.

Table 19.4 Increases (%) per capita

Recession	Visits	Circulation	Reference transactions	Inter-library lending
1990s	32.2	10.3	19.6	58.8
2000s	9.3	10.9	–	75.9

Source: University of North Carolina at Chapel Hill, School of Information and Library Science for the Institute of Museum and Library Services (IMLS).

Circulation is increased even though expenditures for collections decreased in constant dollars per capita (–13.6% in the 1990s and –11.4% in the 2000s). Based on the ALA report (Davis, 2010), there appears to be a slight increase in constant dollars (+0.6%) from FY 2008 to FY 2009. Inter-library borrowing is up because of reduced collection expenditures. Reference transactions have decreased over the past decade, which is reflected in the 2000s recession. From 2003 to 2007, the number of reference transactions decreased by about 3.1% (Davis, 2010). The overall decrease is caused, in part, by access to the Internet, including from the libraries (Griffiths and King, 2008).The mode of visit to public libraries has increased visits even more because of online remote access to library services, which increased visits by as much as 75% and actually facilitates more in-person visits (Griffiths and King, 2008). Visits and services also appear to have increased substantially during the current recession, with an emphasis on supporting job hunting and access to government information.

Attitudes towards library and information science (LIS) education

Surveyed librarians were asked to rate how well their LIS education prepared them for their initial assignment and their current position. The seven-point rating scale varied from 1 – not at all well, to 4 – somewhat well, to 7 – extremely well. Table 19.5 shows the proportion (%) of MLS librarians who rated educational preparation for their initial assignment and their current position at various levels. Average ratings are also displayed.

About half (53.1%) of the MLS librarians reported that their LIS education prepared them somewhat well to extremely well (ratings 5 to 7) for their initial assignment, but fewer (42.6%) rated this level (5 to 7) for their current position. Among the three types of librarian, academic librarians rate the LIS education preparation highest for initial assignment (4.73 versus 4.59 for the other two), but the average drops to 4.25 for their current position. Perhaps the biggest concern is the almost 17% who indicated that their education did not prepare them at all well for their initial assignment: 15%, 17% and 20% of public, academic and special librarians, respectively.

Table 19.5 Proportion (%) and average ratings of how well ILS education prepared surveyed MLS librarians for their initial assignment and current position, by type of librarian (2007)

	Proportion (%) of MLS librarians			
	Public (n=960)	Academic (n=799)	Special (n=304)	All (n=2,063)
Initial assignment				
Not at all well to somewhat well (1–3)	15.40	16.50	19.70	16.70
Somewhat well (4)	31.60	28.80	29.80	30.20
Somewhat well to extremely well (5–7)	53.00	54.70	50.50	53.10
Total	**100.00**	**100.00**	**100.00**	**100.00**
Average rating	4.60	4.73	4.56	4.64
Current position				
Not at all well to somewhat well (1–3)	25.00	26.60	28.50	26.30
Somewhat well (4)	31.30	32.50	28.20	31.10
Somewhat well to extremely well (5–7)	43.70	40.80	43.30	42.60
Total	**100.00**	**99.90**	**100.00**	**100.00**
Average rating	4.31	4.25	4.27	4.28

Source: University of North Carolina at Chapel Hill, School of Information and Library Science for the Institute of Museum and Library Services (IMLS).

Length of experience in the library workforce can have a bearing on how the librarians rate education for both their initial assignment and their current position (Table 19.6).

The ratings for initial assignment increase with years of experience, but decrease somewhat for the current position (with the exception of special librarians). There may be several reasons why the initial assignment ratings increase with experience. One is that librarians were prepared better in the past (i.e. those who have 20 or more years' experience). Also, it could be that some librarians with poor preparation for initial assignment merely left the workforce, thus leaving fewer librarians with 20 or more years' experience in base number reporting. The difference between initial assignment and current position ratings increases substantially with years of experience (0.36 difference across all librarians).

Table 19.6 Proportion (%) and average ratings of how well ILS education prepared surveyed MLS librarians for their initial assignment and current position, by years of experience and type of librarian (2007)

Years of experience	Average ratings (1–not at all well to 7–extremely well)			All (n=2,063)
	Public (n=960)	Academic (n=799)	Special (n=304)	
Initial assignment				
Less than 10 years	4.59	4.58	4.23	4.51
10 to 19 years	4.72	4.69	4.64	4.69
20 or more	4.75	4.86	4.75	4.79
All years	4.60	4.73	4.56	4.64
Current position				
Less than 10 years	4.50	4.34	4.03	4.34
10 to 19 years	4.22	4.22	4.33	4.24
20 or more	4.21	4.20	4.39	4.24
All years	4.31	4.25	4.27	4.28

Source: University of North Carolina at Chapel Hill, School of Information and Library Science for the Institute of Museum and Library Services (IMLS).

Attitudes towards work-related issues

Surveyed MLS librarians rated the importance of and satisfaction with five work-related issues: salary, fringe benefits, type of work done, opportunities for advancement and geographic location. Five-point scales of importance and satisfaction were used, ranging from 1 – very unimportant, to 5 – very important, and from 1 – very dissatisfied, to 5 – very satisfied, with average ratings displayed in Table 19.7.

The nature of the work done is rated highest by far, in both importance and satisfaction, by all three types of librarian, with the exception of satisfaction with geographic location, which was rated higher by special librarians. On the other hand, 'opportunities for advancement' was generally rated lowest in importance and satisfaction. One criterion in assessing the work-related issues is the numeric difference between the average importance and satisfaction ratings. Here, salary has by far the greatest difference, of 0.74 (4.03–3.29). While satisfaction with salaries is not rated the lowest, it is the lowest in difference. The next highest difference in ratings is opportunities for

Table 19.7 Average ratings of work-related issues, by type of librarian

| Work-related issues | Type of rating | Average ratings (1 to 5) | | | |
		Public (n=996)	Academic (n=882)	Special (n=309)	All (n=2,187)
Salary	Importance	4.05	4.00	4.02	4.03
	Satisfaction	3.30	3.31	3.25	3.29
Fringe benefits	Importance	4.02	3.98	4.01	4.00
	Satisfaction	3.58	3.68	3.79	3.66
Type of work done	Importance	4.48	4.34	4.35	4.40
	Satisfaction	4.23	4.21	4.04	4.18
Opportunities for advancement	Importance	3.54	3.44	3.64	3.53
	Satisfaction	3.20	3.00	2.89	3.06
Geographic location	Importance	4.02	4.01	3.98	4.01
	Satisfaction	4.06	4.03	4.13	4.06

Source: University of North Carolina at Chapel Hill, School of Information and Library Science for the Institute of Museum and Library Services (IMLS).

advancement (0.47). When making career choices (e.g., to leave a job) the gap between importance and satisfaction can have relevance.

Attitudes toward librarianship

MLS librarians were asked whether, if they had the opportunity to choose their career over again, they would still choose librarianship. They were given five possible responses: definitely not, probably not, unsure, probably and definitely (with ratings of 1 – definitely not, to 5 – definitely). The results of these ratings are given in Table 19.8.

About three-quarters of MLS librarians say they probably or definitely would choose librarianship again, and this attitude is consistent among the three types of librarian.

Table 19.9 shows that average ratings seem to go down somewhat in the 10 to 19 years' period of experience and then up again. Perhaps some who are dissatisfied with librarianship during this time leave, so that the average ratings increase for those who decide to stay. This result may reflect dissatisfaction with opportunities for advancement identified earlier.

Table 19.8 Proportion (%) and average ratings of whether surveyed MLS librarians would choose librarianship again as a career, by type of librarian (2007)

Type of response	Proportion (%) of MLS librarians			All (n=2,050)
	Public (n=953)	Academic (n=796)	Special (n=301)	
Definitely	41.0	36.4	35.5	38.2
Probably	35.5	36.8	38.9	36.7
Unsure	15.0	16.2	16.3	15.7
Probably not	7.1	8.7	7.6	7.8
Definitely not	1.4	1.9	1.7	1.6
Total	100.0	100.0	100.0	100.0
Average	4.08	3.97	3.99	4.02

Source: University of North Carolina at Chapel Hill, School of Information and Library Science for the Institute of Museum and Library Services (IMLS).

Table 19.9 Average ratings of whether surveyed MLS librarians would choose librarianship again as a career, by years of experience and type of librarian (2007)

Years of experience	Average ratings of choice (1 to 5)			All (n=2,050)
	Public (n=953)	Academic (n=796)	Special (n=301)	
Less than 10 years	4.13	4.05	4.01	4.08
10 to 19 years	3.96	3.88	3.95	3.93
20 or more	4.13	3.97	4.00	4.05
All years	4.08	3.97	3.99	4.02

Source: University of North Carolina at Chapel Hill, School of Information and Library Science for the Institute of Museum and Library Services (IMLS).

An indication of the influence on choosing librarianship again as a career is satisfaction with work-related issues such as type of work done, salary, and opportunity for advancement. Table 19.10 provides such evidence.

Average ratings of satisfaction with type of work done are by far the highest for those who say they definitely or probably would choose librarianship (4.38) and the difference in rating with those who would not choose librarianship is 1.10 average rating (4.38 minus 3.28). With salary and opportunity for advancement, the differences in ratings are

Table 19.10 Average ratings of satisfaction of type of work done, salaries and opportunities for advancement, by whether librarianship would be chosen again as a career, and by type of librarian (2007)

Work-related issues Would choose librarianship	Average satisfaction rating (1 to 5)			
	Public (n=987)	Academic (n=7v3)	Special (n=300)	All (n=2,060)
Type of work done				
Definitely/probably would	4.40	4.40	4.30	4.38
Unsure	3.86	4.01	4.01	3.94
Definitely/probably would not	3.31	3.28	3.21	3.28
Salary				
Definitely/probably would	3.45	3.45	3.62	3.49
Unsure	3.04	3.12	3.11	3.08
Definitely/probably would not	2.36	2.78	2.94	2.63
Opportunity for advancement				
Definitely/probably would	3.34	3.16	3.21	3.25
Unsure	2.93	2.74	2.77	2.83
Definitely/probably would not	2.42	2.37	2.33	2.38

Source: University of North Carolina at Chapel Hill, School of Information and Library Science for the Institute of Museum and Library Services (IMLS).

0.86 and 0.87 respectively, providing an indication that the difference between those who would and those who would not choose librarianship is generally lower than for the type of work done.

Trends in librarian competencies

In addition to determining the future demand for librarians, it is important to know whether the nature of the work is changing in any way and, if so, in what direction. The project survey design team gathered competency statements published by relevant professional associations, as well as its own research to develop a unified list organised into six broad categories: operations/technical services, user services, technology/systems, digital library management, management/administration and general professional. This study asked about the change in importance of various librarian competencies over the previous five years and trends for future importance. The competencies vary according to the functions performed, and their importance varies to some extent by type of library.

The results show that academic and special librarians have very similar, evolving competency requirements while public librarians demonstrate some differences from them. Academic and special librarians tend to place more importance on electronic collections, cataloguing, user training and bibliographic instruction for electronic services and database searching. Public librarians are more focused on collection development, dealing with all types of materials, training and bibliographic instruction in general. When considering technology-related competencies, all three types of librarian have similar perceptions of importance, with public librarians focusing a little more on hardware and systems, while academic and special librarians are more focused on website development. In the area of digital libraries all types of librarian assessed the importance of various competencies in similar ways.

In terms of administrative competencies, academic and special librarians had a little more focus on leadership and policy development, while public librarians were concerned with planning and budgeting, management, and public relations/marketing. Overall, in terms of general professional competencies, all three types of librarian identified as important: positive attitude towards users and colleagues, effective communication skills and critical thinking. Public librarians also noted the importance of behaviour management skills (such as dealing with difficult patrons). Academic and special librarians were especially concerned with the ability to evaluate, select and filter resources. When considering trends in increasing importance of competencies, there was much more agreement across the three types of librarian. Librarians from all types of libraries identified as increasing most in importance:

- web content management skills
- knowledge and skills in training and bibliographic instruction for electronic services
- knowledge and skills to develop websites
- knowledge of computer operating systems
- digital library design skills

- database management skills
- knowledge of mark-up languages
- public relations and marketing skills
- critical thinking for solving library problems.

Public librarians also viewed knowledge of cataloguing principles; knowledge of sources of non-electronic materials; knowledge of foreign languages; knowledge of legal, financial and funding issues; and knowledge of funders' expectations of the library as increasing most in importance. Academic and special librarians also identified knowledge of sources of electronic materials; archives and records management; licence negotiation skills; knowledge of technology network options; ability to evaluate, select and filter information; and making presentations to groups as most increasing in importance.

Conclusion

The future for qualified librarians is strong. There is a continuing need for librarians to reinforce and strengthen their roles as leaders, navigators, organisers, managers and interpreters of the expanding record of human activity and accomplishment in all its forms. However, the library profession and workforce face continued and increasing competition for qualified individuals from the rapidly evolving information industry. Librarians need to recognise that, to remain relevant as society at large becomes much more aware of and engaged with recorded knowledge opportunities, they need to be proactive in monitoring and adapting to change, and to pay considerable attention to positioning and marketing themselves in this environment.

Notes

1. See http://www.libraryworkforce.org for more information.
2. The IMLS study was focused on the need for professionals with a degree accredited by the ALA. The accredited degrees are Master's degrees in librarianship and some information science/management areas. Basically, the accreditation ensures the readiness of the degree holders to hold professional positions in libraries, although they may opt to work in other contexts.

3. The ALA does accredit programmes in Canada and Puerto Rico as well as in the USA.
4. Master's degrees awarded by U.S. ALA-accredited programmes in 2009, as reported to the ALA, totalled 7,179.
5. As of August 2010, there are 21 US institutions and six international members of the iCaucus.

References

ALA. (2008) *Standards for Accreditation of Master's Programs in Library and Information Studies.* Chicago: American Library Association. Online at http://www.ala.org/ala/educationcareers/education/accreditedprograms/standards/index.cfm.

ALA. (2009a) *Public Library Funding and Technology Access Study.* Chicago: American Library Association. Online at http://www.ala.org/ala/research/initiatives/plftas/2009_2010/index.cfm.

ALA. (2009b) *Core Competences of Librarianship.* Chicago: American Library Association. Online at http://www.ala.org/ala/educationcareers/careers/corecomp/corecompetences/index.cfm.

Bates, M.J. (2007) 'Defining the information disciplines in encyclopedia development'. *Information Research*, 12 (4). Online at http://informationr.net/ir/12-4/colis/colis29.html.

Becker, S. and Kinney, B. (2008) *Graduate Information Programs and Accreditation: landscape survey and analysis.* Silver Spring, MD: American Society for Information Science and Technology. Online at http://www.asis.org/Accreditation_Report.pdf.

Berry, J.N. (2006) 'Blatant Berry: can ALA bring change? Disappointed by Gorman's effort to reform library education'. *Library Journal*, 15 September 2006. Online at http://www.libraryjournal.com/article/CA6370229.html.

Berry, J.W. (2002) 'Addressing the recruitment and diversity crisis'. *American Libraries*, 33 (2), 7.

Burnett, K. and Bonnici, L. (2006) 'Contested terrain: accreditation and the future of the profession of librarianship'. *Library Quarterly*, 76 (2), 193–219.

CIBER (Centre for Information Behaviour and the Evaluation of Research). (2009) *The Economic Downturn and Libraries: survey findings.* London: University College London. Online at http://www.ucl.ac.uk/infostudies/research/ciber/charleston-survey.pdf.

Cooper, M.D., Van House, N.A. and Roderer, N.K. (1983) *Library Human Resources: a study of supply and demand*. Chicago: American Library Association.

Davis, D.M. (2010) *The Condition of U.S. Libraries: public library trends, 2002–2009*. Chicago: American Library Association, 2010.

Davis, D.M. and Hall, T. (2006) *Diversity Counts*. Chicago: American Library Association.

Dohm, A. (2000) 'Gauging the labor force effects of retiring baby-boomers'. *Monthly Labor Review*, July.

Dohm, A. and Shniper, L. (2007) 'Employment outlook: 2006–16'. *Monthly Labor Review*, November.

Griffiths, J.-M. and King, D.W. (2008) *Interconnections: The IMLS national study on the use of libraries, museums and the Internet*. Washington, DC: Institute for Museum and Library Services. Online at http://www.interconnectionsreport.org.

Griffiths, J.-M. and King, D.W. (2009) *A National Study of the Future of Librarians in the Workforce*. Washington, DC: Institute for Museum and Library Services. Online at http://libraryworkforce.org/ tiki-index.php.

Harrison, H.D. and Hargrove, M.J. (2006) 'Ageing faculty: workforce challenges and issues facing higher education'. *Business Perspectives*, Fall–Winter.

Hayden, C. (2009) Cover memo transmitting Library Education Task Force Final Report to ALA Executive Board. Online at http://www.lita. org/ala//aboutala/governance/officers/eb_documents/2008_2009eb documents/ebd12_30.pdf.

Hecker, D.E. (2001) 'Occupational employment projections to 2010'. *Monthly Labor Review*, November.

King, J.L. (2006) 'Identity in the i-School movement'. *Bulletin of the American Society for Information Science and Technology*, April–May. Online at http://www.asis.org/Bulletin/Apr-06/king.html.

Larsen, R.L. (2009) 'The iSchools'. In *Encyclopedia of Library and Information Sciences, 3rd edition*. Abingdon: Taylor and Francis. See also http://www.ischools.org.

Lenzini, R.T. (2002) 'The graying of the library profession: a survey of our professional association and their responses'. *Searcher*, 10 (7). Online at http://www.infotoday.com/searcher/jul02/lenzini.htm.

Liming, D. and Wolf, M. (2008) 'Job outlook by education, 2006–10'. *Occupational Outlook Quarterly*, 52 (2), 2–28.

Lipscomb, C. (2003) 'Library supply and demand'. *Journal of the Medical Library Association*, 91 (1), 7–10.

Lynch, M.J. (2002) 'Reaching 65: lots of librarians will be there soon'. *American Libraries*, March. Online at http://www.ala.org/ala/alonline/resources/slctdarticles/reaching65.pdf.

Marshall, J.G. et al. (2009) 'Where are they now? Results of a career survey of library and information science graduates'. *Library Trends*, 58 (2), 141–54.

Myers, M. (1986) 'The job market for librarians'. *Library Trends*, 34 (4), 645–66.

St Lifer, E. (2000) 'The boomer brain drain: the last of a generation'. *Library Journal*, 125 (8), 38–42.

20

The value of libraries: the relationship between change, evaluation and role

Stephen Town

Introduction

What is the relevance and importance of evaluation to the role of libraries and their place in society? This chapter describes how approaches to library evaluation have responded to pressures arising from wider changes in the environment and society, and suggests that the related concepts of values and value will be the key to future approaches. Because behaviour follows measures, changing evaluation frameworks continually shape what libraries are and what they do. The first part of the chapter defines evaluation and argues for its importance in how libraries have defined themselves. The second part identifies some key past trends in evaluation, culminating in the current position of a variety of cross-pressures on libraries to prove their worth. The key question of the value of libraries is posed, with a brief review of some recent responses. Finally, the chapter seeks to offer a route to library value based on broader values, and how this might be characterised within the construct of the transcendent library.

What is evaluation and why is it important?

An assumption implicit throughout this book is that major changes are taking place in society and that these generate changes of requirement in what libraries are and what they do. There appears to be no doubt that libraries have changed substantially in the four decades since 1970, and that evaluation within libraries has tried to keep pace with these changes. Whether the concept of libraries which forms the framework for evaluation has developed apace in the world beyond libraries is more open to question. Libraries are a social construct (see, e.g., Cullen, 2006), but one of our problems is now a lack of clarity and certainty about this shared construct, exemplified in recent trends to rebrand libraries under other names such as 'discovery', 'explore' or 'learning' centres. What is clear is that these shifts in concept will lead to demands for different forms of evaluation and proof of contribution.

What is library evaluation? Some commentators (see, e.g., Brophy, 2006) make no distinction between the terms 'assessment' (as used widely in North America), 'performance measurement' (as used in libraries in the UK and Ireland and broadly understood throughout the world, and also the accepted term in the management discipline) and 'evaluation' (as used in some key works in the past, see, e.g., Lancaster, 1993). A perceived difference between evaluation and measurement was, however, sufficient for some library science publishers in the past to have had titles on each in their lists. The author's position would be that the differences might and sometimes do imply a different understanding of the activity described: assessment seems to the author to actively imply measurement for a purpose; measurement focuses on the activity itself but in relationship to a sense of due form, while evaluation might indicate an activity which offers an answer to a question arising beyond the library's boundaries. However, these terms are, more often than not, used interchangeably, and this chapter will do so.

The focus of this chapter is not the practice of evaluation, except where measurement tools and methods add to an understanding of the overall picture, but what might be termed a meta-level view of what performance measure developments indicate about libraries and their role. Performance measurement is inseparable from performance; performance is inseparable from a consideration of due form; and the assumptions behind the measures, as to what the due form is, help to provide a definition of role. Brophy (2008) records that library performance measurement has evolved rapidly over the last 30 years; but also suggests we are now at a watershed in this field, due to the fact that libraries are changing. Library performance measurement has certainly become a recognised sub-discipline in its own right: a healthy field of research and practice with its own journal; two large-scale international conferences; an extensive international community of practice with a readiness to question, respond to change and often to be well ahead of parent organisations in appreciation of this element of management. It is difficult to do justice to the extraordinary richness of library evaluation, and the author has no choice but to be personally selective in his sources for this chapter. In particular, examples have been drawn largely from the perspective of my own experience of specialist, academic and research libraries, but the conclusions are believed to be applicable to all library sectors and contexts.

It is often stated that measurement is about control, but this is perhaps too narrow a focus. The author's assumption is that there are probably three levels at which evaluation and measurement are used and have influence: firstly, for internal library operational management; secondly, for advocacy, strategy and understanding of the library and its services within its governance or organisational frame; and thirdly, for a broader justification for the role of the library or libraries within communities or societies. It could be suggested that, whilst as a profession we have generated good data and methods for the first, we have not been fully persuasive in the second; and are in danger of failure in the third, at least in some contexts. There would appear to be a greater need now than in the past to positively influence and shape the social imaginary (that is, the view of what our society values, or the institutions that it accepts as fundamental) in a way that strongly incorporates a role for libraries. In particular, the transcendent, collective and connective role of libraries does not play well in an increasingly individualistic, disconnected and fragmented society (as described, e.g., in Putnam, 2000 or Taylor, 2007) or as represented in extreme new technology rhetoric (see, e.g., Negroponte, 1995). Because the prevailing social imaginary consists partly of values, and value measurement should hinge on these shared values, this chapter gives more space to recent work on impact and value measurement and its relation to this third justificatory task of evaluation. It is, however, important to recognise that there are different perspectives outside the West and its privileged élites. The value of libraries to human flourishing seems less in dispute in developing contexts, where the proof that libraries change lives is a given and seems not to require campaigns, straplines or competitions.

Ten years ago, the author questioned whether the performance measurement frameworks that libraries were employing were sufficient, or whether in fact the forms of measurement used actually inhibited performance (Town, 2000), and suggested four hypotheses which might help to frame better measurement. Ten years on, some of these factors have indeed been used to frame new measures, as a result of both external pressures and internal professional recognition. The factors identified then were:

- quality management
- digital development
- library development stage
- staff as a key resource.

These are reflected in some of the trends identified below. A key difference now is that the question of the effectiveness of library evaluation has shifted from an internal professional debate to a broader one, amongst stakeholders, around the justification of libraries themselves. Evaluation is therefore a critically important element amongst other future challenges.

Recent key trends and frameworks

What are the changes to which libraries have been responding in their measurement systems? In order to simplify the answer the author has reduced these to four critical trends. Each produces pressure for a distinctive type of evaluation evidence. These might be expressed as:

1. Digitisation of content and process
2. Quality, customer satisfaction and culture
3. Economic reductionism
4. Worth: value and impact.

The digitisation trend implies that as the main means and forms of communication, publication and knowledge become digital, so measurement and evaluation relating to digital resources and services will be the main concern, and possibly the only measures ultimately relevant. The second trend is exemplified by the wave of quality management that swept through western industry in the final decades of the last century and that subsequently flowed into libraries. This trend encompasses a view that only customers judge quality, and therefore evidence from customers in evaluating service quality will be paramount. The third trend has perhaps been ever present, but has increasingly impacted on libraries when ideologies that label public services as a social evil have held sway, or when the economic context is difficult and efficiencies or cuts are sought. In such times paymasters seek a reduction of libraries to basic financial elements that can be traded off, made more efficient, competed for or removed entirely to balance the books. These three trends together have combined into a fourth narrative which might question the future existence of libraries as unnecessary in a digital world, unresponsive and irrelevant to changing customer requirements, and an uneconomic and declining luxury. To counter these arguments new forms of proof of impact and value become necessary as a basis for a justification of continued investment, or in extreme cases, existence.

Nearly 60 years ago a prescient paper was written which suggested a natural history of the development of academic libraries (Lancour, 1951) and, by implication, the way in which measurement systems might also develop. It suggested a history of three phases of focus for academic libraries: storehouse; service; education. This can be used to characterise the history of evaluation in all library contexts, and supports the idea of the trends above. At the outset the library adopted mainly internal measures, based on the original value proposition of the library as storehouse. This has been followed by the recognition of service and service quality, driven by the broader quality movement, with associated methods and measurement tools. The final and current challenge is to link our measures to the broader aims of our institutions (education, in the case of academic libraries) and society in general. This may of course simplify the picture too much; there has perhaps always been some evaluation activity across the whole spectrum. However, the idea of a progression from the internal focus on physical collections and an agreed set of associated processes, through to more externally focused measures of first immediate customers, and then to a broader range of stakeholder interests, would seem to hold good. This has also moved the focus of evaluation from the immediate and concrete towards the more transcendent contribution of libraries.

Digital developments

It is evident that the content of libraries is changing, due to digital developments, and that this is not simply an exchange of content of one kind for another, but a trend which fundamentally alters traditional processes, usage and library boundaries. Most libraries are still in transition, and the 'print is dead' message is not completely borne out in the current measurement of library activity. Early assumptions about the decline of certain types of library usage (in particular, physical visits) have not been valid, as libraries have renewed their physical offerings, while other measures do show less use of, for example, enquiry services, and less concern for personal service.

The influence of digital developments on library evaluation and measurement has perhaps not been as marked as their influence on libraries generally. Work goes on to count activity associated with digital resources (see, e.g., Shepherd, 2006), and this is of necessity a joint effort across libraries and providers in a way that demonstrates that the boundaries of the library service in terms of delivery and ownership are no longer evident to users. The Association of Research Libraries (ARL)[1] in North America has been a focus for activity around new digital measures, with the creation of a variety of new tools. ARL has also recognised the fundamental content shift in its membership index, removing the size of physical collections from its criteria, which are now based on input measures alone.

There has not yet been as much work on how user behaviour has changed in this context, and there are dangers in simplistic interest in activity alone (Town, 2004). A key requirement for the future will be the re-creation of the fundamental understanding of use which in the past was available from information science studies. Assumptions are currently made about users as 'digital natives' or alternatives, and there is recent work in the academic area (helpfully summarised by Connaway and Dickey, 2010), but until more evidence is collected this evaluation trend has, perhaps surprisingly, not generated the changes of concept on which a different construct of libraries can be based.

Quality

Quality has been a much stronger driver for changes in evaluation, and consequently in the construct of libraries, than have been digital developments. While most libraries remain a hybrid of digital and physical offerings, few libraries would now not categorise themselves first and foremost as a service. This change has perhaps not been much commented on, but it is a radical change from 60 years ago, when service elements were in some places sometimes a distraction from the demands of the storehouse construct. Indeed, it could be argued that the assumption that libraries are now just another service among many within their broader organisations has led to a reduction in the recognition of libraries as transcendent services (alongside others that clearly are not), less priority given to longer-term preservation aspects, and sometimes to the assumption that we are solely a service profession.

From the evidence of a survey of assessment initiatives in academic libraries (Wright and White, 2007; Killick and Stanley, 2009,) the overwhelming majority of new measurement efforts over the past 10 years might be characterised as quality oriented. The main rationale provided by the libraries themselves is the self-generated pressure to understand more about users, proving the point that the internal construct has shifted towards the service ideal. Surveys have been the most commonly used quality tool within the academic context. As an example, the LibQUAL+ survey[2] has been used throughout the world over the last 10 years, providing a reliable, valid and acceptable instrument for research libraries in multinational contexts. The ability to provide benchmarks of user satisfaction and comparison around the globe is an unparalleled achievement. Interestingly, the survey dimensions (information control; library as place; effect of service), and hence the underlying construct of libraries, have remained consistent for several years, in spite of digital developments. These detailed market surveys have now been accompanied, and in some cases displaced, by broader organisational or national surveys. The National Student Survey[3] is an example. A side-effect of this displacement is the reduction of the concept of the library to that encompassed by the single issue chosen for the question, which is either purely instrumental or limited to a single market segment.

Fortunately this reduction has been balanced by the broadening of the quality concept to what might be termed meta-levels. Since Kaplan and Norton's seminal work on the balanced scorecard (Kaplan and Norton, 1996), the concept of a measurement framework reflecting the interests of a number of stakeholders has been attractive to those wishing for a more holistic or strategic approach to measurement. Kennerley and Neely (2002) suggest that organisations perform better with a balanced framework than without, and a number of libraries have taken this up. The Balanced Scorecard application[4] at the University of Virginia shows the strength of this approach as more than just a measurement framework, but rather, a cultural instrument (Self, 2003). Wilson has been working on a cultural framework in order initially to answer the question of whether benchmarking exercises made a real difference to library quality (Wilson and Town, 2006). This study led to the reshaping of a Capability Maturity Matrix from the software industry[5] for library purposes, and suggests that quality improvement needs to be based within a culture that can support multiple improvement projects. The finding that sophisticated tools like benchmarking will be effective only where the culture can absorb and embed the lessons learned is a valuable one, and shows up the way in which quality has led to new constructs of the library, at least within those libraries that embrace it systematically.

Economic and financial measures

The response to the need for financial measures is covered in more detail in the following section. Despite the financial pressures on libraries, standard approaches to costing have not been a strong feature in library evaluation. One recent international benchmarking exercise across a number of research libraries found no consistent approach to costing and financial analysis on which to base comparisons. There is a surprising lack of data and focus on financial measures within our profession. This might simply demonstrate that there are more interesting truths to discover about libraries. However, these truths may be in danger of being submerged in a world which seeks to know the price of everything and the value of nothing. Libraries seem to be very resistant to external pressures to produce a construct of themselves in financial terms, and this could be seen as a weakness rather than a virtue in times of economic constraint.

Worth

In a recent conference, a demand for proof of worth was voiced by a university leader (Lombardi, 2007), which, when developed (Town, 2009a), suggested that there were only two 'bottom line' measures of worth: impact on research (and ultimately research reputation) and impact on the financial bottom line. This rather narrow view can, however, serve as a reflection of the two pressures that have recently been growing in library assessment for impact and value measures that have meaning for broader stakeholders and society. So far in this chapter, the term 'worth' has been used to mean the combination of these two measurement strands, although value might be the more appropriate collective term (incorporating impact). A recent paper based on focus groups with senior UK academic librarians commissioned by the Research Information Network (RIN) generated the following observation (RIN, 2010):

There is a strong feeling among senior librarians that they have failed effectively to communicate the value of their services ... there is an increasing risk that much of what libraries actually do may be invisible in a virtual environment. ... We believe it is important that libraries should be able to show ... that they provide services with demonstrable links to success in achieving institutional goals. Return on investment is thus an increasingly important issue. Libraries need to be more proactive in seeking to understand user behaviour and workflows; and in rigorously demonstrating the value of their activities ... The focus of performance indicators up to now has tended to be on inputs and outputs ... rather than addressing the much harder issues relating to impact and value. ... We believe it is essential that more work is done to analyse the relationships between library activities ... and learning and research outcomes.

This summarises the current challenge for library evaluation, and also hints at some potential answers. In simple terms, it suggests that we need to understand our users better, as this will be a route to value, and we need tools such as return on investment (ROI)[6] to make the link to value and, ultimately, to institutional goals. The next main section will consider some responses to this demand for value and impact measures. This demand for proof of worth is an additional pressure on libraries, and does not reduce or replace the need for the many other forms of assessment in use. There is also an associated danger of reductionist thinking on the part of both stakeholders and librarians in understanding and responding to this pressure, especially when paymasters and others attempt to base these proofs on a limited range of utilitarian or financial measures.

Cross-pressures

The collision of the products of the different themes and influences described above is now everywhere apparent, generating cross-pressures on evaluation for library managers and their stakeholders. In practice, few libraries can or do take a single path in response. Evidence (see Killick and Stanley, 2009) from examples from the UK academic library context is that many different approaches and methods are taken up at different times in a contingent fashion. Library managers and leaders are now regularly assailed by a range of demands or opinions relating to evaluation. To demonstrate these cross-pressures through personal experience during a single week early in the first year of this new decade:

1. A blog suggests that in the new digital age information literacy is the only measure of a library's contribution.

2. An e-mail draws attention to the results of a national student experience survey and demands that it be taken seriously as it may affect student recruitment.

3. A financial benchmarking exercise requires the itemisation of all expenditure on staff in a year to be apportioned to particular categories for comparison with other similar institutions.

4. An academic wishes to discuss the impact of management changes in the cathedral library on both the learning of history students and the reputation of the university in its local community.

5. A presentation is required for a strategic board (which will draw heavily on quantitative survey results) to demonstrate that our plans for new library space will make a measurable difference to student learning.

6. A letter from a grant-awarding body judges the impact of our archives service on research against other services in order to apportion funding.

All this generates an implicit sense of the continuous need for justification of the library, prioritisation within itself and alongside all the other potential methods and techniques of enhancing learning and research.

An observation from the above is that although librarians are constantly admonished that the world has changed and libraries should change, the resulting range of concerns is broadening rather than reducing, and that the more traditional aspects of the service are still valued. The Web may have turned the world upside down, print may be dead, and scholarly publication may be in revolution, but the death of libraries and the end of library evaluation appear to be some way off. This does, however, present opportunities; libraries are not merely passive recipients of these pressures and changes, but active agents with a role in shaping the world, as much as in responding to it.

One way in which this can be done is through narrative. The move from internal operational measures towards more strategic and cultural measures, generated to meet broader advocacy needs, requires a vehicle for communicating these effectively. Brophy (2008) suggests that libraries are being challenged to re-invent themselves within the workflows and lifeflows of their users. Because context is all important, and the context of digital information is complex, new measures must draw rich pictures in order to be persuasive. Brophy's view is that ethnography, self-evaluation and narrative will assist here. Ethnographic approaches have already been adopted, for example at the University of Rochester (Foster and Gibbons, 2007). This could also be seen to flow logically from the simple strictures of total quality management that have emphasised the need for deeper understanding of customers. Narrative leads us, or leads us back to, the question of what story we are trying to tell about our libraries. What choices we make will define the new construct of the library. The next section will consider the potential role of value and impact evaluation in these stories.

Value as a key measure

Around 30 years ago, in an influential paper Orr made the key distinction between 'how good' libraries are, as opposed to 'how much good is done' by them (Orr, 1973). This laid a dual framework: the former reflecting library quality (equated with effectiveness) and the latter reflecting library value (equated with benefit). Orr did not reflect specifically on the philosophy of value, as the paper was a response to perceived pressures to incorporate new management science into libraries, but the distinction between these two aspects thus characterised has held good. While there has been great progress in measurement of quality, measurement of value has remained more intractable and less visited. Later perceptive commentary by Buckland (1982) suggested that this is because what is lacking is coherence, a sense of the whole, in our measurement systems. The emphasis on the former aspect of library goodness, realised primarily through instrumental levels of measurement, has resulted in library evaluation which does not reflect the holistic, collective, connective and transcendent contribution that libraries make.

Thus the challenge of developing value measures has existed for some time, and the resurfacing of a demand for proof of value is not surprising. In the UK and Ireland developing and collating a coordinated response to the demand for value and impact measurement in academic libraries has been through the Society of College, National and University Libraries (SCONUL) Value and Impact Programme (known as VAMP) (Town, 2007 and Town, 2009a). Value and impact might be considered to be two distinctively different facets, but both are clearly about answering the challenge to define the beneficial contribution of libraries. A body of theory and practice existed from previous work in UK further and higher education (Markless and Streatfield, 2008), including the Library and Information Research Group/SCONUL Impact Initiative (Poll and Payne, 2006) on which to draw. The SCONUL Impact Initiative was considered to be the basis for a model for evaluation and measurement in this field. An impact tool was subsequently commissioned, developed and mounted on the VAMP site.[7] The majority of early projects in this programme were related to information literacy, despite an initial desire to concentrate on research impact. However, it would seem that the development of information literacy in individuals is a very good example of the creation of something transcendent which continues to deliver value well beyond the boundaries of the library or parent institution. With the advent of information literacy, the idea of a contribution that was both transforming from the individual's point of view and an addition of transcendent value from the library's perspective has helped to sharpen concepts of impact in a positive way. Work continues in this area, with a tool for research impact being a highly desired product for proof of research library worth.

Turning from impact to value measurement, what follows is a brief review of recent views on value measurement, taken from a presentation to the 2009 Northumbria International Conference (see Town, 2009b). First, a caution made some time ago about the difference between cost and value:

> focusing on cost without being able to demonstrate [service] value and quality … leaves the initiative to people whose chief concern is cost-control or profit: the funders and the vendors. (Whitehall, 1995)

In other words, there is a danger in giving ground to pressures for cost data without a framework which translates costs into value. Whitehall's warning has been largely unheeded in some areas; for example, the lack of any real credible qualitative data on e-resources has resulted in large volumes of academic library budget being handed over to vendors without any corresponding reverse pressure for value-for-money measurement guarantees. Missingham (2005) reviewed a range of recent value studies in libraries. In doing so, she proposed a natural history of value initiatives, suggesting three successive steps:

- activity-based costing for output efficiency
- perceived value based on labour saving
- balanced scorecard pressure for 'hard' value measurement.

Note that this assumes value to be solely an economic question, although Missingham does however also make the key point that the demonstration of value needs to be linked to the organisation's value statements. The paper's conclusions were based on five studies, including the British Library, three US public library systems and a national bibliographic service in New Zealand. These initiatives suggested varying benefit ratios for libraries around the 1:4 to 6:5 levels. Many questions arise from this. Does the variation reflect real differences across communities? Larger libraries give higher returns, but what is the precise level of good? A 1:4 return might appear slight in absolute terms. Missingham concluded that contingent valuation does not provide a 'magic bullet' for library value measurement.

In another study (called a 'meta-analysis') of return on investment, Aabo (2009) considered this to be a new field, and driven by the financial crisis' generating a need for worth estimates in monetary terms. This work is a review of reviews, covering 17 US public libraries and 43 other international initiatives. It found a lack of consistency in methodology, limiting valuation comparisons, but again the scores are generally within the 1:4 ranges. However, 80% of the studies are from the USA, and over 80% are from public libraries, suggesting that this is a particularly attractive technique in some contexts and sectors. The variety of methods included cost-benefit analysis, contingent valuation, and secondary economic impact.

In a North American perspective, White (2007) considered ROI to be an old tool with potentially new uses, and was more directive in his suggestions for application. This paper recognised that use of the tool in libraries has often been defensive or reactive, and echoed the previous conclusions that there is currently no professional consensus on methodology for value determination. White suggests a more internal and instrumental use of the tool for predictive, small-scale investment decision making, for post-implementation value assessment and for introspective use to evaluate unit-to-unit service within the library. A key comment is that these tools could also be applied in more offensive use for library intangible benefits, and this seems an important suggestion, leading towards methods which might answer the need for a more holistic picture of library value.

Kostagiolas and Asonitis (2009) suggested that intangible asset measurement is important because the recognition and evaluation of the full range of the value of assets is key to assessment of overall library value. The valuation of intangible assets will supplement that of real assets, which have tended to be based on the concepts of the library as storehouse, or a set of clearly defined service processes, and therefore do not satisfy the criteria of transcendence or of holism. This paper equates intangible assets with knowledge assets, and these are recognised as difficult to evaluate. However, there are methods for resolving this, and an approach of this type requires an intellectual capital reporting model, using similar tools to those already recognised above, such as ROI and contingent valuation. A key area where this paper broadens the viewpoint towards the holistic and the transcendent is in the recognition of additional dimensions suggested for assessment:

- human capital
- structural capital
- relational capital.

This begins to recognise that there are valuations to be computed not simply for what the library does in instrumental terms, but that there is also a value in what has been built by the library in terms of its staff capability and capacity, in the services built around both real and virtual collections and in the relationships which the library has with both its immediate stakeholders and broader society. Not only are most of these aspects not measured by current frameworks, they are also not yet generally recognised as being objects for measurement and evaluation.

The conclusion from this is that the traditional tools for value measurement will provide only a partial answer to the demand for proof of worth. Economic value tools may be primarily instrumental; offering something new within our current frame of reference, but not providing a transcendental answer of the kind sought. Some of these tools may be better employed internally for individual valuations rather than for a whole library approach, because their frame of reference fails to take into account either intangible assets or broader definitions of value. In other words, one of the reasons that libraries may be undervalued is because the techniques and measures for true and complete valuation are underdeveloped. Because behaviour follows measures, if there are no effective measures for these substantial assets which libraries build and generate, then behaviours will not be directed to maximise these assets. Paradoxically, measures such as satisfaction with library staff derived from surveys actually direct one away from library staff as an asset because users are not in a position to appreciate their true value to the enterprise. This leaves open the question of how best to measure library value. In the next section a potential resolution is offered which might serve to draw the strands of library evaluation together into a new framework based on the relationship between value and values.

Values and value: a possible resolution

The current economic crisis has generated some challenge to the previous dominance of measurement and evaluation based largely on a limited range of economic values and judgements. Libraries which see themselves as a common good can take some comfort from, for example, Professor Michael Sandel's 2009 Reith Lectures (as commented on in a British newspaper editorial; see Guardian, 2009):

> The credit crunch has exposed myriad mirages, demonstrating how the market can get things badly wrong when it comes to valuing things ... when bureaucracies price things which should not be priced, they start trading them off against other objectives, instead of appreciating their absolute obligations.

This offers a reminder that true value cannot be measured by financial measures alone, and that pursuit of a set of such narrow measures can be disastrous when unaccompanied by broader considerations. Consequently, adding a few economic value indicators to our current evaluation methods may not be an adequate response to the demand for value measures. What may be needed is some reflection on value in terms of these absolute obligations.

The lack of persuasive proof of the value added by libraries has hampered their cause; but blame can also be attached to broader leadership, which has been subverted by the same trends towards narrow measurement. The cross-pressure experienced by library leaders in this context has been recognised for some time, and some commentators have described those arising from different value sets:

> Civil society has more to do with attitudes, feelings and symbols ... leadership [sees] an increasing emphasis on values ... value-based management is second only to change management [in importance

> to leaders for continuing education] ... but most organisations consist of different value sets ... there is a focus on the importance of leaders as value creators. (Pors and Johanssen, 2003)

This suggests that there are conflicting values between different trends in public sector management, but that an understanding of values will be critical to effective future performance. Again, these demands do not replace the other many existing cross-pressures for data and evidence arising from earlier management trends, such as the quality movement.

The conclusion is that there is a specific new pressure for proof of value, which libraries have not yet succeeded in developing. However, a response based solely on a limited economic model may not be the answer; rather, there is a need for a broader assessment of the meaning of value; and for a recognition that value is dependent on values sets or systems. This surely offers an opportunity for libraries to represent themselves more effectively within a construct based on values, with clear evidence of how we add value within this overall values system. In other words, library leaders in civil society contexts recognise that there is something more here to libraries and measurement than the immediate concrete dimension. In simple terms, society considers a range of intangible things to be important alongside the economic and the practical; this has something to do with the values of that society; libraries should manage themselves according to values (but there may be conflicting value sets); in this approach, value (to society) is created as a result.

Two questions arise here. How can we link values and value? And how can we measure the value which libraries add to the achievement of these broader values? It is interesting that in most of the literature on library value the link between value and values is unrecognised. This is probably due to the conflation of the idea of value to economic value alone. Values have not been seen as the basis for a framework for measurement, although a values statement is considered a standard requirement by many organisations as part of its leadership framework.

Some more detailed consideration of the concepts of value and values seems relevant here. This is again developed from the 2009 Northumbria presentation (Town, 2009b). Value has been variously defined as worth, desirability, utility; or as the qualities on which these depend; or as estimated worth; or as a financial exchange or other form of equivalent (Sykes, 1982). More generally, value as 'the quality or fact of being excellent, useful or desirable' has been used as a starting point for discussions of value theory, accompanied by conclusions that precise terminology has not yet been obtained (Rescher, 1969). There has been much philosophical debate about value over more than two thousand years, so it is not possible to do full justice to that here. There are some points worth noting from that debate. First, there is ambiguity over what value means. Consequently, value will mean different things to different people. Value is an idea; in other words, it has no independent existence and, like any idea, it can be described as 'arbitrary'; in other words, there is not likely to be a single wholly satisfactory answer to value measurement (Najder, 1975).

For libraries the challenge is to compute value, and because values are manifested, there will be something that we can measure arising from the way values are enacted in our libraries, and the way value is generated as a result.

> Whenever valuation takes place ... values must enter in ... in evaluation an indispensable recourse to underlying values is involved. Values cannot be deduced from ... data or logic ... they have to be chosen. Acts or series of acts are steered by multiple and changing clusters of values. (Williams, 1968)

These quotes suggest that valuation or evaluation assumes a certain set of values, and that values must be chosen. Consequently, according to this, library evaluation should be based on a clear and agreed set of shared values. Because values guide conduct, then the results of this conduct must be observable and potentially measurable. Some value assumptions may have been implicit in some existing measurement frameworks (especially those related to the quality movement), but there is little, if any, discussion in the literature connecting values and performance measurement within a common explicit framework.

There would seem to be a broadly accepted management science view that values and value are connected, and that both are relevant to effective organisational performance:

> Value creation is the objective of every enterprise, every worker and every leader. (Cameron et al., 2006)

Values in the work situation provide purpose to a job on the part of individuals, and motivation is considered to be proportional to the values perceived in the job. Because a value represents a slogan for the rationalisation of action, values provide impetus to correct actions, which then result in value creation. Many libraries have value statements, but it may be that these have not been fully recognised or utilised to support improved performance or to help recognise how value is being added. An example from industry of the way in which this link has been recognised was the IBM experience (Hemp and Stewart, 2008), when the company saw a need to improve 'working together' within to reflect the company's new integrated solutions offerings for the external market. The solution was seen as a new set of corporate values, achieved through a 'Values-Jam', an intranet discussion amongst 320,000 employees to 'weigh in' on the new set of corporate values. Ten thousand comments were received, mainly dissonant and discontented, but the company leadership had the confidence to let the debate run, eventually leading to resurfacing of some original company values lost in the recent transition: dedication; innovation; and trust. Note that these may be difficult to measure, but it was accepted that soft corporate values (and, by implication, measures of those) had to coexist alongside hard financial metrics.

At the University of York Library and Archives, we have used this inspiration to conduct our own values investigation using a Web 2.0 consultation tool, followed by an all-staff conference to settle a new statement of values. This included a recognition of conflicting values sets as characterised by Cameron et al. (2006). While this started out as an investigation of staff values, we extended the question to what users valued or would value about our services. This would make the link between our internal value set and the adding or creation of value for the broader academic community. By asking what users value, instead of what they want, need or rate as satisfactory, we received answers which were surprisingly different from what we had learned through quality approaches.

In terms of the effect on library constructs, a more holistic academic vision of the library as 'a real tangible physical expression of knowledge' emerged, which revealed current weaknesses in our construct of what is needed to deliver the virtual equivalent of former physical libraries. A physical library lays out knowledge in a way that virtual libraries do not, with density steering appreciation of the literature of a discipline. These issues had not been identified through our satisfaction surveys, with their separation of content, service and physical dimensions. The value of the library as the 'intellectual heart, a collection of knowledge made without fear or favour' and as a visible 'celebration of scholarship' raises questions about how we can compute the value of this kind of intangible contribution and reflect it in both library construct and practice.

The student vision also revealed a new set of priorities, much more closely linked with day-to-day pressures and contextual experiences, and suggesting a need for much closer involvement of this group in design and delivery of service. Almost no response to our question suggested economic tools as being particularly relevant to proofs of value, although value for money was an issue for students in an increasingly difficult economic climate. From a student perspective, a construct of the library as a social as well as an academic service came through strongly.

Conclusion: value, values and transcendence

The contribution of library evaluation to the role of libraries and their place in society is likely to be in the development of value and impact measures which demonstrate proof of worth, and which also provide a construct for the future library that is robust enough to withstand future challenges. These measures will be in addition to current frameworks, because these existing frameworks work at the level of operations and within institutions, rather than at the level of fundamental justification or of considerations of worth which transcend these boundaries. The framework for proof of value will arise from consideration of the values of organisations or societies, and will extend well beyond economic value contributions. Some library leaders maintain a pessimistic view that libraries would not have been invented if we had started within the current digital context. This demonstrates precisely the lack of appreciation both of the value that libraries add holistically as a system and of the value generated by our less tangible assets. The quest for value measurement is implicitly a demand for evidence of transcendent contribution. Internally focused evaluation tools will not provide the answers. These broader contributions may relate to individuals, wider groupings or society, and evaluation will require a similarly broad scope to compute their value. A complete and holistic picture of the value of libraries will emerge only through additional work on gaining a better understanding of how users engage with libraries in this changing context, and also on methods for assessing the value of intangible assets which are not the objects of current measurement systems. Only then will the full story of the transcendent library be told.

Notes

1. http://www.arl.org/.
2. http://www.libqual.org/about/about_survey.
3. http://unistats.direct.gov.uk/.
4. www2.lib.virginia.edu/bsc/index.html.
5. http://www.sei.cmu.edu/cmmi/.
6. http://www.investopedia.com/terms/r/returnoninvestment.asp.
7. http://vamp.diglib.shrivenham.cranfield.ac.uk/.

References

Aabo, S. (2009) 'Libraries and return on investment (ROI): a meta-analysis'. *New Library World*, 110 (7/8), 311–24.

Brophy, P. (2006) *Measuring Library Performance: principles and techniques*. London: Facet.

Brophy, P. (2008) 'Telling the story: qualitative approaches to measuring the performance of emerging library services'. *Performance Measurement and Metrics*, 9 (1), 7–17.

Buckland, M.K. (1982) 'Concepts of library goodness'. *Canadian Library Journal*, 39 (2), 63–6.

Cameron, K.S., Quinn, R.E., DeGraff, J. and Thakor, A.V. (2006) *Competing Values Leadership: creating value in organisations*. Cheltenham: Edward Elgar.

Connaway, L.S. and Dickey, T.J. (2010) *The Digital Information Seeker: report of the findings from selected OCLC, RIN, and JISC user behaviour projects*. JISC/HEFCE. Online at http://www.jisc.ac.uk/media/documents/publications/reports/2010/digitalinformationseekerreport.pdf.

Cullen, R. (2006) 'Operationalising the Focus/Values/Purpose Matrix: a tool for libraries to measure their ability to deliver service quality'. *Performance Measurement and Metrics*, 7 (2), 83–9.

Foster, N.F. and Gibbons, S. (eds) (2007) *Studying Students: the undergraduate research project at the University of Rochester*. Chicago, IL: ACRL.

Guardian (2009) Editorial: 'In praise of Michael Sandel'. *Guardian*, 14 October. Online at http://www.guardian.co.uk/commentisfree/2009/oct/14/in-praise-of-michael-sandel?INTCMP=SRCH.

Hemp, P. and Stewart, T.A. (2008) 'Leading change when business is good: an interview with Samuel J. Palmisano'. In: *Harvard Business Review on Strategic Renewal*. Boston, MA: Harvard Business School Publishing.

Kaplan, R.S. and Norton, D.P. (1996) *The Balanced Scorecard: translating strategy into action*. Boston, MA: Harvard Business School Press.

Kennerley, M. and Neely, A. (2002) 'Performance measurement frameworks: a review'. In Neely, A. (ed.) *Business Performance Measurement: theory and practice*. Cambridge: Cambridge University Press.

Killick and Stanley (2009) *Library Performance Measurement in the UK and Ireland*. Washington, DC: Association of Research Libraries.

Kostagiolas, P.A. and Asonitis, S. (2009) 'Intangible assets for academic libraries: definitions, categorization and an exploration of management issues'. *Library Management*, 30 (6/7), 419–29.

Lancaster, F.W. (1993) *If You Want to Evaluate Your Library*, 2nd edn. Champaign, IL: University of Illinois, Graduate School of Library and Information Science.

Lancour, H. (1951) 'Training for librarianship in North America'. *Library Association Record*, September, 280–4.

Lombardi, J.V. (2007) 'On the research library: a comment'. In DeFranco, F. et al. (eds) *Proceedings of the Library Assessment Conference: Building effective, sustainable, practical assessment*, 25–27 September 2006, Charlottesville, VA. Washington: Association of Research Libraries. Online at http://libraryassessment.org/archive/2006.shtml.

Markless, S. and Streatfield, D. (2008) 'Supported self-evaluation in assessing the impact of HE libraries'. *Performance Measurement and Metrics*, 9 (1), 38–47.

Missingham, R. (2005) 'Libraries and economic value: a review of recent studies'. *Performance Measurement and Metrics*, 6 (3), 142–58.

Najder, Z. (1975) *Values and Evaluations*. Oxford: Clarendon Press.

Negroponte, N. (1995) *Being Digital*. New York, NY: Knopf Publishing.

Orr, R.H. (1973) 'Measuring the goodness of library services: a general framework for considering quantitative measures'. *Journal of Documentation*, 29 (3), 315–32.

Poll, R. and Payne, P. (2006) 'Impact measures for libraries and information services'. *Library Hi Tech*, 24 (4), 547–62.

Pors, N.O. and Johanssen, C.G. (2003) 'Library directors under cross-pressure between new public management and value-based management'. *Library Management*, 24 (1/2), 51–60.

Putnam, R.D. (2000) *Bowling Alone: the collapse and revival of American community*. London: Simon and Schuster.

Rescher, N. (1969) *Introduction to Value Theory*. Englewood Cliffs, NJ: Prentice Hall.

RIN. (2010) *Challenges for Academic Libraries in Difficult Economic Times: a guide for senior institutional managers and policy makers*. London: Research Information Network, March.

Self, J. (2003) 'From values to metrics: implementation of the balanced scorecard at a university library?' *Performance Measurement and Metrics*, 4 (2), 57–63.

Shepherd, P.T. (2006) 'COUNTER: usage statistics for performance measurement?' *Performance Measurement and Metrics*, 7 (3), 142–52.

Sykes, J.B. (ed.) (1982) *The Concise Oxford English Dictionary of Current English*, 7th edn. Oxford: Clarendon Press.

Taylor, C. (2007) *A Secular Age*. Cambridge, MA: Belknap Press of Harvard University Press.

Town, J.S. (2000) 'Performance or measurement?' *Performance Measurement and Metrics*, 1 (1), 43–54.

Town, J.S. (2004) 'E-measures: a comprehensive waste of time?' *VINE*, 34 (4), 190–5.

Town, J.S. (2007) 'Value and impact measurement: a UK perspective and progress report on a national programme (VAMP)'. In DeFranco, F. et al. (eds) *Proceedings of the 2006 Library Assessment Conference: Building effective, sustainable, practical assessment*, 25–27 September 2006, Charlottesville, VA. Washington, DC: Association of Research Libraries.

Town, J.S. (2009a) 'Building a resource for practical assessment: adding value to value and impact'. In Hiller, S. et al. (eds) *Proceedings of the 2008 Library Assessment Conference: Building effective, sustainable, practical assessment*, 4–7 August 2008, Seattle, WA. Washington, DC: Association of Research Libraries.

Town, J.S. (2009b) 'From values to value measurement: a metaphysical enquiry'. To be published in *Proceedings of the 8th Northumbria International Conference on Performance Measurement in Libraries, Florence*, 17–20 August 2009.

White, L.N. (2007) 'An old tool with potential new uses: return on investment'. *The Bottom Line: Managing Library Finances*, 20 (1), 5–9.

Whitehall, T. (1995) 'Value in library and information management: a review'. *Library Management*, 16 (4), 3–11.

Williams, R.M. (1968) 'Values'. In: *International Encyclopedia of the Social Sciences*. New York: Macmillan, 1968.

Wilson, F. and Town, J.S. (2006) 'Benchmarking and library quality maturity'. *Performance Measurement and Metrics*, 7 (2), 75–82.

Wright, S. and White, L.S. (2007) *SPEC Kit 303: Library Assessment*. Washington, DC: Association of Research Libraries.

The future of and for library and information services: a public library view

Tony Durcan

Introduction

This chapter is written from the public library perspective at possibly a unique time in the history of the public library service. Firmly embedded within local authorities, UK public libraries, along with other local authority services, are bracing themselves for the most severe budget cuts in a generation, possibly in the post-war period. This is after a recent period of what, paradoxically, has simultaneously seen significant growth alongside a perceived decline in performance.

Central government seems very keen to change public libraries and to stop the perceived rot. The former Culture Minister Margaret Hodge MP (who was on record in 2007 and 2008 as repeatedly saying that libraries should be more like the now closed Borders' book stores[1]) asserted in a newspaper interview in 2009 that 'technological advances and higher expectations of service mean that libraries must move with the times to stay part of the times' (Jeffries, 2010). In 2010, Mrs Hodge concluded a consultation on the public library service's future as part of the long-standing Public Libraries Review, commissioned in summer 2008. The resulting policy statement, *The Modernisation Review of Public Libraries* (DCMS, 2010), was published in March 2010. It did make it clear, after persistent recent rumour and some public anxiety, that there would be no change in the legislative framework and status for public libraries.

To date, the Coalition government's view is similar in this respect, at least. Hampered by funding pressures, the new Culture Minister, Ed Vaizey MP, has had to temper any announcements on public library development. The government has removed Margaret Hodge's commitment to universal free Internet use by the end of 2010 (a modernisation review pledge). The main Coalition development area so far is the Libraries' Improvement Programme, a collection of 10 live case studies exploring different service and governance improvements. The learning from this should be captured by the end of 2010.[2] It will be interesting to see if this will result in a new direction, or at least in a new drive and renewed emphasis for the service.

But whatever powerful (or muddled) challenges await public libraries, in many respects the service nationally is now in a better shape to deal with them than ever before. In the last 10 years there has been huge development in public library infrastructure (People's Network;[3] new buildings; self- and remote service; staff skills) and, whatever one thought of them, the relatively short-term *Public Library Standards* (DCMS, 2001) drove up investment and performance nationally and left behind them a significant improvement legacy. It is true that there are significant negative images around profile, decline in some areas of participation (especially book lending) and poor performance and management in some local authorities.

The main reason why this is a unique time for public libraries is that we have the opportunity to help all local authorities (and the country) to deal with the imminent new austerity. Now is a good time to reinforce our traditional role, and to drive and exploit our potential as the *free* street-corner, village, town and city-centre access points to positive activity, recreation, skills support, information and knowledge. We also have the opportunity, if we are brave enough to take it, to demonstrate the power of strong leadership. Austerity will demand excellent leadership skills to maintain the profile and impact of libraries and to ensure that they develop their unique and high-value contribution to society at a time of increased need. We undoubtedly have great potential here, and this chapter highlights some of the key areas of challenge for the public library and information service.

Future roles and challenges

The future will be an extension of the core books, reading, knowledge, information and space role – within the context of changing media and environments, and much higher customer expectations. The service areas listed below, many if not all interlinked, are challenging. But what is also challenging is that developed and expanding roles will need to be delivered alongside existing core services, at least for another generation. And although it is not mentioned per se, underpinning all of this is the need and ambition for everyone to achieve both a fluency of reading and a fluency of information handling. Even after 150 years, the public library's role in assisting this fluency is not universally acknowledged, though it remains vital.

Change has always been a challenge, but there must now be a culture not just of accepting, but of wanting, welcoming and anticipating change. We must be a sector that relishes and searches out change. One area where this has significant implications and opportunities concerns workforce development. Defining appropriate new technical and professional skills, being brave enough to move away from less-relevant qualifications, keeping skills up to date, anticipating new skill requirements and marrying them with the highest standard of customer service skills and customer-focused attitudes will all be essential. There needs to be a rethinking of the public library skill set.

Reading

For years the future of the printed book has been in doubt (a mythology like that proclaiming the end of the public library service), casting a shadow over the traditional book-lending and reading service. For example, central government's current view is that libraries must wholeheartedly embrace the e-book. Do declining book issues reinforce this view? The printed book remains the traditional tool in delivering fluency of reading. Public libraries in the UK have an unrivalled reading backlist. According to research undertaken for the Arts Council, reading for pleasure is the most popular 'cultural' activity in England (Creative Research, 2009). There has been an explosion in reading groups across the UK and the library sector is supporting further expansion; the number of groups in England and Wales has risen by 149% in the last four years. There are now roughly 10,000 library-linked reading groups in England and Wales, providing 100,000 people with new reading opportunities (The Reading Agency, 2008).

Supporting reading (as opposed to just lending books) will continue to be a core role of the public library service. In addition to the obvious literacy support, reading contributes to well-being, greater knowledge and wider experiences. It stimulates aspiration. Evidence also suggests that reading groups animate important social networks supporting community well-being and cohesion, as well as creating reading activists to spread the message. In addition, community engagement in reading supports social inclusion (BLM and Reading Partnership, 2000; The Reading Agency, 2002; The Reading Agency, 2004).

Different reading formats and media present delivery challenges, but they are issues of choice rather than competition. Public libraries will fully embrace e-books as soon as they have resolved the outstanding issues with publishers (such as copyright, licence fees and download systems); and they will continue to deliver a contemporary reading service as long as they are allowed to do so. As with other service areas, the challenge is to find new ways of encouraging and supporting new reading audiences. There is the challenge of reaching the 40% of people who do not read, and the opportunity to reach the 20% who do read for pleasure, but not through the public library. The priority in social terms must be the 40% of non-readers.

Information

It will be necessary to address the challenges arising from new ways of living and working and from the need to support citizens' thirst for more choice to help them to make informed decisions. One example of this is how to provide the most relevant employment information, in the best format, for a working environment and career map without geographical boundaries. Achieving this successfully requires a step change in terms of information literacy support and its availability. This is an area which seems to receive more attention in academic rather than public libraries. But the Chartered Institute of Library and Information Professionals' definition of information literacy applies equally to all library sectors:

- knowing when and why you need information
- where to find it, and how to evaluate, use and
- communicate it in an ethical manner.[4]

The information literacy needs of people are as critical now as they ever were, and the public library role of dealing with the following is as key as ever. But it is not given a high profile, possibly because it is easily perceived as traditional business – those key issues with which the public library service has always tried to deal. Yet for so many people it is the key route to information fluency:

- the need to know
- knowing you need to know
- how to ask the best question
- how to get the best answers
- using the right formats
- having the right skills and confidence.

What make the information literacy role of public libraries more challenging today are the mass of information available, the digital context and the common view that it is easy for anyone to retrieve just whatever information they want from the Internet. We must work hard, ideally with partners, to provide innovative and creative ways of improving citizens' information skills – and across all formats. To reinforce the point, the recent American report of the Knight Commission on the information needs of communities in a democracy included the following quotation as part of its introduction:

> Information is as vital to the healthy functioning of communities as clean air, safe streets, good schools, and public health. (Knight Commission, 2009)

This articulates powerfully – and in a way not usually seen – the relative strategic importance of information, and does so in a way we should exploit so as to promote and develop our critical role – both present and future – in information provision and support.

Digital library, digital exclusion, and Digital Britain

Digital Britain (DCMS and BIS, 2009), while making little specific reference to public libraries, helps to articulate their digital priorities.

Public libraries help to plug the '21% digital gap' with equipment, connectivity and staff support for the one in ten households that do not have access to a high-speed/broadband Internet connection; the 37% of adults who have no regular access to the Internet; the 50% of adults who do not yet use the Internet to access government information; the 20% who do use the Internet as first port of call for information relating to a health concern; the 12.5 million adults who do not use the Internet. *Digital Britain* identifies three specific client groups for whom the digital divide is widening:

- adults over 65
- socially excluded citizens
- those with few or no qualifications.

Public libraries are a universal and accessible delivery mechanism with a key role to play in executing the national plan for digital participation – but they have to seize the opportunity and gear up. For example, 98% of public library authorities currently help new library members to get online (MLA, 2010). An excellent number, but this has to hit the 100% figure as soon as possible, and deliver with greater pace and quality. Dame Lynne Brindley, the Chief Executive of the British Library, has called for a focus on digital literacy skills. 'We may get the plumbing (broadband) and we may get the poetry (new content) envisaged by Lord Carter,[5] but if we do not have proficiency to exploit the opportunities, such investment will be wasted. We need digital literacy for all – the skills we need as a nation to prosper in the digital world' (Brindley, 2009).

Developing really good digital library and information services will not – and should not – automatically result in predominantly remote use and a corresponding decline in building-based services. For many people, public and shared space (and often space with staff to provide expert support) will still be needed to facilitate access to mediated information, discussions about information choices and options, and peer-group engagement in the digital environment. Offering a digital route to library and information services will not result in less face-to-face service delivery, or save money. This is yet another complexity we need to be prepared for, and another myth we need to dismiss. Digital is something we must provide as a choice, and not just as an alternative – or at least not for some time.

A key challenge will be to understand and respond to the current requirements of contemporary digital users, and to predict their future requirements. Library staff have to engage with the experts – the 'cradle digitals'[6] and the digital producers – to try to work this out in the most effective way. Part of this challenge is scale: we will have to find a way to push the debate, the thinking and the vision at a national level – rather than locally in each of the 151 English library services.

Richard Watson (2009) presents an interesting and – at first – a seemingly contradictory perspective. He seems to dismiss the need for public space in the context of delivering and using digital services: 'One of the ironies of digitalisation is that the more we are connected, the more we become isolated,' and: 'We've traded intimacy for familiarity. We know lots of people but we don't know them well, and we know few people with whom we could discuss a problem. We can get instant news and tweets throughout the day but we don't know our neighbours' names.' Again, this highlights the public library's role, as a universal provider of information, in mitigating against isolation where it occurs, and where citizens want that mitigation.

Watson goes on to say: 'In the UK 5.4 million people work at home. This is why Starbucks does so well — they want somewhere to go. Even in offices people don't communicate, they stare at screens all day. Lunchtime has gone, the dining room has gone, the family sitting around one television has gone.' And finally from Watson: 'the public library, feared moribund in recent years, is in its element because it's about much more than books. It's a quiet and safe community space, an experience that enables you to access expertise from commercially uncorrupt resources, and that's both ethical and resource-friendly' (Watson, 2009). We know that there are more public libraries than Starbucks, and you don't have to buy or pay for anything to use the public library. What an opportunity – to recreate or at least redefine the library as meeting space. The Mechanics Institutes[7] reborn!

Supporting democratic living

The original, radical role of public libraries is often overlooked and appears to have little currency. But where else is the radical in public and community life? Can libraries regain their initial role and reputation of supporting free and radical thinking? If libraries don't offer this, what other organisation can? The ability to read, access and understand the information needed for daily life is critical for everyone. Where will the digitally excluded citizens find the support and opportunity to vote electronically; to shop; and apply for employment online? Where else can they engage equally and freely? And where else is there the balance of literature and information, of printed and digital media? Where else is there the opportunity to research freely, and with the support of objective and expert intermediaries? This is not a new role for public libraries, but it is not seen as a contemporary one. It is a role which must be re-energised to help achieve a more equal society.

Lifelong learning

It is interesting to reflect that an earlier version of the statutory public library service (the 1919 Libraries and Museums Act) resulted from the work of a government Adult Education Committee. Ninety years later, the government's *The Learning Revolution* (DfIUS, 2009) sees the cultural sector, including public libraries, as key to delivering its future informal adult learning agenda. Community facilities will be at the heart of informal learning. The report also identifies e-learning as key, and consequently the need to tackle digital exclusion. UK online centres, many of which are also public libraries, are being asked to take on a new role as championing informal learning. Budget reductions have already begun to hit adult learning generally, and the need to reduce overheads, coupled with the demand for accessible community venues, presents a huge opportunity to exploit the physical library network. Managers need to find ways of accommodating the informal learning role alongside core business, and in an affordable way.

Twenty-first-century space

Not just a challenge, but also an opportunity, as David Vogt and Les Watson also comment in Chapters 9 and 10 respectively: where today can citizens find a safe and free (and hopefully quality) environment in which to talk, to think, to study? Pubs are closing and community centres are reducing in number. Public squares are excellent, but do not offer shelter and security. The best public libraries are akin to top-quality public squares but better, with shelter and security. This is a traditional rather than just a contemporary characteristic. But it must be protected, and developed, and library leaders must harness all their political and negotiating skills to achieve this. The challenge will be to raise the standard of this space, and to maintain it for the future.

Twenty-first-century customers

We have already shifted significantly from the merely responsive 'here it is if you want it' service. Public libraries have spent at least the last 30 years trying to differentiate between various types of customer and potential customer and then tailor services for them. This has been a very positive development, but it is not enough, for at the same time customer expectation has also increased significantly. People want more convenient opening hours, contemporary and regularly updated environments, and more choice in terms of both the service on offer and means of access. Customers also want high-quality products, and they want them on demand, or at least very quickly.

How can we respond to this higher expectation at a time when we will have to deliver even greater efficiencies? Spend on content and infrastructure will almost inevitably be reduced. So public libraries really will need to look at achieving creative efficiencies – through better partnerships, better procurement, more shared services, even more creative thinking on what constitutes a contemporary service. Funders will want to minimise the impact of budget reductions on front-line service. Assuming that budget reductions will be consistent over a three- to six-year period, there is a real challenge to be radical about reducing overheads and sharing management, support and infrastructure costs, regardless of political and geographical differences. Now this really is a challenge for the sector and its decision makers. But if we don't deliver it, budget pressures will probably erode service content and quality irrevocably.

The death of the public library?

In 2009, the journalist Rachel Cooke wrote an article for the *Observer* newspaper that was dramatically entitled 'Time to go into battle to save our world of books' (Cooke, 2009). This was just one of several articles bemoaning the end of the public library service, the shortage of book stock and the perceived loss of the traditional service. No one would dispute genuine concern at the significant decline in book issues. At a time when 60% of the public engage in reading, why do one-third of the readers not get their reading materials from the library service? There is also real concern at the apparently low percentage of budget spent on book stock. But Cooke's view, along with a number of other London-based writers and commentators, is a very élitist, traditional and nostalgic one. Consider, for example, the fuss about Camden Libraries' modernisation proposals in 2008, which entailed providing improved Internet access and relaxing previously draconian rules on eating, drinking and the use of mobile phones (see Muir, 2008; Hamilton, 2008).

Public libraries continue to have reading at their core – for pleasure, for information, for learning and to help participate fully in contemporary life. This is what public libraries did in the 1850s and the 1900s, and what they must continue to do in the 2010s, 2020s and beyond. Personal computers (PCs) and download stations would have been part of the 1850s public library service had they been invented then. They are just the current means of accessing information and reading, and of providing access to all, and especially to those who do not have their own means. Busy banks of PCs, crowded study tables, as well as full bookshelves, may not sit well with some people's 1970s memories (and may seem an irrelevance to those with high-speed access from their home computers), but this is a description of contemporary public libraries at their best.

Reflection

The public library roles discussed here are as valid and important now and for the future as they have ever been. That's the public library manager's view. But it is a tempered view. To deliver core services and to tackle the current challenges of helping to deliver a literate, informed and empowered society in the 'austerity' context, we have to face up to radical change and the relentless pursuit of new opportunity. Many library services are working hard to deliver digital and virtual library services to local customers. This is about giving choice of access, and also about reaching out to those who are much less likely to use services delivered in the traditional, building-based manner but who still need (or would benefit from) a good library and information service. But there is a problem with the UK digital library service. It is, by and large, being delivered in a piecemeal fashion, almost, but not quite, in 151 different ways. Public libraries, ideally with central support and vision from the Department for Culture, Media and Sport (DCMS), need to work together to deliver a national digital library service: what could so easily become the universal, personalised library and information service. This is not proposed by the new modernisation policy paper (DCMS, 2010), so if it is to happen it looks as though the demand and drive for it will need to come from within.

The library estate (the complement to the virtual library service) is another area for radical change and investment (even if only on an 'invest to save' basis). Invest to save would provide initial investment to enable future savings through, for example, more shared services; more partnerships with other organisations (including the voluntary sector); the use of self-service and digital technology to reduce other costs; unstaffed libraries offering books and People's Network services with drop-in information service surgeries. All of these can be delivered successfully, but they require clear thinking and vision. For example, a shared service is more than simply a shared building; there has to be a rigorous debate about what distinguishes public library and information provision from a room of bookshelves and computers. At the same time, library managers have to be open to the potential opportunities provided by other organisations, their buildings and their staff.

Conclusion

To help conclude, here are a few comments from a recent public library conference in Edinburgh, made by the Leader of Newcastle City Council, Councillor John Shipley:

> Libraries come cheap at the price, reducing costs in almost every other problematic area of public spending: policing and crime prevention, vandalism, drug and alcohol abuse, social exclusion. The public library is one of the few spaces that you could go to and not have to spend money. As such, it is becoming the pillar of interaction for citizens, and it's not just to read. Access to information and civic services is a core entitlement – the cost of the library service is a small price to pay to what other parts of a local authority would have to pay if the library service doesn't deliver to its potential. (Shipley, 2010)

To deliver this agenda, public librarians and library managers must look out for and seize any opportunity which allows the service or its resources (including its workforce) to make a recognised contribution to other agendas. Many of us are not good at this – a situation that must change quickly. We need attitude, and the enthusiasm for radical change referred to above. That is the only way to build, harness and maintain the support of key politicians and other influential stakeholders. These are the people we need, especially in the immediate future, to say that our contribution (in proportion to our relatively low municipal cost) is too vital to be reduced.

So, a final comment: the death of the public library? Just as Mark Twain said 'the report of my death was an exaggeration',[8] I firmly believe the same about the much-heralded death of the public library and information service. But to keep it alive and flourishing needs decisive action, vision and energy nationally. We need a clear sense of direction from government and, to be fair, it needs to be stronger than that offered in the new modernisation review. But we also have to replicate that action, vision and energy in every one of the 151 services.

Notes

1. http://news.bbc.co.uk/1/hi/business/8380268.stm.
2. See http://www.culture.gov.uk/news/news_stories/7215.aspx and http://www.culture.gov.uk/news/news_stories/7381.aspx.
3. http://www.peoplesnetwork.gov.uk/.
4. http://www.cilip.org.uk/get-involved/advocacy/learning/information-literacy/Pages/definition.aspx.
5. http://www.timesonline.co.uk/tol/news/politics/article5622452.ece.
6. 'Cradle digitals' are those who have had access to ICT from birth.
7. http://en.wikipedia.org/wiki/Mechanics'_Institutes.
8. http://www.askoxford.com/quotations/2375?view=uk.

References

BML and Reading Partnership. (2000) *Reading the Situation: book reading and borrowing habits in Britain*. London: Book Marketing Ltd.

Brindley, L. (2009) 'Dame Lynne Brindley challenges government on Digital Britain'. British Library Press Room, 21 January. Online at http://pressandpolicy.bl.uk/Press-Releases/Dame-Lynne-Brindley-challenges-Government-on-Digital-Britain-265.aspx.

Cooke, R. (2009) 'Time to go into battle to save our world of books'. *Observer*, 22 March, 5–7. Online at http://www.guardian.co.uk/books/2009/mar/22/saving-british-libraries.

Creative Research. (2009) *The Future of Reading: a public value project.* Arts Council England. Online at http://www.artscouncil.org.uk/media/uploads/Future-Reading-Appendices.pdf.

DCMS. (2001) *Comprehensive, Efficient and Modern Public Libraries: standards and assessment.* Department for Culture, Media and Sport. Online at http://webarchive.nationalarchives.gov.uk/+/http://www.culture.gov.uk/images/publications/libraries_archives_for_all_assessment.pdf.

DCMS. (2010) *The Modernisation Review of Public Libraries.* Department for Culture, Media and Sport. London: HMSO. Online at http://www.culture.gov.uk/what_we_do/libraries/5583.aspx.

DCMS and BIS. (2009) *Digital Britain: final report.* Department for Culture, Media and Sport, and Department for Business, Innovation and Skills. Online at http://www.culture.gov.uk/images/publications/digitalbritain-finalreport-jun09.pdf.

DfIUS. (2009) *The Learning Revolution.* Department for Innovation, Universities and Skills. Online at http://www.dius.gov.uk/assets/biscore/corporate/migratedd/publications/l/learning_revolution.pdf.

Hamilton, F. (2008) 'Public libraries open way for drinks, snacks and mobiles'. *The Times*, 19 September. Online at http://www.timesonline.co.uk/tol/news/uk/education/article4783690.ece.

Jeffries, S. (2010) 'Battle of the books'. *Guardian*, 8 March, 17–20.

Knight Commission. (2009) *Informing Communities: sustaining democracy in the digital age.* The Aspen Institute. Online at https://secure.nmmstream.net/anon.newmediamill/aspen/kcfinalenglishbookweb.pdf.

MLA. (2010) *Role of Public Libraries in Supporting and Promoting Digital Participation.* Museums, Libraries and Archives Council. Online at http://research.mla.gov.uk/evidence/documents/public-libraries-and-digital-participation-mla.pdf.

Muir, K. (2008) 'We need books to sink our teeth into, not burgers'. *The Times*, 19 September. Online at http://www.timesonline.co.uk/tol/life_and_style/education/article4783704.ece.

Public Libraries Act 1919. London: HMSO.

The Reading Agency and BLM. (2002) *Reading Groups and Public Library Research.* Report for London Libraries Development Agency.

The Reading Agency. (2004) *A National Library Development Programme for Reading Groups.* Online at http://www.readingagency.org.uk/new-thinking/newthinking-uploads/Programme_for_reading_groups.pdf.

The Reading Agency. (2008) *Library Reading Groups: explosion in membership*. Online at http://www.readingagency.org.uk/media/press-releases/LibraryReadingGroups.pdf.

Shipley, J. (2010) 'The Physical Library and Regeneration'. Presentation at *EDGE 2010: Global conference pushing the boundaries of public library delivery*, Edinburgh Castle, 25–26 February.

Watson, R. (2009) *Future Files: a brief history of the next 50 years*. London: Nicholas Brealey Publishing.

22

The future of public libraries and their services: a Danish perspective

Hellen Niegaard

Introduction

What kind of conceptual and structural changes are public libraries, as local cultural and knowledge institutions supporting democracy and access for all, currently undergoing? What are the driving forces behind the shift? What kind of strategic response is required? And where are the new and promising models in the pipeline? The answers to these questions, of course, depend on which country you look at. However, many aspects will be universal and therefore the national solutions of one country might be of relevance to others. The following 'look ahead' for public libraries in terms of their value and usage within society reflects current developments, strategic actions and a selection of tangible projects initiated in Denmark to meet 21st-century needs – those of users and those of the society.

The death and rebirth of libraries

Time and again, as the use of information and communication technologies (ICT) has spread, and the Internet, with its global communication, information and search methods, has grown, the death of the library has been proclaimed. In fact, the very same developments may be said to stipulate the need for an institution promoting access to knowledge and cultural expression of quality, and for professional guidance on searching. Rolf Hapel, Director of Citizens' Services and Libraries, Aarhus Municipality states:

If libraries didn't already exist, then new, open institutions as resource centres would have to be invented. The knowledge society presents both traditional and new challenges, accentuating the need for institutions and services that can ensure cohesion, identity creation, lifelong learning, public service supply of culture and literature experiences, and knowledge and competency development. Essentially, [this is] an open, public place with learning facilities and cultural opportunities, including contemporary and competent instruction. As we do have the libraries, let's reconstruct them! (Hapel, 2008)

Re-inventing the public library

The public library is undergoing a paradigm shift, transforming the physical library from a classic book- and shelving-dominated facility to a place of communication: a library offering a variety of connections and relations, including Internet services and network partners, yet still including traditional collections. Globalisation has, during the last 10 to 15 years, together with ICT, gradually changed the classic library forever. The change in media formats and the breakthrough of ICT, including access to online libraries and information services 24/7, have, together with the automation of manual handling procedures and the emergence of extended self-service points and sorting robots, made it essential to change the way libraries are organised and laid out. This applies to public, academic and school libraries – or, indeed, any kind of library.

Why would you need a library when you have the Internet and its billions of pieces of information, music, digitised books, and search engines such as Google? The answer is rather simple, and highlighted in several Danish surveys on library use, of which the most recent was made by Gallup for the Danish Library Association and other Danish organisations in July 2009.[1] Firstly, professional face-to-face guidance, help with finding information, and expertise are still valued very highly by patrons and, in particular, amongst young people. Secondly – if facilities are updated – users still want to come to the physical library. In fact, only about half of the users who visit the library today actually come to borrow material. They come to find inspiration, to work, meet, socialise and just be – in an ambiance of knowledge. Denmark, with its population of 5.5 million, has some 34 million public library visits a year (2008), making the library the Danish cultural institution with most visits per year. The number of book and other loans is declining; however, it still amounts to 50.5 million loans (including renewals) annually, which should be seen in connection with a fast-growing number of e-loans, the total number of which grew in 2008 to around 24 million (visits to home pages and downloads). Users may have changed their media habits, but apparently they still want to use libraries.[2]

These trends may not be so surprising. After all, the library is considered, together with the city hall, schools and hospitals, to be one of society's central and fundamental public spaces, a building that is synonymous with knowledge and access to knowledge. From the very beginning of time, the library has been closely associated with wisdom and with mingling with one's peers – positive attributes valued throughout history and previously associated with powerful institutions such as the state, the church, monasteries and universities, to name but a few. However, the library, its physical premises and its services, are undergoing a complete transformation – a transformation from a classic, print-oriented library, to a modern cultural and learning institution. What strategic initiatives support that transformation?

The Danish situation

The basis of the new public library in Denmark is comprised of several factors, including a change in formal governmental structures in 2007. To understand the impact of these changes it is necessary to understand the function of the Danish public library. It functions, it could be said, under a 'contract' with society, supporting citizens' personal development and learning and, therefore, a permanent democratic development process. The Local Government Reform of 2007[3] reduced the number of Danish municipalities from close to 300 then to 98, and condensed the many counties into five regions. The process led to new library structures amongst the majority of the municipalities and to the closure of more than 100 smaller and decentralised branches. Public libraries are 100% financed by the local municipalities. The state, via the Danish Agency for Libraries and Media, is responsible for library legislation, funding for development projects, inter-library lending systems (including five regional libraries and the State and University Library, Aarhus), plus the national infrastructure Bibliotek.dk[4] – a result of the new law.

The 2000 Act Regarding Library Services,[5] the latest version of the Danish library legislation (which first appeared back in 1920), is the legal basis for the 21st-century public library. It stresses that printed materials, together with digitised and Internet-related resources, are all important for libraries, in order to provide continuous free access to information and knowledge. Denmark is known for its library cooperation and its inter-library lending system. The 10-year-old national database and online service, Bibliotek.dk, enables users to find records of all items published in Denmark, as well as all items found at Danish public and research libraries. The service includes online reservation, and delivery to the user's preferred library. The database is developed and maintained by the Danish Bibliographic Centre (DBC).

Libraries are moving from having collections to having connections. The move is far from complete, as books are still primarily acquired in print, but the end of the Gutenberg era may not be very far away. To access electronic files, libraries subscribe to an Internet access point at the publisher's or distributor's database, and in most cases via extended collective licence agreements. However, copyright and licences must be updated according to libraries' needs. Increasingly, content is available in electronic formats and transaction costs are going down. However, as Harald von Hielmcrone, Danish copyright expert and advisor to the Danish library community, says, there is no free lunch (von Hielmcrone, 2010). The consequence of the move is that libraries will no longer be able to control conditions for access or use and long-term preservation, because use will depend on licence agreements – and what will happen if commercial database owners go out of business?

The emerging new media landscape and the change in cultural behaviour and media habits as a result of social networking and similar sites such as Wikipedia,[6] MySpace,[7] Facebook[8] and Twitter[9] – do not replace the library. The so-called Google generation, people born or brought up in the Internet age since the mid 1990s, is upon us; they are taking up not only the new media, but also traditional media like books. So too are previous generations, according to the BibliotekGallup 2009 survey, and another Danish study of 2008 by the private research company Firstmove.dk, which states that the 'library has become a trendier place than cafés'.

The e-society is here, at least in Denmark, and ICT is playing an increasing role in the everyday lives of Danes, in accordance with the Danish Globalisation Strategy 2006[10] for the aims of local government reform and the ongoing quality reform, Modernisering.dk.[11] Three out of four Danes are daily users of the Internet; about 86% of Danish families have a computer in their home, 83% have Internet access and 76% have broadband connections.[12] Internet social networking services with user-created content, such as Facebook, are extremely popular. And more than half of the population (52%) download digital material, and the number is increasing. This is also the case in libraries, as noted earlier, while at the same time they continue to use traditional printed books.

Policies for the new library

All in all, these trends have put a great deal of pressure on local library systems, as they now have to navigate between the need for traditional, classic library services and the need for new, digital and online-based services: all this at a time of limited financial resources. These are trends which have made the Danish Library Association do a number of things. First, since 2006, the Association has urged its members – 90% of the Danish municipalities – to develop local, politically approved policies and strategies for the necessary development of the local library service. Second, around the same time the Association started lobbying for a new, common national vision for the public library. And third, in 2008 it published a book, *Biblioteksrummet* (Danmarks Biblioteksforening, 2008), on new library concepts and the need to update existing libraries or build new ones. The publication was updated and translated into English in 2009 as *Library Space*. Finally, the Danish Library Association, in cooperation with other Danish library organisations and with the Nordic Library Associations, discussed copyright and licence issues in order to identify means to guarantee future access and long-term preservation.

In 2009, the then Minister of Culture, Carina Christensen, established a fast-working committee on 'The Role of the Public Libraries in the Knowledge Society', with a call for a new national vision, made in the context of local government reform and the closure of decentralised library branches. The committee's work produced recommendations, not legislation. It submitted its report, 'The Public Libraries in the Knowledge Society',[13] in late March 2010. The report analyses the current situation of libraries. It states that 'The local government reform in 2007 had major consequences for the library service. The number of libraries decreased and the remaining libraries grew in size.' Furthermore, it looks at the changes in use and media etc. The committee looked at:

- traditional services

- literature dissemination

- digital infrastructure and interaction with traditional services

- digital dissemination of cultural heritage and licensed information resources

- models for different types of learning and inspiration activities

- new partnerships and the competence of library staff.

It chose to address both the general societal requirements relating to libraries' and users' more concrete needs by setting out a number of recommendations for future library developments.[14] The recommendations are divided into five areas of action:

- open libraries

- inspiration and learning

- the Danish Digital Library

- partnerships

- professional development.

Currently, one of these issues in particular is being discussed, namely, the possibilities of and ways to establish the so-called Danish Digital Library, 'a common digital mediation to the Danes' – offering a single access point for digital media such as films, games, music and literature.

Library space

Through the publication of *Library Space: inspiration for buildings and design* (Niegaard, Lauridsen and Schulz, 2009), the Danish Library Association wants to stimulate a rethinking of library layout and construction – to encourage the municipalities, as library 'owners', to work towards new library buildings of high quality, flexibility and creativity, as well as to have the courage to seek new directions in design, architecture and urban location. And furthermore, to position the public library as a visible and powerful asset of the 21st century's democratic knowledge society. Many articles reflect the way in which the public library is radically changing, in terms of both services and buildings, from a book- and product-orientated place to a user-orientated place. They also illustrate how developments in ICT, user behaviour and cultural experiences call for a transformation not only of the library building but also of the library concept (see, for example, Hapel, 2009; Niegaard, 2009; Thorhauge, 2009; also see Berry, 2006). The book, written by Danish and foreign architects, library managers and specialists, is a practical guide for all parties involved in preparing for a new or updated library – from architects and designers, politicians and other decision makers, to library management and staff – and, last but not least, the users. What does it take to create the library building of tomorrow? Nobody seems to have all the answers to that question, but one thing is certain – all library stakeholders, public authorities and universities will have to re-evaluate not only their services but also their library buildings in order to ensure an effective and sustainable library service.

Developments and examples

The new library building

Today, the library promotes experience and learning through lectures, story-telling, debate meetings, homework cafés and interactive gaming – for children, teenagers and adults. The citizen expects much more than metre after metre of shelving and printed materials. Besides books, they come for music, films, games and Internet-based services. Even the library architecture, design and layout must be something special: often buildings have iconic qualities. Additionally, public libraries are now frequently being established or re-invented in collaboration with new partners, as, for instance, the *KulturOen Middelfart* (Island of Culture, Figure 22.1), housing library, cinema, restaurant and tourism office.

In many countries, plans for new buildings are now emerging that aim to ensure full-scale classic *and* virtual services and to provide attractive public libraries. Denmark is no exception, and two projects are currently seen as models for the new library and are attracting attention beyond the borders of Denmark. Conceptually, they are very different. One represents the experience library par excellence and is situated in a shopping mall (The Metropol) on the main street in Hjoerring; this library opened in 2008. The second is Mediaspace, Denmark's largest public library building, a landmark structure planned to brand Aarhus as a city of knowledge and culture when it opens in late 2014 or early 2015. It is to be built on the urban harbour front.

Figure 22.1 *KulturOen Middelfart (Island of Culture)*

Photo: Hellen Niegaard

The two projects may be different in nature, but they both represent the concept of the public library as a meeting place for democracy and a community building, that 'third place' the American sociologist and anthropologist Ray Oldenburg defines as 'not home nor job (or school) but an open meeting place for all'. In his 2008 book *The Great Good Place*, Oldenburg argues that 'third places' are central to local democracy and community vitality, as public places on neutral ground where people can gather and interact. The two projects reflect the ideas on urban space of Danish architect and professor of urban design Jan Gehl and his belief in good-quality public spaces (Gehl and Gemzøe, 2004). Because in a society that is becoming steadily more privatised the public component of our lives is disappearing, it is therefore increasingly important to make cities inviting, so that we can meet our fellow citizens face to face and experience directly through our senses. Public life in good-quality public spaces is an important aspect of a democratic life and a full life.

Using a series of future scenarios has transformed the main library in Hjoerring into a genuine experience library.[15] The new main library is an attraction not so much in terms of the building itself, but more because of its conceptual design and layout. It is approximately 5,000 sq m and is situated in the central shopping mall, called Metropol, a building complex designed by Schmidt, Hammer, Lassen Architects. The library interior was developed by the library staff in close cooperation with the interior architects Bosch and Fjord. The interior design is very attractive and different from traditional models, including: an anarchistic Red Ribbon, a range of very colourful, inviting seating arrangements, a number of interactive features for children, stages, lounge, orange study rooms and thematic areas, and pleasant classic library features – which all promote experience, learning, games, play and contemplation – all in one large room. The Red Ribbon runs here, there and everywhere, guiding users around the library, while at the same time offering displays, seating space and much more (Figure 22.2).

It works: people flock to the library and library usage has doubled since its opening. People love the atmosphere and the characteristic smell of old books, which of course are also to be found here, together with plasma screens showing the latest news in unexpected ways. Free access

Figure 22.2 *A Danish Experience Library, opened 2008: Hjoerring's main library*[15]

Photo: Laura Stamer/Bosch & Fjord. Reproduced courtesy of Hjoerring Public Libraries.

to poetry, philosophy, facts and fiction, including new media and online services, and not least the professional guidance of 'outgoing' librarians help users to find what they are looking for. A fine balance has been established between exciting experiences and a vivid environment, without turning the library into a shallow 'Tivoli'.[16]

The vision: Mediaspace,[17] Aarhus (opening 2015) – in Danish *Multimediehuset* – is designed to be a flexible and dynamic sanctuary for everyone in search of knowledge, inspiration and personal development; the attractive library will be the core of the building, and will offer a diversity of media. It will be an open, interactive and accessible learning environment supporting democracy and unity. With its unique location on the New Central Waterfront where the Aarhus Canal meets the harbour, the new main library will be one of the future landmarks of Aarhus, Denmark's second-largest city (Figure 22.3). The architects Schmidt, Hammer, Lassen have designed an inviting and remarkable building that will set new standards for public libraries in Denmark. Mediaspace will, in addition, house Citizens' Services and a number of its (as-yet unidentified) partners. The space comprises approximately

Figure 22.3 *The Library of the Future: Mediaspace will open early 2015 in Aarhus*

Illustration: Schmidt/Hammer/Lassen Architects. Reproduced courtesy of Aarhus Main Library.

18,000 sq m for library purposes and 10,000 sq m as a potential area reserved to house private companies and other third-party activities on the future harbour bastion. New urban spaces will be designed on the bastion around Mediaspace, while car parking, local trains, arrival halls and other utilities will be established on the bastion or nearby. The project was approved by the government in 2003 and many players are involved in its preparation. A series of interactive features have been developed and tested already, together with Innovation Lab Katrinebjerg and the Alexandra Institute/Aarhus University. In 2009, an extensive process of identifying ideas for the new building was initiated, involving both user groups and partners engaged in the project.

Why invest in libraries now?

Why? To guarantee citizens and patrons an up-to-date and satisfactory library service combining the physical and the online library. Because, as mentioned above, a set of more or less universal circumstances emphasises the growing need for either new buildings or the redesign of existing building layouts in order to provide an efficient and satisfactory library service. There are other organisational reasons, such as the need to make the user self-sufficient via self-service solutions, not only when borrowing and returning material, but also when searching for and retrieving relevant information and media. Moreover, another reason is a need to update the way library technical processes are organised, arising from the change from manual task management to automation. Furthermore, libraries can enhance the progress of the society that they are intended to serve. 'Libraries and Urban Development – creativity, innovation and experience' (*Biblioteket i byudviklingen – kreativitet, innovation og oplevelse*)[18] is the title of a Danish research project by the Royal School of Library and Information Science, the Realdania Foundation and other partners, including the Danish Library Association.

Both internationally and domestically, there is an increasing focus on local growth strategies and how each city or region can position itself. In Denmark, the municipalities have been increasingly competitive and diverse in recent years, and today stimulating cultural opportunities are an important factor when it comes to attracting and retaining users. At the same time, the 98 municipalities are part of the 2007 Local Government Reform, the starting point of which was to create more sustainable municipalities through new, larger organisations, whereby each must create and develop its own identity. It is the overall understanding of the project that the library holds great potential in this context: the library can play an important role both as a stage for cultural events and as a laboratory for creativity and innovation. The library can be the identity created by its diverse cultural activities, and at the same time it promotes information and knowledge through technology, materials and dissemination. The project aims to highlight how the library can contribute to and strengthen the visibility of cities and municipalities, while at the same time supporting the needs of citizens for public venues, meaningful experiences and creative challenges.

Local self-service libraries

In recent years, Danish public libraries have faced many challenges. One of the most visible has been the closure of more than 100 branch libraries across the country, in the suburbs and in rural areas, as a result of budget cuts and the trimming of library structures in many of the recently merged municipalities. These closures have left many local users dissatisfied with a situation that is contrary to the recommendations of the Danish Library Association, which advocates longer opening hours. The idea that libraries should be open and accessible at all hours for the convenience of users led to extra funding for decentralised projects from the Ministry of Culture in March 2009, and to a number of new, decentralised 'open self-service' local libraries. Here, libraries are staffed for a limited number of hours, while users have access to the unstaffed library at all other hours via a card key system. This service has, in fact, been very well received by users, due to the much longer opening hours.

New partnerships and reaching out

Society's recognition of the public library's role as an axis and a fulcrum for local citizens' personal development, democratic learning and community building has in recent years led to new services of social importance, providing Citizens' Services at the library, services stimulating language and integration, and services stimulating e-learning. The public library is open to and for everybody, regardless of income, race, gender and status. Citizens of all ages are welcome to gain access to information and cultural expressions that they may consider relevant.

Citizens' Services

The Local Government Reform of 2007, as well as merging municipalities, also included a number of changes to public services. For libraries, it meant new partnerships with public authorities and Citizens' Services, offering a limited number of 'city hall' citizen assistance units at local level in association with so-called local libraries. The idea is to create a single gateway to the public sector at local level, and to take advantage both of the public libraries' expertise in providing public information and of their longer opening hours. Two models of organising Citizens' Services dominate today: either there are two separate services next to each other, sharing premises, or there is one service point where the staff are shared and the service is integrated with the library. The service as such has faced some criticism from some library professionals and politicians fearing for the neutrality of the library. However, the concept seems to be established in a growing number of libraries.

News Library

In fact, decentralised library services are increasingly being established in collaboration with other local players from public health and job services (community centres), along with local cultural centres, cinemas, sport facilities and museums. In 2009, Denmark's – and maybe the world's – first News Library opened: Midtown, a partnership between Herning Bibliotekerne and the local Media and Newspaper House (*Biblioteket I Midtbyen*[19]), a library with very few (new) books and based on access to news. Users seem to like it.

Net services

Danish libraries have developed a wide range of net libraries serving all Danes. Among the most used are: Bibliotekvagten.dk[20] (online reference service), Finfo[21] (service to immigrants), Litteratursiden.dk[22] and netmusik.dk.[23] A new portal for children, Pallesgavebod,[24] was launched in August 2010. The trend is to create online professional library services and guidance together with the services also allowing users to contribute. To optimise use of data, DBC, with Copenhagen Libraries (*København Kommunes Biblioteker*/KKB) and Aarhus Public Libraries (*Aarhus Kommunes Biblioteker*/AAKB), has created a common communication platform based on Open Source. The vision is to allow individual libraries to use the platform freely in all possible contexts. AAKB, KKB and DBC collect data in a 'well', so that the libraries can all access the data and use it in whatever context they need. Library access via mobile phone is another facility under development.

ICT learning campaigns

Public libraries have gradually begun cooperation with other public authorities and players. Since 2007, the Danish Library Agency for Libraries and Media's focal point for a 'competence development network' has become an active partner with Danish public libraries in a national campaign to strengthen citizens' knowledge of public, digital self-service solutions, as for example TAX.dk,[25] and the nationwide borger.dk[26] (citizen.dk), which is the official gateway to the public authorities on the Internet, providing access to all 98 municipalities. ICT affects all parts of Danish society and developments in this area have had an impact on economic growth. All citizens should benefit from the digital potential. It requires access to basic ICT infrastructure, and also that citizens possess the necessary ICT skills to enable them to use the digital services. The Ministry of Science, Technology and Innovation is therefore focusing on spreading the availability and use of ICT within Danish society, one example being through a number of national campaigns in which the public libraries are playing an active role. Two campaigns in 2009–10 involving public service TV channels, Learn more IT (*Lær mere IT*) and To the Keyboard (*Til Tasterne*) included the libraries as professionals, search-instructors and ICT access points.

Learning activities

A brand new project, in conjunction with Danish TV, is the Academy of the Danes – promoting lifelong learning. Ever since the first public libraries were established more than a century ago, supporting personal learning and development has been a central task related to democratic support. Today learning activities are increasing. Helping and instructing patrons in their Internet searching has been professionalised and now almost all libraries offer a number of ICT courses – some via campaigns, some not. One development, informal learning programmes, has recently led to criticism by local political parties because they fear 'unfair competition from the free-of-charge library services'. The Danish Library Association sees the situation as an opportunity to combine competencies and encourage the two sides to work together at local level in order to stimulate citizens' need for lifelong learning.

Democracy development

A recent example of another type of democratic support takes the form of collaboration between one of the public service TV channels and the public libraries. It gives viewers an opportunity to ask questions to 'this week's top politicians' either through their own webcam or through library facilities. Once a week from February 2010, DR2's news programme *Deadline17*, via an agreement with the Danish Agency for Libraries and Media and with 10 major libraries around the country, helps individuals to submit questions to the politicians. The intention is to involve a greater number of libraries.

Homework cafés

Library services supporting integration take many forms. Over the past three years homework cafés have popped up all over Denmark, offering young children adult homework assistance. The target groups are primarily first- and second-generation Danish children whose parents are not always able to assist with daily homework in Danish. The Ministry of Culture and the Ministry of Integration support homework assistance for all young people as part of the libraries' work with integration. An important outcome has been the creation of 130 cafés across the country. The evaluation of the three-year-old project shows that thousands of children and young people from ethnic minorities have been helped to achieve success in school. In total, the cafés received over 30,000 visits during the three years of the project. Some cafés have also been teaching parents, so as to help them to help their children with homework. The popular cafés are organised at the library and staffed by volunteers. An online version of the service was opened in 2008 and attracts, amongst others, teenage boys, who find this solution more convenient. The Danish Agency for Libraries and Media supported the projects through special funds derived from the Ministry of Culture and the Ministry of Social Affairs.

Bookstart

Children love to read bedtime stories with their parents, but some families have no tradition of this, nor any kind of reading traditions to stimulate children to read for themselves. Likewise, they may just not have the money and do not attend libraries. Since March 2009, public libraries across the country, in cooperation with local social authorities, have offered free book parcels to children in less fortunate areas. It is a priority project, funded with DKK16 million between 2009 and 2012 and run by the Danish Agency for Libraries and Media. The children receive a book parcel on four occasions; first at the ages of 6 months and 12 months, when librarians visit the family at home. When the child is 18 months old, the families are invited to collect the parcel at the library, and when the child reaches his/her third birthday, the fourth book parcel is given, this time at the day-care institution in the local area. Besides book parcels, the project offers language-stimulation activities for children, and advice to parents about children's language and reading. Bookstart is a key to reading and the pleasure of reading, and it is intended to help children gain good language skills before they reach school age, so that they are ready to learn to read.

The last third

During 2009 the then Minister of Culture, Carina Christensen, launched a new cultural strategy entitled Culture for All. Its essence: art and culture are important factors in the Danish community and, to ensure our cohesiveness as a nation, we must not resign and accept that about one-third of all citizens cannot be seen as users of cultural facilities and institutions. The strategy recommends cross-cultural outreach initiatives to attract 'the last third' of the population, or at least to ensure that cultural institutions and services are known to all. For many years, Danish public libraries have debated how to reach out and how to market library services much more efficiently.

Conclusion: marketing a must

Rethinking the library concept is clearly far from enough. To make the transformation and the new concept known is another urgent task. Marketing and branding the re-invented library is a serious challenge for library management, library associations and other players in the sector. Nothing is as it used to be within the library sector, and yet everything is still the same – and that has created a good deal of confusion. In early 2008, Danish national media stimulated a vigorous debate about libraries 'throwing away books to create spacious user areas', which was inspired by a modernising project in Copenhagen Main Library by then head of the library Ms Pernille Schaltz. In summer 2009 a similar debate arose in southern Sweden, when Malmoe Main Library started a weeding process as part of transforming the library and rethinking spaces and refurbishing. It was an unfortunate situation, with public debate concentrated on protecting the vision of the library as 'the book house', as in the Gutenberg model – otherwise known as the printed book – rather than focusing on what is important to both users and society, namely, the new role of the library and the way libraries of the future will fulfil a role as local, modern places of knowledge and cultural experience.

Of course, some things are essentially the same. The fundamentals of the public library in Denmark, and in the western world more generally, are as they have been, it would seem, for the last hundred years or so: to identify, purchase, classify and make available all relevant materials – of quality and/or of current interest. Today, however, 'purchase' does not mean buying and collection building alone. It also means purchasing licences – mostly in package form – and access to all kinds of relevant information and files, whether in the form of e-books or MP3 files for download, or in the form of links to certain services on the Internet. Therefore, it can be claimed that the role of the public municipal library is the same today as it was yesterday and probably will be for the foreseeable future, and this causes confusion. Nevertheless, at least seen from a Danish and western perspective, the public library concept is changing and definitely taking a new direction in the 21st century.

The marketing of the new library – increasing visibility and awareness of both its physical and its digitised and online services – is high on the Danish political agenda: nationally, as a priority of the central development funds; locally, as a way to create greater understanding among decision makers, politicians and library owners of the necessary transformation; but not least to promote the use of new services and licences to users, and to guarantee an efficient return on investments in licensed materials. As the Swedish example illustrates, it should be high on the agenda everywhere.

The Danish Library Association and the library sector are now discussing the recommendations of the Committee on the Role of Public Libraries in the Knowledge Society, mentioned earlier in this chapter, and how these might improve the dissemination of the idea of the modern public library.

Notes

1. http://www.dbf.dk/ – BiblioteksGallup 2009.
2. See Danish Library Statistics 2009 by the Danish Agency for Libraries and Media, *Folke-og Forskningsbiblioteksstatistik 2009*, at http://www.bibliotekogmedier.dk/biblioteksomraadet/statistik/indberetning/.
3. http://www.kl.dk/English/Local-Government-Reform.
4. http://bibliotek.dk.
5. http://www.bibliotekogmedier.dk/English.
6. http://www.wikipedia.org/.
7. http://www.myspace.com/.
8. http://www.facebook.com.
9. http://twitter.com/.
10. http://www.netpublikationer.dk/um/6648/html/chapter01.htm.
11. http://www.modernisering.dk.
12. http://www.dst.dk/publikation.aspx?cid=14039.
13. http://www.bibliotekogmedier.dk/fileadmin/publikationer/publikationer_engelske/Reports/The_public_libraries_in_the_knowledge_society._Summary.pdf.
14. http://www.bibliotekogmedier.dk/publikationer/publikationer-paa-engelsk/.
15. http://www.hjoerring.dk – Biblioteket.
16. Tivoli (also called Tivoli Gardens in English) is a famous amusement park and pleasure garden in Copenhagen, Denmark. The park opened on 15 August 1843 and is the second-oldest amusement park in the world, after Dyrehavsbakken in nearby Klampenborg. http://www.tivoli.dk.
17. http://www.multimediehuset.dk/english.
18. http://www.db.dk/cks/proj.htm.
19. http://www.herningbib.dk/om-biblioteket/midtbyen.
20. http://biblioteksvagten.dk/.
21. http://finfo.dk.
22. http://litteratursiden.dk.
23. http://netmusik.dk.
24. http://www.pallesgavebod.dk/.
25. http://www.tax.dk.
26. http://www.borger.dk.

References

Berry, J. (2006) 'Gale/LJ Library of the Year 2006: Salt Lake City public library – where democracy happens'. *Library Journal.com*. Online at http://www.libraryjournal.com/article/CA6341871.html.

Danmarks Biblioteksforening. (2008) *Biblioteksrummet*. Online at http://www.dbf.dk/Default.aspx?ID=5164.

Gehl, J. and Gemzøe, L. (2004) *Public Spaces – public life*. Copenhagen: Danish Architectural Press, 2004.

Hapel, R. (2008) *Annual Report 2008: citizens' services and libraries*. Aarhus Municipality, Denmark. Online at http://www.multi mediehuset.dk.

Hapel, R. (2009) 'Reconstruction of the library'. In Niegaard, H., Lauridsen, J., and Schulz, K. (eds) *Library Space: inspiration for building and design*. Copenhagen: Danish Library Association.

Niegaard, H. (2009) 'Digital drive and room for contemplation', in Niegaard, H., Lauridsen, J. and Schulz, K. (eds) (2009) *Library Space: inspiration for building and design*. Copenhagen: Danish Library Association.

Niegaard, H., Lauridsen, J. and Schulz, K. (eds) (2009) *Library Space: inspiration for building and design*. Copenhagen: Danish Library Association.

Oldenburg, R. (2008) *The Great Good Place*. Oldenburg, MA: Marlowe and Co. Publishing.

Thorhauge, J. (2009) 'Library service for children in the future'. In Niegaard, H., Lauridsen, J. and Schulz, K. (eds) *Library Space: inspiration for building and design*. Copenhagen: Danish Library Association.

Von Hielmcrone, H. (2010) 'Digital Libraries'. Paper presented at the *Nordic Conference on Libraries and Copyright*, Oslo, Norway, 1–2 February.

23

Library landscapes: digital developments

Derek Law

Introduction

This chapter looks at the future in terms of the kind of landscape in which libraries will operate. This will inevitably be a landscape that is dominated by the Internet and the new kinds of provision and usage that are possible in a digital world. The chapter investigates key aspects of digital libraries and the relationship between digital libraries and knowledge creation and use in different communities. It considers the view that there is an urgent need for libraries to develop a strong online presence, in addition to the physical building, in order to remain relevant in today's online world – especially because they are social institutions, rooted in social communities. The chapter looks at a range of current and likely future communication tools, including wikis, blogs, social networking and podcasting, and looks at how to develop a range of resources that will best meet the needs of the library population.

Societal change

The notion that the world is changing fundamentally and that the digital natives have arrived is hardly novel, but once it enters the heart of the establishment we must grant a new gravitas to the presumption of such change. The way in which church and state have both arrived at this conclusion now leaves little room for the sceptic. The Catholic Church has adopted this view. For World Communications Day 2010, Pope Benedict XVI developed the notion of cyber priests. He proposed a new commandment for priests struggling to get their message across: 'Go forth and blog.' The Pope, whose own presence on the Web has grown massively in recent years, urged priests to use all multimedia tools at their disposal to preach the Gospel. This message can be found not only on Facebook, but also on the papal website Pope2You.[1]

At almost the same time, the Lord Chief Justice of England[2] has called for a rethinking of trial by jury to meet the abilities of the Internet generation (Gibb, 2009). He believes that individuals no longer have the ability to listen to sustained oral presentations for hours on end and then draw valid conclusions. This in turn reflects a world where jurors are increasingly in trouble for such things as using Google Maps[3] to view crime scenes – and not only in the United Kingdom (Schwartz, 2009). The world is increasingly populated by the aliterate, for whom reading and writing in the way that past generations have understood these activities are becoming optional lifestyle choices and not the normal requirement of the intelligent individual. The aliterate expect:

- instant gratification
- convenience (which is seen as superior to quality)
- images, which are at least as important as text
- that if it's not on the Web, it doesn't exist
- cut and paste, which is preferable to original thought
- just enough material for the task in hand, not everything (Law, 2006).

Perhaps the ultimate (if slightly tongue-in-cheek) application for this attention-deficit-disorder generation is the Ten Word Wiki.[4] Rather like the haiku,[5] it attempts to distil, if not wisdom, then at least information, in exactly 10 words.[6] Nor is this change unique to libraries. The virtual collapse of the local newspaper industry has been chronicled by the much-admired Clay Shirky (2009), and his central theme has been transposed neatly:

> If you want to know why ~~newspapers~~ *libraries* are in such trouble, the most salient fact is this: ~~printing presses~~ *library buildings and services* are terrifically expensive to set up and to run.

> Society doesn't need ~~newspapers~~ *libraries*. What we need is ~~journalism.~~ *access to information.*

When we shift our attention from 'save ~~newspapers~~ *libraries*' to 'save society', the imperative changes from 'preserve the current institutions' to 'do whatever works'.[7]

This is the landscape in which libraries must now operate; a landscape in which the maps of the past are of little value but the central tenets of our professional geography remain relevant – if in need of complete rethinking. Librarians have always believed passionately in the concept of service. But there is now a need for a complete reversal of thinking, and successful libraries will have to build their services around the user's workflow; libraries must be available to users when and where needed, rather than users be expected to visit the library at times convenient to the organisation.

Different communities, different responses

Although the communities that libraries serve may require different responses, it is the case that the underlying issues are the same. The Ithaka Report (2009) makes the unhappy if unsurprising comment that 'basic scholarly information use practices have shifted rapidly in recent years, and as a result the academic library is increasingly being disintermediated from the discovery process, risking irrelevance in one of its core functional areas'. This is just as true of students as it is of researchers, but while academic staff feel that they need libraries to buy materials to support research, students are much more likely to need support services to teach them how to undertake research and to find the relevant materials that the library already owns or has access to.

Digital content

In a recent Research Information Network (RIN) study that considered key issues for researchers and the links that needed to be forged with librarians (RIN, 2010a), a number of useful points were made which reach to the heart of the challenges that have to be addressed. Libraries have tended to focus either on purchasing digital content or on digitising the paper collections they already possess. Of course it is arguable that the explosion of purchasing of electronic journals and e-materials has been in response to researchers' needs. Another RIN report (RIN, 2010b) examined how researchers interact with journal websites and what the impact of this has been. It concluded that researchers show significant expertise when using e-journals, that they find the information they need quickly and efficiently, and that greater spending on e-journals was linked to better research outcomes. But there has been almost no debate on born-digital content and how the huge explosion of such content should be collected, organised and managed. Academic staff increasingly see librarians as managers of the purchasing process rather than as collection builders in support of research (Ithaka, 2009). Yet collection building and, more particularly, the aggregation of resources at a system level does demonstrate one of the elements we can contribute to a digital future. Dempsey (2009) reflects on this in relation to the long tail, and links it to classic librarianship:

> It is not enough for materials to be present within the system: they have to be readily accessible ('every reader his or her book', in Ranganathan's terms), potentially interested readers have to be aware of them ('every book its reader'), and the system for matching supply and demand has to be efficient ('save the time of the user').

It is time for libraries to develop agreed strategies for digital collection development. Thus far efforts have been somewhat piecemeal and have tended to focus on digital repositories. Initially seen as tools for collecting research output, there has been a growing realisation that repositories could be one of the key building blocks of future library development hosting a whole range of types of digital resources. But this has to be coupled with an understanding of a raft of what may seem obvious infrastructural elements to librarians but are not necessarily so to scientists: long-term archiving, bibliographic control, metadata, version control, authority control, audit trails, usage data, IPR management, navigation and discovery, delivery and access.

Matching user support to user needs

As research environments become more complex, it seems sensible to explore how far scientists can manage their own infrastructure and how far they need support to manage this, in exactly the same way as estates professionals, human resources professionals and health and safety professionals manage elements of research support. What seems destined to become a classic case of not managing information happened in 2009–10 at the University of East Anglia, where the science underpinning climate change was challenged because the information had not been properly managed. This need to manage information has in some libraries led to a revisiting of the concept of the subject librarian, now described as 'embedded'. There is even a neat coinage of 'feral' librarians[8] for those working in librarian positions but without library qualifications. Kesselman and Watstein (2009) judge that 'embedded librarianship is one of the prime tenets of a user-centered library'. It is only by experiencing at first hand exactly how users manage their information, their information seeking and their workflows that librarians can begin to design and offer services that truly add value and are responsive.

Student use of libraries

An Online Computer Library Center (OCLC) survey of 2006 should have given librarians pause for thought. It showed that:

- 89% of students use search engines to begin a search
- 2% use a library website
- 93% are satisfied or very satisfied with this approach to searching
- 84% are satisfied if they are librarian assisted.

This reduction in satisfaction when librarians intervene does not suggest that all the effort going into information literacy training has been productive. This may reflect traditional approaches and what has been called the 'eat spinach syndrome'. When all that a student seeks and requires is just enough information for the task in hand or a short cut to the answer, library staff still insist on showing them how to undertake the task properly. The minatory approach requires the user to do it properly or not do it at all; eat your spinach, it's good for you. This is no doubt well intentioned and worthy, but obviously it does not reflect what users want. Much more effort is needed to identify and then meet user needs, rather than holding on to the past.

If librarians wish to be real stakeholders in the teaching and learning process, this will require a fundamental rethinking and refashioning of the concept of user support. The key will be the ability to add value. Not just to manage collections of learning objects; to manage and preserve the wiki and blog spaces; to manage the content links and licensing – these are all well within existing library competences – but to provide the hotlinks and metadata which will allow the user to navigate with ease.

Work by the Centre for Information Behaviour and the Evaluation of Research (CIBER) in 2007 clearly demonstrates that users significantly overestimate their skills and their ability to manage information. Students will often give up after their initial searches (assuming that they have completed the research process), believing that if it's not instantly discoverable on the Web, it doesn't exist. Easier access to full-text articles and content online also seems to have changed students' cognitive behaviour. Rather depressingly for librarians, such easier access is allied with very short spells of time spent on reading the material. Electronic content encourages browsing, cutting and pasting – almost certainly accompanied by increased plagiarism. However, there is more than a suspicion that this is usually done through ignorance rather than malice. Research by the CIBER group is unequivocal in its findings, which are based on huge volumes of log analysis (Nicholas, 2009). The shorter an item is, the more likely it is to be read online. If it is long, users will either read the abstract or squirrel it away for a day when it might not be read (digital osmosis). Users seem to prefer abstracts much of the time, even when given the choice of full text. In short, they go online to *avoid* reading (Nicholas, 2009).

Now libraries might argue that they have always embraced a service philosophy. Perhaps the change that is needed is to recognise the requirement to offer what users need, when and where they need it, rather than to provide services that we think they should have. An excellent example of this approach is the University of Hong Kong, where a major rethink of how the library identified need and responded to users led to major changes in the way it operated and was staffed, and has transformed the concept of service (Sidorko and Yang, 2009). The review was aimed at positioning the library as a key player on campus in terms of teaching and learning support. Each organisation will produce different solutions to meet local needs, but the emphasis at the University of Hong Kong on a client-centred approach is striking.

Libraries and an online presence

Libraries were some of the earliest adopters of computing, and have a history of systems development stretching back almost 50 years. In truth, what we largely engaged in at first was the mechanisation of existing processes; nonetheless, librarians have been receptive to change. But it may be the case that they misread the Internet. Huge effort and investment was put first into Online Public Access Catalogues, and then into websites, based on the premise 'If we build it, they will come'. Librarians imagined they were building hubs which would attract users, only to discover that in reality they sat not at the centre but at the edge of users' digital worlds. Users largely bypassed these complicated facilities in favour of the ease of searching that Google provides.

It is not then clear that we have learned the lesson that, if our users don't want it, we shouldn't make it. Arguably, we need a much clearer understanding of the larger forces at work before developing specific tools. Librarians have rushed to become involved in social networking sites, but few have stood back to observe the large societal forces at work. The issue of how online collectivism, social networking and popular software designs are changing the ways in which people think and process information raises the question of what becomes of originality and imagination in a world that prizes 'metaness' and regards the mash-up as 'more important than the sources who were mashed' is largely undiscussed in the professional literature, but is producing serious thinking elsewhere (Kakutani, 2010). Librarians have engaged in almost every fad from Facebook to Second Life without perhaps considering how service philosophy should change beyond a rather hackneyed concept of being where the users are. And yet there are examples of good practice, at least in isolation. Kelly (2008) has suggested that the key definers of social networks for libraries are:

- application areas where users can easily create content
- syndication/alerting technologies which share news
- a culture of openness which makes content available for sharing and reuse
- a culture of trust which encourages the sharing of content, bookmarks and discussion
- social sharing services which share images, bookmarks and stories
- and social networking which allows everyone to implement the above.

These concepts really need to underpin any decision to use the tools described below, or else we run the risk of further littering the Web with inactive library blogs, lifeless virtual library communities and out-of-date Facebook pages. The following partial list of tools and examples shows the very mixed response from libraries.

Apps

Libraries have been quick to explore and exploit mobile technology as a development tool. There are a growing number of library apps for the iPhone. These start with simple information sources giving addresses and opening hours. Others begin to offer access to the library catalogue. OCLC's WorldCat offers access to a range of libraries and shows where the nearest copy of a work may be found. This has been further enhanced by linking to a shopping price comparison tool. Users can scan a book barcode with the RedLaser app on an iPhone and find WorldCat.org results. The app uses the WorldCat Search API[9] and WorldCat Registry APIs[10] to deliver results for libraries nearby, complete with contact information and driving directions.

With the launch of DukeMobile 1.1, Duke University Libraries (Mobile Libraries Blogspot, 2010) now offers the most comprehensive university digital image collection specifically formatted for an iPhone or iTouch device. It includes about 32,000 images of photos and other artefacts from 20 collections that range from early beer advertisements to materials on San Francisco's Haight-Ashbury scene in the 1960s and covering women's history, early American sheet music, Duke history and other topics. Although a growing number of scholarly institutions offer images and other material online, Duke University Libraries is the first to offer collections that take advantage of the iPhone's design, navigation and other features. Others will follow these examples, which are based as much on using the tools that users have as on exploiting any specific social space.

Blogs and the Twitterati

One approach popular with librarians is the use of tools that require active posting of information and thoughts. Librarians have embraced Twitter with the passion of a first schoolroom crush. Apparently no conference is complete without its Twitter feed. However, it is much more difficult to discover good examples of the use of Twitter by libraries in support of their users. It is estimated that some 300 US libraries have Twitter feeds, while in the UK only 400 librarians are active on Twitter. The use of Twitter by library services was discussed in the *Guardian* (Flood, 2009). Behind the headline describing libraries promoting specific books, author events and closing times, it becomes clear that the principal (and not unimportant!) use is by librarians tweeting to other librarians.

Blogs have been much better used by librarians. These can be informative, whether in terms of news or descriptions of services, and some excellent examples exist. A good example of what issues are exposed comes from The Blogging Libraries wiki.[11] First created in 2006, and apparently not updated since, it contains links to excellent and interesting active blogs – and also to the deceased and moribund. What is most difficult to establish is whether these blogs are popular with – or even useful to – users and how they integrate with users' work habits.

Delicious and shared bookmarks

The interest in social bookmarking is that these tools are, in effect, user-provided content. Easily the most popular of these is delicious.[12] The Mélange blog[13] provides a wonderful example of its use. It shows the value of tag clouds, succinctly describes why social bookmarking is useful, provides links to good examples and displays many responses and comments.

Facebook

The wonderfully named Feral Librarian reviews the academic library experience of Facebook.[14] There are a large number of library Facebook sites. Although these are fashionable, it is again very difficult to discover whether they are valued by users. They appear in the main to provide a new channel for standard information on facilities and opening hours and are typically a new space for providing old information.

Podcasting

Huge numbers of universities have now developed podcasting as a method for delivering lectures. As this is a relatively recent phenomenon, many fewer have established reliable mandated routes for the long-term preservation of such material. Others have chosen to make material available through iTunesU.[15] This service from Apple provides a comprehensive solution to making current lectures available. What is much less clear is how material will be archived in the very long term and how rights will be managed.

Second Life

Many libraries have 'opened' on Second Life.[16] They do seem to be valuable in offering reference services in particular, although one might easily see this as a way of exploring the use of e-books. However, there is a lingering worry that the original users have moved on and that spaces such as these are now largely occupied by the suits and the pornographers (Collins, 2010 and Somma, 2010). Whether and how libraries (and indeed their parent universities) disinvest in Second Life and move on may provide an instructive lesson in dealing with obsolescence.

Wikipedia

A great deal of intellectual snobbery surrounds whether this user-created encyclopaedia is a tool that should be encouraged or not. Whatever the presumed merits of Wikipedia[17] as compared with traditional encyclopaedias, it is much larger and much more quickly updated than they are. The huge number of hits that it receives makes it quite clear that it is a preferred starting point (at least) for researching new topics. In practice too, a study conducted by Giles and published in *Nature* (Giles, 2005) showed it as only marginally worse than the *Encyclopaedia Britannica* for the accuracy of its scientific information. The exercise revealed numerous errors in both encyclopaedias, but among 42 entries tested, the difference in accuracy was not particularly great: the average science entry in Wikipedia contained around four inaccuracies; *Britannica*, about three. Some libraries have responded imaginatively. When the Bodleian Library discovered inaccurate entries relating to some of its treasured special collections, it assigned staff not simply to correct the errors but to provide hotlinks through to relevant related material (Thomas, 2008). This imaginative approach is much more valuable than simply putting a library entry into Wikipedia, as many organisations have done.

It is clear that social networking, popularly lumped together as Web 2.0, has had a profound effect on the ways in which users communicate and on how they seek information for whatever task is in hand. The danger for libraries is that, as they move to occupy these spaces, they find that users have moved on to the next space. What libraries must really do is try to develop a more theoretical or philosophical understanding of their role in supporting users in such environments, irrespective of the particular product at hand. For the moment, the approach seems to be to treat these as new spaces for providing traditional information rather than as new ways of communicating.

Aggregation of content

Libraries have always acquired content that is distinguished because of the collections that are formed, rather than necessarily by the value of individual items. The Internet has allowed the possibility of aggregating content from numbers of collections and sources to provide meta collections. Libraries can then add value through the provision of federated searching, metadata tagging and linking to tools such as Google Maps which can enrich the underlying sources. A large number of projects have dealt with aggregation, usually of content, but also of skills, in ways which attempt to combine resources to meet the needs of users. Each is appropriate in its own context, although many motivations are displayed. The key consideration in each is the way in which value has been added and to what extent. The following are good examples of quite different approaches.

The Europeana Project[18] is fairly overtly a political project and a response to the dominance of Google. Its key goal is to be multilingual. It brings together over six million cultural objects, appears to use size as its defining goal and is organised by the museum, archive and library community.

Project Nines (Networked Infrastructure for Nineteenth-Century Electronic Scholarship)[19] involves the (largely American) scholarly community, which has peer reviewed over 600,000 objects brought together from 118 sites for nineteenth-century scholarship and aims to:

- serve as a peer-reviewing body for digital work in the long 19th century (1770–1920), British and American
- support scholars' priorities and best practices in the creation of digital research materials
- develop software tools for new and traditional forms of research and critical analysis.

It has, arguably, strong content, but is weaker on information management skills.

Project Bamboo[20] focuses on tools rather than content, and involves both the support and academic communities. It aims to be a multi-institutional, interdisciplinary, and inter-organisational effort that brings together researchers in arts and humanities, computer scientists, information scientists, librarians and campus information technologists to tackle the question: 'How can we advance arts and humanities research through the development of shared technology services?' The project is mapping out the scholarly practices and common technology challenges across and among disciplines to discover where a coordinated, cross-disciplinary development effort can best foster academic innovation.

The University of Texas has chosen a more traditional approach, combined with a novel attitude to born-digital material, as a way of meeting institutional academic goals. It is a rare example of collection building combined with web tools ranging from Google Maps to video clips of interviews (Heath, 2009). It has a clear set of priorities:

- bulk harvesting of human rights sites from the World Wide Web
- custom harvesting of human rights themes from the Internet
- preservation and disclosure of born-digital documentation.

It applies archival principles ranging from selection to dark archiving of material relevant to outstanding trials, e.g. in Rwanda, and it relates the collection quite explicitly to the mission of the institution.

Libraries as place

Although there is a strong and growing literature on digital and hybrid libraries, librarians remain curiously (perhaps sentimentally?) fond of the concept of library as place. It can be a place to promote enduring values (Weise, 2004); it is 'the centerpiece for establishing the intellectual community and scholarly enterprise' (Freeman, 2005); and a place to see and be seen while working privately (Gayton, 2008). The positioning of the physical library in the student environment is clearly articulated, although researchers and academics have long since abandoned the library as a place of first resort, in favour of the Internet. Yet very little thought has been given to the cost of that physical environment. Possession of a library is an unquestioned and therefore uncosted part of the infrastructure of being a university. Very little thought has been given to the cost of running libraries – beyond staffing budgets. But this is beginning to surface as an issue, if only in the light of green agendas, which have become fashionable as institutional budgets have come under pressure. In most organisations it is the practice to top-slice utility bill costs from the corporate budget before sub-allocating to departments. Libraries are unusual in that they tend to occupy a whole building, and so attributing utility costs to them is quite straightforward, if very unusual (Law, 2009). The results are surprisingly large and should lead us to consider exactly why we spend so much on preserving materials, particularly those materials commonly held elsewhere.

Ironically, universities will tend to be places where there is a broad spectrum of ecological sophistication and where academic departments work on sustainable design and operations. Yet practices as simple as materials recycling and attempts to move to carbon-neutral footprints remain far removed from library orthodoxy. Some work is beginning on this area and it is to be expected that the green movement in libraries will grow as budgets decline (Mulford and Himmel, 2009; Green Library, 2010).

Virtual libraries

While libraries as place remain close to the heart of most information professionals, at least some have followed a quite different route, moving towards a virtual library. One of the earliest adopters of this was the University of Phoenix, which has had an online campus since 1989 (Jackson, 2010) and an online library since the mid 1990s. With some 37,000 online journals, almost 30,000 e-books, 114 databases and 20 million articles, it can rival any traditional library in terms of its content. Other libraries have since embraced this route in whole or in part, but what Phoenix has perhaps principally done is to show both that libraries without place are viable – and also that they do need professional management and staffing.

Conclusion

As the many examples used in this chapter show, librarians have the capacity and the curiosity to embrace and employ the latest digital tools and services. Rethinking the concept of service is also well within the competence of librarians. The science fiction writer William Gibson famously declared that the future is already here, it's just not evenly distributed.[21] Each of the applications and tools described in this chapter has been adopted, embraced and enthusiastically championed by many librarians. What is less clear is that this has been done as part of an overarching philosophical redefinition of what libraries should be, whom they should serve and how, rather than as a well-intentioned and enthusiastic attempt to modernise an existing product. The fear must be that most libraries are trying desperately to cling to outmoded notions of what customers really want and are being ever more inventive and efficient in so doing; for there is another, but much less palatable, future for libraries. The story is often told of the end of the typewriter. In 2000, the president of Smith-Corona, at the closing of the company's very last plant, gathered together the remaining employees and told them that on that day the company had the highest-quality product with the lowest defect rate, greatest customer satisfaction levels and lowest return rates it had ever produced. And then he told them that they had 'perfected the irrelevant' (Roner, 2009). Libraries too run that risk. There is a wealth of imagination, innovation and inquisitiveness within the library profession. The real challenge is whether the innovators and early adopters can inspire their colleagues to embrace these developments as central to the future of the profession and not have them seem the ephemeral and transient gewgaws of an eccentric fringe.

Notes

1. http://pope2you.net/.
2. http://www.judiciary.gov.uk/about-the-judiciary/judges-magistrates-and-tribunal-judges/biographies/biography-lcj.
3. http://maps.google.co.uk/.
4. http://www.tenwordwiki.com/.
5. http://dictionary.cambridge.org/dictionary/british/haiku.
6. http://theridiculant.metro.co.uk/2010/02/ten-word-wiki-for-when-wikipedia-is-just-too-long.html.
7. http://chrisbourg.wordpress.com/2009/03/19/shirkys-newspaper-ideas-applied-to-libraries/.
8. http://chrisbourg.wordpress.com/.
9. http://www.oclc.org/worldcatapi/default.htm.
10. http://www.worldcat.org/devnet/wiki/Services.
11. http://www.blogwithoutalibrary.net/links/index.php?title=Welcome_to_the_Blogging_Libraries_Wiki.
12. http://delicious.com/.

13. http://angelacw.wordpress.com/2007/06/04/delicious-libraries/.
14. http://chrisbourg.wordpress.com/2008/10/16/our-library-facebook-page/.
15. http://www.apple.com/education/itunes-u/what-is.html.
16. http://secondlife.com/.
17. http://www.wikipedia.org/.
18. http://europeana.eu/portal/.
19. http://www.nines.org/.
20. http://projectbamboo.org/.
21. http://www.guardian.co.uk/books/2007/aug/12/sciencefictionfantasyand horror.features.

References

CIBER (Centre for Information Behaviour and the Evaluation of Research). (2007) *Information Behaviour of the Researcher of the Future*. London: CIBER. Online at http://www.jisc.ac.uk/media/ documents/programmes/reppres/ggworkpackageii.pdf.

Collins, B. (2010) 'Whatever happened to Second Life?' PCPro. Online at http://www.pcpro.co.uk/features/354457/whatever-happened-to-second-life/print.

Dempsey, L. (2009) *Libraries and the long tail: intro*. Online at http://orweblog.oclc.org/archives/002020.html.

Flood, A. (2009) 'Libraries tap into Twitter'. *Guardian*, 24 June. Online at http://www.guardian.co.uk/books/2009/jun/24/libraries-twitter.

Freeman, G.T. (2005) *The Library as Place: changes in learning patterns, collections, technology, and use*. CLIR Report No. 129. Online at http://www.clir.org/pubs/reports/pub129/freeman.html.

Gayton, J.T. (2008) 'Academic libraries: "social" or "communal?" The nature and future of academic libraries.' *Journal of Academic Librarianship*, 34 (1), 60–6.

Gibb, F. (2009) 'Lord Judge calls for jury system that caters for computer generation'. *The Times*, 21 October. Online at http://business. timesonline.co.uk/tol/business/law/article6882947.ece#cid=OTC-RSS&attr=989864.

Giles, J. (2005) 'Internet encyclopaedias go head to head'. *Nature*, 438, 900–1. Online at http://www.nature.com/nature/journal/v438/n7070/ full/438900a.html.

The Green Library (2010) http://thegreenlibraryblog.blogspot.com/.

Heath, F. (2009) *Human Rights: the challenge of documentation in the digital age*. Online at http://digital.casalini.it/retreat/2009_docs/ heath.pdf.

Ithaka (2009) *Faculty Survey 2009*. Online at http://www.ithaka.org/ithaka-s-r/research/faculty-surveys-2000-2009/faculty-survey-2009/?searchterm=faculty%20survey%202009.

Jackson, A. (2010) *The University of Phoenix Library and eLearning Materials Provide Vast Resources Anytime, Anywhere for Working Learners*. Online at http://www.phoenix.edu/uopx-knowledge-network/articles/case-studies/uopx-library-elearning-resources-anytime-for-working-learners.html.

Kakutani, M. (2010) 'Texts without context'. *New York Times*, Books section, 21 March. Online at http://www.nytimes.com/2010/03/21/books/21mash.html?scp=1&sq=kakutani&st=cse.

Kelly, B. (2008) 'Web 2.0 and social networks for museums, libraries and archives: an introduction'. Online at http://www.authorstream.com/Presentation/briankelly-71604-web-2-0-social-networks-museums-libraries-ukoln-mlaeastengland20080701-web20-education-ppt-powerpoint/.

Kesselman, M.A. and Watstein, S.B. (2009) 'Creating opportunities: embedded librarians'. *Journal of Library Administration*, 49 (4), 383–400.

Law, D. (2006) 'Back to basics: a-literacy, the Boolean gene, convergence and the long tail'. *Electronic Library*, 24 (6), 729–31.

Law, D. (2009) 'An awfully big adventure: Strathclyde's digital library plan'. *Ariadne* (58) Online at http://www.ariadne.ac.uk/issue58/law/.

Mobile Libraries Blogspot (2010) 'Library Digital Collections? There's an app for that'. Online at http://mobile-libraries.blogspot.com/2009/06/library-digital-collections-theres-app.html.

Mulford, S. and Himmel, N. (2009) *How Green is My Library?* Santa Barbara, CA: Libraries Unlimited.

Nicholas, D. (2009) 'What is beyond books and journals? Pointers from CIBER's Virtual Scholar programme'. *Beyond Books and Journals: 3rd Bloomsbury Conference on e-publishing and e-publications*, 25–26 June. Online at www.ucl.ac.uk/infostudies/e-publishing/e-publishing2009/2a-nicholas.ppt.

OCLC (Online Computer Library Center). (2006) *College Students' Perceptions of Libraries and Information Resources: a report to the OCLC membership*. Dublin, OH: OCLC.

RIN (Research Information Network). (2010a) *Ensuring a Bright Future for Libraries*. Online at http://www.rin.ac.uk/our-work/using-and-accessing-information-resources/ensuring-bright-future-research-libraries.

RIN. (2010b) *E-journals: their use, value and impact.* Online at http://www.rin.ac.uk/our-work/communicating-and-disseminating-research/e-journals-their-use-value-and-impact.

Roner, L. (2009) 'The 10 Most Common (and Dangerous) Forecasting Mistakes'. *Eyeforpharma*, 5 March. Online at http://social. eyeforpharma.com/story/10-most-common-and-dangerous-forecasting-mistakes.

Schwartz, J. (2009) 'As jurors turn to Web, mistrials are popping up.' *New York Times*, 17 March. Online at http://www.nytimes.com/2009/03/18/us/18juries.html?_r=2.

Shirky, C. (2009) *Newspapers and Thinking the Unthinkable.* Online at http://www.shirky.com/weblog/2009/03/newspapers-and-thinking-the-unthinkable/.

Sidorko, P. and Yang, T. (2009) 'Refocusing for the future: meeting user expectations in a digital age'. *Library Management*, 30 (1/2), 6–24.

Somma, R. (2010) 'The decline and fall of Second Life'. *Ideonexus.* Online at http://ideonexus.com/?s=the+decline+and+fall+of+second+life.

Thomas, S. (2008) 'I've looked at life from both sides now'. Paper presented at the 10th Fiesole Collection Development Retreat, Fiesole, 27–29 March. Online at http://digital.casalini.it/retreat/retreat_2008.html.

Weise, F. (2004) 'Being there: the library as place'. *Journal of the Medical Library Association*, 92 (1), 6–13.

24

Towards Library 2.0: building the library of the future

Sarah Porter

Introduction

Higher education has seen a huge increase in student numbers over the last 20 years, to the point that some libraries have had to change substantially in the way that they operate. Libraries face increased competition and are no longer seen as the single source of research and learning resources. Social and technical trends have changed the global context for information and resources as users create, own and manage their own content and systems. Librarians and information professionals need to understand some of the major strategic challenges that their institutions are facing and to think creatively about how they can best plan to support the core learning, teaching and research needs of their users. This analysis and planning should be carried out across the whole institution in order to cross the traditional boundaries and take an institution-wide approach. National shared services and the potential of cloud computing[1] can offer opportunities, but must be considered carefully.

The context for change

We are at a point in time where people need to think differently about academic libraries. Libraries are faced with the challenges of reduced resources, and ever-growing expectations from end-users, in a world where the ubiquitous search engines have created an impression that all content is available at the click of a mouse, instantly and for free. Global and national changes in political and financial circumstances mean that this challenge is made more urgent; some libraries are now fighting for their survival. At the same time, there have been dramatic changes to the provision of information, which means that we are now in an environment that could not have been predicted some years ago. Librarians face stark and difficult choices about the future direction in which they should go. There are urgent decisions to be made.

Technology provides huge opportunities for libraries to provide their services in new and innovative ways. At a time when students are often also employees, and lifelong learning is a significant leisure pursuit for many after retirement, technology can enable the library to provide its services to users at a time and in a place that suits the user and their lifestyle. Services and resources no longer have to be offered by the library itself, and the use of digital versions of resources in the place of hard copy offers up exciting opportunities for outsourcing of services to other providers. Libraries have started along this road already through their use of remotely hosted publisher-owned resources as part of the large-scale move to subscribe to electronic journals (e-journals). There is potential for much more here, and each library will need to choose where it wishes to position itself within the spectrum of options that are available. However, this opportunity also presents a threat. Libraries are being challenged to redefine their role and purpose within the changed world of distributed, uncoordinated information provision. Libraries are no longer the only doorway to information; nor are librarians the gatekeepers of a walled garden.

A changing education and research landscape

Higher education (HE) in the UK has seen dramatic changes since the early 1990s. These changes have had a marked impact on many universities, such that some are barely recognisable as their pre-millennium selves. Two major government policy initiatives have led to this change. In 1992, through the 1992 Higher and Further Education Act, the most recent wave of 'new' (or post-1992) universities was created (Office of Public Sector Information, 1992). This single change doubled the size of the university sector more or less overnight. Not only did it increase the size of the sector, it also meant that the sector was far more diverse, with traditional, well-resourced institutions with long academic records and significant research income now sitting alongside new organisations that sometimes suffered poor funding and had limited resources. The other dramatic change has been the increase in numbers of undergraduate university places, led by the then UK government target of 50% participation in HE by 18- to 25-year-olds.[2] This target led to the universities' implementing policies on widening participation, so that participation in HE in England increased gradually to reach 43% of 17- to 30-year-olds by 2008. Student numbers had increased to over 2.3 million by 2008 (HESA, 2009). These trends have meant that many libraries have had to cope with far higher student numbers, but without proportionate increases in funding. Universities have diversified their strategies in order to widen participation, engage with employers, retain students and pursue regional alliances.

Looking to the future, in addition to possible, unknown changes to government policy, there are other changes that HE is likely to have to face over the two decades to 2030. Changes in demographics are predicted by organisations such as the Higher Education Policy Institution (HEPI) to pose a big challenge to the sector during the coming years up to 2025 as the size of the population that traditionally makes up the student community, those aged 18–25, declines. This demographic challenge is a particular concern for some regions of the UK where the population faces particularly significant drops in this age range. Figures published recently by HEPI suggest that the north-east and north-west of England, Yorkshire and the Humber and the West Midlands will face particular declines (HEPI, 2008). This may lead to increased competition between institutions for student numbers and may encourage institutions to diversify, trying to attract students by offering courses online, by specialising or by merging with other institutions in the region (Universities UK, 2008).

Collaboration between organisations has also increased. It is now more common for universities to work together where they share strategic goals and to coordinate resources. In some cases, this leads to mergers and the rise of regional universities such as Leeds Metropolitan University, which delivers many of its programmes through a network of about 20 colleges in the north of England and in Northern Ireland.[3] In other cases, the collaboration is national rather than regional, for example that between the Russell Group institutions.[4] Higher education is spreading out into other sectors, with further education colleges now offering a substantial level of HE provision, and a growth of relationships between universities and commercial companies, such as Kaplan, which offers franchised undergraduate degree courses that are accredited by UK universities such as the University of Essex.[5] This blurring of the boundaries around the traditional university is characterised as the 'edgeless university' (DEMOS, 2009).

Table 24.1 summarises four of the major current strategic goals for universities and the challenges that these can provide to the university library.

Changes in university libraries

In response to these system-wide trends, the period since the mid 1990s has seen immense and revolutionary change in university libraries. The Electronic Libraries Programme was funded by the Joint Information Systems Committee (JISC) and began in 1994 through three phases of funding and development, ending in 2001. The programme was designed to help UK university libraries to transition from the traditional, print-

Table 24.1 Summary of major strategic goals for universities

Strategic goal for university	Current challenges for libraries
Maintain strong research focus	Specialist collections to acquire and maintain Research outputs to manage and promote
Attract most able students and postgraduates	Specialist, high-end support Specialist resources High-end technology and storage space Specialised study areas for postgraduate and group work
Recruit and retain large numbers of students	High quantity and easy availability of most popular resources Fast, efficient services that can cope with heavy demand Flexible opening hours Zoned working spaces to cope with large numbers and wide range of students Social space, important for part-time and mature students
Deliver courses through partnership with business and other organisations	Professional, high-quality working spaces Flexible licensing arrangements – on- and off-site access Expertise in key subject areas that are most relevant to partner organisations

based environment to a new environment that embraced technology. It focused funding in 12 areas:

- electronic document delivery
- electronic storage of books and journals (digitisation)
- electronic journals
- on-demand publishing and the electronic book
- awareness and training
- navigational tools
- pre-prints and grey literature
- electronic short loans
- images
- hybrid libraries
- large-scale resource discovery
- digital preservation.

Lorcan Dempsey (2006) has suggested that we consider the programme as covering two main areas – 'discovery to delivery' and 'repository and content management'. This list provides a useful reflection of the transition the libraries have made since the mid 1990s and allows us to draw some conclusions about how much the library has already adapted to the new environment and how much further there is to go (Duke and Jordan, 2006).

The first observation is that the hybrid library (see, e.g., Sykes, 2009) is now the reality for all and no longer a topic for exploration. Many of the repository and content-management issues are solved – electronic storage of books and journals, e-journals, pre-prints and grey literature and electronic short loans would now generally be considered to be problems that have been solved, notwithstanding that there are still challenges in how they are funded and sustained. JISC has made further investments in the creation of institutional repositories and, while the repositories are not yet being used to a satisfactory degree either to store resources or as a source of materials, the infrastructure is now mostly in place. On-demand publishing and e-books are still under exploration but are well-understood problems where demand is not yet sufficient to drive full-scale solutions in most institutions. However, issues of resource discovery at an institutional level still remain unsatisfactory. The explosive growth of the 'giant' search engines has perhaps exaggerated the need for libraries to think creatively about how to tell their users where resources can be located, and to remind users that the library is their main access point to authoritative sources of information.

So, as we move into the increasingly fragmented and demanding information world, what are the main challenges for libraries, and how should they prioritise their investment in the coming years? Leaders in universities are asking themselves hard questions about their future priorities. Universities are becoming more businesslike in their approach to the provision of HE and asking questions that challenge traditional assumptions about how a university is organised and how it operates from day to day. Libraries need to play their part in responding to the change that has started and that is set to continue for some years. It is essential to understand technical and social trends in order to respond successfully.

Current technical and social trends

Technical and social trends are converging as technology becomes ever more firmly embedded into people's lives. There is a constant interaction and ongoing, rapid development between habits of use influencing new technology, and vice versa. Technology is no longer controlled by a single, centralised owner but is instead owned by everyone; everyone contributes to content and services, as well as owning tools (JISC, 2009a). User expectations have changed hugely, reflecting the way that users interact with technology in the course of their social and business activities. As the JISC/SCONUL (Society of College, National and University Libraries) Library Management System study of 2008 states: 'Today's library users expect speed and immediacy of information discovery, one-stop access to aggregated services, user-generated open content, and personalised, workflow-related delivery to the desktop' (SCONUL, 2008). Pervasive technology and fast networks mean that the concept of sharing a service can be stretched to encompass a wide range of options. Current trends such as cloud computing and virtualisation are building upon these technical capabilities and taking us 'back to the future', to a world of outsourced storage and client-server architectures. The advantages of using remote storage and applications that are owned and maintained by someone else are fairly obvious – storage can be made available 'on demand' rather than the institution having to plan to purchase additional capacity, to house and maintain it; and the institution can, in theory, reduce its need for applications expertise in-house by using software that is delivered by a third party in 'the Cloud' (Yanosky, 2008).

These trends in user behaviour and technology have now converged very rapidly to bring us to a place where there are exciting examples of collaboration taking place around the world using networked technologies of all kinds – hand-held, personal devices of all shapes and sizes being used frequently to share user-created content such as photographs through websites like Flickr,[6] as well as community participation in collection-development or research projects. For libraries, this new environment provides both an opportunity and a threat. As Lorcan Dempsey said in 2006, 'we tend to focus on the impact of technology on libraries, however the real long-term issue is how technology will influence how library users behave and what they expect' (Dempsey, 2006). Coupled with changes in the strategies of our institutions and the unpredictable change in the external environment, is a need for libraries to be flexible and to respond to opportunities as well as to threats.

Planning for Library 2.0

So how can the library help to support the changes that are needed in HE in order to make it more effective and efficient? How can the library help to build the future? The answer to this question will be different for each institution, but the general principles remain the same. Senior library staff need to engage with the strategic planning of the institution in order to understand where the institution is trying to go in the future, and so as to ensure that the library is supporting this strategy as effectively as possible. In order to adapt to the different pressures and opportunities in the funding environment, universities are increasingly giving different levels of importance and priority to the traditional agendas of education, research and outreach. All university services, including libraries, have to respond to these changes, and in some cases have to reprioritise their services in order to meet the institutional strategy. As institutional priorities change, we see that libraries are changing to support these priorities.

A question that regularly surfaces in discussions on the future of the library is the issue of the library management system (LMS). Many information professionals are dissatisfied with the current products and wish to think about future options. There is a general sense that the LMS is not providing all that it might do in order to improve efficiency, support processes better and improve the user experience. The JISC and SCONUL conducted a research study in 2008 to ask questions about how information professionals saw the future of the LMS. The conclusion of the study was that LMS are only part of the picture and, in fact, may soon be retreating into the background when put into a context of multiple sources of data, global search engines and user-owned devices. Libraries need to work together in order to rethink what they need in terms of systems and processes:

> There is consensus that the time is right for intensified dialogue about the nature and function of the modern HE library, its systems and processes. It is especially timely to explore consortia and other partnership arrangements to increase critical mass and network effect, whilst potentially reducing system and service costs. (SCONUL, 2008)

In the fast-changing world in which we now find ourselves, where information flows freely from multiple sources to multiple users, it is perhaps short sighted to place too much emphasis on reviewing and replacing the LMS. Instead, the library needs to consider how all of the information systems of the institution can support the ways in which users want and need to do their learning, teaching and research. Table 24.2 sets out some of the new challenges for libraries in the face of the system-wide change that we have discussed above, reflecting the prevailing changes in user requirements. For each of the key institutional strategic areas – research focus, student recruitment and retention, employer engagement – there are implications for current and future library services. The table summarises some of these trends, the challenges that they present and their implications for library services.

In order to plan for future requirements, libraries will need to assess whether these new developments should be included in its strategy. The questions below provide examples of some of the key questions that will need to be addressed when planning the future of the library.

Encouraging use of library resources

Do we provide a single information source to provide simple access to all resources: licensed, open access and in-house? Have we tested this solution with end-users to ensure that it meets their requirements? Is it being promoted by teaching and student support staff? Do research staff and graduate students know about it and does it meet their needs?

Table 24.2   Current trends and implications for library service provision

Strategic area	Trends and new challenges	Implication for library service provision
Strong research focus	Maintaining a balance of high-quality resources from a range of subject areas Poor user satisfaction with library resources, lack of awareness of what is available Management of university's research publications through a repository or set of repositories New research tools that support the researcher's work from anywhere on or off campus and are used by research groups that cross institutional boundaries	Need to consult with user groups regularly and explain the library's acquisitions strategy Need to provide a single information source to provide simple access to all required resources: licensed, open access and in-house Requirement for accessible, flexible repository infrastructure with the capability to interface with national and international repositories is required[7] Need to integrate library systems with tools such as virtual research environments (VREs) that are being adopted either by research departments or centrally. Requires coordination with other departments in order to meet expectations
Supporting most able students and postgraduates	Provision of dedicated work and collaborative spaces for postgraduates only – real and virtual High-specification computers for personal research Research tools and support for the creation of research publications	Library systems need to integrate with tools such as VREs[8] that are being adopted, either by research departments or centrally. Need for coordination with other departments in order to meet expectations. Departments may need guidance on how to manage information resources within the VRE or how to manage resources outside the VRE (e.g. in repositories)
Recruiting and retaining large numbers of students	Fast, easy access to popular, heavy-usage resources Online learning platforms that can be accessed remotely and that provide a single point of entry to all resources Need to access resources using mobile devices	Need to interface with student record systems, and possibly other systems such as financial data Library platforms may need to be upgraded or replaced in order to interface with new systems and be able to deliver content in formats suitable for the devices that students wish to use
Delivering courses through partnership with business and other organisations	Licensing arrangements that allow other users to access library resources Support for learners through a personalised learning system that supports their learning process (e.g. an e-portfolio system)	A genuinely personalised learning system needs to interface with a number of other existing institutional systems and may require the acquisition or licensing of new systems. The library will need to work with other departments in the institution to establish the ownership of and responsibility for personalised learning support systems. Requirement to conduct user needs to alter or replace systems so that they can meet needs

Publishing and managing the institution's research outputs

Do we have in place adequate repository infrastructure, plus the capability to interface with national and international repositories? Can our repository content be found by external search engines? Do we have a strategy for managing research data?

Supporting the university's research strategy

Does the library's strategy support the university's research strategy? Are we helping to raise the profile of researchers by highlighting world-class research? Are we aware of whether researchers are using new research tools? If so, do they interface with the library systems and repositories?

Supporting learning and teaching

Do we know what learning platforms are currently being used? Do we know which are being planned for the future? Can our library and resource systems interface fully with learning platforms? Are we able to support personalised learning systems? Can we support on- and off-campus learners and non-traditional learners?

Working across university services and functions

For a number of years now, some universities have redefined their internal structures to include new 'converged' models for the provision of key, user-facing services. These services are arranged in a variety of typical groupings. These include:

- bringing together administrative and IT services
- bringing together library and IT services
- bringing together student services and the library; or bringing together all student-facing services into one large department that may include IT, libraries, estates, parking.

I do not intend here to explore the pros and cons of the various models, but rather to note two important factors. Firstly, that changes to the university 'business' mean that there may be impetus to change the way that the university provides its service, in order to be more efficient and more coherent to the end-user. This can lead to some quite radical changes to structure and governance. Secondly, the traditional boundaries between the spheres of operation of some of the key university services are less relevant and, increasingly, cannot be maintained in the new world of pervasive technology. Students depend on technology for increasingly large elements of their social and educational activities; it is neither viable nor efficient to maintain separate access systems and data depending on whether they are paying their library fines, contributing to an online course discussion, planning a work placement or working on a class research project.

Some examples of crucial systems that require working across traditional departmental boundaries are provided in Table 24.3.

There are an increasing number of key, corporate systems that are not owned clearly by a single department. Institutions need to take a holistic

Table 24.3   Examples of institutional systems that require cross-departmental collaboration

System requiring cross-departmental collaboration	Reason why
Access and identity management systems	Students and academics wish to have a single identity for using all university systems, rather than to to maintain separate information for use of library systems
Learning management systems or VLEs	Digital library resources should be made available to students through their course web pages Students wish to search library resources (or be automatically directed towards them) from their learning system or portal, rather than having to use separate systems
Institutional repositories for research outputs and data	Libraries have the knowledge and experience to build good information and resource management systems, but they will not always be considered as the best place to store research outputs, so this needs to be achieved through partnership
Customer relationship management (CRM)	Libraries need both to use information about 'customers' and to provide information about their users for the CRM

approach to analysing their systems in order to identify possible problem areas. Libraries need to be at the heart of this planning process in order to support institutional change and make best use of available resources.

An institution-wide approach to planning systems

For some time, institutions have been encouraged to look at developing whole-institution strategies for planning and implementing their IT systems. Programmes such as the Information Strategies Initiative[9] ran from the mid to late 1990s in order to help universities to understand the current state of their information systems and processes and to take a more strategic approach to planning their future development, based on information needs. Many of the lessons that emerged from that initiative are still relevant today and are worthy of review and analysis.

A more recent trend has been to use enterprise architecture (EA) approaches to analyse and plan systems and processes. If used properly, EA will allow the institution to understand its current systems and processes and to plan how to use them more effectively and strategically. This can allow the institution to make an informed decision about the viability of outsourcing all or part of its library and IT systems. An enterprise approach to systems will also allow better use of the information held within those systems. For example, drawing together all sources of information about an individual student into a single 'dashboard' so that the course tutor can understand more about that individual's study habits, and so provide more timely support. Or a single research management system that allows any staff member to see which current research projects are running, which grant proposals have been submitted, digital versions of research publications (in draft or final form), each research-active member of staff's profile, and perhaps even access to research data. Or a single, integrated content management interface that allows a user to access from one place all the digital resources that the institution holds. Keeping an up-to-date map of all systems puts the institution into a better position when it needs to respond to changes, such as budget reductions, or when it wishes to replace a system. An accurate, up-to-date map of enterprise systems will also allow an institution to identify those systems that might be appropriate for outsourcing, for provision through a shared service or for replacement. To analyse all institutional systems and processes is a big undertaking and needs full institutional support in order to be successful. The JISC publication *Doing an Enterprise Architecture* (JISC, 2009b) gives a good overview of the concepts of EA, explains why it is important to future planning for universities, and gives three examples of institutions that have piloted this approach.[10] EA will work only if it is led by the organisational strategy and fully supported by senior staff in the institution.

Other trends: new models for delivery of services

Each library needs to drive forward its own strategy for responding to the changes afforded and challenges posed by the digital environment, including the choice of where it makes sense to share infrastructure, services and even people. At the same time, we know that there is huge potential in coordinating activity between libraries. The UK library sector has a strong track record in taking this approach, but we can do much more – and now is the time to put this into place. This ethos and long experience is aligned with government agendas to look at increasing efficiency within any area of the public sector by encouraging the sharing of services between organisations. The intention is to reduce unnecessary duplication of functions, to improve efficiency and, of course, to reduce costs. There are a variety of ways to provide and operate a shared service: it may be collaborative effort between two institutions that are located in the same city, for example; it may be a service offered by one institution to others over the network; or it may be a commercial service that is bought in by the institution. When planning for the future, all libraries need to consider which services they need to retain in-house, which they might buy in from commercial providers or from other institutions, or whether they might collaborate with others to develop a new system.

Shared services

The concept of shared services is not new and is, in fact, a model that has been widely used by libraries for a number of years. The inter-library loans system is one example of a successful shared service that started because of recognition by library professionals that they had more to gain by collaborating to share limited print resources, and so reduce the amount of resources that each library had to hold, than by competition. Here too, libraries have been ahead of the curve: the revolution from print to digital journals happened in the 1990s, so libraries are comfortable with the model of purchasing critical content that is hosted outside the institution – indeed, outside the country in some cases. Using IT to underpin a shared service means that many of the traditional problems with sharing print resources are removed. We no longer have a single copy of a resource, nor do we have to wait for it to be delivered to us. Resources can be duplicated, and held in many locations at the same time.

Shared services may be delivered through a variety of models. They may be delivered on a geographic basis, where institutions that are located close to each other and that have a reason to collaborate may decide to share a service. Technology makes other options also possible, such that institutions that already work in partnership may decide to share a service. Another model is for an institution with a particular area of expertise or resource already in place, such as high-performance computing or a large data centre, to provide a service to others. The number of shared services in the UK is at present limited, though there is potential to develop more and the Higher Education Funding Councils have invested in studies to explore the options here, including the possibility of sharing LMS and research data systems. A useful briefing on shared services is available from the JISCInfoNet website (JISCInfoNet, 2010).

Outsourcing and remote hosting of systems or content (using the 'cloud')

Another current trend which is perhaps of more immediate interest is the option of outsourcing systems and applications and remote hosting. A common term to describe this trend is 'cloud computing'. With cloud computing, the institution has the option to outsource some or all of its systems or applications to a third party. Cloud services range from the provision of storage space, with no associated applications or processing, to hosting software remotely. In the library world, the range might be from outsourcing a server farm to using a remote installation of an LMS instead of running the LMS locally. This trend has been picked up by suppliers of library systems. Many are discussing the option of providing their systems as a hosted service to libraries, either by hosting a single instance of the software for an institution on a remote server or by providing cloud services. Libraries have a long history of using remotely hosted content as a core part of the provision that they make to end-users – for example, online journals hosted by publishers. However, there are different challenges in hosting the LMS in this way, in particular because the LMS may be integrated with local processes, such as with the virtual learning environment, and this integration will be more difficult to accomplish if a remotely hosted system is used.

Many university IT departments are already using some cloud services by outsourcing student e-mail to remote systems such as Googlemail. This is a business decision based upon balancing the ever-increasing and insatiable demand for e-mail storage space against the relatively low risk of outsourcing a non-critical system. It is interesting to note, though, that the same institutions are not all choosing to host the staff e-mail remotely, as here the risk of loss of service or infringement of data protection rights is at present considered to be too high.

What does this mean for libraries?

At a time of economic challenge, the concept of sharing services or outsourcing services rather than duplicating functions within every library becomes a serious option. In the UK, national programmes have been set up to explore which of these functions might best be delivered through shared services. At present, the main shared services that are available are content hosts which provide content that is delivered at a national level. This includes national services that are currently provided to all universities by the JISC, such as the two national data centres, EDINA and MIMAS, as well as content provided by publishers and others. Exploratory work is under way at present to identify the potential for other shared services, including shared LMS, a national research data management system and shared data centres.

The changing role of the librarian

There is an irony in the fact that technology now allows valued resources such as quality-assured journals to be accessed from multiple points of use all over the globe and users are often unaware of the precise set of connections and permissions that allow them to access the right resource at the right time – and are also not aware of the role that the library may have played in facilitating their access. Perhaps librarians and information professionals should accept this change in emphasis, and retreat into the background, but this approach is increasingly risky in an environment where any centralised spending of resources is scrutinised, and is compared with investment in research and other facilities. 'There are challenges for libraries because you can see some institutions thinking at some stage – can we do without libraries altogether. Is it just to buy licences so users can access work online?' (DEMOS, 2009).

Librarians have essential skills and experience that are needed to guide their users through the information sphere. Their traditional skills are still needed – and are still being used – but they need to reposition themselves within a changed world. However, there are increasingly broad ranges of user requirements that either the library needs to try to satisfy, or about which it needs to make choices regarding which of the users are to be given preference. Libraries now have to work in different ways, and this is likely to be even more so in the future. Depending on the strategic decisions that are taken by the managers of libraries, librarians may now find themselves having to take on completely new roles and responsibilities. A librarian may now need to:

- be an expert negotiator
- have deep and up-to-date knowledge of licensing and copyright
- know how to integrate disparate information, learning and research systems
- know how to outsource some of their core library systems without losing control of their data or infringing data protection legislation
- have project management skills that will allow them to deliver collaborative projects across multiple institutions and even across national boundaries
- develop expertise in ergonomics and workspace design.

These changes to the role of the librarian require a thorough analysis of the future workforce requirements to go hand-in-hand with the overall strategy for the department, and which may identify a need for investment in re-skilling the workforce. Library leaders need to commit resources to developing multi-skilled, flexible 21st-century information professionals.

Conclusion

HE in the UK has undergone substantial and remarkable expansion since the passing of the Higher Education Act in 1992. This change has coincided with the global trend towards working, playing, researching and learning in a networked environment where technology is used in a highly mobile, personalised environment. Content is now sourced from multiple providers and the concept of the 'walled garden' of knowledge has been overtaken by the trend for open publishing of varied types and quality of content on the Internet. Increasing amounts of research and teaching are conducted using technology, and so we are seeing a 'data deluge' of content.

Libraries have responded to these challenges in various ways, but in the main by focusing on institutional strategies and supporting the main focus of the institution, whether that is to support large numbers of undergraduates, to engage with employers and private providers or to maintain a lead in research. Technology provides ways to help the institution to meet these challenges, but libraries need to make choices about where to prioritise investment in order to do so.

Technology takes no account of boundaries, and so the academic library can no longer operate in a silo within the institution. Increasing numbers of institutional systems need to be planned and owned across traditional divisions. Libraries need to be involved in planning these systems and ensuring that good practice is used to manage and organise information. EA is one approach to analysing and planning systems across the whole institution, although a genuine time commitment and, more importantly, support from the organisation's leaders are needed if this is to have sufficient support and buy-in to make it successful.

Apart from this, we are seeing increasing fragmentation of the institution's 'infosphere' as the creation, ownership, management and access to digital content rests largely outside the direct sphere of the library. In addition, new systems are being planned to manage and use this content; many of these systems are being planned outside the library and, sometimes, without the knowledge of the information professionals within the institution. Information professionals need to make efforts to understand the trends in user behaviour and the resulting systems that are being created and used, if they do wish not to find themselves marginalised. New, creative approaches to thinking about the library are needed if we can ever hope to build Library 2.0.

End-note: engagement with national and international debate

JISC is working with thought leaders in the library world to debate the following questions: what might a UK library infrastructure look like in 5 or 10 years' time – at a local, regional and national level? To move from the present library to what is required in the future is an immense challenge at three levels: people, processes, infrastructure. JISC will use the outcomes from the debate to guide institutions in how to plan their futures. The library sector is encouraged to engage with this debate in order to shape its own strategy and to help guide the HE system towards a confident and sustainable future. Information is available from http://www.jisc.ac.uk/.

Notes

1. http://en.wikipedia.org/wiki/Cloud_computing.
2. http://www.bis.gov.uk/assets/biscore/corporate/docs/h/09-1452-higher-ambitions-summary.pdf.
3. http://www.leedsmet.ac.uk/run/.
4. http://www.russellgroup.ac.uk/.
5. http://www.kaplanopenlearning.org.uk/pr-online-foundation-degree-launch.html.
6. http://www.flickr.com/.
7. The JISC's repositories programmes are investigating many of these issues and provide examples of good practice. Information is available from http://www.jisc.ac.uk/.
8. The JISC has funded three VRE programmes. Information is available from http://www.jisc.ac.uk.
9. A summary of the work of the Information Strategies Initiative is available at http://www.jiscinfonet.ac.uk/infokits/strategy/jisi/guidelines-what.
10. Available from http://www.jisc.ac.uk/media/documents/techwatch/jisc_ea_pilot_study.pdf.

References

DEMOS. (2009) *The Edgeless University: why higher education must embrace technology*, London: DEMOS.

Dempsey, L. (2006) 'The (digital) library environment: 10 years after'. *Ariadne*, 46. Online at http://www.ariadne.ac.uk/issue46/dempsey/.

Duke, J. and Jordan, A. (2006) *Impact Study of the JISC Electronic Libraries Programme*. Bristol: Joint Information Systems Committee.

HEPI. (2008) *Demand for Higher Education to 2029*. Oxford: Higher Education Policy Institute.

HESA. (2009) *Students in Higher Education Institutions*. Cheltenham: Higher Education Statistics Agency.

JISC. (2009a) *Higher Education in a Web 2.0 World*. Bristol: Joint Information Systems Committee. Online at http://www.jisc.ac.uk/publications/generalpublications/2009/heweb2.aspx.

JISC. (2009b) *Doing an Enterprise Architecture*. Bristol: Joint Information Systems Committee. Online at http://www.jisc.ac.uk/media/documents/techwatch/jisc_ea_pilot_study.pdf.

JISCInfoNet. (2010) *What are Shared Services?* JISCInfoNet Online at http://www.jiscinfonet.ac.uk/infokits/shared-services/.

Office of Public Sector Information. (1992) *Further and Higher Education Act 1992*. London: HMSO. Online at http://www.opsi.gov.uk/acts/acts1992/Ukpga_19920013_en_1.

SCONUL. (2008) *JISC and SCONUL Library Management Systems Study*, London: Society of College, National and University Libraries. Online at http://www.sconul.ac.uk/news/lms_report/lmsstudy/section1.pdf.

Sykes, J. (2009) 'Hybrid library management'. In Baker, D. and Evans, W. (eds) (2009) *Digital Library Economics: an academic perspective*. Oxford: Chandos.

Universities UK. (2008) *The Future Size and Shape of the Higher Education Sector in the UK: threats and opportunities*. London: Universities UK.

Yanosky, R. (2008) 'From users to choosers: the cloud and the changing shape of enterprise authority'. In Katz, R.N. (ed.) *The Tower and the Cloud*. EDUCAUSE. Online at http://www.educause.edu/thetowerandthecloud/PUB7202m.

25

Library 2050

Chris Batt

Introduction

'Walk out with me toward the Unknown Region ... no map there nor guide'.[1]

We cannot know the future. We cannot even be certain that libraries have a future beyond the next few years. We may believe they will remain of high value to society, but that belief alone gives no guarantee of survival. I cannot show you a picture of what Library 2050 will look like, but I will suggest ways to map the route; to demonstrate new approaches to sustaining long-term value in our evolving society. To do this I will consider the future for libraries and information services through the lens of my PhD research,[2] begun during 2009. The research is a comparative study of traditional policies and practices for collecting, curating and disseminating knowledge in support of public policy and the growing range of freely available knowledge resources on the Internet. The study includes all creating, curating and disclosing institutions: schools, colleges, universities, museums, libraries, archives, public service broadcasters, government departments and agencies. The objective is to answer the following question: 'In what ways will digital technologies and the Internet as channels for knowledge and learning change approaches to public policy formulation, implementation and delivery?' Rather than emphasising traditional institution-centric priorities, crucial to the research is understanding the flow of knowledge within public policy and the downstream value that is delivered. While any useful outcomes remain some way into the future, the approach and initial work may help to position the practical concerns and uncertainties of service managers within a broader frame of reference. Across the cadre of institutions listed there is currently little collective debate about future possibilities. In my view, even the smallest impetus that can be given to changing that situation is a move in the right direction.

If libraries did not exist, would someone invent them?

This question is at the same time both trivial and fundamental. It is trivial in the sense that, for library workers and users, libraries are real and tangible, and there are just so many better things to do than deal with hypothetical questions. On the other hand, on a number of levels, as a 'null hypothesis' proposition demanding proof by contradiction, it is *the* fundamental question of meaning for libraries and information services. Self-evidently the question is absurd, since libraries and information services of many types do exist and can claim by tradition and by current actions to be delivering significant value to their users. The library as a public good is ubiquitous in developed countries and an aspiration in those still developing. Collective action to gather together physical containers of knowledge (books, journals, images, recordings and so on) for the general benefit of users, whether university, school or the public at large, has a history counted in centuries and is deeply embedded within our culture (Rose, 2001; Blacker and Moore, 2006). In fact, until recently, that embedding has been so deep that libraries as essential public good services tended to be 'normalised' – an invisible expectation in the same way that turning on a tap produces safe drinking water. Consider, for example, public perception of English public libraries as reported in studies separated by more than 30 years. In *The Effective Library*, the 1976 report of the Hillingdon project on public library effectiveness, in response to the statement 'It would be a great loss to the community if there were no public libraries', 86% of public library users strongly agreed – a percentage exactly matched by the responses from the sample of non-users (Totterdell and Bird, 1976). In 2006, the BBC reported[3] the results of a study of Essex Libraries that concluded, 'Essex County Council found that a majority of respondents thought libraries were a sign of "a civilised, caring, responsible society". Users and non-users alike said society would lose out if services closed.' In addition, a study on public libraries from the UK research company MORI[4] for the Audit Commission, and which draws on surveys dating from 1998 to 2000, demonstrated that just fewer than 50% of non-users were satisfied with their public library services (MORI, 2002). This evidence is merely presented to show that community value of the public library seems to be rooted as much in belief of general value as in specific, personal assessment of the services provided.

In the past, the belief in public libraries' being a 'good thing' has underpinned justifications for their continued provision, just as the academic library as a physical storehouse of and guide to knowledge has been seen as the foundation on which education and research are built. As recently as March 2010, in the government's *Modernisation Review of Public Libraries*, Margaret Hodge, the then Minister for Culture, included in her introduction the following words:

> The public library service ... guards against the tyrannies of ignorance and conformity, and its existence indicates the extent to which a democratic society values knowledge, truth, justice, books, and culture. (DCMS, 2010)

Fine words, originally published in *American Libraries*[5] in 1995 and revised in 2000. However, while the words restate well the traditional values of the library within society, a lot has happened in the first decade of the new millennium that makes vital a re-appraisal of what might be the long-term role(s) of libraries of all types. Across that 10-year period, the changes that will be discussed below have touched all aspects of personal and social life, causing significant uncertainty about whether and how it is possible to plan services beyond the short term. Quite how to plan imaginatively for three to five years ahead remains a big question within the public sector, and if that is the case, why or how can one think further out? Internet guru Jaron Lanier was recently interviewed about his book *You are Not a Gadget: a manifesto*.[6] Reflecting on how the future might unfold, he made the telling point that it is easier to predict what things might be like in 50 rather than (say) 10 years' time. A longer time horizon enables people to describe how they *wish* things to be rather than how the current determinism of economics, technology or social change will define them for us. It is in part for this reason my research is directed at possible futures up to 40 years ahead and why this chapter bears the title 'Library 2050'. Like me, some readers may be able to look back 40 years and ask: if the roles and missions from the 1970s have stayed pretty much the core of services today (as I think they have), why should they change in the next 40 years? Are they not long tested and relevant, despite the changes in media and in connectivity?

My search for an answer to those questions is at the core of my research. What will the library be for, be doing, in 40 years' time? What are the things you do now that should be distilled and preserved for the future; the roles and tasks that should continue, however technology might develop, and which are so demonstrably vital to the social fabric that policy makers will want to pay for them? Furthermore, how are those roles and tasks unique to the library? I cannot resist making the point that, apart from the use of the word 'books', the quote above from *American Libraries* would fit just as well the museum, the public service broadcaster, even the university. For that and other reasons, the future library mission will need to make explicit what the unique defining roles are; what the library can deliver that no other institution, public or private, is able to deliver.

To return to the question that heads this section, we may define several challenges to be addressed. First, to describe clearly what is the unique, long-term public value delivered by the library (the mission), and second, to identify who are the key influencers to be persuaded of the importance of that value to wider public policy, and how best to influence them. Confidence in answering the challenge which the null hypothesis proposition invites should make possible the collective authentication of core mission(s) and consequently demonstrate trajectories to maximise future public value. This latter question of approaches to advocacy is something to which we will return at the end of the chapter. First, it is important to examine the reasons why long-term mission clarity and public worth are more essential than ever before, and the extent to which future success will depend on the justification of library-like services as a collective mission (a coalition) or the continued separate development of roles across different institution and service types. These issues will be addressed in the next two sections.

Turbulent times

Today, more than ever before, public sector managers are expected to justify the expenditure of taxpayers' money; what value is delivered for the investment made? Within this section three significant external factors in this will be briefly described. They will highlight both the challenges facing public sector libraries and the first step towards understanding approaches to the demonstration of future public value.

Supply: market competition

The decade of the 1960s was a period of opportunity for many library services, both public and academic, with investment in new buildings and a sense of growing opportunity for the library to play an increasing role in the formal education and informal learning of society. Indeed, around that time the increasing popularity of the public library was blamed for the final demise of commercial circulating libraries such as Boots Booklovers Library, which, by the end of the decade, were finally gone. No direct correlation is suggested, and certainly the growth of the book club also had an impact (Drabble and Stringer, 2003), but the public library was able to flourish where commercial competition could not. There are, of course, good reasons why the collective management and supply of knowledge, free at the point of use, in support of education, informal learning, business, personal development and community well-being should be cherished as a universal entitlement; issues that have been addressed by John Feather in Chapter 5. My point in raising the issue here is to contrast the emergent dominance of the public library in the 1960s and libraries' subsequent 30 years unchallenged as guardians of that entitlement with the heterodox landscape of digital choices that now face the citizen.

I have reviewed elsewhere the evolving relationship that the UK public library service has had with digital technologies between 1985 and 2010 (Batt, 2009a), based on the six national surveys of IT in public libraries that I undertook between 1985 and 1998 (Batt, 1985; 1987; 1990; 1992; 1994; 1998) and my involvement with the People's Network Project[7] and subsequent national developments such as Reference Online.[8] In the review of developments I highlighted two phases of change. The first phase, up to the year 2000, I called 'Status Quo Plus'. During this period, libraries adopted and adapted their services using technology to improve efficiency (circulation control), effectiveness (CD-ROM and online reference tools) and service innovation (public access to the Internet). The second phase I called 'Status Quo 2.0', for the obvious reason that the past decade has been dominated by the growth of social networking. Libraries of all types, alongside many other sectors, have engaged and experimented with how these new tools can enrich and enhance service delivery.

Other developments have encroached on the traditional roles of libraries over the past decade. The impact of file sharing, iPod and iTunes on the recorded music industry, the slow birth of the e-book, Wikipedia,[9] Google[10] (and now knowledge engines such as Wolfram Alpha[11]),

Amazon[12] and the whole 24/7 thing, all in one way or another eat into the service propositions of which libraries have felt ownership in the past. While nobody can yet predict the future impact that these will have on public institutions such as libraries, it must be evident that these new media and new 'always on' delivery technologies will, at least, change how libraries deliver their services. In my view, given the market turbulence, 'Status Quo 2.0' has been the right strategy to follow. Incremental change reduces the risk of 'backing the wrong horse' and provides continuity for users and service providers alike. However, there will be tipping points when more radical change is necessary. The shift towards electronic resources in academic institutions has brought both challenges and opportunities to university libraries, and the announcement that two libraries at Stanford University will soon be bookless may be a precursor of more radical changes in other places (Krieger, 2010). It is certainly the case that the future will bring more challenges rather than fewer to the libraries sector, and it will be essential that the sector be able collectively to demonstrate, with more apparent routes to knowledge and ideas, what is the unique service proposition.

Demand: society and digital culture

The flip side of this is the level of impact of digital technologies and networking on the behaviours and expectations of individuals, communities and society. There is no shortage of opinions, ranging from the utopian to the dystopian. To give just two examples, Shirky (2008) presents a compelling case for the unlocking of talent and energy through social networking and crowd-sourcing that will transform people and society, while in the opposite corner Keen (2007) argues passionately that the increasing involvement of amateurs in music, media and other disciplines is undermining the trustworthy skills of the professional, whether journalist, artist or librarian. Debates about the power of the professional and the power of social action are not new (see, e.g., Illich, 1973), but there is growing evidence that digital technologies are creating permanent change in cultural forms, and in people's consequent behaviours and expectations. The evidence so far suggests that this may have a growing impact on how knowledge is created and accessed, and may therefore call into question the services that libraries have traditionally provided and the tools and techniques they have used to organise knowledge.

In his review of the individual and society in the digital age, Luke Tredinnick (Tredinnick, 2008) identifies a number of changes in cultural forms that are taking place, three of which will be mentioned here. First of all, digital technologies facilitate *participation*. Through e-mail, social networking sites, blogging, crowd-sourcing and citizen journalism, the barriers to free expression have fallen dramatically, alongside a growing engagement with the reuse and recycling of cultural assets – the 'mash-up'. The result is to challenge the traditional primacy of the book as a secure container of knowledge, since no longer is the work of the author 'bound', literally and metaphorically, in one place:

> The credibility of cultural artefacts in the modern age was in part influenced by the indexical association between content and form, and incorporated a conferred credibility forged in the link between the original creative act and the mechanical reproduction that acted as a kind of shorthand in the evaluation of individual artefacts or information ... with the separation of material and form, this extrinsic means of validating knowledge has become more problematic. (Tredinnick, 2008)

This extract touches also on both the second and third of the changes. The second is the very apparent *fragmentation* of the forms and locations of knowledge and information. Today, the long-form book and the journal article are still relevant, but knowledge is now embedded in the blogosphere, in discussion groups, e-mails, on websites and all the other digital tools of sharing. The third change to note is the trend towards *disintermediation*:

> While in the age of publishing and mass media control over the apparatus of mediation became largely synonymous with control over discourse, digital technologies increasingly place power over the creation, dissemination and the use of content in the hands of consumers. With disintermediation, the status of information and the relationship between the apparatus of mediation and control over knowledge begin to shift. (Tredinnick, 2008)

This is a view reinforced by Stephen Page, chief executive officer of Faber, in a recent post to the *Guardian* Books Blog:

> Publishers also have to explain what value they are bringing to the relationship between writers and readers, a conversation that is

made far more transparent through digital media and digital texts. (Page, 2010)

Assuming that these trends continue, those managing libraries are going to have to consider not just how digital technologies can support existing core activities, but also some fundamental questions about the role of the library worker as gatherer, curator and intermediary of knowledge in this new, fragmented landscape.

There is a final and more practical point to make about the demand side: look at what is happening around you, on trains, in offices and in homes. The smart phone, the iPad and the Kindle, increasing media channels and social networking are changing people's behaviours and expectations. The question is not whether Tredinnick's interpretation is right or wrong, but how quickly the reality of change will bring libraries of all types to a tipping point.

Public policy and public value

There was perhaps a time in the past when justifications about the provision of libraries such as 'indicates the extent to which a democratic society values knowledge, truth, justice, books, and culture' (DCMS, 2010) *might* just be sufficiently compelling to sustain investment. The provision of public good services is, after all, rooted in political choices, and within democratic societies, free access to knowledge and ideas touches at the very heart of the relationship between the individual and society. In recent years, with increasing competition for limited public funds, managers have been expected to place their service performance within a framework of indicators and outcomes that can be aggregated into assessments of costs and benefits. It is self-evident that the ability to apply such approaches successfully will vary across the diversity of public service provision. While the performance of the UK's National Health Service in reducing the mortality rates from a certain disease may be both quantifiable and a powerful message to politicians and the public, it may be tougher to show the value of the public library as a community place, or the vital role played by large collections in university libraries in research and the creation of new knowledge. Furthermore, as we have seen above, there is also competition from the products and services available in the private/commercial sector that impinges on functions that were in the past delivered unchallenged. Whether or not this competition is genuine and will be long lasting remains unclear, but it certainly makes imperative the need to find ways to demonstrate beyond doubt the individual and collective value that the libraries sector provides to society. There are a number of criteria that may be applied to the justification for public investment. *Creating Public Value* (Moore, 1995) presents an analysis of the steps to understanding and demonstrating public value, successfully bridging the divide between the academy and practical experience. The book describes a number of facets that help to contribute to the definition of public value. Moore suggests that only where there is obvious market failure can value be achieved by the provision of public services that are deemed necessary for society. Harking back to earlier comments about the dominance of the public library over the circulating library illuminates this issue. Of course, we have also already noted that there are now areas of activity where there is a growing competitive market – iTunes, rather than renting CDs or movies from the public library, the 24/7 reference resources on the Web, and so on. This suggests again that the libraries sector will need to define and agree how the service proposition articulates a route through this more complex landscape so as to show where the public value rests.

There are two other factors to be mentioned that offer some opportunity for building that collective argument. The first is the *economies of scale* that are possible where a large number of resources can be coordinated collectively. Here, the richness of the total library collections in the public sector – academic, school, public and other information services – represents a corpus of knowledge that even the likes of Google Books[13] cannot match and are unlikely to. The recent Department for Culture, Media and Sport (DCMS) *Policy Statement on Public Libraries* (DCMS, 2010) includes the following as a part of the core offer it envisions:

> Access to the national book collection – any book from anywhere: Order any book through your library (even out of print books).

Given that whatever happens to the future prospects of the book as the container of knowledge, it will certainly be the case that books remain a core resource for many years. The guarantee of access to anything, anywhere, is a unique proposition that currently the private sector is unable to match. Sadly, at present, the mechanisms that make such access possible publicly are less available than used to be the case when schemes of cooperative inter-lending covered the country. That was not full access to the national book collection, but it could be achieved now, with cooperation across the whole sector and some investment. There is a further practical constraint, however, to promoting the uniqueness of this service. It is the fact that in some public library authorities the cost of requesting not-in-stock items is higher and often slower than purchasing the item second hand through Amazon. So the public value of the DCMS's aspiration will be tempered by private sector competition for some materials some of the time; which takes the edge off the unique public value argument (Drahos and Braithwaite, 2002).

The third factor is *trust,* and this sits at the heart of what libraries in their present form aim to achieve. In the future, it would seem, managing trusted resources will be a fundamental role in a society where access to knowledge is a vital component of living. Yet, there is again challenge both in the public perception of services such as Google and Wikipedia as sources of knowledge, and in the means by which the libraries sector can show collectively and convincingly that what it does is uniquely different.

Playing consequences: all for one or free for all?

Despite describing a range of challenges to the traditional position of the libraries sector, it is certainly the case that libraries are still able to demonstrate large and loyal audiences. Set against that are the external factors that will challenge sovereignty and the viability of services in coming years; factors over which the leaders of the libraries sector may not have much control. Whether there will be a tipping point, when the status and positioning of the library service shifts radically up or down, remains a matter for conjecture. Yet, in relation to factors such as market competition, digital culture and public policy, as I write this in a week that began with the announcement of £6 billion of cuts in public spending (HM Treasury, 2010), as only the first step in the UK government's austerity programme, and ended with the global launch of the Apple iPad,[14] there are definitely powerful external forces abroad.

If this tells us anything, it is that the libraries sector collectively, or the various component parts separately, needs to have an absolutely clear and compelling story to tell about roles and value in the short- and medium-term future. That requires two things: services that demonstrably provide unique public value, and the capability to 'sell' that value to the right people. The most obvious defining feature across the whole of library history has naturally been collecting, organising and making available recorded knowledge, and, as we have seen, so far, despite the encroachment of digital services in areas such as scholarly journals and public search engines, the building and curation of collections of books remains core to the library mission. We need to remember, if or when radical change takes place through the shift to e-books and other forms of electronic delivery, that it may be decades before there is no longer a need to provide access to legacy collections of the printed word. Even were Google Books and other digitisation projects to get close to 100% coverage, which is unlikely, a sustained culture change would still be required for the book to become so marginalised as to make access to the published heritage unnecessary. Will that be sufficient justification for retaining places called libraries that people can actually visit? I do not think so; not within consideration of other routes to delivery. For example, Amazon has already demonstrated how cost-effective a centralised service of selection and delivery can be. Could such a centralised approach produce a better and more sustainable service, providing 'access to the national book collection' (DCMS, 2010)? In time, when rational solutions have been found to establish a balance between intellectual property rights and access to knowledge, a more practical strategy might be to scan the printed word on demand.

Libraries have always been much more than just collections of recorded knowledge. They are places of encounter, places for individual and convivial learning; they are sources of information and guidance, and places of escape. Yet building that 'destination' concept into the value proposition needs to be justified in terms of what is the particular value 'library-ness' adds. It will never be enough to justify retention on the basis of substitution: the village needs a community centre, the undergraduate needs somewhere to study. We have already noted the changes that Stanford University is implementing to remove physical collections from two of its specialist libraries. Does the space that remains continue to be a library? Or is it just another place to sit and gain access to remote electronic resources? School libraries are not ubiquitous, despite strong argument to the contrary (see, e.g. SLA, 2010), and consequently many public libraries are able to argue their essential role in *supporting* learning both inside and outside formal education. Yet the evidence of recent years suggests that the case has not convinced policy makers to ensure that public libraries are adequately funded to provide any consistent substitute following on from the closure of school libraries (see, e.g. Ward, 2010).

To answer those questions calls for a change in how the role of the library is developed and is presented both to those within the sector and to those outside – users, policy makers and so on. The key step is to reject the notion that location and service are inextricably bound together. This is a generalisation, since libraries of all types have offered outreach, remote access and, recently, the tools of social engagement. However, I would suggest that the case for libraries in the short to medium term be presented around three sets of activities – the place of encounter, the networked service and the agency of development and progress. I wrote about this in 2008 (Batt, 2009b), when I examined this set of activities in relation to the development of the English public library service. I believe now that it offers the means of creating a much-needed building block for the future, a forum for the discussion of future roles and responsibilities across the whole of the sector. At present such a forum does not exist. To take two examples, the current Libraries of the Future project[15] appears not to consider relationships with public or school libraries as a core component of the study, while the DCMS *Policy Statement* (DCMS, 2010) fails in the same way to recognise the opportunities that might arise from building a collective future. What sense does that make in a world where everyone thinks the answer is Google?

So, the answer to the question 'all for one or free for all?' is quite simple. Sustaining debate around institutional architecture – public library, school library, academic library and so on – will bring only short-term fixes, where some libraries are able to justify their value more than others. What would be the effect if tomorrow the statutory duty to provide public libraries were repealed? Is it only the law that defends the line? Long-term security of access to knowledge for all will come from debate around why lifelong access is of public value to everyone, rather than how that access should be delivered; shifting attitudes away from institutional roles to build a common mission for the libraries sector as a whole is long overdue, and we all share responsibility for that failure.

This is your future: towards Library 2050

Beyond Current Horizons was a project run by FutureLab[16] with a mission to 'build a set of long-term and challenging scenarios for the future of education 2025 and beyond in the context of socio-technical change'.[17] The final report (Facer, 2009) summarises a wide-ranging programme of work, with contributions from leading educationalists. Yet the three most interesting, tangible outcomes are not the report, but a toolkit, six scenarios for the future and a three-minute animation.[18] Two minutes into the animation we are told that by 2030:

> institutions traditionally seen as separate such as home, work, shopping mall, school, work place and college will merge and blur due to economic pressure and changes in the way people use technology.[19]

If a genuinely collective debate can be started about the value of access to knowledge, surely here is a short cut to starting it. In *Six Rules for Effective Forecasting*, Paul Saffo (2007) says that 'we routinely overestimate short-term change and underestimate long-term change', and this seems to me to sum up well the state of current debate about the future of libraries. I am confident that what Beyond Current Horizons has to say about the merging of schools with other institutions will not be immediately palatable to many teachers and parents. However, the approach follows Jaron Lanier's view (Lanier, 2010) that decoupling present realities from future possibilities offers a powerful mechanism to build debate around basic principles, rather than the defence of a perpetual status quo.

Naturally, I cannot draw a picture of the 2050 library in its various manifestations, any more than the work of Beyond Current Horizons was able to do for schools and education. My research has a long way to go and addresses a broader agenda than just the future of libraries. I can, however, suggest some key concepts and behaviours that might inform collective debate about strategic options for a dramatically different long-term future. Earlier, I referred to the core function of the library as a storehouse of and signpost to knowledge and, with increasing cultural fragmentation, the aggregation and disclosure of knowledge resources for public value may be more important than ever. Yet there will remain the need to show not just how public value may be delivered, but why the value is essential to public policy. What does public access to knowledge achieve? Today's language of value – improved education, understanding, confidence, creativity, better communities, happiness, healthiness, fun and so on – may remain relevant, but lacks a collective coherence, not least since the policies it supports are mainly unconnected, being guarded in many different government silos. In my view, collective coherence will be a critical success factor in gaining future traction in public policy, and it is therefore a core part of my research programme. My hypothesis is that all exchange relationships taking place across the 'knowledge/user boundary' should demonstrate to advantage the acquisition of knowledge; the user gains some value. To put it another way, the exchange has the effect of changing the receiver in some way that contributes to overall societal value. An act of learning takes place, whether formal, informal, just out of the cradle or close to the grave. Discussion, unfettered by the traditional shackles of organisational architectures, addressing how libraries might *collectively* support that exchange between knowledge and learning through life is already overdue.

Knowledge and learning are compelling policy concepts, but the libraries sector cannot claim sole ownership. The educational infrastructure, museums, archival collections and even public service broadcasters rightly claim chunks of the territory and the recent study by National Institute of Adult Continuing Education (NIACE) on the future for lifelong learning provides the beginnings of a broader strategic view into new priorities and relationships (NIACE, 2009). Nevertheless, if the 'merging and blurring of institutions' message of Beyond Current Horizons is right, the strategic debate will need to be wider than just the library in 2050. Already, the university sector is reaching out into communities through crowd-sourcing projects such as Galaxy Zoo[20] and the Great War Archive.[21] Listen to Martin Bean, the Vice Chancellor of the Open University, talking about his mission to create 'megaphones of informal learning' through channels such as iTunesU[22] and YouTube;[23] reaching everyone (Bean, 2010). His view is that, through their lives, people should be able to move easily between formal and informal learning, depending on their particular need. His 'megaphones' are a first step towards bridging that gap. By 2050, will the traditional university have turned itself inside out, as Bean is suggesting? What would that mean for the collection and management of public knowledge? The UK's Open University has, of course, had long associations with public service broadcasting. In considering how organisational relationships might change, mention must be made of *A History of the World in 100 Objects*, the partnership between the BBC and the British Museum.[24] To me, this provides a glimpse of a future where the power of broadcast media will increasingly be a compelling route to knowledge resources of all types; informal learning writ large.

Conclusion

Such developments give clues as to future possibilities, but there is as yet no mechanism to coordinate debate or provide the helicopter view across the whole landscape of public knowledge and learning. When it arrives, it will be essential that the library sector can present a strong message of collective coherence. Were a mechanism for debate and coordination to be created, what might be the outcomes? At the top level, the expectation must be an informed and knowledgeable society. A society where learning is normalised within everyday life from cradle to grave, where appropriate knowledge resources are managed, trusted, accessible to all and relevant to their needs and recognised as a core public good. With or without our current economic pressures, the delivery of that knowledge through digital technologies will be important, and that will call for new organisational architectures and relationships to manage, aggregate and present knowledge to the user. The need will be not for the duplication of resources – increasing reliance on digital access will make that unnecessary – but for the re-presentation of trusted knowledge for the particular need. In my view, that is the heart of what knowledge management skills will demand and the place where the future library worker should be. Many of the existing skills of organisation, description and curation of knowledge will be required, but decoupled from geography and recast in partnerships with the skills of the broadcaster, the marketer and the educator.

What of place, the physical destination in the wider knowledge sector? For the broadcaster, audiences have always been virtual. For the historical collection, the physical objects can communicate in ways that virtual simulacra will never achieve, although their digital representations may offer unique and popular interpretational value.[25] In my view, at this stage, the physical nature of the library, the museum, the university and so on is a second-order question, subject first to the development of a collective view of public knowledge and learning in the long term. It may well be the case that people will continue to want places to meet, places of encounter; places of convivial learning and 'library-ness' should be in all of them. Critical now is collective ownership of a unique and robust service proposition – a confident definition of 'library-ness' that fits and complements the wider public knowledge landscape, free from the weight of how things are now. The sooner that case emerges and the advocacy is translated into strategic policy, the more chance there is of achieving that informed and knowledgeable society to which the libraries sector has always aspired.

Notes

1. Walt Whitman, 'Whispers of Heavenly Death', no. 2. The Walt Whitman Archive, eds E. Folsom and K. Price, http://www.whitmanarchive.org/published/periodical/poems/per.00051 (accessed 14 February 2011).
2. http://www.digital-futures.org/Digital_Futures/Working_papers.html.
3. http://news.bbc.co.uk/1/hi/5105580.stm.
4. MORI merged in 2005 with Ipsos to create IpsosMORI.
5. http://www.ala.org/ala/alonline/resources/slctdarticles/12wayslibraries.cfm.
6. RSA webcast: http://www.thersa.org/events/vision/vision-videos/jaron-lanier-you-are-not-a-gadget.
7. http://www.peoplesnetwork.gov.uk/.
8. http://www.mla.gov.uk/what/support/online.
9. http://www.wikipedia.org/.
10. http://www.google.com.
11. http://www.wolframalpha.com/.
12. http://www.amazon.co.uk.
13. http://books.google.com/.
14. http://www.bbc.co.uk/news/10176138.
15. Sponsored by the British Library, JISC, SCONUL, Research Information Network and Research Libraries UK, http://www.futurelibraries.info/content/.
16. http://www.futurelab.org.uk/.
17. Beyond Current Horizons website, http://www.beyondcurrenthorizons.org.uk/.
18. http://www.futurelab.org.uk/resources/multimedia/video/Video1589.
19. *Ibid.*
20. http://www.galaxyzoo.org/.
21. http://www.oucs.ox.ac.uk/ww1lit/gwa.
22. http://www.open.ac.uk/itunes.
23. http://www.youtube.com/user/TheOpenUniversity.
24. http://www.bbc.co.uk/ahistoryoftheworld.
25. See, e.g., the British Library's Turning the Pages service, http://www.bl.uk/onlinegallery/ttp/ttpbooks.html#.

References

Batt, C. (1985) *New Technology in Public Libraries: a survey.* Winchester: Public Libraries Research Group.

Batt, C. (1987) *Information Technology in Public Libraries.* Winchester: Public Libraries Research Group.

Batt, C. (1990) *Information Technology in Public Libraries 1989.* Croydon: Public Libraries Research Group.

Batt, C. (1992) *Information Technology in Public Libraries*, 4th edn. London: Library Association.

Batt, C. (1994) *Information Technology in Public Libraries*, 5th edn. London: Library Association.

Batt, C. (1998) *Information Technology in Public Libraries*, 6th edn. London: Library Association.

Batt, C. (2009a) 'From punched tape to wifi and beyond'. In *Wifi in UK's Public Libraries Survey 2009*. London: Civic Regeneration.

Batt, C. (2009b). 'Political realities and the English public library system'. In Smith, K. (ed.) (2009) *The Politics of Libraries and Librarianship: challenges and realities*. London: Chandos.

Bean, M. (2010) Keynote address at *JISC Conference 2010*, London, 12–13 April. Online at http://www.jisc.ac.uk/events/2010/04/jisc10.aspx.

Blacker, A. and Moore, P. (2006) *The Cambridge History of Libraries in Britain and Ireland: Volume 3*. Cambridge: Cambridge University Press.

DCMS. (2010) *The Modernisation Review of Public Libraries*. Department of Culture, Media and Sport. London: HMSO.

Drabble, M. and Stringer, J. (2003) 'Libraries, circulating'. In *The Concise Oxford Companion to English Literature*. Oxford: Oxford University Press.

Drahos, P. and Braithwaite, J. (2002) *Information Feudalism: who owns the knowledge economy?* London: Earthscan.

Facer, K. (2009) *Educational, Social and Technological Futures: a report from the Beyond Current Horizons programme*. Bristol: Futurelab.

HM Treasury. (2010) 'Government announces £6.2bn of savings in 2010–11'. Press release 24 May. Online at http://www.hm-treasury.gov.uk/press_04_10.htm.

Illich, I. (1973) *Tools for Conviviality*. London: Harper and Row.

Keen, A. (2007) *The Cult of the Amateur: how today's Internet is killing our culture*. London: Doubleday.

Krieger, L. (2010) 'Stanford University prepares for "bookless library"'. Online at http://www.deseretnews.com/article/700036147/Stanford-University-prepares-for-bookless-library.html.

Lanier, J. (2010) *You Are Not a Gadget: a manifesto*. London: Allan Lane Press.

Moore, M.H. (1995) *Creating Public Value: strategic management in government*. Cambridge, MA: Harvard University Press.

MORI. (2002) *Perceptions of Libraries: desk research conducted for the Audit Commission*. London: Audit Commission.

NIACE. (2009) *Learning through Life: inquiry into the future for lifelong learning*. Leicester: National Institute of Adult Continuing Education.

Page, S. (2010) 'Apple iPad: will it lead to a reading revolution?' Online at http://www.guardian.co.uk/technology/2010/may/28/apple-ipad-launch-publishing.

Rose, J. (2001) *The Intellectual Life of the British Working Classes*. London: Yale University Press.

Saffo, P. (2007) 'Six Rules for Effective Forecasting'. *Harvard Business Review*, July–August.

Shirky, C. (2008) *Here Comes Everybody: how change happens when people come together*. London: Penguin.

SLA (School Libraries Association). (2010) *Submission from the School Library Service to the School Library Commission*. Online at http://www.sla.org.uk/sla-school-library-commission-submission.php.

Totterdell, B. and Bird, J. (1976) *The Effective Library: report of the Hillingdon Project on public library effectiveness*. London: Library Association.

Tredinnick, L. (2008). *Digital Information Culture: the individual and society in the digital age*. Oxford: Chandos.

Ward, H. (2010) 'Closure of another library service speaks volumes'. *Times Educational Supplement*, 7 May. Online at http://www.tes.co.uk/article.aspx?storycode=6043014.

Index

9 781843 341314